Socialization and Personality Development

Socialization and Personality Development

SECOND EDITION

EDWARD F. ZIGLER
Yale University

MICHAEL E. LAMB
University of Utah

IRVIN L. CHILD
Yale University

New York   Oxford
OXFORD UNIVERSITY PRESS
1982

Library of Congress Cataloging in Publication Data
Main entry under title:
Socialization and personality development.
Includes bibliographies and index.
1. Socialization.   2. Personality.
I. Zigler, Edward Frank, 1930–   .   II. Lamb, Michael E., 1953–   .   III.
Child, Irvin Long, 1915–   .
HQ783.S568   1982   303.3′2   81-16981
ISBN 0-19-503076-1   AACR2
ISBN 0-19-503077-X (pbk.)

Printing (last digit): 9 8 7 6 5 4 3 2 1
Printed in the United States of America

We dedicate this book to a great episode in the history of social science, the Institute of Human Relations at Yale University (1931–1960), and to its pioneering students who brought the theories of psychodynamics, learning, and culture together, and thus immeasurably furthered understanding of socialization and personality development:

John Dollard	Neal E. Miller
Leonard W. Doob	O. Hobart Mowrer
C. S. Ford	G. P. Murdock
Clark L. Hull	Robert R. Sears
Mark A. May	John W. M. Whiting

Acknowledgments

The authors would like to acknowledge their special indebtedness to Winnie Berman for her careful and insightful work on this book. Thanks are also extended for the important work of Maria Leveton and Greg Bialecki.

Contents

Part One

1. Introduction, 3

2. Socialization, 10

3. Major Theoretical Perspectives, 20

4. Mechanisms of Influence, 37

5. Socialization—Then and Now, 44

6. Approaches to the Study of Socialization, 47

7. Becoming a Social Individual, 50

8. Gender Identity and the Development of Behavioral Sex Differences, 55

9. Moral Development, 62

10. Achievement Motivation, 67

11. Aggression, 70

12. Social Cognition, 74

13. Major Sources of Influence, 78

14. The Effects of Divorce, 96

15. Intracultural Variation, 99

16. Intercultural Variation, 117

17. Atypical Development, 127

18. Conclusion, 153
    References, 156

Part Two

Determinants of Development

1. Future Research on Socialization and Personality Development, 185
   EDWARD ZIGLER AND VICTORIA SEITZ

2. Principles of Psychological Development and Response to Art, 200
   IRVIN L. CHILD

3. My Brother, My Self, 206
   DONALD DALE JACKSON

4. Conception, Pregnancy, and Birth: The Politics of Infancy, 213
   FREDA REBELSKY, CAROLLEE HOWES AND JOANNE KRAKOW

5. Divorce, A Child's Perspective, 223
   E. MAVIS HETHERINGTON

6. The "Elastic Mind" Movement: Rationalizing Child Neglect?, 234
   ALBERT ROSENFELD

Atypical Development

7. Personality Determinants in the Behavior of the Retarded, 238
   EDWARD ZIGLER AND DAVID BALLA

8. The Syndrome of Early Childhood Autism:
   Natural History, Etiology, and Treatment, 246
   BARBARA K. CAPARULO AND DONALD J. COHEN

9. Mainstreaming: The Proof Is in the Implementation, 253
   EDWARD ZIGLER AND SUSAN MUENCHOW

Child Rearing

10. On Being a Parent, 258
    EDWARD ZIGLER AND ROSA CASCIONE

11. What Can "Research Experts" Tell Parents about Effective Socialization?,
    268
    MICHAEL E. LAMB

12. Relation of Child Training to Subsistence Economy, 274
    HERBERT BARRY III, IRVIN L. CHILD, AND MARGARET K. BACON

13. Paternal Influences and the Father's Role: A Personal Perspective, 281
    MICHAEL E. LAMB

14. Come Back, Mister Rogers, Come Back, 287
    JEROME L. SINGER AND DOROTHY G. SINGER

15. Stop Picking on Big Bird, 290
GERALD S. LESSER

16. Controlling Child Abuse in America: An Effort Doomed to Failure, 292
EDWARD ZIGLER

Early Childhood Intervention Efforts

17. Project Head Start Becomes a Long-Distance Runner, 299
LAURA L. DITTMANN

18. The Yale Child Welfare Research Program:
Implications for Social Policy, 306
LESLIE A. RESCORLA AND EDWARD ZIGLER

19. IQ, Social Competence, and Evaluation of Early Childhood Intervention
Programs, 317
EDWARD ZIGLER AND PENELOPE K. TRICKETT

20. A Vision of Child Care in the 1980s, 329
EDWARD ZIGLER AND MATIA FINN

Index, 341

Part One

I

Introduction

Human development is a remarkable phenomenon. During the 70 years or so that each of us lives, we pass through a succession of metamorphoses that are common to us all. At the same time, each of us changes in ways that are distinctive and unique. The changes are as diverse and far-reaching as one could imagine. They extend from our size, strength, and the way we look, through changes in our ability to assimilate, process, and understand information, to the way we behave toward and understand other people. Physical, cognitive, and personality development each continue throughout our lives, although the most rapid and dramatic developments occur during infancy and childhood.

Several of the biological and social sciences have as their goal the understanding of human development. Developmental psychologists like ourselves focus on the development of human behavior, which we define broadly so as to include both overt behavior and unobservable mental behavior. Today, however, psychologists specialize even further, choosing to study perceptual or cognitive or sociopersonality development exclusively. In this book, we shall emphasize social and personality development, considering other aspects of development only to the extent that they help us to understand personality development. Let us, therefore, briefly describe the central concerns of each of these specialized areas of investigation and theory.

Perception involves using our memory of previous encounters with stimuli to flesh out or supplement the actual stimulus information. Consequently, *perceptual development* refers to changes in the ability to take in and process information from the environment. *Cognition* refers to the further use we make of this stimulus information and *cognitive development* to changes in our understanding of relationships among objects, persons, and events—how they affect one another, what they do, how they can be used, etc. *Social and personality development*, finally, refers specifically to the emergence of a characteristic way of relating to other people, perceiving their intents, and imputing motives and goals to them. Both perceptual and cognitive processes are necessarily involved in this, although students of socialization are most concerned about the way individuals perceive and think about people rather than things. Students of personality also focus on individual differences in motivations and behavior—particularly social behavior.

Students of socialization are concerned with analyzing the way people come to behave in a manner that permits them to get along successfully in the culture in which they live. Learning to behave in this fashion is by no means as simple as it sounds. Every society has a large and distinctive set of rules prescribing, proscribing, or diversifying the behavior of its members. There are rules regarding honesty and morality, the control and display of aggression, sexual behavior, public and private behavior, achievement, dependency, and modes of address and communication, and these rules vary from one society to the next. The rules are not the same for everyone in a society, of course, and vary according to the situation and its social definition. For any one person, customary behavior varies with the position that person occupies in relation to others. A woman has different expectations for the way she will act toward her child, her husband, or her employer and expects different behavior from each of these when they are interacting with her as their mother, wife, or employee. Nor are most social rules absolute; some few are rigid, but most allow for a great deal of variation in the extent and the way in which people's behavior conforms, and even in whether people are ever clearly aware of the rules.

Many of a society's rules refer to skills or modes of action which diversify a person's behavioral potentialities beyond those given by simple biological development. (A prime example is provided by language: a language is a set of rules whose mastery permits not only more differentiated communication with others but also a greatly increased capacity for thought, fantasy, and planning.) Socialization refers to the processes through which the culture's rules of conduct are learned. The focus of those who study personality development is a little broader, for they are concerned not only with the acquisition of behavior that is regulated by societal norms but also with the individual differences in social style and behavior that make each person recognizably unique. Our goal in this book is to describe the processes by means of which socialization and personality development are achieved.

Most developmental psychologists today acknowledge that development continues throughout the life span. While we are children, first parents and later teachers and peers make concerted efforts to shape our behavior by example, by instruction, or by the discriminating use of rewards and punishments. Whether or not anyone deliberately attempts to shape our behavior, furthermore, all of our early experiences provide opportunities to learn how others expect us to behave and what types of behavior are rewarded. Throughout our adult lives, too, we enter new situations, undertake new responsibilities, and adjust our social styles and our definitions of ourselves in response to these changing demands. Most adults, for example, marry and become parents; many undergo divorce and the death of a spouse. All these experiences influence our personality development. Unfortunately, this realization is fairly recent; most of the major theories of socialization focus primarily on the events that occur during childhood, and few explicitly consider the formative importance of adult experiences. This is probably because societies develop comprehensive means of socializing young children; the socialization of children is viewed as one of the primary responsibilities of parenthood. Parents try to mold their children's morals; they aim to make them masculine or feminine, hardworking and ambitious, or gentle and nurturant, and so on. Many theorists seem to believe that a "core" personality is established early and that adult experiences produce minor (perhaps predictable) variations from the core, although no one would acknowledge quite so extreme a view of personality development. By contrast, some few maintain that people generally reach adulthood with their personalities still extremely malleable despite the effects of prior experiences. In any event, most of the research we shall review in this volume deals with the socialization of children.

One's conceptions of how long personality development takes and of when the most formative periods occur partially determine which experiences and socialization agents one focuses on. Some theorists emphasize very early experiences, and so consider only members of the family as significant influences. Others conceive of a longer process, and so consider a succession of teachers and a changing peer group as well. Still others emphasize institutional expectations when we take jobs, social expectations and pressures regarding spouses and parents, and so on.

This topic has been especially controversial in the last few decades. Following the lead of psychoanalysts, it became a truism among developmental psychologists that early experiences were especially important in the determination not only of personality but also of intellectual potential (e.g., Bloom, 1964; Bowlby, 1951; Freud, 1940). This belief not only affected theoretical assumptions and the focus of research efforts but also had major practical implications. Maternal employment and day care were deemed harmful to young children, while intervention efforts designed to improve the educational performance of disadvantaged children were focused on the preschool years. When it was concluded—erroneously—that Head Start programs for 4- to 5-year-olds were unsuccessful, some argued that this was because these programs began too late in the children's lives (B. White, 1975). The first few years were thus perceived as "critical periods"; psychologists believed that if developmentally necessary experiences were not provided, the ill effects could never be eliminated by later substitute experiences—the damage was irreversible. (The same applied, of course, to enrichment during critical early periods.)

This belief in the special importance of early experiences has been roundly criticized (Clarke & Clarke, 1976; Rutter, 1972), and it is now evident that the unique emphasis on early experience was misguided. Early experiences are certainly important, but so are the experiences that follow them (Lamb & Campos, 1982; Zigler & Seitz, 1982b). It is naive to believe that positive early experiences inoculate children against all harmful consequences of later adverse experiences, just as it is incorrect to conclude that one can never remedy the effects of adverse early experiences. As Zigler and Valentine (1979) argue, there are so many critical periods in development that almost every age is critical, and so the concept is not terribly useful. Consequently, if we are to understand the processes of socialization and personality development, we must consider formative experiences at all ages, as well as the wide range of socialization agents within and beyond the family.

The above paragraphs imply that socialization depends on what happens to us, on the impact of our experiences in the course of development. Actually, the process by which socialization occurs is itself one of the basic issues addressed by students of socialization. Why are people the way they are? Were they born that way or with a tendency to develop thus? Or did they become that way because of their experiences? If experiences were significant, what sorts of experiences were influential? Any events, or only encounters with other people? Do those who shape us know they are influencing our personalities, or do they often act unwittingly? Will people always be as they are, or will they continually grow and change? If they continue to change, is there some core element that will remain unchanged, providing some basic, lifelong continuity? When did the person become the way she or he is now, and why? These are the types of questions of interest to those who study personality development and socialization.

Outline of the Book

In the next section of Part 1, we will say a little more about the field and describe recent changes in the way psychologists approach the study of socialization and personality development. Historical changes in the field are discussed again in Section 5. These changes deserve attention because they have implications for the way this book is organized, compared, for example, with the way it would have appeared if it had been written as little as a decade earlier. Without question, psychologists have taken new and rather distinctive stands in relation to some central issues in the last decade. We will describe these issues and their history in section 2, for the recent revision of the field is testimony to the essential importance of these far-reaching issues. Though they involve philosophical stands, there can be no doubt concerning the way each scientist's philosophy determines what he or she studies and the way he or she approaches the field.

Then we turn from philosophical considerations to disciplinary perspectives. Section 3 briefly reviews the contributions of the seven schools and/or approaches that have contributed to our understanding of socialization and personality development. We consider these in rough historical sequence, beginning with classical psychoanalysis and ending with the evolutionary biological approach that has recently attained prominence. Each of these approaches takes a different stand on the basic philosophical issues described earlier, and each has chosen a slightly different way to construct a picture of the complex processes involved in the establishment of individual personality. Some are diffident about individual differences and focus on cultural consistencies, whereas others focus their closest attention on the origins of individual differences. Such differences in focus have produced a situation whereby many of the alternative approaches are not necessarily contradictory but may instead be viewed as complementary perspectives.

Similarities as well as differences among the major approaches are set in clearest relief in Section 4, where we describe the major processes or mechanisms used to explain *how* societies, institutions, and the individuals within them change and mold the behavior of others. Despite the diversity of approaches reviewed in Section 3, we see here that they all rely upon a limited number of mechanisms of influence in their descriptions of the socialization process. Their stand on the basic philosophical issues described in Section 2, however, has a remarkable impact on the way these mechanisms are described. It is sometimes difficult to recognize the same mechanism when it has been described in the terminology of two different schools of thought and integrated into a framework involving different formative processes and a different "model of man."

The processes of influence are described in general terms applicable to all human beings in all societies. They are thus used to explain socialization in many societies and within the various classes or castes that make up each society or nation. The content of what is taught differs, however, inter- and intraculturally. We will discuss inter- and intracultural variation in Sections 15 and 16 after completing a discussion of the major aspects of socialization. In a series of rather detailed sections (7 through 11), we will take a generally topical rather than chronological approach, dealing with each of the major areas of socialization—social development in infancy, the development of sex differences, moral development, achievement motivation, and the socialization of aggression—in turn. A chronological approach is not terribly appropriate for discussions of socialization, because each aspect of socialization is learned or developed over an extended period of time.

Consider, for example, the socialization of girls and boys into feminine and masculine sex roles (Section 8). Boys and girls are treated differently from birth, and deliberate efforts to shape their behavior begin before children are able to talk. As children enter the peer group, attain puberty, start dating, get married, and become parents, they encounter new demands and efforts to shape their behavior. As a result, the definitions of masculinity and femininity are refined in accordance with the changing responsibilities the individuals face. The point is that we are socialized into sex roles throughout our lives, and it is thus impossible to identify any one phase of life and say, "here is where sex-role development occurs."

Discussion of the major aspects of socialization is followed by consideration, in turn, of the major sources of social influence on personality development (Section 13). In this section we review evidence concerning the effects, on diverse aspects of social and personality development, of parents and siblings, the media, peers, teachers and schools, and day care. In the succeeding sections, we discuss a variety of deviations from the "normal" developmental processes described thus far. We start with a review of the effects of divorce on the development of children (Section 14). This evidence is of steadily increasing social relevance, since divorce is now a common event in contemporary industrialized countries: recent statistics indicate that nearly one-third of children under 18 in the United States experience the divorce of their parents (Bronfenbrenner, 1975b; Glick, 1979).

Although all societies and subcultures have rules regarding morality, sex roles, achievement, dependence or independence, the rules themselves—and often their mode of enforcement—differ from culture to culture and between classes and ethnic or religious groups within cultures. We will refer to these variations while discussing the major focal areas of socialization and will consider these variations exclusively in Sections 15 (intracultural variation and intervention programs) and 16 (intercultural variation).

In the final substantive section, we discuss atypical development. We focus on four topics here—developmental psychopathology, mental retardation, intellectual giftedness, and child abuse—which are chosen because of their social relevance and their implications for understanding the socialization process.

The second part of this book consists of a collection of articles on various topics concerning socialization and personality development. These articles highlight issues discussed in the first part of the book, providing details and illustrations of concepts which could not be covered at length in Part 1. The readings are grouped into four categories: determinants of development, atypical development, child rearing, and early childhood intervention efforts. "Determinants of Development" includes selections on infant and child development, sex differences, self-concept, and genetic and environmental influences on development. Grouped under "Atypical Development" are articles considering mental retardation, education of the handicapped, and childhood autism. Under the heading of "Child Rearing," parenting, intercultural variation, influences of television, effects of divorce and the problem of child abuse are considered. Finally, selections in the section "Early Childhood Intervention Efforts" deal with such topics as day care, the Head Start program, and the evaluation of intervention efforts.

2

Socialization

Chief Concerns and Goals

Each of us enters the world in the same humble way: as a small infant, rather helpless and poorly coordinated. On that day, we begin a dramatic lifetime of change and development. Even if we focus only on aspects of social and personality development, the agenda facing the newborn infant is complex, extensive, and demanding.

The human newborn possesses a set of reflexes and behavioral propensities that differ from those of other species and allow it to engage in simple yet significant social interactions with other people (Bowlby, 1969). The ability to cry, for example, is inborn, and it is effective in attracting adults to the infant when it is most in need of their ministrations. Social and personality development begins with simple transactions such as these. In most encounters, for example, the baby has an opportunity to look at the face of its caretaker—something which, we find, is remarkably interesting to even the youngest of babies (Sherrod, 1981). From repeated opportunities of this sort, the baby develops first the ability to distinguish between people and objects and thereafter the capacity to recognize specific individuals. These may seem to be elementary steps, but they are certainly essential parts of the process of becoming a functioning member of society.

The repeated tendency of caretakers to relieve the infant's discomfort (biological and psychological) has two major consequences (Lamb, 1981a, 1981b). First, the infant's concept of the caretaker begins to take shape as the infant learns that certain smells, sights, sounds, feels, and events go together consistently. Of greatest interest to students of socialization is the formation of a relationship with the caretaker as the infant learns (a) that the caretaker usually responds in a predictable way, and thus is reliable or trustworthy, and (b) that his or her interventions are usually ameliorative, which ensures that a positive, affectionate relationship is formed rather than an aversion. Second, the infant forms an important—perhaps the most basic—concept of itself at the same time and as a result of the same interactions that lead it to form conceptions and expectations of the caretaker. Specifically, the infant learns that by crying, it can cause things to happen. In other words, the baby learns that it is an effective social being, not simply a passive organism at the mercy of other uncontrollable agents and events. (We will discuss these topics in greater detail in Section 7.)

Caretakers, of course, vary. Some are highly responsive and sensitive, while others are less so. Variations in the way they behave largely account for variations in the type of relationship established between themselves and their infants (Ainsworth, Bell, & Stayton, 1974). These variations in the quality of attachment presumably affect the children's attentiveness to the pressures and demands of their parents, which are there to be sensed as soon as the infant realizes that other people exist. In the view of most socialization theorists, the first major conflicts between parents and children occur when parents attempt to control their children's toileting behavior. However, there is probably nothing especially important about toilet training in itself, since the demands that basic biological functions be controlled begin at the same time as demands that the child take a more independent role in this (and other) area(s), as well as suggestions regarding the types of activities that are deemed appropriate for children of his or her age and sex. Suddenly, a whole array of limitations on children's freedom are imposed. For the young child, the demands must seem bewildering and contradictory. At the same time that it is being encouraged to play independently, for example, it is told to respect the personal property of others and to take heed of warnings from those who are older and stronger. Yet the rule is not transitive, for the child who attempts to dominate those who are younger learns that bullying is forbidden and that the rules governing the protection of personal property are modified by others governing the control and display of aggression. The rules would seem impossibly complex were there not many other people displaying relevant behavior to watch and imitate (Bandura, 1977). Conformity is also facilitated by the development of cognitive and communicative competence, for as children grow older, they can learn abstract rules or principles that govern behavior in a wide range of circumstances. Thereafter, as students of moral development repeatedly point out (Hoffman, 1970b), the task is to teach the child the exceptions and deviations tolerated by the society in recognition of other, and more abstract, principles.

Each of us reaches adulthood with a good understanding of our society's basic rules, and long before that, we each develop a characteristic personality or social style. The individual differences that constitute our distinctive personality in part involve variations in the extent to which we conform to social norms—how masculine or feminine we are, how eager we are to achieve, to be dependent, to be perceived as moral, to be nurturant and gentle. It also involves characteristics such as how at ease we feel in interacting with others, both strange and familiar, how fluently we interact with others, and how capable we are of interpreting other people's behavior and monitoring our own behavior in light of this.

As we survey the people around us, each behaving most of the time in accordance with remarkably complex norms, we cannot help wondering how this considerable conformity arises. Equally, the diversity of individual styles demands that we contemplate their origins. Although students of socialization have developed a science around these issues in the last 50 years, the basic questions with which researchers deal are several millennia older than the discipline. Philosophers have long speculated about the way in which socialization proceeds, pondering the relative importance of inborn differences and experiential history as determinants of development. This issue has perhaps been less important to parents, who are perennially more concerned about the extent to which they can socialize their children efficiently. Responding to this, experts have advised parents how to raise their children at least since the time of Sparta, and probably since long before that. Those who study socialization scientifically today know that there still exists an eager audience of parents, many of whom are disappointed by the limited progress scientists have made in a half-century of intensive research. In part, progress has been slow because socialization is enormously complex: it often seems that "progress" simply involves finding that the complexity is even greater than we had thought. More commonly, though, it is because the interests of scientists and parents are rather different. Students of socialization aim to understand precisely *how* norms or rules are communicated to, understood by, and internalized by those who are the targets of socialization. The nature of the rules themselves is of less consequence to scientists than are the processes by which they are learned, the sources of individual differences in adherence to them, and the origins of characteristic social styles. For many parents, of course, the priorities are reversed, with attention focused more on the aims of socialization than on how to achieve them.

Enduring Philosophical Issues

To say simply that *socialization* refers to the processes by which individuals become distinctive and actively functioning members of the society in which they live is to define the field in a fashion that avoids dealing with some basic philosophical issues that cannot be ignored. Every scientist, every philosopher—indeed, every parent—takes an implicit or explicit position with respect to these issues, and it is time we discussed both the issues and their relevance.

The first issue has to do with the origins of sociability and social behavior. How important are the forces of biology and environment? Is each child born with certain propensities, and how important are these innate tendencies relative to the attempts by parents, teachers, and peers to shape the individual's behavior? This issue is an ancient concern; it was addressed explicitly by Aristotle and may well have occupied the attention of philosophers before him. Related to it is another issue that poses a slightly more specific question: what role do individuals play in their own socialization? Are they passively shaped, or do they actively influence what is done to them? Is the message of socialization always simple, or are there variations in the extent to which individuals interpret and apply the message? Are children taught, or do they seek to learn?

Even if children have innate tendencies, what sort are they? Do humans tend automatically toward what is good or prosocial, or are they perhaps innately evil or egotistical—organisms who must be tamed if they are to function in a society of cooperating individuals? This too is an issue about which there has been extensive speculation over the years.

Finally, there is an issue that has the fewest philosophical forebears but nevertheless elicits different responses from proponents of the major theories: is there a particular period (perhaps early in life) during which humans are especially amenable to influence by their experiences? Any theorist's answer to this question prejudices his or her depiction of the socializing environment. Briefly, the longer the period over which experiences are deemed formative, the greater the number and variety of socializing agents whose influence must be considered.

Let us now consider each of these issues in turn.

Nature Versus Nurture;
Heredity Versus Environment

Throughout most of this century, American psychologists have tended to emphasize environmental influences at the expense of biological ones. The major reason for this is probably sociopolitical rather than scientific. Particularly in the twentieth century, citizens of the United States have viewed destiny as something to be fought for and seized by every individual. At the turn of the century, this was a new, young country in which all things seemed possible given the necessary will and determination. This national optimism fostered a view of the person as shaper rather than shaped. Thus it seemed reasonable to many when Watson claimed it was possible to make any child, regardless of genetic heritage, into any kind of adult; Watson's promise was consistent with the national philosophy. In such a philosophical climate, it would seem heretical to claim that biological factors contributed to or determined individual destiny, for such a view would implicitly state that all were *not* created equal, that individuals differed in potential, and that innate differences constrained the manner and extent of each person's development.

A contrary note was sounded by a Yale pediatrician named Arnold Gesell, who was the most prominent American exponent of a maturationalistic perspective in this century. Gesell, who was trained first as a psychologist and then as a physician and embryologist, believed that behavioral capacities unfolded over time in the same way that certain physiological events occurred in a fixed sequence during the prenatal phases of development. It is to Gesell that we owe phrases like "she's at that awkward stage," "he'll grow out of it," and "the terrible two's." In his best read works, Gesell emphasized these uniformities, while not doubting that biological factors could also give rise to individual differences. He achieved enormous popularity among the lay public, although he was never that popular among professionals.

Both Watson and Gesell were firmly committed to their positions, and their followers maintained this zeal during the succeeding decades. Looking back on the statements made prior to 1960 concerning the nature-nurture issue, therefore, one gets the impression that the two groups of extremists clung to their beliefs unyieldingly. In fact, however, a growing number of psychologists adopted more moderate positions when framing their own perspectives. In 1958, Anastasi published a paper that succinctly summarized the interactionist position that was becoming increasingly persuasive. Anastasi pointed out with special cogency that both hereditary and experiential influences were important, since every aspect of development was determined by a complex interaction between biological (inherited) and environmental (experiential) factors. Without either, there could be no development. In view of the constant interaction between these two sources of influence, she continued, it makes little sense to argue about how important either factor is relative to the other; the joint effect is not equivalent to the sum of the two separate parts. In a review published several years later, Zigler (1970a) restated these conclusions.

Anastasi's claim regarding the interactive role of biological and environmental forces seemed to summarize the assumptions of many psychologiosts, and since

1958 it has been common (for textbook writers, especially) to say that the nature-nurture issue has been resolved. Unfortunately, as we shall observe shortly, many psychologists give only lip service to this resolution while stressing one source of influence (usually the environmental) at the expense of the other. Further, none of the major theories gives sophisticated and careful attention to the exact nature of the interaction between the two sources of influence.

Related to the nature-nurture controversy is the question of whether socialized behavior is mediated by enduring personality traits or by environmental situations; this, too, is a question of internal versus external determinants of behavior. On the one hand, it would be argued that a person will exhibit certain traits in all situations, and on the other, that a given person will exhibit different traits depending on the situations in which he or she is involved. According to the latter view, it would not be meaningful to speak of an "honest" person, because a person may be honest in one situation but not in another. For example, people are more honest when cheating is likely to be noticed or (to use a different type of example) more quiet in churches than at football games (Mischel, 1969, 1973). In this view, knowledge of a situation is a better predictor of behavior than knowledge of a person.

Several criticisms of this situational approach to personality have been pointed out by Zigler and Seitz (1978). First, behavior is often more significantly affected by a person's interpretation of a situation than by the situation itself (Bowers, 1973), suggesting that internal factors are crucial mediators of behavior. Second, people select or create their environments: people who hate violence tend to avoid situations in which aggression is likely to occur, while hostile people may seek out just such situations. Even a reexamination of the evidence on which the situationist position was based (Burton, 1963) revealed more consistency across situations than was originally found. Further, Zigler and Seitz raise a question about developmental continuity in personality traits: while these traits appear to be enduring, they may be expressed differently at different ages, and this makes long-term assessment somewhat problematic.

Active Versus Passive Views of the Child

One of the most significant changes in socialization theory in recent years has been in the conception of the child's role in socialization. The shift has been from a view of children as passive to one of children as active in shaping the course of their own development. Learning theory, for example, held children to be passive in the socialization process, simply reacting to reinforcement and punishment, which determined the nature of the adults they would become. In the psychoanalytic framework, children were seen as vulnerable to traumatic experiences whose effects could last a lifetime (Zigler & Seitz, 1978). Recent evidence, however, suggests that children play an active role in socialization. As Zigler and Seitz discuss, one line of evidence comes from a study of infants, who are surprisingly competent even just after birth (Kessen, 1963) and, moreover, whose development is affected by biological predispositions which cannot easily be changed by caretakers. A second line of evidence comes from cognitive-developmental theorists' demonstration that children are active in selecting experiences and in directing their own intellectual growth.

Whereas a passive conception of the child yields research which assumes a unidirectional (parent to child) influence in socialization, a view of the child as active necessitates consideration of both parties in the parent-child relationship. Thus, research has moved from emphasizing caretaking practices and their effects on children to considering infants' effects on parents and the establishment of stable patterns of interaction (Bell, 1968; Freedman, 1974; Thomas & Chess, 1977). Similarly, as Zigler and Seitz (1978) note, effective parenting is no longer considered to derive from a single type of practice but, rather, from responsiveness to particular infants' styles and empathic understanding of infants' needs (Ainsworth et al., 1974; Baumrind, 1975; Blehar et al., 1977; Schaffer & Emerson, 1964; Thomas et al., 1968). One major result of the shift in conceptualization of the child is the realization that the outcome of socialization is not the sole responsibility of parent or child but depends on both.

Natural Good or Evil?

The third philosophical issue which we will discuss concerns the debate over whether innate human tendencies are good or evil. Several centuries ago, this debate coexisted with that over the nature-nurture issue discussed above. The argument over natural good and natural evil has been resurrected recently by some of the popularizers of ethology and sociobiology (e.g., Ardrey, 1967; Montagu, 1968; Morris, 1967; Wilson, 1978), but for most of this century, the debate lay dormant. There were many reasons for this: the widespread denial of any "natural" (i.e., biologically determined) tendencies; the widespread interest in individual differences rather than normative trends; and the desire of psychologists to avoid value judgments when constructing the science of psychology.

In the seventeenth and eighteenth centuries, however, the issue of natural tendencies was a very real one. The question which concerned philosophers and theologians was whether people are born selfish beasts whom civilization makes human or with an inherent humanity which civilization corrupts. Most Christian theologians—particularly Calvinists, for example—believed that children were innately evil, manipulated by the devil. Socialization involved delivering their souls to God, and this required a long and vigorous effort to subdue basic evil instincts. Even the philosopher Locke (1693), who is better known for his claims regarding the importance of experiential factors and the irrelevance of biological ones, implies in his treatises on child rearing and education that whatever biological forces existed were likely to be negative. Of course, this only accentuated further the necessity for extensive efforts on the part of parents and other socializers. Another philosopher, John Hobbes, wondered how socialization was possible at all, in view of the base animal nature he attributed to human beings.

Jean-Jacques Rousseau (1762), the Swiss-born philosopher, was the most prominent proponent of the opposing view—that people are innately good and that society makes them evil and egotistical. We owe to Rousseau the concept of the noble savage—the moral and happy person who was spared the influence of modern culture and so was able to develop to his or her full and glorious potential. Rousseau scoffed at the notion that any program of socialization fashioned by humans could ever achieve as much as the "forces of nature." His major work, *Emile* (1762), so shocked and unsettled the governments and societies of Europe with its scathing attack on cultural institutions that Rousseau spent the remaining 16 years of his life as a fugitive or in exile.

Although not phrased in such absolute terms, the issue of natural good or evil remains important to contemporary socialization theory. In one view, children are seen as ultimately selfish and instrumental, desiring only to fulfill basic needs, while their parents try to inculcate in them consideration for other people. In another view, empathy and concern need not be taught but develop naturally if children's physical and emotional needs have been satisfied. Sociobiologists offer yet another view, arguing that altruism, for example, arises as a function of genetic relatedness among individuals.

With regard to this issue, the change in recent years has been to a more positive view of the child. Zigler and Seitz (1978) illustrate this trend with a reference to psychoanalytic and learning theories of development. Both of these theories were, some 25 years ago, based on a negative image of children's motivation for development. Freudian theory assumed that positive motives, such as love, derived from more basic negative and self-interested ones, such as failing to receive protection or food. Learning theorists such as Dollard and Miller (1950) and Hull (1952) argued that the motivation for behavior was to be found in the desire to reduce unpleasant tensions caused by biological needs. In contrast, recent developments in these fields reflect a more positive attitude. For example, neo-Freudian psychologists have argued that adaptive and positive behaviors are not derived from primitive instincts but exist on their own (e.g., Hartmann, 1958). Personality theorists such as Allport (1955), Maslow (1954), and Rogers (1951) have discussed positive intrinsic growth tendencies and see self-actualization (within the framework of society) as the goal of socialization. White (1959, 1960) postulated an inherent effectance motivation. On the learning theory side, recent investigators have been concerned with positive, adaptive behaviors such as curiosity and exploration and have viewed these as independent of biological drives (Berlyne, 1960; Harlow, 1953). In general, recent researchers seem to hold positive characteristics as predominant and have tended to look for positive changes in attempting to understand human development.

Length and Breadth of the Socialization Process

The third philosophical issue, which we now discuss, is particularly pertinent to contemporary efforts to account for individual differences in personality. This issue, already mentioned in the introductory section, concerns the length of the period during which socialization is believed to be an important formative influence. Some theorists have focused most of their attention on events during a very narrow phase (usually one that occurs early in life), while other theorists have described a much longer and slower process. Those who focused on narrow "critical periods" argued that children were uniquely susceptible to environmental influences on both social and cognitive development during these predetermined periods, and believed that behavioral plasticity was much less after these early critical periods had passed. As a result, their theories and researches focused almost exclusively on early experiences (later experiences were interesting only as outcomes of earlier formative experiences), and they proposed that early interventions alone were likely to make any reasonable impression.

    As we shall see in the next section, the two theories that laid greatest stress on the role of early experiences in shaping socioemotional development—psychoanalysis and psychoanalytically oriented ethological theory—focused almost exclusively on parents as agents of socialization. Following their lead, most other theorists wrote only about parental influences, though their theoretical positions did not necessarily demand this. Most anthropologists and sociologists have always considered the influence of multiple agents of socialization, but psychologists have until recently followed Freud's lead and have regarded early (intrafamilial) experiences as uniquely important. Recent workers within social learning theory, however, have discussed the influence of socialization agents encountered by the child after it moves from its sheltered position within the family to contact with peers and teachers, and this broader perspective is evident in later sections of this book. In 1975, Urie Bronfenbrenner (1975b, 1977), a prominent psychologist, argued that developmentalists had erred in placing too much attention on the "micro" environment (i.e., the family) and too little attention on the "meso" and "macro" environments (i.e., institutions in the wider society). Bronfenbrenner's critique stimulated a number of endeavors in which attempts were made to place the child's development in a broader context (e.g., Belsky, 1981; Bronfenbrenner, 1979; Cochran, 1977; Garbarino, 1977).

Another change in socialization research has been to consider periods of life other than childhood. In contrast to the characteristic theoretical emphasis on children and adolescents, Erikson's (1963) life span view of development addresses the need to examine developmental crises at all stages of life. Recent researchers, too, have begun to study development during the period from young adulthood to old age (Birren & Schaie, 1977; Eisdorfer & Lawton, 1973; Goulet & Baltes, 1970). Brim and Wheeler (1966), for example, have argued that the socialization for the new roles which adults must continually adopt occurs at the time these roles are adopted rather than decades earlier. We might expect similar factors to affect adult and childhood socialization, although in adulthood parents would no longer be the primary socializing agents. Zigler and Seitz (1978) suggest that as children are active in their own socialization, and change themselves according to their own self-definitions, adults may be involved in their own socialization to an even greater extent. For example, these authors point out that decisions made in adulthood, such as to change careers or marriage partners, appear to arise partially from self-defined goals.

A decision about whether or not to place special emphasis on early experiences has far-reaching implications for the development of theory concerning socialization and personality development. First, as noted already, it determines which and how many agents of socialization must be considered, and this in turn determines how complicated the explanation must be. Second, it forces the theorist to consider whether there is continuity or stability in development. Do earlier experiences determine enduring outlines of personality physiognomy, while details are filled in by later experiences? Or do later experiences completely paint over the products of early experiences, resulting in a developmental trajectory marked by extreme discontinuity? Or do different sorts of experiences affect different aspects of development at different times, so that there is perfect continuity within rather specific areas? Most researchers sidestep this issue by considering only one set of influences at one stage of development, but in the long run no successful theory can adopt this strategy.

3

Major Theoretical Perspectives

In this section, we will consider seven perspectives or approaches that have been prominent during the twentieth century. Some of these perspectives are now largely of historical interest only, whereas others remain popular today. We will discuss these perspectives in rough chronological order, though we shall deviate from this sequence when theoretical links between approaches make the chronological organization inappropriate.

As Zigler (1963a) argued several years ago, all of the major theories that continue to dominate developmental psychology are not really theories at all. They are, rather, approaches, points of view, or perspectives, most of which fall short of the basic definition of a theory: a set of statements providing clear-cut and testable predictions. As the following brief review indicates, testability is a major problem with prominent developmental theories. Some are descriptive only, eschewing explanation; others attempt explanations that are scientifically untestable; still others make scientifically testable predictions but do not discuss or attempt to explain the psychological and behavioral changes across the life span that are the principal concerns of *developmental* psychology.

Psychoanalysis

This approach must head our list both because it was the first approach to gain prominence and because it has been the most influential theory—the yardstick by which other theories have been compared and contrasted (Hall & Lindzey, 1978). Thus, the impact of psychoanalytic theory on the study of socialization has been both direct and indirect. One direct theory on the contribution has been in the form of hypotheses generated from Freud's focus on relationships in the family and on the significance of child-rearing practices. An indirect influence is evident, for example, in the work of the neo-Hullian learning theorists (e.g., Dollard, Miller, Mowrer, Sears), who used learning theory to examine areas of social development such as aggression and dependency, which they felt psychoanalytic theory had identified as most important (Zigler & Seitz, 1978).

The psychoanalytic approach was developed in Vienna by Sigmund Freud around the turn of the century. Freud was a neurologist by training who became aware of the power of psychological factors when he and a colleague, Breuer, found that emotional factors could be totally debilitating—paralyzing—and yet could be relieved by hypnosis. Later, Freud decided that hypnosis was not necessary: it was sufficient for the patient to recall and relive the events that were the cause of the emotional blockage.

Freud's clinical work led him to the idea that most of his patients' problems could be traced to events (long forgotten) that had occurred early in their lives. As a clinician, Freud's primary goal was to alleviate his patients' symptoms, and his attempts to do this led him to focus on the earlier events or experiences that appeared to be responsible for existing symptoms. This resulted in a set of notions about the origins of personality patterns—notions that combined to form a theory of psychosocial development, albeit based on contact with a small number of neurotic patients. We will discuss here only those aspects of the theory particularly relevant to understanding its application to the study of socialization.

In Freudian theory, development is a function of both biological maturation and experience—notably, the subjective interpretation of experience. Freud's personality theory is based on the assumption of unconscious mental processes which affect every part of life and on the assumption that all mental events are causally related (the principle of psychic determinism). The motivation for behavior is seen to stem from internal or instinctual needs, of which Freud's later theory postulates two major categories: the life instinct (which seeks to preserve the individual and, more generally, the species) and the death instinct (which, when turned outward, is a destructive force). These instinctual forces are held to be universal, but their "objects," or the conditions which satisfy the needs, vary for different individuals. According to Freud, psychic energy becomes cathected, or invested, in a mental image of an object or person with the degree of cathexis depending on the importance of the object or person. Freud called the constructive force, or psychic energy, associated with the life instinct *libido*.

Freud believed that personality structure has three parts, and the successive development of these is of relevance to understanding some of the assumptions of psychoanalytic theory to which we have referred (especially the negative view of the child). The original mental function—the sole process in infants, and the one from which all others derive—is the *id*, a totally unconscious store of psychic energy associated with the instincts. The id does not have a conception of reality; it seeks only immediate gratification (either in a real object or in a fantasized one). The development of a rational mental function, the *ego*, occurs as an infant grows and needs real means of satisfaction. The ego then mediates the conflict between id and reality, but it is important to remember that it is a secondary function which grows out of the id. Finally, during childhood, a third region of mind develops out of the ego: the *superego*, a representation of cultural values and standards. While the ego is partially conscious and partially unconscious, the superego is largely unconscious and is an uncompromising opposing force to the id.

Perhaps of central importance in the study of socialization is Freud's postulation of developmental stages. Freud believed that these stages occur as a result of maturation and the direction of children's psychic energy: as children grow, different parts of the body become the focus of libidinal needs. This concept of *stages* notes that different experiences will be most salient for children of different developmental levels. While the stages are seen to occur naturally, their primary importance may be found in their representation of the child as especially susceptible, during brief definable stages, to experiences of a certain type. Thus, Freud's theory is actually a fairly sophisticated interactionist one.

Freud described five such phases of development. During the *oral phase*, which lasts over the first 2 years, oral experiences (particularly those associated with feeding) are most influential. During infancy, the child forms its first affectionate social relationship to the person consistently associated with the pleasures of feeding—its mother, Freud assumed. Both good and bad oral experiences are believed to have long-term influences on personality. Here, as in other phases, Freud explained the events in terms of a complex set of processes involving the interrelated dynamics of motivations and fantasies and the three psychic structures (the id, the ego, and the superego) competing for control over the individual's behavior.

The *anal period* follows the oral phase. The focus of primary gratification shifts to the anal region in this phase, so that urination and excretion now bring the greatest pleasure to the child, and the parents' attempts to toilet-train the child are the focal point for the major socializing influences. According to psychoanalysts, obsessive compulsions and marked messiness in adults have their sources in negative experiences during this phase.

Instead of the oral and anal areas, the primary sources of gratification and pleasure during the *phallic period* (4.5 to 7 years, approximately) are the genitals. During this phase, the child has fantasies of sexual relations with others—particularly the opposite-sex parent—and this sets the stage for a major event known as the *Oedipal situation* (Mullahy, 1948). This event has to be described differently for boys and girls. According to Freud, each young boy at this age fancies himself as his mother's lover. He is afraid, however, of his rival for the mother's love—father—and fears that the father may castrate him in revenge. According to the theory, the boy believes that this is a realistic fear because his interpretation of the anatomical differences between the sexes is that women have lost their penises, presumably by castration. To guard against this possibility, the boy identifies with his father, attempting to emulate his morals, standards, principles, etc.; the child reasons that the father would not be vindictive toward someone like himself. Psychoanalysts attribute to identification the internalization of the masculine personality and strict morality; resolution of the Oedipal situation is held to be the basis of the superego and, so, is a highly important part of psychosocial development.

The girl's experience during this period, in Freud's view, is rather different from the boy's. Like the boy, she discovers the anatomical differences between boys and girls, but instead of castration anxiety, she experiences penis envy—believing she once had a penis which has been removed by her mother. She decides that the only way to regain a penis is to share it with a lover (or have a baby as a penis substitute), and so, she sets out to attract the attention of a male, the prime candidate being her father. Since the father clearly loves the mother, the daughter chooses to identify with the mother as a means of securing her father's affection. Freud believed that this motive to identify is not as strong as the motive (castration anxiety) prompting identification in boys and, as a result, that the internalization of the sex role and morality is never as far-reaching and complete in girls as it is in boys. Freud regarded these events as inevitable in both boys and girls. When fathers are not present to complete the Oedipal triangle, for example, Freud suggested that the child would create fantasy parents.

The tumultuous phallic period is followed by a period called *latency* (from 7 to 11 or 12 years)—a phase of relative quiescence. Then follows the *genital period*, beginning around puberty, during which the foundations of heterosexual relations are established. Freud had much less to say about these two later phases, apparently believing that the oral, anal, and phallic phases were of greatest formative significance.

Most of Freud's followers have adopted this belief in the special importance of early experiences. A major exception is Erik Erikson (1950), who has been perhaps the most widely read neo-Freudian. Like Freud, Erikson believes in stages of development, but he describes eight stages occurring between birth and death. Instead of emphasizing a shifting locus of gratification, Erikson claims that each developmental stage is characterized by an *issue* which can be resolved either well or badly. The stages and the positive and negative resolutions are described in Table 1. According to Erikson, the manner in which each issue is resolved has

Age	Positive and Negative Resolutions
Infancy	Basic trust vs. mistrust
Toddlerhood	Autonomy vs. shame
The preschool years	Initiative vs. guilt
Middle childhood	Industry vs. inferiority
Adolescence	Identity vs. diffusion
Young adulthood	Intimacy vs. isolation
Adulthood	Generativity vs. stagnation
Maturity	Ego integrity vs. despair

implications for the way in which future issues can be resolved, producing a snowballing effect. In the early stages, the successfulness of resolution depends in large part on the behavior of parents and other caretakers. Later, individuals themselves have a more direct impact on resolution, although the strength of the personality developed in previous experiences is of course critical. Like Freud, Erikson emphasizes feeding experiences during the first 2 years, but the major issue concerns the establishing of a trusting relationship between infant and caretaker. As far as toilet training is concerned, Erikson emphasizes the battle of wills between parent and child that occurs when the child tries to assert its independence from parental demands. Erikson does not believe that the Oedipal situation characteristically occurs; instead he describes the key issue of the third period as one of initiative vs. guilt. Furthermore, Erikson obviously believes that the period of formative experience is far longer than Freud suggested, for he describes stages and issues continuing throughout life. Unfortunately, although he identifies issues, Erikson has not indicated what experiences are especially influential in the various stages, nor has he specified mechanisms of influence. Erikson has paid less attention than Freud to the dynamics of psychological functioning.

Psychoanalysis provided the first deterministic theory of development and represented the first appreciation by psychologists that formative experiences occurred as early as infancy. Despite the contributions of this theory to socialization research, however, it has decreased in importance in this country over the years. One reason for this is that many psychoanalytic propositions are difficult or—because the theory deals with unconscious mental processes, which are by definition inaccessible to research—even impossible to test. Another reason for the decline of psychoanalytic theory's influence, suggested by Zigler and Seitz (1978), is that the theory's negative view of children's development is incompatible with the increasing recognition of children's active, exploratory nature: in a psychoanalytic framework, positive characteristics such as play and curiosity would have to be derived from more basic negative ones such as the repression of libidinal tendencies.

Social Learning Theory

Although psychoanalysis was developed in Europe, it rapidly drew the attention of psychologists in the United States (Kessen, 1965). Although some prominent Americans (such as G. Stanley Hall) were impressed by the depth and power of psychoanalysis, most saw the extensive focus on unconscious mental processes as a step back toward the barrenness of introspection. As has been indicated above, however, the rejection of psychoanalysis was not total; it was the mention of unobservable processes that was objectionable, not the ambitiousness and apparent explanatory power of the theory. Thus, for example, Watson's view of personality development was greatly influenced by psychoanalysis, even though he led the attack on the mentalistic elements of both psychoanalysis and introspectionism in his famous *Behaviorist Manifesto* (1913). Watson shared Freud's rather negative view of human tendencies and proposed a similar tension reduction model of psychodynamic function. All that psychologists could and should study, Watson argued in his *Manifesto*, was observable behavior. Consequently, the socialization of the child was best viewed as a series of learning experiences: if one simply studied the way in which any child had been treated by its parents, one would understand why it later behaved as it did. If there were similarities between the developmental courses of different children, this could be attributed to similarities in the way they had been treated rather than to biologically determined stages. Every person was viewed as completely pliable. Behaviors that were associated with negative events or consequences dropped out of the child's repertoire, whereas those that had positive consequences or associations were more likely to be repeated in the future. The problem of socialization was, essentially, how children are taught to become the right kind of adults (Zigler & Seitz, 1978).

Watson himself left academic psychology while still young, and his empirical contributions to the study of personality development are limited to the demonstration that a phobic fear can be conditioned simply by the association of neutral stimuli with fear-provoking stimuli (Watson & Raynor, 1920) and the parallel demonstration that phobic fears can be deconditioned (Jones, 1924). Much of Watson's writing was directed toward parents rather than academic psychologists (Watson, 1928). Watson did not elaborate a detailed theory, although he stimulated the development of more detailed accounts by Skinner (1938, 1974, 1978) and Bijou and Baer (1961, 1963), who are the best-known living proponents of a deterministic stimulus-response theory of socialization. Skinner's theoretical system, in its applied form of behavior modification, has gained some popularity as a child-rearing technique (Zigler & Seitz, 1978).

Prior to Skinner and Bijou and Baer, however, another influential school of learning theory took shape at Yale University under the guidance of Clark Hull (1943, 1951, 1952). Whereas the Skinnerians consider only reinforcement, punishment, and contingent association as the learning mechanisms involved in socialization, the Hullians introduced the notion of *drives* and proposed that drive reduction was the most important form of reinforcement. Children, like all mammals, were believed to have a set of primary drives (e.g., for food), the reduction of which was reinforcing. The first social relationship between infant and mother, argued the Hullians, was formed because the mother was repeatedly associated with relief of the infant's hunger. They proceeded to show that many of the events described by psychoanalysts could be translated into *drive reduction learning mechanisms* (Dollard & Miller, 1950; Miller & Dollard, 1941). This permitted one to explain the developmental issues Freud had defined without relying upon unconscious, unobservable, and thus unverifiable mental processes and fantasies in the explanations.

In addition to a small set of *primary drives* (defined by their biological significance), Hull and his colleagues developed the notion of *secondary drives*. Secondary drives are established through repeated association with primary drives. One example will suffice. Hunger is a primary drive, and being fed is thus reinforcing. If the same individual consistently feeds the infant, then proximity to that person will become the goal of a secondary drive, and proximity to that person will become reinforcing. Among older children, approval can also become a secondary reinforcement in this way.

Further, Hull and his colleagues noticed that Freud frequently referred to identification in his descriptions of personality development, and they realized that reward and punishment were probably not sufficient explanatory processes on their own. Thus the Yale theorists introduced to learning theory the notion of *imitation* (Dollard & Miller, 1941; Sears, 1951). We learn a great deal, Hull and his colleagues argued, by observing other people perform certain behaviors (see also Mussen, 1967). We imitate them because we find it rewarding to do so (others may reward us, or we may reward ourselves in their absence because we are like them). Thus reward is still involved in learning and shaping the behavioral performance, but the first performance is not randomly determined or prompted by some basic drive—it is the consequence of imitation. The Hullians, however, eliminated the motivational dynamics implicit in Freud's discussions of identification, replacing it with a simpler motivation—pursuit of reward.

Drive reduction theory was influential until the late 1950s, when it fell from favor. There were two reasons for this. First, students of learning found an increasing number of exceptions to the tight but complex laws of learning developed by Hull and his many collaborators (see, for example, Harlow, 1953). Second, and of greater relevance to developmental psychologists, Harlow (Harlow & Zimmerman, 1959) showed that infant monkeys formed relationships not to surrogate mothers who were associated with the reduction of primary drives (hunger) but to surrogates who provided contact comfort. The attempts by theorists such as Berlyne (1963) to defend the drive reduction orientation against Harlow's criticisms proved unsuccessful. Today drive reduction theories have few adherents among those studying socialization and personality development.

The most prominent learning theory extant today is the *social learning theory* of Bandura and Walters (1959, 1963a; Bandura, 1962, 1969, 1977). Bandura and Walters argue that many of the behavior patterns that children learn were never taught in the tedious, step-by-step manner involved in the shaping of behavior by reinforcement and punishment. Rather, they propose, children learn from simply observing other people—they *imitate*. Bandura proposes a two-phase *model* of *imitation* or *identification*. The first phase is that of *acquisition:* the child learns whatever it sees performed by others. Of course the child sees many contradictory patterns of behavior, and many of the behaviors it observes are never imitated (i.e., acted out by the child). The second phase, *performance* of a learned pattern of behavior, depends on a number of factors: the identity of the original model (children are more likely to remember and perform the behavior of nurturant and powerful models than those of people they don't like or respect), the consequences for the model (was he or she rewarded or punished for the behavior?) and the consequences for the child (punishment or reinforcement) when he or she attempts to emulate. Bandura's social learning theory thus considers reinforcement and punishment, but mainly as influences on performance rather than as influences on acquisition.

By introducing the mechanism of imitation, social learning theorists have developed a more plausible perspective on the complexity of socialization than would be represented by a theory concerned only with punishment and reinforcement. It becomes reasonable to conceive of children learning roles rather than the component behaviors. Still, social learning theory has its problems. Yando, Seitz, and Zigler (1978) have criticized the nondevelopmental nature of social learning theory, arguing that behavior is mediated by different processes at different ages, and that imitation depends on motivational factors and cognitive and motor skills which change with development. Furthermore, since both boys and girls see both male and female models, how do they choose sex-appropriate models? How otherwise do they learn specific, appropriate sex roles when there is little evidence that parents reinforce and punish children consistently for sex-stereotyped behavior? These issues were taken up by Kohlberg (1966), whose cognitive developmental theory we shall consider later. Before doing so, however, we should consider a perspective that has also been influential, although it has contributed less than these others to our understanding of the processes of influence.

Anthropology

The discipline of anthropology emerged a century ago as an attempt to record and understand the diverse customs of peoples and cultures throughout the world. Among the customs to which it turned attention were those surrounding the development of children. Anthropology carried the promise of testing whether the "universal" developmental phases and processes psychologists discussed were indeed universal, rather than characteristics of the Western cultures in which the psychological theorists were immersed (Kardiner, 1939, 1945; Whiting, 1941). It was clear to many anthropologists that Western social scientists had a very narrow view of socialization—a view that was circumscribed by their own experiences and cultural presumptions. Anthropologists argued—correctly, we believe—that one might come to understand abstract principles of socialization more easily if one focused on unfamiliar cultures rather than solely upon one's own.

As reports returned from the field, it became clear that there was enormous societal diversity, and this led anthropologists to stress the importance of cultural rather than biological factors as sources of influence on personality development (Barry, 1969; Whiting & Child, 1953). On the other hand, similar issues seemed to be central in most cultures, and this suggested that there were biological forces behind development also. In addition to its contributions to the search for universals, furthermore, anthropological data offered *natural experiments* of influences on socialization—for example, in its documentation of extreme or unusual cases. Zigler and Seitz (1978) note one such example in the effect of cultural change on an African tribe, the Ik: external destruction of traditional societal practices resulted in a breakdown of family structure, near-abandonment of care for children, and the disappearance of personality qualities such as affection and concern (Turnbull, 1973). A major problem with anthropological evidence, however, is that data are usually correlational, so when cultural differences are observed, it is difficult to determine their cause. Also, recent researchers have become sensitive to the problem of ethnocentricity on the part of Western-trained observers (Cole & Brunner, 1971; Cole et al., 1971; Tulkin & Konner, 1973).

Several lessons have been learned from the anthropological perspective. First, students have been forced to be more cautious and to refrain from ready descriptions of universal principles. The anthropological perspective has also taught us that there are many ways of achieving the various goals of socialization and that different cultures often rely upon different means for achieving common goals. On the other hand, anthropologists have not described new and novel mechanisms, and they tend to describe socialization at the level of culture rather than at the level of the individual (Barry, Bacon, & Child, 1957; Barry, Child, & Bacon, 1959). Thus, their contributions to psychological theories of socialization have not been extensive.

A promising shift has occurred, however, in the anthropological research of recent years. Anthropologists have increasingly turned to a cognitive rather than a behavioral view of culture, seeing a culture as a people's shared mode of experiencing and understanding the world. Clifford Geertz (1973, p. 89), a leader of this movement in anthropology, defines *culture* as "an historically transmitted pattern of meanings embodied in symbols, a system of inherited conceptions expressed in symbolic forms by means of which men [and women] communicate, perpetuate, and develop their knowledge about the attitudes toward life." This view of culture poses, of course, a major question about socialization: How do individuals acquire the pattern of meanings that characterizes their group? If anthropologists come to search for the details of an answer to that question, their work will interact in new ways with the psychological study of socialization. This new approach to cross-cultural research has also been emphasized by Michael Cole and his colleagues (Laboratory of Comparative Human Cognition, 1979). We discuss their own and related work in a later section on "Intercultural Variation."

Cognitive Developmental Theory

The cognitive developmental approach to personality is largely associated with the work of Piaget (see Piaget, 1970) and, as implied by its name, focuses on cognitive growth. In this approach, development is viewed as a systematic process consisting of a universal sequence of stages. The environment is seen as playing an important role in development, but it is held that the environments in which children grow almost always provide the experiences necessary to foster development. Furthermore, in the cognitive developmental approach, the child plays an active role in development. Cognitive structures mediate between the environment and the child's responses. According to Piaget, these structures continually develop with the child's new experiences: when new knowledge cannot fit into an existing structure (or *schema*), children modify their schemas to handle the new experience. In this manner, children pass through stages of cognitive functioning, each of which is characterized by a type of reasoning which subsumes and builds on that of the previous stage. The thought of children, then, is qualitatively different from that of adults. In the cognitive developmental framework, motivation for behavior is seen as an inherent cognitive characteristic rather than as derived from biological needs or from external rewards.

Zigler and Seitz (1978) note several criticisms often leveled against the cognitive developmental approach. First, cultural and experiential factors are underemphasized in the determination of thought processes. In this regard, it must be recognized that cognitive developmentalists assume the process of thinking (e.g., memory capacity, information processing) but not the content to be invariant and age related; the content of thought differs between children and between cultures. Another criticism has been that the cognitive approach emphasizes intellectual at the expense of affective development. Finally, in the search for a normative sequence of cognitive development, this approach has given relatively little consideration to individual variability.

The cognitive developmental approach has grown rapidly and is currently an extremely influential one for socialization studies. Although Piaget was primarily concerned with the development of thinking in children, his theory also has implications for socialization and personality development. Piaget himself discussed only one aspect of personality development—the changing concept of morality (Piaget, 1932). Essentially, he proposed that there was a shift around age 7 from obedience to moral precepts in order to avoid punishment or to obtain approval, to obedience out of a realization that smooth social functioning depended on everyone's adhering to a common set of rules. He attributed this shift to a change in the way the child was able to think about the world.

Many years later, the cognitive developmental approach to moral development was updated by Kohlberg (1958, 1963). Kohlberg claimed that there were six (later changed to five) universal stages of moral development; not all people reached the highest stage (actually, very few do), but no one could reach this stage without first passing through the lower stages. There was a hierarchical sequence of stages, each of which represented a different way of thinking about society and its rules and a different way of justifying obedience and disobedience. We will discuss the details of these stages later; here, it is important simply to note that Kohlberg drew the attention of psychologists to the fact that with age there occurs a change in the way children conceive of socialization and social rules. One cannot, therefore, simply see children as homogeneous, pliable organisms, as the social learning theorists seemed to believe. Children have minds, Kohlberg pointed out, and any viable theory of socialization had to recognize this even if it did not accept Kohlberg's notion of universal stages of social cognition.

Kohlberg was particularly critical of Bandura and Walters' theory of observational learning, which was widely popular when he developed his theory. Social learning theorists, argued Kohlberg, failed to consider that children might be motivated to imitate certain models in preference to others. Sex-role learning was a case in point. Around the age of 6 or 7, Kohlberg (1966, 1969) argued, children realize that their sex will remain constant throughout their lives. This realization, coupled with the recognition that society prescribes distinctive modes of behavior for males and females, leads children to search out same-sex models to imitate. This motivated search for appropriate models explains why children selectively imitate same-sex models and thus learn "appropriate" behavior patterns. Kohlberg's theory builds upon both cognitive developmental theory and observational learning theory in arguing that we need to consider characteristics of both the model *and the observer* (particularly his or her cognitive developmental status) when seeking to explain the acquisition of complex patterns of behavior,. This is an important contribution. Zigler and his colleagues (e.g., Achenbach & Zigler, 1968; Kohlberg & Zigler, 1967; Yando et al., 1978) have likewise argued that one needs to consider the cognitive developmental level when describing personality development and socialization. The specific mechanisms are discussed below in the sections "Cognitive Factors" and "Mental Retardation."

The study of social cognition, which has risen to prominence since the mid-1960s, exemplifies another way in which cognitive development affects social development. Students of social cognition are concerned about the ways in which children come to understand and evaluate the behavior, intentions, and dispositions of other people. One basic capacity has to do with the recognition that other people, by virtue of their location, roles, and experiences, often perceive the world differently from oneself. In order to interact competently, one must take these differences into account and tailor one's communications accordingly. Very young children are egocentric and incapable of placing themselves in another's position so as to understand a different perspective. This inability to take another's role also limits the capacity to empathize with others, which is another topic of concern to students of social cognition. Another area of interest is the development of person perception. Researchers have shown that as children grow older, they come to describe stress in terms of less concrete and more psychologically complex factors such as motives and traits. The research on social cognition is discussed more fully in Chapter 12.

Recently, cognitive psychologists have suggested that the notion of *scripts* may be a useful concept for students of socialization to consider. By taking part in social life and by observing the interactions of others, a child learns a great deal about what people of his or her group ordinarily do in various situations. A child develops a *script*, as psychologists have recently come to say (Abelson, 1981), for what happens when it's time for lunch, or when you meet a stranger, and so on (Nelson & Gruendel, 1981). These scripts reflect cultural regularities in what the child has observed or lived through, so when the child's actions are influenced by them, the scripts serve as cognitive mediators of the socialization process. Scripts as an aspect of cognitive learning have been applied by Gagnon (1973) to sexual socialization in our society and by Tomkins (in press) to the development of emotional life generally. In transactional analysis (a form of therapeutic practice and associated theory), the term *script* has been used to restate in cognitive terms the importance that psychoanalysis claims for childhood experience as an influence on adult personality (Steiner, 1974). Blind adherence to the scripts learned in childhood hinders the development of new behavior better adapted to unexplored realities of adult life. Even the prevention of cognitive learning may affect socialization. For example, a child who is prevented from learning about sex, or is isolated from contact with people of other religions or ethnic groups, is socialized in the direction of incompetence or unreadiness and comes to lack appropriate knowledge of what to expect in potentially sexual or transethnic situations.

Normative-Maturational Approach

Between the 1930s and the 1950s, an important approach to development was the charting of growth as a function of age. As mentioned earlier, Gesell, a major proponent of this approach, viewed behavioral capacities as unfolding in a sequence over the course of time. Thus, a given child's socialization could be assessed with reference to normative trends, the typical occurrence of certain behaviors at certain ages (such as talking at 2 years). Studies by Gesell and his colleagues (Gesell, 1937; Gesell & Ilg, 1943) and the California Growth Studies (see Jones et al., 1971) provided such data against which children could be viewed. Zigler and Seitz (1978) suggest that the influence of the normative maturational approach declined as a result of the emergence of extreme environmentalism in American psychology. They note, however, an indication of a revitalization of this approach (Kagan & Klein, 1973) and suggest, in light of the renewed attention to biology in the late 1970s, that maturation may again play a role in socialization theories. Zigler and Seitz caution that both maturation and environment must be utilized to explain the processes of socialization.

Behavior Genetics

Whereas Gesell attempted to describe normative developmental trends as products of innate biological factors, behavior geneticists look to *inherited differences* as sources of individual differences among people. Much of the empirical work conducted by proponents of this approach has focused on the genetic determinants of intelligence, and the claims of people like Arthur Jensen (1969), Hans Eysenck (1971), and Richard Herrnstein (1971) have elicited a storm of vitriolic protest (e.g., Kamin, 1974). However, the efforts of behavior geneticists have not been limited to research on intelligence; they have also considered many other aspects of personality and appearance.

Behavior geneticists believe that genetic factors may limit the reaction range of a given trait for an individual—the range of possible phenotypes which can be expressed by the individual's genotype. Genetic factors set limits on the possible outcomes for the individual, and environmental factors determine where, within the range, the individual will fall. Thus, variation both in genetic and in environmental factors may be important, and their relative weight may vary from one trait to another or from one population to another. In most investigations, the goal of behavior geneticists is to determine the *heritability* of particular traits: that is, they aim to determine how much of the variance in a given trait is attributable to genetic influences, how much to experiential/environmetal influences, and how much to the interaction between these two sources of influence. This is done by comparing the degree of resemblance between people who differ in their degree of biological relation to one another. If a trait is entirely determined by genetic factors, siblings should be fairly similar, since they share, on average, half of their genes, while monozygotic (i.e., identical) twins should be identical since they share all their genes. A test of such predictions is known as a *consanguinity study*, the commonest version of which involves a focus on twins, notably on the differences between monozygotic and dizygotic twins of the same sex. If the trait is genetically determined, the dizygotic twins should be more similar than ordinary siblings; if the dizygotic twin pairs are as similar as monozygotic twin pairs, a strong environmental determination of the trait would be suggested.

Using this strategy, behavior genetics have shown convincingly that a variety of traits, including intelligence, extraversion-intraversion, persistence, and sociability, are to some extent heritable. However, it is also very clear that the heritability of most aspects of personality is much less than the heritability of intelligence. In view of the difficulty of establishing simple large effects of environmental factors, too, this suggests that an interaction between genetic and environmental influences may be especially important in their effects on personality and emotional development.

Behavior geneticists and those who study biological influences on personality propose that inherited factors can influence development in three main ways. First, an individual can inherit a tendency to behave in a certain way, and this tendency may remain as a long-lasting phenomenon. For example, an individual may inherit a tendency to be introverted and will thus be characterized by introversion throughout his or her life. Second, inherited dispositions may affect the way an individual responds to potentially influential experiences. Faced with novel challenges, for example, one individual may withdraw whereas another may actively attempt mastery. These individuals would be affected very differently, although both faced the same challenge and had equivalent opportunities to benefit. Third, inherited characteristics may affect the way that others behave toward the individual and so allow each person to shape—at least in part—his or her own formative experiences. For example, an even-tempered, "easy," and attractive infant may elicit more attention and affection than her unattractive and irritable brother, and as a result of all the stimulation, she may develop more rapidly and become more sociable than her brother (Lamb, 1982b). Students of socialization have written a great deal recently about similar instances of children shaping or contributing to their own development (e.g., Bell & Harper, 1977; Lewis & Rosenblum, 1974).

The interest in children's contributions to their own socialization has accompanied a more general resurgence of interest in the importance of biological influences on development. Researchers have demonstrated that a number of aspects of personality—including susceptibility to psychotic breakdown (Gottesman & Shields, 1972; Meehl, 1962; Rosenthal, 1971), and intraversion-extraversion (Matheny, 1980; Scarr, 1969) are at least partially determined by heredity. The publication of results from the New York Longitudinal Study (Thomas & Chess, 1977, 1979; Thomas, Chess, & Birch, 1968; Thomas et al., 1963) was influential in persuading many psychologists how important inherent personality characteristics were. Thomas and his colleagues argued persuasively that children were born with personalities or styles—which they called *temperaments*—and these temperamental differences had a major influence on psychological development. The researchers focused attention on the difference between babies whose parents found them "difficult," those who were "easy," those who were "slow to warm up," and those who were "average." Difficult infants, as one might expect, were most likely to need psychotherapeutic counseling as they grew up, but Thomas and his colleagues found that developmental problems were not inevitable even among these children. The key determinant of whether or not development would go awry was the "mesh" between the child's temperament and the parents' personalities. Thus both environmetal and inherited factors had to be taken into account when explaining personality development.

The results of the New York Longitudinal Study suggested that experiences could not be considered in a vacuum; they had to be considered in light of the individual's inherited dispositions. This finding captured in concrete and compelling terms the importance of the interaction between heredity and environment (as represented by the parents' personalities). On the other hand, such studies do not explain the *processes* of socialization and the mechanisms whereby interaction takes place.

Ethology and Behavioral Biology

Finally, we consider another perspective giving emphasis to innate biological factors. The difference between the ethologists and the behavior geneticists is that the former consider specieswide propensities and predispositions, whereas the latter are concerned about determinants of individual differences. Proponents of the ethological perspective enlarge upon the fact that humans, like all other animal species, are born with behavioral tendencies that enhance their own likelihood of survival and the chance of the species surviving (Hinde, 1974). An example pertinent to socialization involves complementary tendencies in infants and their caretakers. Even though human infants are more helpless than the young of any other mammalian species, they are equipped with some behaviors of significance for survival (Bowlby, 1969). Babies cry, for example, when distressed, and infant cries are very effective means of eliciting attention and help from adults. The system of signal (cry) and response (approach and pick up) is programmed into the species so that helpless infants are guaranteed the adult interventions they require if they are to survive.

The above example points to the relevance of ethological concepts (in this case, instinctual response systems) for the study of socialization. Concepts such as imprinting and critical periods have proven important to research on human social attachments (Bowlby, 1969; Klaus et al., 1972) and on sex-role identity (Money et al., 1957). Zigler and Seitz (1978) point out that there has been a general increase, in recent years, in the exchange of theory and methodology between the study of animals and of humans. For example, naturalistic studies of animal behavior have suggested possible genetic bases for certain human social behaviors, including maternal behaviors (Fossey, 1971; Goodall, 1965). On the other hand, knowledge of human behavior has stimulated, for example, attempts to discern the possible existence of Piaget's sequence of cognitive stages in nonhuman primates (Jolly, 1973) and the attempt to find cognitive abilities believed to be exclusively human (e.g., language, self-awareness) in animals other than humans.

Ethologists have provided a way of looking at the behavior of both adults and infants, learning how to determine what is meaningful and what is of less significance. In addition, ethologists point toward the fact that certain behaviors are reinforced only by specific complementary responses, rather than by generalized reinforcers as the learning theorists once proposed (Rajecki, Lamb, & Obmascher, 1978). And they suggest that there are constraints on learning, ensuring that some things are learned easily because they are of significance to individual survival, whereas other associations not of biological significance are learned slowly, if at all (Hinde & Stevenson-Hinde, 1973). Although the writings of many popularizers of ethology (e.g., Ardrey, 1967; Morris, 1967) suggest other-wise, ethologists are not nativists—they do not believe that our behavior is in-nately preprogrammed. They simply emphasize that social development depends on *both* species-specific tendencies and individual experience. We shall show later how their perspective has affected the way psychologists think about social and personality development in infancy.

4

Mechanisms of Influence

The theoretical perspectives reviewed in the previous section provide very different models of humans and human development. They differ with respect to the fundamental issues reviewed earlier (Section 2), as well as in relation to other issues. Nevertheless, when one examines them closely to determine what modes of influence they propose, one finds that all the theories that are still influential today consider one or more of the following simple mechanisms: maturational unfolding; innate predispositions; reinforcement and punishment; cognitive development and learning; and imitation. A major difference among them has to do with the role attributed to motivational factors. In this section, we discuss these mechanisms in detail, where possible contrasting their portrayal by different theorists.

Maturational Unfolding

Maturational unfolding has been proposed by psychoanalysts, cognitive developmentalists, and ethologists to explain developmental phenomena, although the role attributed to unfolding differs from one perspective to another.

For cognitive developmentalists, stages occur in a fixed and predetermined sequence determining *how* the child conceptualizes its world but not the content of the concepts. In other words, the stages refer to qualitative rather than quantitative or concrete factors. Between 7 and 10 years of age, for example, children have rigid views of social norms, whether they pertain to moral behavior, sex roles, or games. By early adolescence much more flexible conceptions develop in all of these areas.

For the ethologists, what develops maturationally is a special readiness for certain types of learning, not specific behavior patterns per se. There are, in other words, critical periods when certain associations are most readily formed. The psychoanalysts, too, propose varying sensitivities during discrete developmental phases to certain types of experiential influences (e.g., the oral, anal, and phallic phases). But Freud went beyond this to suggest that if the normative experiences did not occur on time, the child created them in fantasy. This perspective is thus more deterministic than the cognitive developmental and ethological perspectives. However, no contemporary perspective is quite as deterministic as Gesell's (1928) was. Gesell proposed that whole patterns of behavior (e.g., "negativism") emerged in a predetermined sequence. As noted earlier, Gesell's unwillingness to consider individual differences reduced the popularity and explanatory significance of his approach.

Social learning theorists do not consider maturational unfolding in their explanations of development.

Innate Predispositions

Innate predispositions have been discussed by ethologists and proponents of the behavior genetics approach. They take one of three forms, being viewed (1) as the sources of lifelong personality traits, (2) as one influence determining how and how much the child will be affected by particular experiences, or (3) as factors affecting the way the socializers treat the child in the first place. In recent years, Sameroff (Sameroff & Chandler, 1975; Sameroff & Harris, 1979) has proposed a transactional approach to the study of socialization. Sameroff notes that both socializer and child have particular individual characteristics when they enter each interaction, and both are affected by each encounter, thus entering the next encounter from a different starting point. This is an important thing to bear in mind when formulating explanations of personality development, although the transactional perspective does not really help us to understand *how* each interactant is affected.

Rewards and Punishments

Rewards and punishments are the simplest and commonest ways of influencing the behavior of any organism. One group of theorists, the Skinnerians, conceive of socialization largely as a process of building up patterns, piece by piece, through reinforcement and punishment. Among other theorists, while none would deny that reinforcement and punishment can affect behavior, most argue that socialization is too complex and far-reaching to be explained on the basis of these mechanisms alone. Consequently, a number of elaborations have been offered. Drive reduction theorists have tried to overcome this problem by introducing the concepts of primary and secondary drives so as to explain the establishment of motivational factors which guided future learning. Social learning theorists regard reinforcement and punishment as factors affecting the performance of whole roles or scripts, not simply individual items of behavior. Ethologists talk of constraints on learning which facilitate some associations while making others difficult if not impossible to form; given these constraints, rewards and punishments are sometimes effective and sometimes not. Cognitive developmentalists point out that the same things are not reinforcing or punishing for all people because each individual's conceptions determine how they understand and interpret their experiences.

Imitation

Imitation, like reinforcement and punishment, has been discussed by most theorists, regardless of orientation; a review of imitation, as it pertains to developmental psychology, has recently been published by Yando, Seitz, and Zigler (1978).

Psychoanalysts like Freud (1905, 1921), while not taking imitation in general as a problem of interest to their theories, have had much to say about children's imitation of their parents and about selective imitation of one parent rather than the other. According to psychoanalysts, children of both sexes initially identify with, and are thus motivated to imitate, their mothers, but this changes during the Oedipal phase. At this point, boys become fearful of their fathers and identify with them as a defense, whereas girls' identification with their mothers is reinforced. Many psychologists have drawn hypotheses regarding the effects on the motivation to imitate of variations in the quality of the parent-child relationship (e.g., Hetherington, 1965; Hetherington & Frankie, 1967).

Cognitive developmentalists like Piaget (1962) and Kohlberg (1966, 1969) have also described factors accounting for developmental changes in the desire to imitate others. Piaget (1962) had the most to say about developmental changes during infancy. He portrayed imitativeness as a characteristic of infant cognitive capacities but described rather than explained this early appearance of imitativeness and how it changes with age. Kohlberg (1969), by contrast, presented a clear theory, portraying imitativeness as a manifestation of an urge to become *competent*. He expected imitation to increase with age between 3 and 5 years of age and then to decrease with age, and to be most directly related to mental age rather than chronological age. Kohlberg's theory is thus related to competence theories (such as that of White, 1959, 1960), which postulate an intrinsic motivation to behave competently, often referred to as *effectance motivation*. The notion of an intrinsic competence motivation also underlies Zigler's *outer-directedness* formulation (e.g., (Yando & Zigler, 1971; Zigler & Yando, 1972), which considers the extent to which different people use external cues to guide problem solving. This formulation predicts that imitativeness should vary in relation to the complexity of a task and the child's consequent need for cues from others about how to perform; as the child develops, problem solving becomes less dependent on external cues and more a matter of internal cognitive processing.

Social learning theorists like Bandura (1962, 1969, 1977) distinguish between the acquisition and performance of behaviors learned by imitation. Acquisition is affected by the attention the child gives to the model (and thus by factors influencing attention, such as the salience and nurturance of the model); performance, on the other hand, is affected by the reinforcement or punishment seen to be received by the model or by the child when it attempts to imitate. Aronfreed's (1969) elaboration of the social learning formulation emphasizes the affective context in which the behavior is observed. In contrast to these attempts to apply reinforcement theory in a way which is adequate to understanding imitation, some doctrinaire reinforcement theorists have argued that the very concept of imitation is superfluous or mistaken. Gewirtz and Stingle (1968), for instance, deny that anything new can be learned through observation. Learning occurs, they say, only when overt performance, which occurs by chance or through direct training, is followed by extrinsic reinforcement. This view has had less impact than any of the others on developmental psychologists, perhaps because its assumptions seem at variance with everyday observations concerning the pervasiveness of imitation and the eagerness of children to imitate.

In their reformulation, Yando et al. (1978) portray imitation as an important mechanism whereby children learn how to behave competently. They agree with Bandura's fundamental assumption that many behaviors are learned, without direct training, by means of imitation. However, they criticize the nondevelopmental nature of social learning views of imitation and propose that one has to consider both the cognitive developmental level of the child and the nature of the relationship between the child and the model when explaining imitation. In a study reported in their book, these authors examine imitation in children of four age groups, on four different tasks which were given with three types of instruction, each designed to affect differentially the motivation for imitating (i.e., telling a child to play a game any way versus saying that there was only one correct way). The results of this study suggest the role of development in mediating the likelihood of imitation, motivation to imitate, and ability to recall modeled behavior. For example, more imitation occurred in the older groups after instructions were given emphasizing finding the correct solution, but the 4-year-olds displayed comparable amounts of imitation regardless of the type of instruction. Similarly, older children imitated more behaviors which were relevant to the task, while younger children imitated both relevant and irrelevant behaviors. These findings suggest that younger children are generally more dependent on imitation as a problem-solving technique, while the degree to which older children use imitation depends on situational demands. The model of imitation proposed by these authors involves a synthesis of the social learning and cognitive developmental perspectives. It is important to recognize that the perspectives of social learning, cognitive developmental, affective, and psychoanalytic theorists are, for the most part, complementary rather than contradictory where imitation is concerned.

Cognitive Factors

As we have repeatedly mentioned, cognitive factors also play an important role in the mediation of socialization. Each individual has a unique understanding of or perspective on the world, and children's conceptions differ in characteristic ways from those of adults. These conceptions determine how individuals interpret what they observe and what happens to them, and this determines what they find reinforcing/punishing, as well as who they choose to imitate (Kohlberg, 1966, 1969). These factors have been discussed above in our consideration of other mechanisms of influence because cognitive factors affect all of them in one way or another.

Even apart from these interactions with the other mechanisms we have considered, however, cognitive learning has a basic importance of its own as a mediator of socialization. From their experiences, children learn how to behave in some common everyday circumstances. These scripts reflect cultural regularities, and when children's behavior is influenced by them, the scripts serve as cognitive mediators of the socialization process (Abelson, 1981; Gagnon, 1973).

Other important correlates of cognitive development have been discussed by Zigler and his colleagues. Many of these are related to the assumption that children are intrinsically eager to be and to become competent, and thus enjoy challenges. However, a child who is less competent than his or her peers may develop strategies that increase the appearance of competence. Outer-directedness may begin here, for instance, in a tendency to watch one behavior of others and the surrounding circumstances closely in order to improve one's own performance (Achenbach & Weisz, 1975; Achenbach & Zigler, 1968). While it is partly a means of genuinely improving competence, this leads at times to learning only the outward simulation of a competence one really lacks. Another consequence of a child's being relatively less competent than peers may be the development of an expectancy of failure, which leads children to stop even trying to succeed (Cromwell, 1963). These and related characteristics have often been discussed in relation to personality development in the mentally retarded (see Section 16), whose cognitive limitations are especially threatening to their sense of competence.

Self-image disparity—that is, the disparity between individuals' perceptions of themselves as they actually are and their idea of what they would like to be—has also been considered from a cognitive developmental perspective (Achenbach & Zigler, 1963). Katz and Zigler (1967) proposed and demonstrated that self-image disparity is correlated with developmental level because the ability for cognitive differentiation (and thus the ability to distinguish among various potentialities) improves with mental age and because the capacity to experience guilt also increases with age. This finding was later replicated by Phillips and Zigler (1980). The cognitive developmental explanation of self-image disparity, and the finding that disparity increases with cognitive maturity, are especially interesting because such disparity had previously been viewed as an index of personality maladjustment (Rogers & Dymond, 1954).

Considerable attention has been given to Kohlberg's notion that conformity to cultural expectations for one's gender is largely a product of the knowledge one seeks out—that self-socialization into an appropriate sex role, in short, depends on the cognitive development out of which that quest emerges. Kohlberg (1966) proposed, and Kohlberg and Zigler (1967) established, that there is an increase in sex-role adoption around the mental age of 6 or 7 which accompanies children's first realization that their gender is an unchangeable characteristic. This realization induces in them an effort to minimize the discrepancy between their behavior and the culturally approved behavior by seeking out appropriately sexed models. Slaby and Frey (1975) demonstrated, in accordance with this prediction, that children start paying increased attention to same-sex models after they achieve *gender constancy* (i.e., the cognitive awareness that their gender is immutable).

Finally, Zigler, Levine, and Gould (1967) proposed that humor, too, has a cognitive developmental basis. Children find things most amusing when the stimulus makes a cognitive challenge or demand at the upper limit of their ability to understand. Again, this tendency is related to the notion of intrinsic effectance motivation.

Motivational Factors

One major dimension of difference among these theories has to do with the role attributed to motivation. Psychoanalysis is essentially an attempt to account for all of human behavior—basic human nature and the specifics of individual personality—in motivational terms, although it is not always clear where the motive force comes from. Several theories give motivation an important place while not, like psychoanalysis, giving it absolute predominance. Cognitive developmentalists, for instance, are much concerned with accounting for developmental shifts in motivation (Kohlberg, 1969), and drive reduction theorists attempt to explain how motives themselves can be socialized (Mussen, 1967). In the views of all these theorists, the child learns and acts upon the impetus of its own motives; thus the child is an active shaper of its own destiny. Reinforcement theorists like Skinner (1938), and to a lesser extent social learning theorists like Bandura (1977), on the other hand, consider motivation to be excess theoretical baggage and view the child as passively manipulated by outside conditions. Since motives are mentalistic concepts, which they eschew, Skinner and Bandura refrain from invoking such concepts, preferring instead to focus on the characteristics and behavior of the stimulus or socializing agent.

5

Socialization— Then and Now

Some major changes in the way developmental psychologists approach the study of socialization have occurred within the last two decades. As earlier reviews of research on socialization make clear (Child, 1954; Zigler & Child, 1968), interest in the study of socialization had its first great expansion during the 1950s. Unfortunately, the extraordinary interest in the processes of socialization at that time brought with it some simplistic assumptions which made progress during those years very limited.

As Richard Bell (1968; Bell & Harper, 1977) pointed out in a critique of the earlier decades of research on socialization, it was widely assumed by psychologists that influences on the socialization process were always unidirectional, with environmental influences and parental practices and characteristics affecting child development. Seldom recognized was the possibility that children are not passive in their development and that children's characteristics might be antecedents rather than consequences of the parents' behavior. There were, of course, exceptions to this tendency; some of the books published during this period (e.g., Whiting & Child, 1953) contain lengthy discussions of the alternative propositions. In general, however, it was rare for researchers and theorists to note that influences were usually bidirectional—that children affected the way their parents behaved. Rare, too, was serious recognition of the fact that different children might be affected differently by the same parental behavior. We now know that influences on the socialization process are usually bidirectional, and that in either direction the effect depends upon characteristics of both child and parent.

The assumption that the direction of influence was from parent to child had implications for the way earlier research was conducted. The vast majority of studies were correlational in nature; in simply finding that some feature of child behavior tends to go with some feature of parent behavior, they provided no evidence about the causes of this association. The basic assumption that parent behavior must be the causal agent left researchers satisfied with their simple interpretation of antecedent parent behavior as the cause of consequent child behavior and prevented them from planning the more complicated studies that would be needed to evaluate the complex and varied causal sequences involved. As research findings accumulated, however, a distressing tendency toward nonreplication became evident (Caldwell, 1964; Yarrow, Campbell, & Burton, 1970), and it was frequently ascribed to the overly simple design of studies based on the unidirectional assumption about causation.

Even if researchers had been more cautious than they were about the direction of effects issue, however, the findings of the studies conducted during this era would still be questionable. There were two other major flaws in most of this early research. First, most researchers obtained information about both parents' and children's characteristics from a single source—usually the parents. Thus the data being correlated were not independently gathered, and the confounding this represented may account for the modest empirical relationships found. In other words, there might be essentially no relationship between the two characteristics, yet a statistically significant correlation might be found because information about the two was nonindependent. Only a few of the best investigators of that era recognized what most researchers now acknowledge—namely, that data must be gathered from independent sources if we want to ensure reliable and valid findings.

Second, many researchers were content to ask parents or children how they behaved or what they believed without questioning the reliability and veracity of self-reports. Over the intervening decades, however, we have obtained substantial evidence that what people say they do may be little related to what they actually do (Yarrow, Campbell, & Burton, 1968). People tend to describe their behavior so that it sounds more like the socially approved pattern, or they may honestly describe their intentions without recognizing the difference between what they say and what they do. Ironically, when the deficiencies of self-reports became known, new deficiencies were introduced. Most researchers switched from interview to observational sources of data out of a general distrust of any data obtained from interviews or questionnaires, but in fact parental reports are a valuable and sometimes essential aid in understanding what we see in observations. As Parke (1978) and Lamb (1982a) have recently stressed, interviews should be used to supplement what we learn through observations; they should not be seen as alternative forms of data gathering. Most investigators today agree that we need to use multiple techniques to assess the attitudes and behavior of both parents and children.

Although perhaps of lesser importance, a third operational assumption may have hampered progress in the 1950s. This was the assumption that parents were so much more important than other possible socializing agents that teachers, peers, and others need be accorded little attention. The resultant failure to consider agents who may supplement or weaken familial influences may also help account for the disappointing legacy of these years of enthusiastic investigation.

It is sad that the work of an earlier era should be so flawed, because some of the studies themselves (e.g., Kagan & Moss, 1962; Sears, Maccoby, & Levin, 1957; Sears, Rau, & Alpert, 1965) were more ambitious in conception than most that are conducted today. They involved large numbers of parents and children, and many of them were longitudinal investigations. The exigencies of funding make large longitudinal studies uncommon today, even though they are the only way we can really study socialization effects, and we now have available the statistical tools to make data analysis more conclusive than it was formerly.

The inconclusiveness of the earlier studies probably hastened the decline from popularity of research on the effects of socialization. Although we have seen a revival of interest in the 1970s, the field itself is now very different. The research is methodologically better: multiple and interactive sources of influence (both inside and outside the family) are considered, multidirectionality of influence is assumed, and correlational strategies are supplemented by experimental ones. The questions asked today are much more refined and precise. As a result, however, they do not always relate to broad meta-theoretical issues, and the concepts studied are often defined in such idiosyncratic ways that they are not readily related to constructs discussed and investigated by others.

In reviewing the evidence for this book, we have attempted to synthesize the best of the old and the best of the new. We will discuss the results of earlier studies when their findings have stood the test of time and replication and when they bear on issues or questions that are central to contemporary theory regarding socialization. Before doing so, however, we will briefly discuss the two research strategies that are currently dominant.

6

Approaches to the Study of Socialization

Experimentation

A great deal of the research being conducted today involves the application of experimental methods to the study of social and personality phenomena. The major advantage this brings is the opportunity to control other possible influences on the variable of interest and, by manipulating these selectively, to determine how influential they are. In practice, this usually involves developing analogs of reality in which researchers establish and maintain control. As a result, there is usually uncertainty about the legitimacy or validity of generalizing to the real world from the artificially constructed analog situations and the operational measures employed in studying them. In testing the effects of nurturance on the effectiveness of a model or socializing agent, for example, experimenters often arrange for a "nurturant" confederate to praise a subject two or three times, whereas a "neutral" confederate who is present with a control subject simply stands silently. Does the marginal friendliness of an unfamiliar adult really elicit feelings and behavior that are qualitatively similar to the emotional supportiveness of a familiar adult (e.g., a parent)? Even when the experimental analog is impeccable, we are able to determine only what might be the case: we are never able to determine whether the effect demonstrated is actually of any formative significance in the process of development. By showing, as many researchers have, that children will imitate the aggressive behavior of a model, we learn only that some aggressive behavior might be learned by imitation. We have no idea how much of the aggressive behavior any individual evinces was acquired in this way. Since only nonexperimental field studies can assess this, we can see that successful and adequate study of socialization must involve both experimental and field approaches. These are complementary approaches, not alternatives.

Experimental studies are essential to the confirmation of the clear-cut predictions that successful theories must provide (Zigler, 1963a). The entire direction of effects controversy, for example, would never have arisen if experimental techniques had been used to determine whose behavior influenced whom. Field studies can suggest how antecedents and consequences are related to the real world, but experiments are necessary to test the hunches formed in the field.

Field Studies

In most field studies, researchers assess a variety of constructs in the real world and determine whether variations in one or more tend to occur simultaneously with changes in another. Unlike the experimental method, the variations have arisen naturally rather than being deliberately produced by the researcher. Some type of correlational technique is used to assess the degree of co-occurrence of variation in the constructs concerned, but there is no way of determining whether variations in one construct *cause* variations in the other and, if so, what the direction of influence is. Researchers who work in the field rely upon a variety of techniques of measurement (observation, interview, or analog measure), and measurement in the field is usually more extensive than it is in experimental studies. However careful the measurement, field studies are always inconclusive where causality is concerned. Experimental studies then become useful in assessing the direction of causality by systematically varying the putative determinants and observing the effects on the dependent measure.

In recent years, critics like Bronfenbrenner (1977, 1979) have challenged the idea that experimental studies can be at all useful. They have argued that many experiments conducted by developmental psychologists not only fail to elucidate causality in any meaningful way but contribute very little of *any* value. The major problem, according to Bronfenbrenner, is that many experiments lack *ecological validity* (that is, relevance to the real world) because they involve the behavior of children interacting briefly with strange adults in strange situations. Bronfenbrenner urged that ecological validity should be of greater concern to developmental psychologists, and his critique has certainly effected a noticeable improvement.

Bronfenbrenner did developmental psychologists a service by reemphasizing the importance of validity. He may have overstated his case in implying that *all* laboratory-based experimental research lacked ecological validity, however, just as experimentalists had overstated their case by arguing that field studies are necessarily inconclusive. As Parke (1978) pointed out, laboratory studies need not be experimental, and field studies need not be naturalistic (they can be experimental). Consequently, it is important to distinguish between *where* a study is done and the *research strategy* involved. Validity should be a primary concern for all researchers, regardless of whether they rely upon the experimental method or not. Moreover, as Weisz (1978) argues, complementary use of diverse methodologies such as laboratory and field approaches is most likely to yield durable and generalizable principles of development which remain valid across changes in time, culture, and cohort. Each approach has strengths and weaknesses, and while exclusive use of either may weaken the force of findings, conclusions may be bolstered if research of both types presents a common result.

Major Aspects of Socialization

The processes affecting socialization which we described in Section 4 are neutral as far as content is concerned. This means, as we shall show in the next five sections, that all aspects of personality development appear to be affected to some extent by each of these mechanisms. Socialization is extremely complex; each aspect of personality is multiply determined, the product of influences exerted by many agents via several processes. This theme will be evident throughout the following sections, in which we discuss current thinking about the development of several major aspects of personality: attachment in infancy and social development (Section 7), gender identity and the development of behavioral sex differences (Section 8), moral development (Section 9), achievement motivation (Section 10), and aggression (Section 11).

In addition to being neutral with respect to content, the processes of influence are also independent of class and culture: they are (presumably) involved everywhere in the transmission of social rules. On the other hand, the content of what children learn in the course of their socialization varies quite substantially from one class or culture to the next. In the next five sections, we discuss intracultural (class) and intercultural variation only when there are sufficient data available to make clear statements. In later sections, we will review the research and evidence concerning intercultural (Section 16) and class (Section 15) differences in the process of socialization and in its outcomes.

7

Becoming a Social Individual

Despite our general intention to discuss development topically rather than chronologically, we shall start with a discussion of infancy. Development in infancy is characterized by a number of socially important milestones. In our discussion, however, we will for the sake of simplicity emphasize two superordinate themes—the development of a multifaceted concept of self and the development of social concepts and relationships with others.

As we noted earlier, development in infancy was largely ignored by developmental scientists until Freud declared, early in this century, that childhood experiences—including those that occurred in the first 2 years of life—were of formative developmental significance (see, for example, Freud, 1940). Freud declared that the oral zone was the primary source of gratification in infancy and, consequently, he emphasized feeding experiences. If an infant was fed indulgently, Freud and his followers proposed, it would develop an incorporative oral personality (later showing its fixation by excessive oral habits such as gumchewing, overeating, garrulousness, etc.), whereas an infant whose experiences were unpleasant might develop an oral aggressive personality marked by excessive verbal criticism. The Freudian thesis here was based on a small number of patients, but it elicited an enormous number of studies focused on the relationship between early feeding practices and later personality. Some of these studies were conducted by analysts, others by learning theorists eager to show simple relationships between maternal and child behavior. Researchers of all persuasions evidently were impressed by the availability of a deterministic explanatory model which provided readily testable predictions. Most frequently, researchers investigated the effects of mode of feeding (breast or bottle) and/or timing (demand or schedule) on adjustment and oral personality characteristics. The products of several decades of research in this area were disappointing: as Caldwell (1964) noted in a major review, no consistent relationships were found between feeding practices and later personality.

This outcome made it clear to researchers that there was more to early caretaker-infant interactions than simply feeding; consequently the overall affective quality of the relationship came under scrutiny. Erikson (1950) proposed that the central task for the infant was to form a trustful relationship with its caretaker (typically, its mother), while the mother's task was to behave in a manner that facilitated the development of a trusting relationship. Many psychoanalysts, in fact, agree with this deemphasis of feeding (Escalona, 1968; Mahler, 1969; Sanders 1962) and have long done so, focusing instead on the *sensitivity* of the mother's behavior. Unfortunately, operational definitions of sensitivity are rare, and the process whereby maternal sensitivity is supposed to affect the infant is not well described (Lamb & Easterbrooks, 1981). Thus although there is general agreement about the formative significance of maternal sensitivity, there is little clarity about what constitutes sensitivity.

The absence of demonstrable relationships between maternal feeding practices and later infant personality is often interpreted (as it was by Caldwell, 1964) as a flaw in psychoanalytic theory. As the psychoanalysts point out, it is unfair to draw such a conclusion from the data, because research psychologists and social learning theorists tested only distorted simplifications of psychoanalytic theory. Whether the more complex predictions are true awaits further study, but such study seems unlikely at this point, since the interests of researchers and theorists have shifted in the last two decades.

A significant advance came when Bowlby (1958, 1969) and Ainsworth (1967, 1973) developed *attachment theory* by drawing on ethology for explanations of some of the processes described by the psychoanalysts. Discarding the psychoanalytic notion that infants form relationships to those responsible for physical gratification, Bowlby suggested that human infants, like the young of most species, are born with a number of simple, organized behavior patterns whose common function is to facilitate the attainment and maintenance of proximity or contact between defenseless, helpless infants and protective adults. He noted that human infants are so motorically incompetent at birth that they cannot move toward or cling to adults, but they can summon adults to approach by crying, and later they can entice adults to stay near by smiling. Recent studies confirm that the smiles and cries of infants have precisely these effects on adults (Frodi, Lamb, Leavitt, & Donovan, 1978; Murray, 1979). Adults are biologically predisposed to respond to the infant's signals in an appropriate fashion—providing the protection, comfort, and care that the infant needs. For example, when adults hear a baby crying, they are most likely to move toward it and pick it up (Bell & Ainsworth, 1972), and this is the most effective way of soothing it (Korner & Thoman, 1970, 1972). Ainsworth and her colleagues operationally define parental sensitivity as the propensity of the adult to respond to infant signals promptly, empathically, and with the "biologically appropriate" response (Lamb & Easterbrooks, 1981). It is their repeated responsiveness that accounts for the formation of enduring infant-caretaker bonds.

Attachments develop quite slowly because of the infant's limited cognitive capacities. However, adults are not similarly handicapped and can become bonded to their infants much earlier. Klaus and Kennell (1976) have argued that there is a sensitive period right after delivery when mothers are best able to bond to their infants. Mothers who bond during this phase, Klaus and Kennell argue, promote healthier development and attachment in their infants. Recent careful studies, however, have failed to substantiate Klaus and Kennell's hypothesis (see Lamb & Hwang, 1982; Leiderman, 1978; for reviews). Parents—both mothers and fathers—begin to form bonds to their infants from their first encounters, regardless of whether the first interactions take place 1, 8, 20, or several hundred hours after delivery.

In the first month after birth, a baby cannot discriminate among individuals, and so it behaves in an indiscriminately social fashion, showing no preference for familiar over unfamiliar persons. Once it becomes able to differentiate between its parents and other people at about 2–3 months of age, the infant starts to respond more positively to the mother and father, but since it does not yet have the cognitive capacity to remember them when they are not present (Piaget, 1954), attachment theorists posit that a true attachment has not yet formed. The realization at about 6–8 months of age that people exist even when they are not visible or audible signals a new shift in the nature of the caregiver-infant relationship. In the view of attachment theorists, this is when true attachments first exist. The formation of attachments is indicated by the fact that the infant may now cry when left by the attachment figure, and it seeks proximity to and comfort from that person preferentially.

Recent research shows that babies form attachments to both of their parents at about the same time (Lamb, 1977b). While this may not seem like a particularly striking finding, it is only recently that psychologists have begun to acknowledge the role that fathers play in their children's emotional development on a day-to-day basis. Rather, fathers have typically been viewed as necessary in biological and economic terms, and deleterious effects of father absence have been examined, but in considering emotional development the focal point has been the mother-child relationship. Specific treatment of the father's roles in child development will be undertaken in a later section on family influences (Section 12).

What is significant here is the fact that infants form attachments to their fathers even when the amount of time they spend together each day is small—in fact, fathers in typical American families spend no more than an average of 10 hours a week with their children. This suggests that it is the *quality*, not the *quantity*, of interaction that is important in the development of attachment relationships, and that a great deal of interaction is no guarantee of optimal quality. On the other hand, parents must spend some minimal amount of time with their children in order for normal attachment to develop—although the amount of time is unknown. In any case, the distinction between quality and quantity of care is also relevant to a consideration of multiple caretaking in day care. In this case, the distinction is at the heart of the controversy surrounding the popular belief that development will be deleteriously affected if children do not spend their early years with one exclusive caretaker. Evidence relating to this question is not conclusive, but it suggests that day care *need not* harm children's social development. The problem of day care will be treated in greater detail below (Section 12).

When we say that infants above 6–8 months of age are *attached*, we mean that they focus their proximity and contact-seeking behaviors on some specific individuals whom they *trust* to provide the appropriate responses to their needs. The trust has developed because of the consistency, predictability, and appropriateness of the individuals' behavior in the past (Lamb, 1981a, 1981b). However, not all parents are equivalently sensitive in their responses to infants, and this affects the degree of trust the infant later has in them (Ainsworth, Bell, & Stayton, 1974): attachment theorists refer to variations in the degree of trust as *variations in the security of attachment*. Ainsworth and Wittig (1969) developed a procedure for assessing security of attachment in 1- to 2-year-olds. This procedure allows one to observe how infants behave toward their parents when distressed (Ainsworth, Blehar, Waters, & Wall, 1978). Infants whose parents have been sensitive turn to their parents for comfort when distressed. When parents have been insensitive, babies may avoid, rather than seek, contact and comfort, or else they may behave ambivalently—both seeking and angrily rejecting contact. The way the baby behaves toward any individual reflects the degree of trust in that relationship and thus the way the particular parent earlier behaved toward the infant (Lamb, 1981a, 1981b).

This account of the development of early relationships is complicated because it involves an interactionist explanation. Biological predispositions in infants and adults play a role in shaping the transactions which themselves shape the relationship. The repeated association of infant signals and behaviors with particular biologically appropriate or complementary adult behaviors paces the development of the relationship. Simple learning is involved, but biological predispositions determine which responses will be reinforcing and, so, which adult and infant behaviors are most likely to become associated.

Although the security of attachment dimension refers to the infant's attitude toward specific attachment figures, this attitude is later generalized to other people, so that the security of the initial attachment affects the way infants respond to unfamiliar people such as peers and strange adults (Easterbrooks & Lamb, 1979; Main, 1973; Pastor, 1980; Thompson & Lamb, in press; Waters, Wippman, & Sroufe, 1979). In the course of its early social interactions, moreover, the infant is also developing a concept of itself. Over time, the infant comes to recognize that when it cries (for example), predictable responses ensue (e.g., it is picked up). From repeated experiences of this sort, the infant develops the notion that it is effective—that it can affect what happens to it and so, in a sense, exert control over its experiences and destiny (Lamb, 1981a, 1981b). A belief in one's efficacy is the beginning of a concept of self as something worthy, and this, too, is related to behavior in Ainsworth's procedure. Thus we find that securely attached infants, having greater perceived effectance, are later more persistent and enthusiastic in the face of novel challenges than are the less securely attached infants who have lower perceived effectance (Arend, Gove, & Sroufe, 1979; Matas, Arend, & Sroufe, 1978).

In sum, infants develop fundamental concepts both of themselves and of other people. With regard to others, they develop some basic social expectations which amount to varying degrees of trust in specific people. These expectations then appear to be generalized to less familiar people, guiding children in their initial encounters with strangers of all ages. As far as a self-concept is concerned, children appear to learn from their earliest social interactions—those involving adult responses to their cries and similar signals—that they are effective social agents who have at least some control over their own experiences.

8

Gender Identity and the Development of Behavioral Sex Differences

Two themes lie at the core of contemporary research and theorizing concerning the differential socialization of boys and girls: one concerns children's development of appropriate gender identities, and the other concerns sex differences in children's behavior. As the concepts of gender identity and gender (sex) role are frequently confused, it is important to define them clearly at the outset. The concept of *gender identity* refers to the child's knowledge of its gender and of the fact that its gender is permanent (Kohlberg, 1966). For most (but not all) theorists, *secure gender identity* implies that the child feels comfortable with its gender and would not want to change it (Money & Tucker, 1975). By contrast, *sex roles* pertain to a society's rules concerning how males and females are expected to behave. Secure gender identity does not necessarily imply a high degree of conformity to the society's sex-role standards. In fact, these two variables may have a negative rather than a positive correlation. A person who has an insecure gender identity may try especially hard to conform to sex-stereotyped norms, while a person who has a secure gender identity may feel comfortable violating these norms, unthreatened by possible conclusions others may reach about his or her gender identity. Gender role and gender identity do not develop synchronously, so it is important to consider each concept separately.

One useful perspective on the development of gender identity has been provided by John Money (Money & Ehrhardt, 1972). He has spent many years studying the development of hermaphrodites (i.e., children born with both male and female gonads) and of children showing a discrepancy between their chromosomal and anatomical sex. (For example, medication taken by pregnant women caused some girls to be born with penises, although their internal sex organs were female and they were chromosomally female.) Sometimes these anomalies are identified long after birth, and their discovery is followed by surgery to change external anatomy to agree with true sex. This surgery is accompanied, of course, by an effort to reassign the child from the sex it had been mistakenly assigned at birth to its true biological sex. From an analysis of such cases, Money concluded that the third year of life represented the end of a sensitive period. Prior to this age, children adjusted to their newly assigned sex without difficulty. If reassignment was delayed, however, difficulties and maladjustment were frequent. It thus appeared that gender development goes quite far in the first 2 years of life. Unfortunately, it was not possible in these clinical studies to identify the factors accounting for this early development. Presumably, differential treatment of the two sexes by parents is involved. We know, for example, that parents treat boys and girls somewhat differently from an early point in their lives (Block, 1976). Fathers' behavior may be most important, both because they seem more concerned than mothers about sex differentiation (Aberle & Naegele, 1952; Bronfenbrenner, 1961; Goodenough, 1957; Heilbrun, 1965; Sears, Maccoby, & Levin, 1957; Tasch, 1955) and because they treat infants in such a way as to make themselves more salient to infant sons and less salient to infant daughters (Lamb, 1977a, 1980; Lamb & Lamb, 1976).

Money's claim that gender identity is established in infancy contrasts to Kohlberg's belief (Kohlberg, 1966; Kohlberg & Zigler, 1967) that a cognitive appreciation of gender identity must involve the same cognitive capacity as the ability to conserve. According to Piaget (1970), conservation is not possible before 6 or 7 years of age, and so Kohlberg proposes that this is the age at which true gender identity or *gender constancy* is acquired. According to this theory, gender identity is largely a cognitive construct, and it does not really matter how or from whom the relevant information is acquired. Thus although the parents probably play an important role—repeatedly noting the child's sex by buying toys and clothes selectively, using appropriate pronouns, etc.—sufficient information could probably be received from the media, teachers, or other children. Kohlberg's concern is with the child's reconstruction or interpretation of the information, not its source. The important realization for the child is that gender is stable across time and situations. Kohlberg and Zigler (1967) reported some evidence that conservation of one's own gender occurred only following acquisition of a general ability to conserve, but other researchers have reported contrary findings. Thompson (1975), for example, found that 3-year-olds appeared aware of the constancy of their own sex, and Slaby and Frey (1975) found that by 5 years of age gender constancy appeared to have been established. It is clear that young children learning to speak use appropriate gender-defining pronouns and terms by the third year of life. Nevertheless, Kohlberg, Slaby, and Thompson all place the development of gender identity considerably later than does Money.

These two approaches are difficult to reconcile because the cognitive construct of gender constancy or identity as studied by Kohlberg and the cognitive developmentalists is not the same as the psychological adjustment implied by the concept of security of gender identity, which is central to Money's thinking. Security of identity is not relevant to Kohlberg since he is concerned with a normative developmental milestone. A child may "know" he is a boy, yet feel dissatisfied or uncomfortable with this, thus having an insecure gender identity despite an awareness of gender constancy.

As far as those who study sex-role development are concerned, the establishment of gender constancy (in Kohlberg's sense) permits more extensive involvement on the part of the child in self-socialization. Knowing that it is a girl (or boy), in other words, the child begins to seek out appropriate sex models to imitate (Kohlberg, 1966; Slaby & Frey, 1975). In this way, the child learns how to behave in a socially approved fashion. For students of sex-role development, the processes underlying the establishment of behavioral sex differences are of primary interest. Self-socialization is only one such process, and many of the other sources of influence begin to exert their effects much earlier.

Logically, a concern with the origins of behavioral sex differences begins with consideration of innate sex differences. Several researchers have looked for sex differences in the behavior of newborn infants, but few have been reported with any reliability. Male infants may be somewhat more irritable than girls, but even this finding is controversial (Bell, Weller, & Waldrop, 1971; Moss, 1967; Richards, Bernall, & Brackbill, 1977).

Considerably more attention has been focused on postnatal differences in the treatment of boys and girls. Although there is certainly no unanimity on this score (Maccoby & Jacklin, 1974), there is sufficient evidence that boys and girls are treated somewhat differently from birth (Birns, 1976; Lewis, 1972b; Moss, 1967) and that the magnitude of the differences increases with age (Block, 1976, 1979). For example, it appears that mothers talk to girls more than to boys (Endsley, Garner, Odom, & Martin, 1975; Lewis, 1972a, 1975; Moss, 1967), and this may explain why girls are verbally precocious. On the other hand, it may be that mothers talk to girls more because girls are more verbally responsive—making the mothers' behavior a consequence rather than a cause of sex differences in their children's behavior. In the first few months of life, boys receive more attention (holding, tending) from their mothers than girls do—perhaps because boys are more irritable (Lewis, 1972a; Moss, 1967). By the end of the first year, boys seem to receive more encouragement to explore and be independent (Lewis, 1972b); not surprisingly, male toddlers explore further and for longer periods than their female peers (Ley & Koepke, 1975; Rheingold & Eckerman,

1970). Parents exercise the large musculature of boys more than girls, and they tend to buy toys that provide "appropriate" degrees of physical stimulation for boys and girls (Rheingold & Cook, 1975).

In many cases, parents may not even realize that they are treating boys and girls differently; they may simply think they are responding appropriately with the stimulation the children prefer. Several studies (Condry & Condry, 1976; Rubin, Provenzano, & Luria, 1974), for example, have shown that adults perceive and interpret children's behavior differently depending on what sex they think they are. These distorted perceptions may lead parents unwittingly to treat even a baby distinctively according to its gender. As children grow older, however, conscious and deliberate differentiation becomes more likely, as parents are guided by somewhat different goals in the socialization of sons and daughters (e.g., Fagot, 1974) and these goals seem more relevant to the current life of older children. From the preschool years on, parents tend to reinforce girls for behaving in a stereotypically feminine fashion and to reinforce boys for "masculine" behavior (Fagot, 1974; Langlois & Downs, 1980). When sex-inappropriate behavior occurs at this time, it is seldom punished (Langlois & Downs, 1980), but sanctions may become more predictable and intense later on (Block, 1976, 1979). Social learning theorists believe that people tend to reinforce others for behavior high in their own behavioral repertoire. If this is true, fathers would have a special impact on sons and mothers on daughters. In any event, both parents continue to shape their children's behavior as the children grow older. Block (1976) has presented evidence indicating that parental concern over the sex appropriateness of their children's behavior increases over time—perhaps being most intense during early adolescence. Adolescence is, of course, an important time for the formation of heterosexual relationships and the choice of careers, and both of these developments involve intensified concern over sex-stereotyped behavior and aspirations. The adolescent's own realization of the implications of behavior in these regards doubtless supplements the efforts which Block showed parents making at this time; the pressure to conform is both internal and external.

However they learn about sex-differentiated standards—and it is surely the case that parental influences are supplemented by friends, relatives, and the media (especially television)—boys and girls certainly behave very differently by the time they enter nursery school. Boys by this time prefer physically robust games and play with vehicles (Fagot, 1977; Fagot & Patterson, 1969; Lamb & Roopnarine, 1979), whereas girls prefer more sedate games, dolls, and "playing house." In the nursery school environment, furthermore, children come into contact with new sources of influence—peers and teachers. Generally, these sources of influence supplement the parents' efforts unless the latter have been trying to inculcate non-sex-typed values. Like most parents, teachers reinforce children for gender-appropriate activities (Fagot, 1975, 1977). Meanwhile, children as young as 3 years of age (the youngest in whom the question has yet been studied) reinforce and punish one another selectively: sex-appropriate behaviors are reinforced and sex-inappropriate behaviors are punished (Fagot, 1977; Fagot & Patterson, 1969; Lamb, Easterbrooks, & Holden, 1980; Lamb & Roopnarine, 1979). The cues provided by a child's peers are clearly effective (Lamb & Roopnarine, 1979; Lamb et al., 1980): punished activities are terminated promptly and reinforced activities are prolonged. Furthermore, it appears that demands for children to behave in a gender-appropriate fashion have a greater effect than comparable demands that children behave in a gender-inappropriate fashion (Lamb & Roopnarine, 1979; Lamb, et al., 1980). This suggests that young children already know what is considered gender-appropriate and what is considered inappropriate behavior; the reinforcements and punishments seem to serve primarily as reminders of these rules. These data provide further reasons to question Kohlberg's conclusion that one's gender is not salient prior to 7 years of age. Although Kohlberg's postulation clearly requires qualification, some change does seem to take place in children's understanding of the importance of socially approved behavior around the time they enter school (Kohlberg, 1966), and self-socialization may increase as a result. In general, this means that children become especially attentive to the behavior of people of the same gender—perhaps even seeking out gender-appropriate persons to imitate (Maccoby & Wilson, 1958; Slaby & Frey, 1975).

Children prefer to play with peers of their own gender from the time they are introduced to the peer group (Asher, Oden, & Gottman, 1977), partially because they are encouraged to do so by parents and teachers and also because they prefer playing with children who have interests similar to their own. This increases the likelihood that children will engage in gender-appropriate activities. It also means that children spend much of their time in the company of gender-appropriate models. Interestingly, Serbin and her colleagues (1977) have shown that when teachers encourage mixed-sex interaction, the usual sex segregation can be eliminated. However, once teachers stop doing this, children rapidly return to same-sex groupings.

Although we know from a multitude of experimental studies that children *can* learn from the behavior of models (Bandura, 1977), we do not know how great a role same-gender models play in the acquisition of sex-typed behavior. Certainly, same-gender models are ubiquitous: they are to be found in the peer group, in the family, on television and in the movies, and at school. We do have some basis for conjecturing what kinds of models are most likely to be observed and imitated, thanks to several studies by Bandura and his colleagues which focused on a variety of effects of models' characteristics (see reviews by Bandura, 1969, 1977; Mussen, 1967). Models who are nurturant and/or powerful are likely to be especially salient to children. This fact may make family members (e.g., parents) likely identification figures: they are usually nurturant and affectionate toward their children, and they are likely to control the resources children value (i.e., they appear powerful). Not surprisingly, therefore, the absence of a same-sex parent may have a greater impact than the absence of any other potential gender-appropriate model; boys who don't have fathers, for example, may be less "masculine" than boys who do (see Biller, 1974, 1981, for reviews). Boys are also more likely to identify with warm and accessible fathers than with distant and inaccessible fathers (Mussen, 1967). Unfortunately, there have been few studies of parental identification in girls, although it may be relevant that girls whose mothers work (contrary to the feminine sex-role stereotype) develop less traditionally feminine sex roles themselves (see Baruch & Barnett, 1978, and Hoffman, 1974, 1979 for reviews). Sons of working mothers are also less traditional in their sex-role attitudes (Hoffman, 1977), underscoring the fact that sex-role attitudes are not learned exclusively by identification with gender-appropriate models.

Throughout this discussion of the development of sex-typed behavior, we have emphasized the influences of exogenous socializing agents and of cognitively mediated tendencies toward self-socialization. These two factors are the ones usually emphasized by contemporary psychologists, who tend to discount a third kind of potential influence—the direct effect of endogenous biological forces. There is some evidence that puberty brings an intensification of gender-appropriate behavior (Feldman & Nash, 1978; Feldman, Nash & Cutrona, 1977; Frodi & Lamb, 1978; Nash & Feldman, 1981), but we have little basis as yet for judging how much of this intensification is a direct consequence of the masculinization or feminization of behavior by the pubertal surge of hormones; much of it seems likely to be indirectly mediated by the other two kinds of processes. Lamb (Frodi & Lamb, 1978; Lamb & Urberg, 1978), in arguing for this indirect mediation, points out that physical changes at puberty alter the way others behave toward the individual and also increase his or her concern about sex, sex-typed behavior, and attractiveness to the opposite sex. Hormonal changes increase the interest in sexuality and thus strengthen concerns for behaving appropriately so as to be attractive to members of the opposite sex (Matteson, 1975). All these indirect effects might account for the emergence of sharper sex differences at puberty.

Children who mature early are exposed to all of the pressures mentioned longer than their later-maturing peers, and this may account for some of the reported differences between early and late maturers. Early maturers appear to be more self-assured, more socially skillful, more conservative, and more conventional in attitude than late maturers (Jones, 1965; Jones & Mussen, 1958; Medinnus & Johnson, 1969; Mussen & Jones, 1957).

These findings are also relevant to Nash and Feldman's (1981) functional role theory of gender development. This theory notes that internal and external pressures to conform to sex-role stereotypes wax and wane at different stages of the life span. Most researchers agree that puberty is one time when parental and peer group pressures intensify, as do the individual's desires to behave appropriately so as to obtain heterosexual success and peer group approval. Internal desires to conform to external (i.e., societal) expectations also seem to increase around the time of initial parenthood, leading to a marked increase in sex-differentiated behavior at this stage too (Nash & Feldman, 1981). In both puberty and early parenthood, the phases of notable concern over conformity to sex-typed expectations are preceded and followed by phases during which this concern is less marked. How masculine or feminine an individual appears varies from time to time in accordance with the varying salience that sex-role conformity has for the individual's own self-concept and for others' evaluations or opinions (Nash & Feldman, 1981). Notice that from this perspective, biological influences may be significant even though they are indirectly mediated.

It should be clear from this brief discussion that sex-differentiated behavior is acquired through a lengthy and complex process. Sex-role standards are taught by parents, teachers, and peers, and both the salience and intensity of their demands vary over time, as does the individual's motivation to conform. The individual's cognitive status and motivations determine the degree of commitment to self-socialization. Finally, biological factors may directly account for some sex differences in behavior and, more generally, by influencing the individual's appearance and motives, they may affect both self-socialization and socialization by others into gender-appropriate behavior. Changes with age are not monotonic, moreover; the tendency to behave in a gender-appropriate fashion neither mounts regularly across the life span nor reaches a plateau and then remains stable. Rather, the tendency to conform to sex-role standards waxes and wanes across the life span in response to variations in one's own and others' expectations and pressures.

9

Moral Development

According to psychoanalytical theory, moral standards are acquired, as is a desire to conform to society's sex-role standards, during the phallic phase of development in the resolution of the Oedipal complex (Freud, 1905, 1950). In the case of the young boy, resolution of the Oedipal complex involves an attempt to placate the father's presumed aggression (and to reduce the potential for castration) by identifying with him. In identifying with the father, the boy strives to copy his masculine behavior and to internalize his standards and moral precepts. The girl, meanwhile, identifies with her mother in order to attract and win her father's approval and love. The girl's envy is far less powerful a motivating force than is the boy's fearful anxiety. For this reason, Freud suggests, boys internalize much stricter moral standards than girls do. Unfortunately, objective verification of these notions is at best very difficult and uncertain, since they refer to events said to be commonly experienced but almost uniformly repressed into the unconscious. Partly for this reason, but perhaps also because of accumulated doubt about whether these events do occur as Freud thought, students of moral development seldom refer to the Oedipal complex today in their attempts to explain either uniformities or individual variations in moral development.

Cognitive developmental theorists—Piaget and Kohlberg—also propose that moral development occurs in stages, though the stages they describe do not resemble Freud's two stages. Piaget (1964) argued that moral development really involves developing an understanding of the nature of social rules. Instead of studying children's understanding of major social norms, therefore, Piaget chose to study their understanding of simpler rules that had more relevance to them. He focused on developmental changes in understanding the rules of the game of marbles. Piaget questioned children closely about the rules of the game while ostensibly seeking some training, and he reported three broad stages in the comprheension of rules. Very young children (3 to 6 years of age) seemed to have no understanding of the nature and purpose of rules; they changed and applied rules unpredictably. Later (6 to 10 years of age), they began to regard rules as unquestioning standards that were derived from external powers (God, parents) and had to be obeyed scrupulously—even though the adherence was not always apparent to Piaget! Finally (at age 10 to 12 years of age), children realized the consensual nature of rules. Rules were seen simply as agreements so that the game could proceed smoothly. Similarly, it was recognized that societies made rules for themselves in accord with consensual goals.

Although he was impressed by Piaget's cognitive developmental emphasis on the development of moral reasoning and judgments, Kohlberg (1958) later criticized the stages Piaget described. From his own research, Kohlberg concluded that there were six rather than three stages of moral judgment to be considered, although because so few people satisfied the criteria of the highest stage. Kohlberg later merged this stage with stage 5. These stages are described in Table 2. In the first two stages, according to Kohlberg, the child does not understand morality; it simply obeys rules in order to avoid punishment and obtain approval. The next two stages are stages of conventional conformity. The individual recognizes that rules are prescribed to facilitate smooth functioning of the society, but there is still a perception of rules as precepts that emanate from a higher legislative authority. Unlike the stage 1 or 2 individual, the stage 3 or 4 person obeys because it is in society's interests to do so, not simply because of personal wishes. However, even in stages 3 and 4, people do not recognize their role in the formulation of the rules. In the fifth stage, by contrast, rules are seen as the products of social consensus; their arbitrariness is recognized. Finally, in stage 6—a stage attained by few—the individual recognizes certain universal principles (justice and equality) and feels it is necessary to disobey rules that violate these ethics.

With the exception of this last stage, the stages described by Kohlberg (like those of Piaget) are content free. That is, the nature of the rules is irrelevant to recognition of a stage; how people think about rules is what matters. Even the way in which people behave is not of concern in recognizing stages; the kind of justification or rationale provided for a moral decision is the basis for determining the individual's stage of moral reasoning.

Kohlberg's theory of moral development is certainly the best-known contemporary theory, and its contributions to the study of development and socialization have been great. The visibility of the theory, however, has also made it the focus

Table 2 Kohlberg's Stages of Moral Reasoning

Level I—Preconventional: Behavior dominated by hedonistic considerations and conformity with the rules of those who are most powerful

Stage 1—*Heteronomous morality.* Physical consequences of the action define its badness; punishment and reward control behavior

Stage 2—*Instrumental behavior.* Individual pursues his or her own needs and lets others pursue theirs within the limits of equitable exchange

Level II—Conventional: Obedience and loyalty viewed as desirable ends in themselves

Stage 3—*Mutual interpersonal expectations.* Individual tries to please others in the environment, seeking to be viewed as good

Stage 4—*Social system and conscience.* Rules are defined by institutions of the society; obedience is viewed as a civic duty.

Level III—Principled (Postconventional): Attempt to define moral values and principles that are valued in themselves

Stage 5—*Social contract.* Rules result from the process of consensual definition; they are essentially arbitrary, but it is only fair that all obey the laws defined by the majority so as to ensure the smooth functioning of society

Stage 6—*Universal ethical principles.* Some moral principles are not arbitrary; they have universal significance and supersede societal rules when conflict results

---

From Kohlberg (1976).

of critical evaluation. In one critique, Kurtines and Greif (1974) concluded that both the reliability and validity of Kohlberg's system were suspect. Most importantly, they argued that the empirical evidence failed to confirm the presence of a clear hierarchical stage sequence and showed that people do not operate consistently at a particular level. The empirical evidence, in fact, was more consistent with Piaget's postulation of just three (rather than five or six) stages. Siegal (1980) suggests that despite such problems, Kohlberg's approach is useful because it characterizes types of moral reasoning which develop in adolescence and adulthood—periods which are not dealt with in Piaget's theory. Siegal argues, however, that Kohlberg's theory has by no means subsumed Piaget's, but that both offer useful proposals for the study of moral development. Perhaps because of the critiques of Kohlberg's theory, moral development has become a less popular topic for research in the last few years. Many of the studies that have been published have employed a more reliable technique than Kohlberg's clinical method for assessing the stage of moral reasoning attained by an individual (Rest, 1975, 1976), and we may hope for firmer knowledge in the future than is presently available.

The focus on moral judgment or moral reasoning that is characteristic of the theories proposed by Piaget and Kohlberg contrasts to the focus of theories proposed by other psychologists, such as Aronfreed and Hoffman. Whether or not they agree that moral reasoning changes with age, these researchers are especially interested in the behavioral implications of developmental changes in morality. Although students of socialization have been influenced by Kohlberg's theory and have conducted numerous studies of moral reasoning (e.g., DePalma & Foley, 1975; Lickona, 1976), there has been (and continues to be) much interest in the development of moral behavior and the determinants of individual differences in moral behavior. In these regards, Kohlberg's theory has not proved very useful. Two approaches—one exemplified and described by Aronfreed (1968) and one propounded by Hoffman (1970a, 1970b)—are more relevant than is Kohlberg's to the analysis of moral behavior.

According to Aronfreed, children learn which forms of behavior are approved and which are disapproved largely in accordance with the well-understood laws of learning. At first, children behave "morally" only because they have come to expect reinforcement for doing so and punishment for behaving otherwise. Although the process is not clear, children are then said to internalize the rules. This means that they start to reward and punish themselves for conformity to or deviation from social rules, so that their behavior is monitored by this internal conscience. Most researchers who adopt this view of moral development focus their attention on how well this internalized conscience operates and attempt to identify the factors associated with variations in its effectiveness. Although social learning theories like Aronfreed's emphasize the role of fathers in the internalization of moral standards, there is no good evidence that fathers are especially important determinants of moral development (Greif, 1976; Hoffman, 1981). Since mothers are usually more involved in day-to-day supervision and correction, in fact, they may be more influential (Hoffman, 1970b, 1981). Parents who are warm, set high standards, and are consistent in their discipline tend to have more moral children than parents who do not (Hoffman, 1970a; Hoffman & Saltzstein, 1967).

Hoffman (1960, 1970b) has focused attention on the type of disciplinary strategy parents adopt, drawing a distinction between punitive and inductive techniques. Parents who emphasize the consequences of transgression of rules (a punitive strategy) are not very successful in making their children behave morally. Induction has proved to be a more effective strategy (Hoffman, 1970b). Inductive discipline involves focusing the child's attention on the effects of misbehavior on the victim of the transgression rather than the negative consequences for the child itself. By encouraging empathy with those who have been wronged, parents seem to make children feel more guilty when they do wrong (suggesting that they have better internalized consciences), and this in turn makes them act more morally (Hoffman & Saltzstein, 1967). The superiority of inductive discipline over love withdrawal (a technique focusing the child's attention on the fact that the parent's respect and love are contingent on the child's behavior) has also been demonstrated in several studies (see Hoffman, 1970b, for a review).

In research on the antecedents of moral behavior in children, the most common strategy involves interviewing parents about their disciplinary strategies while asking children about their behavior. This reliance upon self-report measures is somewhat unfortunate because there is a danger of selective reporting, and consequently some researchers attempt to supplement these data with additional "objective" reports (e.g., by parents and teachers) concerning the children's behavior. Behavioral observations have rarely been used in studies of moral behavior and its parental antecedents, even though an early study by Hartshorne and May (1928; Hartshorne, May, & Maller, 1930; see Burton, 1963) showed that behavioral measures were reliable provided adequately large samples of behavior were observed. Further, there has been little consideration of the extent to which other socializing agents supplement or weaken parental influences. Teachers, media personalities, and peers all communicate moral standards, and of course all provide models for children to emulate. There is substantial evidence that children behave in a more altruistic or prosocial fashion after observing models who behave in this way (Mussen & Eisenberg-Berg, 1977; Rushton, 1980; Staub, 1978, 1979). It is hard to assess the relative importance of observational learning and simple (i.e., operant) learning. However, Bryan (1975) has shown that children are more likely to pay attention to what models do, rather than what they say, when there is a discrepancy between precept and behavior.

10

Achievement Motivation

In the last few years, achievement motivation has received much less attention than either moral development or sex-role development. This was not always the case; achievement motivation was of great interest to researchers during the 1950s. Further, there is renewed interest today in the origins and consequences of individual differences in achievement motivation.

Most discussions of the antecedents of achievement motivation emphasize a combination of identification and reinforcement mechanisms. In general, high achievement motivation appears to result when parents encourage their children to act independently and praise their performance. Such parents tend to set high standards for their children, but they also set high standards for themselves, thus providing models of achievement and aspirations for excellence.

McClelland and his colleagues (1953) reported such findings in an early study of college students whose achievement motivation was assessed by analysis of their responses on the Thematic Apperception Test (TAT). In this test, a person is shown ambiguous pictures and is asked to respond to each by telling an imaginative story suggested by the picture. High achievement imagery in these stories was produced by young men who reported that their parents had maintained strict standards which they enforced severely. Unfortunately, the subjects were the only sources of information, so the data concerning achievement motivation and parental behavior were not independent of one another. Winterbottom's (1958) study was an improvement; achievement was assessed from imagery in stories told to 8- to 10-year-old boys, and child-rearing patterns were assessed by administering a questionnaire to their mothers. Winterbottom found that high achievement was associated with reports that the mothers encouraged independence at an earlier age and provided rewards when the boys behaved independently. Further, the parental practices reported when the boys were 8 to 10 years old predicted (i.e., were correlated with) measures of the boys' achievement motivation several years later (Feld, 1959). These findings were questioned by Rosen and D'Andrade (1959) on the grounds that the encouragement of independence which Winterbottom assessed was not the same as the encouragement of achievement. By observing parents and their sons, Rosen and D'Andrade found that when parents (especially fathers) had high aspirations and expectations for their children and encouraged them to act independently, the children themselves had higher aspirations. In any case, the findings of all these studies are consistent with the summary statement provided early in this section, that high achievement motivation appears to result when parents encourage and praise their children's independence. Notice, incidentally, that all of the major studies of the antecedents of achievement motivation focused only on boys. Could it be that researchers implicitly assumed in the 1950s that achievement motivation was not a salient goal in the socialization of girls?

In the studies reviewed so far, the investigators attributed variations in achievement motivation to the parents' behavior. However, the consequences of the child's efforts to achieve are also important, and this issue has been of greatest interest to later students of achievement motivation. Thus, children who experience many failures adopt a life-style oriented toward the avoidance of failure rather than the achievement of success (Cromwell, 1963). Similarly, children who experience a great deal of failure in their daily lives develop a style of problem solving characterized by dependence, outer-directedness, and a willingness to be satisfied with limited accomplishments (e.g., Achenbach, 1966; Gruen & Zigler, 1968; Sanders, Zigler, & Butterfield, 1968; Turnure & Zigler, 1964).

The individual's history of successes and failures has also been the focus of several more recent studies concerned (under the influence of modern social psychology) with the manner in which the child attributes responsibility for his or her successes and failures (Dweck, 1978; Weiner, 1972, 1974). In an early study, Dweck (1975; Dweck & Reppucci, 1973) found that after being asked to solve several insoluble problems which they did not know were insoluble, children began to see themselves as incompetent or helpless, so that when they were given fairly easy problems to solve, they did not even try. This inability to attempt to solve problems (or to affect the environment in general) because of repeated experiences of unavoidable failure and so of ineffective responses is called *learned helplessness*. By training children to attribute failure correctly to external factors (e.g., the difficulty or insolubility of the problems), therefore, it should be possible to prevent this debilitating impact on achievement motivation (Dweck, 1975).

This realization has led to interest in how children develop attributional styles. Dweck's research, for example, has indicated that teachers subtly (and probably unwittingly) encourage boys and girls to develop different attributional styles (Dweck, Davidson, Nelson, & Enna, 1978). When girls are praised, it is for neatness or other irrelevancies, rather than for the accuracy of their work. By contrast, boys are praised for their ability when they succeed. Similarly, when boys fail to solve problems correctly, teachers accuse them of not trying, whereas when girls fail, the failure is attributed by teachers to the girls' inability. As a result, girls develop concepts of themselves as incompetent, and so, like the children in Dweck's (Dweck & Reppucci, 1973) first study, they may develop learned helplessness and thus lose their motivation to try (Dweck & Gilliard, 1975). Meanwhile, boys are implicitly and repeatedly told that they have the necessary ability to succeed, and that they simply need to apply themselves more diligently. This is likely to enhance the achievement motivation of boys. Interestingly, feedback from peers did not have the same effect on attributional styles as feedback from adults (Dweck & Bush, 1976).

Dweck and her colleagues have studied only teacher-pupil and peer interactions, so we do not know whether parents also encourage boys and girls to develop sex-differentiated attitudes toward achievement through their attributions for success and failure. It is clear, however, that the attitudes and values of both teachers and parents, as well as the child's history of successes and failures, all contribute to the development of achievement motivation.

11

Aggression

Of all the aspects of socialization we have discussed here, aggression is rendered most complex because it is a value-laden concept. Most discussions of the development of aggression consider it to be a negative characteristic, one which parents do not wish to encourage, although the United States culture continues to value certain types of aggression in the guise of assertiveness and independence. In our discussion, we will focus attention on the more extreme antisocial forms of aggression.

In popular parlance, aggression is a characteristic whose emergence parents and other agents of socialization seek to prevent. This fact reflects the common perception that there is a natural tendency for humans to behave aggressively and that socialization agents have to teach the control of aggression. This belief is also evident in some of the major theories. Psychoanalysis, for example, portrays aggression as the outward direction of the negative or death *instinct*. More recently, several ethologists, most notably Konrad Lorenz (1966), have claimed that humans are naturally aggressive and that this behavior trait has adaptive significance. Sociobiologists such as Wilson (1975, 1978) and Barash (1977) have also suggested that males are innately more aggressive than females. This suggestion has been supported by psychologists who believe that the aggressiveness of males can be attributed to the effects of greater levels of testosterone (Maccoby & Jacklin, 1974). Significant correlations between hormone levels and measures of aggression are consistent with this formulation, as are studies indicating that prenatal administration of testosterone to female monkeys makes them more aggressive (Phoenix, Goy, & Young, 1967). Maccoby and Jacklin (in progress) are currently attempting to determine whether the amount of testosterone present at birth is related to the individual's aggressiveness in early childhood. It is important to recognize, however, that males are not always more aggressive than females (Frodi, Macauley, & Thome, 1977). Furthermore, even if there are biological tendencies toward aggressive behavior in some or all humans, it does not mean that aggressiveness cannot be influenced by experience and learning (Harlow & Mears, 1978).

In fact, most psychological research on aggression focuses on the experiential origins of individual differences. For several years, Patterson and his colleagues (Patterson & Cobb, 1971; Patterson, Littman, & Bricker, 1967; Patterson & Moore, 1979) have been investigating the family histories of young children (mainly boys) who are referred for treatment because they are aggressive and out of control. One intriguing finding is that although the parents disapprove of the boys' behavior and try to eliminate it, their own behavior actually reinforces the behavior and so maintains it. In many cases, for example, aggressive behavior elicits parental attention. In other cases, a vicious spiral occurs, with escalation of the child's behavior provoking an escalated parental response, and so on. By modifying the way parents respond to their children's aggressive outburst, Patterson and his colleagues have been able to reduce the incidence of aggressive behavior. (Teachers, too, could influence the incidence of aggression by structuring the environment so as to maximize positive social interaction; Patterson et al., 1967.) Sears, Maccoby, and Levin (1957), in fact, had shown much earlier that the pattern of parental reinforcement and punishment controlled the aggressiveness of children's behavior: parents who punished outbursts of aggression had children who were less aggressive. Unexpectedly, however, Sears (1961) found in a follow-up of the same children that the children whose parents were punitive were later more, rather than less, aggressive than their peers. Sears suggested that the punitive parents actually provided their children with models of aggressive behavior and that the greater aggressiveness of some children in middle childhood was a consequence of identification or imitation. This finding nicely illustrates the complexity of determinants of personality and underscores the need for careful replication before hasty conclusions are made about the origins of any aspect of development.

Whereas there have been relatively few studies of the operant control of aggressive behavior, there have been countless studies focused on the acquisition of aggressive behavior through observational learning (imitation). Bandura and his colleagues (Bandura, 1962, 1969, 1973, 1977; Bandura, Ross, & Ross, 1961, 1963; Bandura & Walters, 1959, 1963a, 1963b) have repeatedly argued that most aggressive behavior is learned in this way, and many studies have confirmed that observing aggressive behavior increases the likelihood that the observer will behave aggressively—particularly when the behavior is instrumentally effective in attaining desirable goals. The characteristics of the model also affect the likelihood that it will be imitated: in general, models who are nurturant, powerful, or in some way like the observer are more likely to be imitated than are other models (Bandura, 1973, 1977).

Unfortunately, these studies show only that aggressive behavior *can* be learned by observing aggressive models—not that it is usually or even sometimes learned in this way. Nevertheless, the striking replicability of this finding has contributed to a widespread concern about the potentially harmful effects of observing violent and aggressive behavior on television. With one notable exception (Feshbach & Singer, 1971), the findings have been surprisingly consistent: there is a substantial correlation between the amount of violent television watched and the individual's aggressiveness (Murray, 1980; Murray & Kippax, 1979; Stein & Friedrich, 1975; present comprehensive reviews). These correlational findings have been supported by experimental and longitudinal studies showing that the direction of effects indeed runs from viewing violent material to aggressive behavior, rather than the reverse. In a major study, for example, Eron and his colleagues (1972; Lefkowitz, Eron, Walder, & Huesmann, 1977) showed that the aggressiveness of 18- and 19-year-olds was better predicted by the amount of violent television they watched about 10 years earlier than by their earlier aggressiveness. The tenor of these findings has been replicated in studies throughout the world, as Murray and Kippax (1979) point out in their recent review. Eron's study also indicated, however, that the harmful effects of viewing violent material could be offset if parents clearly communicated disapproval of aggressive behavior (Dominick & Greenberg, 1972).

The research on the observational and operant learning of aggressive behavior has been concerned with explaining why certain people tend to be more or less aggressive than others. A rather different focus characterizes the proponents of the frustration-aggression hypothesis and its modern derivatives. Originally proposed by a group of psychologists at Yale in the 1930s (Dollard, Doob, Miller, Mowrer, & Sears, 1939), this hypothesis was inspired by earlier psychoanalytic predictions and sought to explain *when* aggression would occur. Essentially, the original formulation proposed that people would behave aggressively when they were frustrated. Berkowitz (e.g., 1974) later modified the theory, proposing that any arousal (not just frustration) can promote aggressive behavior in certain circumstances. These circumstances involve the presentation of cues that have previously been associated with aggression or are aversive to the individual. Such conditioned cues effectively elicit aggressive outbursts when people are frustrated or otherwise aroused. Research shows that the presence of weapons is an eliciter of aggression (Berkowitz, 1968, 1974; Berkowitz & LePage, 1967), as is any aversive or unattractive characteristic of a potential victim (Berkowitz & Frodi, 1979).

Presumably, one could fruitfully study the individual histories that result in the formation of aggression-eliciting cues, but this has not been attempted. Berkowitz's modification, like the original frustration-aggression theory, remains essentially nondevelopmental in nature.

In sum, research on aggression has been focused on three distinct issues. Led by sociobiologists and ethologists, some theorists have argued that innate predispositions make humans, especially males, aggressive. However, the fact that humans are naturally aggressive does *not* mean that any individual's aggressiveness cannot be increased or decreased by experience. Social learning theorists, using both experimental and field approaches, sought to determine how aggressive behaviors are learned and who is likely to behave aggressively. They have demonstrated that aggressive behavior can be learned by imitation of both live and televised models. Finally, social psychologists like Berkowitz have sought to specify when aggressive outbursts are most likely to occur. Very little of the research has been developmental in nature.

12

Social Cognition

Research on social cognition has also attained prominence in the last two decades (Shantz, 1975). By definition, students of social cognition are especially interested in development of the capacity to take another's role and in developmental changes in children's perception and explanations of inferences about other people's behavior.

Interest in the capacity to take another's role was initially created by Piaget's (1926, 1970) claim that until about 7 years of age, children were not able to recognize that people who view a three-dimensional physical scene from different vantage points will see the scene differently (Piaget & Inhelder, 1956). By extrapolation, Piaget argued that younger children would also have trouble appreciating that in social interactions people have different perspectives simply because their experiences are different and they are differentially informed about crucial facts. These deficiencies in young children's understanding were considered by Piaget to be examples of the *egocentrism* of preoperational children. This sort of egocentrism obviously has major implication for social interaction. In order to communicate effectively, it is often necessary to tailor our statements to the receiver's knowledge and understanding. Thus when speaking to young children, for example, adults generally employ simpler terms, speak more slowly, and repeat themselves more than they would when speaking to adults (Snow, 1972). Egocentric children would not be able to do this when interacting with others whose maturity or perspective differs from their own, and communicative failures should thus be common. According to Piaget (1926), the capacity for role taking develops slowly as a result of interaction with peers in middle childhood. Because peers do not try to accommodate to one another as adults do when interacting with children, peer interaction forces children to role-take in order to ensure satisfying interaction.

It is generally agreed today that Piaget overstated the egocentrism of young children and exaggerated the sharpness of the developmental decline in egocentrism. Young children are not wholly egocentric, and the developmental changes appear to occur gradually during the preoperational stage of development (i.e., between 2 and 7 years of age) rather than occurring suddenly at the transition from the preoperational to the concrete operational phase around age 7.

Evidence for these claims comes from diverse sources. In one important study, Shatz and Gelman (1973) observed 4-year-olds interacting with adults and with younger (2-year-old) children. Contrary to Piaget's assertion, the 4-year-olds modified their speech patterns when talking to the 2-year-olds, just as the adults did when talking to the children. Similarly, Garvey and Hogan (1973) reported that preschoolers were capable of playful communication in which they listened to and took into account their partners' comments and behaviors. Both studies thus demonstrated that young children were not wholly egocentric; rather, in everyday situations, they seemed to recognize and respond appropriately to the special needs and expectations of their interactive partners.

Another type of role taking was demonstrated by Marvin and his colleagues (Mossler, Marvin, & Greenberg, 1976) in 3- and 4-year-olds. In this study, an experimenter told the child a story while the mother was out of the room and then asked the child whether the mother knew what happened in the story. The 2-year-olds were invariably egocentric in that they assumed that their mother knew what happened. The 4-year-olds, by contrast, were usually not egocentric: most recognized that their mother could not know what happened since she was out of the room when the story was told. The 3-year-olds appeared to be in a transitional phase, since some behaved egocentrically and others nonegocentrically.

Empathy—the capacity both to recognize and to share the emotion of others— is a skill which depends on development of the capacity to place oneself in another's position. Again, Piaget predicted that the ability to empathize would not emerge until around age 7, and again it seems that Piaget underestimated the capacities of younger children. By 4 years of age, most children seem capable of predicting the emotional reactions of other children in common situations (Borke, 1971, 1973; Mood, Johnson, & Shantz, 1974). For example, they correctly infer that children will be happy when given a desirable new toy and either sad or angry if the toy is then snatched away. However, it is not until much later that children can not only infer another's emotion but actually *feel* the same emotion that the other is experiencing (Chandler & Greenspan, 1972). Evidence like this has led Selman (1980; Selman & Byrne, 1974) to suggest that the capacity to empathize and to role-take develops gradually from early childhood to adolescence through six stages, each of which involves an improvement in the child's cognitive ability to reason about others' internal emotional states. The implication is that the capacity to behave empathically does not emerge suddenly but develops slowly as a consequence of both cognitive development and social interaction. As a result, children may appear nonegocentric in some simple or common situations (e.g., those studied by Shatz & Gelman, 1973) while still appearing unempathic and egocentric in other more cognitively complex tasks (e.g., those studied by Piaget, 1970). Egocentrism is not something like the ability to walk independently, which you either do or do not manifest. Because different measures of egocentrism, empathy, and role-taking abilities are not equally complex and do not demand the same reasoning capacities, it is not surprising that performance scores on the different measures are poorly intercorrelated (Ford, 1979; Rubin, 1973).

Research on children's perceptions of others has revealed similarly gradual developmental changes. By asking children and adolescents to describe people they know, both Peevers and Secord (1973) and Livesley and Bromley (1973) reported substantial changes with age in the types of descriptions provided. Young children (e.g., kindergartners) tend to describe others by reference to their concrete behavior toward the subject (e.g., "she gives me candy"), whereas other-oriented dimensions become more common with age. Young children tend to use fairly undifferentiated adjectives (e.g., "kind," "nice"), whereas older children and adolescents used more informative and differentiated dispositional descriptions (e.g., "she's always ready to help people who're in trouble"). Whereas younger children tend to describe concrete incidents, older children tend to draw more abstract and general inferences from the concrete events. Inferences about psychological states (e.g., motivation) became more common with age. Similarly, when asked to view and then describe brief vignettes, 6-year-olds tend to focus on the events themselves ("he hit the girl"), whereas 9- and 12-year-olds are much more likely to explain or interpret the events (e.g., "he hit the girl because she made him angry by teasing him") (Flapan, 1968).

Students of social cognition have also studied the capacity to infer intentions (i.e., whether an action was accidental or intended) and motives (e.g., whether the actor was trying to help or to aggress against another). Consider the following prototypical vignette (Piaget, 1932). A little boy is helping to clear the table and accidentally trips, breaking several cups. Another child is trying to steal from the cookie jar when he slips and breaks one cup. Which child is naughtier? Most children under the age of 6 or 7 consider the first child to be naughtier because he caused more damage, whereas most adults (and older children) consider the second child naughtier because he was engaged in a forbidden activity when the accident occurred. Young children, Piaget argued, evaluate others' behavior according to the magnitude of the consequences, whereas older children base their evaluations on the actor's motives and intentions.

As with egocentrism and empathy, it now seems that Piaget underestimated the capacities of young children. When the actors' intentions are clearly specified, most 5½-year-olds not only recognize the intentions but take them into account when judging the actors' naughtiness (Armsby, 1971; King, 1971) or generosity (Baldwin & Baldwin, 1970). Cross-sectional studies indicate that children first develop the capacity to distinguish intentions and only later the capacity to infer motives (Irwin & Ambron, 1973). When the relevant information is vividly and clearly presented, however, this capacity may emerge surprisingly early. Berndt (1977), for example, found that kindergartners did not differ from college students in their capacity to take into account the condition that elicited an aggressive act. Thus they evaluated more negatively a person who hit someone who provoked the aggression by jeering and teasing than a person who hit someone who was trying to help. These findings about the ability to infer motives and intentions when evaluating the behavior of others have obvious implications for the study of moral development, as children cannot evaluate and reason about transgressions without the ability to understand and distinguish consequences, intentions, and motives.

13

Major Sources of Influence

The Family

Traditionally, psychologists have assumed that parents are the most influential agents of socialization. The reasons for this appear to be quite simple: early experiences are often viewed as most important, and during the early years children in Western cultures are mainly found in the care of their parents. Furthermore, Western cultures specifically assign to parents responsibility for socializing their children. Other institutions (e.g., school) are given authority *in loco parentis*, implying that parents have ultimate authority and discretion where child rearing is concerned. During the 1960s, increasing emphasis was placed on the very earliest experiences—those taking place during infancy—and this led to a special focus, not only on parents but more particularly on mothers.

We pointed out earlier that children develop characteristic social dispositions or orientations during infancy largely as a consequence of the infants' learning about the predictability of their caretakers' behavior (Ainsworth et al., 1978; Lamb, 1981a, 1981b). These orientations toward others in the social world shape the children's behavior in initial encounters with unfamiliar people and thus may have a long-term impact on their integration into the world beyond the family (Easterbrooks & Lamb, 1979; Main, 1973; Thompson & Lamb, in press; Waters, Wippman, & Sroufe, 1979). In addition, children are first exposed to social norms—those concerning moral behavior, conventions (e.g., how to eat, be clothed), and sex-stereotyped behavior—during the early years, and presumably these norms are taught by parents. By the time children first enter extrafamilial groups (e.g., in nursery school) most have a good understanding of how they are expected to behave (Hoffman, 1970b). As far as morality is concerned, they know the rules, even though they may deviate when they have no fear of being caught. Their behavior is clearly sex-typed, and they administer punishments and rewards to peers who deviate from these prescriptions.

There are many reasons why parents should be effective agents of socialization. Not only do they spend a great deal of time with their children, but they are also powerful—in that they are big, strong, and control the environment, at least as far as their children are concerned—as well as nurturant. Perceived power and nurturance are factors known to increase the salience of models as well as the informativeness of the rewards and punishments meted out (Bandura, 1977; Mussen, 1967). Whether or not psychoanalysts correctly define the reason for this, most children strive very hard to imitate their parents' behavior and obtain their parents' approval (Mussen, 1967). In addition to identifying with the same-sex parent, therefore, children strive to obtain approval from the opposite-sex parent by complementing their behavior—a form of role learning (*reciprocal role learning*) described by Helena Deutsch (1944), Talcott Parsons (1954, 1958; Parsons & Bales, 1955), and Miriam Johnson (1963) as especially important for sex-role learning in girls. Finally, parents influence socialization by controlling access to other potential sources of influence. They decide whether and when their children will go to nursery school, and if so, which one; they control what television programs (if any) their children watch; they determine whether teachers are esteemed or derogated, and at least through middle childhood, they determine who their children spend time with outside school hours.

Although parents may be most influential during the early years, the introduction of children to other agents of socialization (the peer group, teachers, etc.) does not signal the end of parental influence, as many discussions implicitly and incorrectly assume. It simply means that other agents now supplement or modify the parents' influence (Lamb & Baumrind, 1978). At the same time, the child's developing cognitive capacities change the way norms and guides are interpreted.

Since there is every reason to expect parents to have a major influence on socialization, it is both surprising and disappointing how little evidence of this exists. During the 1940s and 1950s, as noted earlier, a number of large-scale studies were designed to determine how parental socialization techniques affected aspects of personality development (Becker, 1964; Martin, 1975). Apparently because of the rapid cultural changes taking place in these decades, the major findings (those concerning class differences in socialization and disciplinary practices) of several of these studies seemed contradictory, and all yielded relatively little evidence of enduring parental influences on school-aged children (Bronfenbrenner, 1961; Yarrow, Campbell, & Burton, 1968). Although with the benefit of hindsight it is possible to attribute these findings to methodological deficiencies, such as the reliance on maternal interviews for evidence regarding both parental and child behavior, this does not amount to satisfactory evidence that parents do influence children in the predicted fashion.

More recent studies have attempted to remedy the methodological defects of these early studies while also adopting a strategy of using multiple convergent techniques for assessing both parental and child behavior in order to maximize reliability and validity. The best of these studies are being undertaken at the University of California-Berkeley, directed by Baumrind (1971, 1975; Lamb & Baumrind, 1978) and the Blocks (Block & Block, 1980). Although the Blocks have yet to publish a report detailing the relationships between parental and child behavior in their longitudinal study, Baumrind has documented the relationships at one age. She has shown that socially competent preschoolers (i.e., those who are enthusiastic, outgoing, assertive with peers, and nonintrusive with adults) have parents who adopt an authoritative parenting style, which involves setting firm guidelines for children but providing well-articulated reasons for the restrictions imposed. Of course, it is not clear whether the parental behavior causes the children's behavior rather than the reverse: only analysis of the longitudinal data will clarify this. Future reports by Baumrind and the Blocks promise to elucidate parental effects on child development.

While most studies of *parental* behavior focused largely on *maternal* behavior, many studies undertaken during the 1950s and 1960s attempted to explore paternal influences on child development by comparing children whose fathers lived with the family to children whose fathers did not (see reviews by Biller, 1974, 1981; Lamb, 1976, 1981c). Paradoxically, some of the best available evidence concerning familial influences on young children comes either from these investigations of what happens when socializing agents are lacking completely (i.e., the father absence literature) or of when they are providing deficient models of social relationships and behavior (i.e., the marital discord literature). The latter evidence will be discussed in Section 13, "The Effects of Divorce."

In the area of father absence, most researchers reasoned that fathers represented male models and primary disciplinarians and focused on the effects of father absence on boys. In general, studies in this area showed that boys raised without fathers tended to be less masculine than those whose fathers were present. The effects were especially marked when the fathers' absence began in the first few years of the children's lives (Hetherington & Deur, 1971). As several reviewers (e.g., Biller, 1974, 1981; Herzog & Sudia, 1973; Lamb, 1976, 1981c; Shinn, 1978) have pointed out, many of these studies failed to control for a number of factors often correlated with father absence—such as social class, economic and emotional stress on the custodial mother—and so it was not clear how much of the effect observed could be attributed to the absence of a role model and limit-setting disciplinarian. Several more recent studies have been more careful methodologically, and they have yielded comparable findings. In an interesting study, furthermore, Hetherington (1972) showed that the development of girls whose fathers were absent was also affected. Adolescent girls whose fathers had died were especially timid in interaction with males, whereas girls whose parents had divorced were usually forward and aggressive with males. Since several other studies had shown few effects of father absence on young girls, it seemed that the effects of father absence on girls were evident only in adolescence, whereas the effects on boys were evident far earlier. Of course, these findings do not mean that all children who experience father absence will necessarily face such difficulties. Clausen (1978) suggests that the most crucial factor in mediating children's general emotional development is not father absence per se but the way a mother interacts with her children—her ability to spend relaxed time with the children, her reaction to the stresses of raising children alone, and the type of day care used.

As has been noted, studies of socialization have tended to equate "parent" with "mother." It has finally become clear, however, that fathers have a significant impact on their children's development under normal circumstances as well as by default in the event of the father's absence. Not only do children develop attachments to their fathers (Lamb, 1977b), but the relationships between a child and each parent are qualitatively different. In one study, Lamb (1977b) found that mothers and fathers play differently with their 7- to 13-month-old infants and hold them for different reasons. Fathers in this study were more likely to play vigorous, physically stimulating, and unpredictable games, while mothers generally played conventional ones (e.g., peek-a-boo, pat-a-cake). Moreover, fathers were more likely to hold babies to play with them or when the babies wanted to be held; mothers more often held their babies for caretaking (feeding, diapering) or to restrict the babies' exploration. These findings suggest that fathers engage their children in unique interactions which broaden the scope of the children's social experience.

Fathers also interact differently with their children than do mothers in relation to differential sex treatment. After children are 2 years of age, fathers begin to withdraw from daughters and pay special attention to sons (Lamb, 1979); children—especially boys—then come to develop a preference for the same-sex parent. Fathers' effects on sex-role development appear to continue, as indicated by the findings discussed above in relation to father absence and by Lamb's (1976) finding that highly nurturant fathers enhance masculinity in sons and femininity in daughters.

In terms of overall adjustment, fathers appear to have an effect both in themselves and in potentially compensating for limitations of mothers. One study found that children with adjustment problems had both mothers and fathers were less well adjusted, less friendly, and less democratic than the parents of well-adjusted children (Peterson, Becker, Hellmer, Shoemaker, & Quay, 1959). Of the maladjusted children, those who were aggressive tended to have fathers who were weak and ineffectual, while those who were shy or felt inferior tended to have dictatorial and unconcerned fathers. Another study found that children whose parents were not very nurturant and were either very strict or very lax had difficulty adjusting to nursery school. Adjustment was easier, however, when either the mother or father was nurturant and firm (Bloom-Feshbach, Bloom-Feshbach, & Gaughran, 1981).

As Zigler and Cascione (1981) point out, fathers also have indirect effects on their children through their relationships with their wives. Several studies have shown, for instance, that marital strife and hostility have adverse effects on the personality adjustment of children (Graham & Rutter, 1973; Power, Ash, Schoenberg, & Sorey, 1974; Rutter, 1971, 1973, 1974, 1979; Rutter, Cox, Tupling, Berger, & Yule, 1975; West & Farrington, 1973, 1977). In fact, marital discord may be more damaging than living with a single parent (Lamb, 1981c). One indirect effect may be seen in Pederson's (1976) finding that mothers appear to be more effective in feeding their babies when their husbands are supportive and less effective when tension or conflict is present in the marital relationship. Generally, parent-child relationships may reflect tendencies within marital relationships: when parents are critical of each other, they tend to express more negative feelings to their children as well (Pederson, Anderson, & Cain, 1980).

Just as marital roles can affect parental ones, parental roles can influence the relationship between husband and wife. It appears, for example, that marital satisfaction can increase when parents share caretaking. One study by Bloom-Feshbach (1979) found that fathers who were involved in child care reported improved marriages after the birth of a child, while fathers who were less involved reported that the birth detracted from the marriage. Zigler and Cascione (1981) discuss a possible explanation of this finding, which stems from the fact that marital satisfaction tends to be higher when couples share activities. When a child is born, mothers typically become more involved with child care and engage in fewer activities with their husbands. If parents share child care, however, this can become another shared activity and enhance, rather than decrease, marital satisfaction. Also in this regard, the quality of mothers' care improves if fathers are involved in child care and the mothers' burden is thereby reduced.

A major problem with studies designed to investigate parental effects on child development is that they tend to view the family in isolation without seriously recognizing the extent to which parental influences are supplemented or contradicted by other agents of socialization. Bronfenbrenner (1979) has argued with particular agents outside the family, focusing not only on their direct influences on children but also on any indirect influences they exert via their effects on the parents' behavior. A similarly broad view of the influences on child development is implicit in the recent recommendation by Keniston and the Carnegie Council on Children (1977) that to improve the lot of children in the United States, the government should initiate a number of economic reforms designed to affect parents and working mothers. In the next few pages, we describe other potentially significant agents of socialization—the media, the peer group, teachers and schools, and day care.

The Media

Over the last three decades, a new and powerful influence on children has emerged—television. Shortly after its introduction in the early 1950s, television was viewed simply as a harmless form of entertainment, but developmentalists gradually became concerned about its possible effects on viewers. Particular concern was voiced about children when it became apparent how much time they were spending watching television. There is tremendous individual variation, of course, but the average child watches 3 hours every weekday and more on weekends (Lyle & Hoffmann, 1972). The most serious concerns about television viewing have centered on the possibility that frequent exposure to televised aggression and violence would increase the aggressiveness of viewers—especially young ones.

Experimental studies, most notably those conducted by Bandura and his students, suggest that there may be good reason for this concern (see Bandura, 1973, for a review). Most children appear to imitate the aggressive behavior they observe on specially prepared television films—indeed, they are as likely to imitate a model on film as a cartoon character or a live model (Bandura, Ross, & Ross, 1963). Furthermore, although the nurturance of a model usually affects the likelihood that it will be imitated, nurturance did not affect imitation in this case: almost all children imitated aggression (Bandura & Huston, 1961). Countless other studies have confirmed the powerful effects models have on the behavior of viewers (Murray, 1980; Stein & Friedrich, 1975). Observational learning or imitation takes place regardless of the fact that viewers are usually not rewarded for imitating what they see. Usually the performance of behavior learned by viewing models depends on whether the child is reinforced or punished for performing the imitative behavior. However, neither the consequences to the model or the observer nor the motives of the model affect the likelihood of imitating aggressive behavior (Bandura, 1973; Stein & Friedrich, 1975).

The reliable demonstration that children would indeed imitate the behavior—particularly, it seemed, the aggressive behavior—of televised models in the laboratory led to the initiation of field studies designed to determine whether regular television programs had similar effects. The Surgeon General of the United States commissioned several extensive reports on this topic, and we can only provide a brief summary of the findings here (Comstock & Rubinstein, 1972a, 1972b; Comstock, Rubinstein, & Murray, 1972; Murray, Rubinstein, & Comstock, 1972; Rubinstein, Comstock, & Murray, 1972). Essentially, those who view violent television programs do appear to be more aggressive than those who do not. Although many studies did not directly assess the direction of effects (i.e., it was not clear whether aggressive people like to watch violent programs or whether viewing violent programs makes people more aggressive), there are some studies that have clarified this issue. Let us discuss, for example, a longitudinal study conducted in New York State by Eron and his colleagues (1972; Lefkowitz, Eron, Walder, & Huesmann, 1977). In this study, the researchers obtained reports from parents and teachers about the behavior, personality, and aggressiveness of third-grade students, reports from parents about their parental practices and their attitudes toward television, and reports from students and parents about the amount and type of television watched. From these data, it was confirmed that there was a relationship between the amount of violent television viewed and the aggressiveness of the individual, although of course the direction of effects remained uncertain. To remedy this uncertainty, Eron and his colleagues obtained further information about the subjects when they were 19 years old and sought to determine what accounted for later aggressiveness. They found that earlier aggressiveness was one factor, but so was the earlier preference for violent television programs. Evidently, they concluded, televised violence did have long-term negative consequences. Several other projects have reported similar conclusions, and it is now widely agreed that television can have harmful consequences (Murray & Kippax, 1979). These are not inevitable, however, even when children do watch many violent shows regularly. The attitudes of their parents are crucial. If parents make it clear that they disapprove of the violence portrayed, adverse effects on the children's aggressiveness can be avoided (Dominick & Greenberg, 1972).

Although most researchers focus on the potentially harmful effects of television viewing, beneficial consequences are also possible. Social learning theorists note that children merely imitate the behavior they observe. If the modelled behavior is violent or aggressive, they are likely to behave aggressively. If prosocial or altruistic behavior is modeled, however, they should become more altruistic. As in the research on the imitation of aggressive behavior, this prediction has been confirmed using both specially prepared films and regular television programs. In one interesting study, for example, Coates, Pusser, and Goodman (1976) compared the effects of two children's programs, "Sesame Street" and "Mister Rogers' Neighborhood," on the behavior of preschoolers. "Sesame Street" is noted for the frequency with which characters give one another both punishing and rewarding responses, whereas "Mister Rogers' Neighborhood" is noted for the rewarding responses (Coates & Pusser, 1975). Coates et al. (1976) found that the children who watched "Mister Rogers' Neighborhood" reinforced one another in the classroom more often after a period in which they were shown this program daily, whereas many children who watched "Sesame Street" meted out more rewards as well as punishments after the "intervention."

Both "Sesame Street" and "Mister Rogers' Neighborhood" have additional goals. "Mister Rogers' Neighborhood" draws upon Erikson's theory of child development in determining both the content and style of presentation, although there have been no investigations of its effectiveness. "Sesame Street" focuses on educational goals and aspects of cognitive development, and the producers of the show have made regular efforts to evaluate the effectiveness of the material presented (Ball & Bogatz, 1970). Unlike "Mister Rogers' Neighborhood," however, "Sesame Street" has been severely criticized by some researchers (e.g., Singer & Singer, 1976) because of its fast (attention-getting) pace. The Singers argue that the rapid pace of "Sesame Street" harms reflectiveness and the imaginativeness of children's play. Lesser (1974), one of the researchers involved in the preparation of "Sesame Street," sharply disagrees with this assertion.

Peers

The peer group is another significant source of influence on children's development. Indeed, as increasing numbers of children are enrolled in group-care facilities because both of their parents work, peer group influences are probably being exerted earlier and earlier and thus may be becoming increasingly influential. Reviews of the extensive research on peer influences have been published by Hartup (1970, 1976, 1977, 1980) and Asher, Oden, and Gottman (1977). These reviews conclude, on the basis of large number of experimental studies, that children are readily influenced by the behavior of peer models. Aggressive, altruistic, competitive, and moral behaviors have all proven susceptible to influence by the behavior of models, although there are few data available to indicate how enduring these effects are or how commonly they occur outside structured experimental situations. By contrast, there are data available from both experimental and naturalistic studies revealing that children as young as 3 years of age reinforce and punish one another for sex-appropriate and sex-inappropriate behavior and that these responses effectively shape the recipients' behavior (Lamb & Roopnarine, 1979; Lamb et al., 1980). These findings underscore the extent to which peers supplement parental influence and, by acting upon the norms or rules (e.g., for sex-typed behavior) learned from their parents and the media, further influence the behavior of other children. Some have suggested that peers may be especially important agents of socialization because they have much less flexible notions of what is acceptable than adults do (Kohlberg, 1966, 1969). Thus a boy who plays "house" is likely to receive more scornful responses from his peers than from his parents.

The desire to obtain peer approval is not confined to early childhood, although much of the recent research has focused on this period. We do not know whether there are changes (either increases or decreases) over succeeding years, but peer approval is important around the time of puberty, when children attempt to adopt more mature sex role and enter into heterosexual relationships (Conger, 1978; Matteson, 1975). Lamb and Urberg (1978) suggested that adolescents are increasingly sensitive to their peers' attitudes because they are unsure of exactly how they should behave and so fall back upon conventional stereotypes and rely upon others to provide cues by which they can shape their behavior appropriately. There is substantial evidence (anecdotal and scientific) that conformity to the norms and standards of the peer group is extremely marked in adolescence (Conger, 1977). As we grow older, furthermore, the peer group remains a primary reference group and a source of pressure and influence (e.g., Nash & Feldman, 1981). The primary driving force behind fashions and fads, for example, is the motivation to behave or dress in conformity with currently approved standards. The pressures of peer group expectations may also be one reason for the increased concern about conformity to conventional sex-role stereotypes around the onset of parenthood (Lamb, 1978a; Nash & Feldman, 1981).

For the most part, peers supplement the influence of parents and the media by providing additional pressure toward conformity with conventional norms and standards. In addition, however, peers have an influence on social competence that may be uniquely important. In early childhood, peers alone provide interactions on an equal footing, for relationships with adults are necessarily asymmetrical (Hartup, 1978; Mueller & Vandell, 1979).

The effects of peer contacts on the development of social competence are also clear. In nonhuman primates, we know that juveniles raised without peers are socially deficient. They never learn the behavioral cues that permit group interactions to remain peaceful, and so they may aggress against or fail to submit to dominant animals, risking attack and serious danger. Peer relationships, argue Suomi and Harlow (1975, 1978), provide the context in which monkeys learn to control and modulate aggressive behavior. Likewise, animals raised without peers do not learn how to interact with same- or opposite-sex individuals, and so even if they are not killed by the group, they seldom have success mating (Suomi & Harlow, 1975).

Of course, deprivation of peer contact cannot be introduced experimentally in human research, but evidence of its effects is available from studies of children who are found to be already socially isolated from their peers (Asher, Oden, & Gottman, 1977; Hartup, 1980). These children, like the experimental animals, are characterized by social incompetence. They are deficient in the knowledge of ways of responding to others' initiatives, of making friends, of initiating and maintaining interactions, and so on. In the case of the children, it is not clear whether they are spurned by others because of prior social incompetence or become incompetent because they are deprived of formative interactions with peers. Recent experimental research, however, shows that when socially isolated children (i.e., those who are seldom nominated as friends in sociometric surveys) are given special coaching in role-taking skills, their social competence improves, as does their popularity in the peer group (Oden & Aher, 1977).

The effects of isolation (unpopularity) and social incompetence are likely to be cumulative. Deprived of interaction with peers, children lack the contacts by which social skills are learned and practiced; without these skills, they are unable to enter into interactions with peers on an equal footing, thus becoming more isolated, and so on. Asher, Oden, and Gottman (1977) reviewed a substantial body of evidence indicating that socially isolated children have greater than normal probabilities of maladjustment in school, low achievement, delinquency, and a later need for psychotherapy of some sort.

Teachers and the School

Once children start attending school, the primary influence of their parents begins to wane as peers and teachers become more influential. Like peers, teachers tend to supplement the pressures and demands of parents; they too both encourage and model conventionally approved behavior. In addition, however, educational institutions have a more salient concern with achievement and academic performance. Although parental attitudes are important in this area, it may be one in which teachers are especially important.

One significant impact of school experience may be on children's motivation to learn and on their assessment of their own abilities. Researchers have gathered substantial evidence over the last several years that children develop expectancies about their abilities as a result of their experiences (Balla & Zigler, 1982; Cromwell, 1963; Gruen & Zigler, 1968; Sanders, Zigler, & Butterfield, 1968; Turnure & Zigler, 1964). Children who fail frequently begin to see themselves as incompetent and lose the motivation to try (Seligman, 1975). By contrast, those who are used to succeeding approach novel problems as challenges in which they are motivated to succeed. These motivational orientations have a tendency to become self-fulfilling: if children are not motivated to apply themselves enthusiastically and persistently, then they are likely to fail again, further reinforcing the damagingly negative self-concepts.

Recent analyses of how motivational dispositions are established draw upon attribution theory (e.g., Heider, 1958; Kelley, 1973; Weiner, 1972, 1974). According to this theory, individuals attribute successes and failures to either ability, effort, or uncontrollable factors such as luck. If people fail at a task, for example, they can conclude that they lack the requisite ability or that they simply did not try hard enough. In the former case, they are likely not to try when faced with similar problems in the future, while in the latter case they are likely to try even harder, knowing that if they do, they may be successful.

In a series of interesting studies which we mentioned earlier, Dweck (1978; Dweck et al., 1978) has shown that children may develop attributional styles as a consequence of their teachers' attitudes and comments. Unfortunately, furthermore, teachers appear not to teach all children similar styles. Instead, it seems that they attribute girls' failures to lack of ability and boys' failures to lack of effort, while attributing boys' successes to ability and rewarding girls in irrelevant aspects of the performance (e.g., neatness). As a result, Dweck argues, girls come to see themselves as incompetent, and their achievement motivation declines. Earlier studies indicated that social class differences might have similar origins: lower-class children come to believe that they will fail in whatever they do, and so they lose the motivation to try (Lefcourt, 1976; Phares, 1976). These social class differences and their origins are discussed further in Section 15, "Intracultural Variation."

Another way in which teachers may affect children—the *Pygmalion effect*—was described by Robert Rosenthal (1966; Rosenthal & Jacobson, 1968) several years ago. Rosenthal administered tests to groups of children and then identified for the teachers those children who could be expected to improve during the year. Actually, these "bloomers" were randomly chosen and did not differ from the rest of the children in any known way. Nevertheless, when Rosenthal retested the children some months later, the bloomers were indeed performing better. Rosenthal referred to this as a *self-fulfilling prophecy*—arguing that the teachers' expectations had led them to give more attention to the bloomers. This experimental demonstration of the importance of teachers' expectations has been widely criticized, and some researchers have failed to replicate the finding (Barber, 1974; Barber & Silver, 1968). Clashoff and Snow (1971) present a number of methodological problems with the original study which cast doubt on the findings, and nine subsequent studies (reviewed by Baker & Christ, 1971) failed to find an increase in children's IQs resulting from modifying teachers' expectations—although they indicated that children often did better schoolwork when teachers expected more of them. There is much evidence, however, that teachers' behavior is influenced by their expectations: they pay more attention to children considered intellectually promising and less to children of whom their expectations are low. In both cases, the expectation may prove self-fulfilling prophecies. Rosenthal and Jacobson underlined the importance of teachers' expectations, and enough studies have replicated their findings to make it evident that teachers' expectations *can*—but do not always—exert a powerful influence on their pupils' performance. Presumably this effect is not limited to achievement but touches broadly on the socioemotional and motivational aspects of the pupils' personalities. An example may be seen in a recent study of Caparulo (1980) which focused on the mainstreaming of mildly retarded children. This study showed that children developed lower expectancies of success and became increasingly outer-directed if their teachers had negative attitudes toward mainstreaming and had taken few special education courses, as compared with initially similar children whose teachers were prepared for mainstreaming and held positive attitudes toward it.

During the heyday of the "environmental mystique" in the 1960s, schools were widely viewed as a means of effecting major socially desired changes in children's lives, personalities, and intellects. For example, educational enrichment was one facet of President Johnson's War on Poverty, a program designed to eliminate the effects of poverty. As preschool-age children were held to be particularly susceptible to environmental influence, a major focus was on preschool intervention programs; these programs will be discussed in detail in a subsection below on "Intervention" (section 14). What is relevant to the present discussion, however, is the overall importance of schools as agents of socialization and the potential impact of educational intervention on children of various ages and socioeconomic groups. Of particular importance is the controversy which developed in the late 1960s and early 1970s, when the failure of educational intervention was widely touted. Two volumes—one published by Coleman and his colleagues in 1966 and the other by Jencks and his colleagues in 1972—contributed most to the belief that schools had little impact—even on intellectual performance. Both Coleman and Jencks claimed that demographic characteristics of the family of origin were much more important than characteristics of the schools, although neither research group systematically investigated any outcomes other than IQ and achievement. In contrast to these pessimistic conclusions, the only large-scale attempt to assess a variety of outcomes, conducted in London by Michael Rutter and his colleagues (1979), concluded that schools indeed make a difference—for better or for worse—in the lives of children.

Although they have an important impact on children's socialization, as do all of the socializing agents we have considered, the influence of the schools does not operate in isolation. Schools both reflect and contribute to the shaping of social attitudes: they change to meet current social climates, and they serve as implicit models for family practices. Thus, schools may play a role either in perpetuating or combating social problems. For example, as we will consider in a later section (16), schools presently seem to aid in perpetuating child abuse through their use of corporal punishment; they could, however, help alleviate the problem of abuse by providing models of nonviolence. In general, the effects of schools on children have led some researchers to the belief that schools provide a logical base for intervention efforts aimed at primary prevention of the social problems facing all children—that is, for taking steps to avoid the occurrence of problems rather than waiting to treat their symptoms (Zigler, Kagan, & Muenchow, 1982). Zigler, Kagan, and Muenchow argue that schools have a stake in primary prevention, since even the narrowest goal of education (academic performance) can be thwarted by larger social issues—e.g., when large numbers of students do not receive adequate health care. Not only do these authors suggest that the goals of primary prevention are compatible with broad goals of education, but they argue that schools could be most effective agents because they reach all children, regardless of socioeconomic class.

Schools vary in quality, goals, and atmosphere, but the fact that they are not always murturant and supportive places is suggested by the occurrence of school vandalism and truancy (Zigler, Kagan, & Muenchow, 1982). Further, since the role of the schools has primarily been restricted to dealing with cognitive functions, teachers and administrators do not tend to emphasize social and psychological development. Perhaps most notable is the fact that teachers, who traditionally establish classroom environments, often define their roles narrowly (Zimiles, 1967). In contrast, a concern with children's lives in broad terms would require a fundamental shift in emphasis to one in which schools would aim (directly) to prepare children for life with both cognitive and affective learning and (less directly) would facilitate utilization of services (such as health care) which are basic requisites of healthy development (Zigler, Kagan, & Muenhow, 1982). Because schools are but one source of socialization, it would also depend on an integration of schools, families, and communities. There is evidence, for example, that direct parent involvement in schools has benefits for parents, children, and schools alike, including improvements in children's academic achievement (Lopata et al., 1969; Mann, 1975); personal benefits to parents (Adams, 1976); and improved staff morale, school climate, and curriculum development (Davies, 1978). Also, Lightfoot (1978) suggests that suburban schools are superior in quality to inner-city ones not only because of relative affluence and availability of resources but because the values of (middle-class) parents and suburban schools are consonant, while those of (lower-class) parents and inner-city schools are not.

Further considerations relevant to intervention efforts in schools may be found in the previously mentioned subsection on "Intervention" (Section 14). Although that discussion deals particularly with children from economically disadvantaged backgrounds, the principles outlined there are of importance to the role of schools in the socialization of all children.

Day Care

The final source of influence on development we will consider is day care. While not every child experiences day care, as more and more women enter the work force and continue working once they have children, more children are placed in some type of day-care setting. This growing number of children makes it important to consider day care as a socializing agent.

The effects of day care are, as yet, not well established, but we might expect them to depend on a host of factors including type of care, quality of relationships with parents and alternate caregivers, type of interaction with peers, cognitive stimulation, and so on. Day-care arrangements vary tremendously, from large institutions to a single babysitter in a child's home. This variability presents a major complication for research on the effects of day care, making it difficult to reach an objective assessment of general effects. In part, the variability is a result of the fact that treatment of day care in the United States has been more affected by political and economic concerns than by consideration of children's needs. While it would seem that the paucity of evidence on the effects of day care along with the recognition that child development depends on the quality of interactions between children and their caretakers should be reason to emphasize quality standards in existing programs, developmental considerations are continually weighed against economic ones when it comes to legislation. For example, the implementation of new Federal Interagency Day Care Requirements, designed to ensure fundamental standards such as provision of nutritious meals and safe staff/child ratios, was blocked in an alleged money-saving measure by the United States Senate (Zigler & Goodman, 1980). Consequently, because of the limitations of the old standards (Cohen & Zigler, 1977), the day-care needs of many children remain unmet, the lack of national standards enables unsafe practices to occur in some states, and the quality of day care which children receive is largely a matter of individual families' luck in finding and being able to afford satisfactory arrangements. This situation is in contrast to that in several other countries, which provide degrees of child care ranging from kindergarten for all 5-year-olds in Israel to nurseries for children over 45 days old in Cuba (Wald, 1978). In contrast to the American practice of offering isolated services to low-income families, furthermore, many foreign countries maintain a comprehensive child-care system, including health services as well as day care (Kamerman & Kahn, 1978; Roby, 1973).

Political concerns are also evident in the history of the United States government's relation to day care. During World War II, for example, the federal government facilitated states' provision of day care because women were needed to work for national defense, but the day-care centers closed after the war, when women were no longer needed—or wanted—in the work force. At that point, public antagonism toward employed mothers was prevalent, and the only options open to women who remained employed (as many did) were private centers, babysitters, and relatives. The situation changed somewhat with the political emphasis of the early 1960s on equal opportunity, but in this context day care was generally seen as a service to the poor and so did not carry much political weight. The increasing momentum of the feminist movement has been a primary factor in fostering the view that all mothers should be entitled to day care. This view is far from unanimous, however: right-wing political groups oppose governmental support of day care, equatting it with sacrifice of the family to communal styles of child rearing (Zigler & Goodman, 1980). The evaluation of day care's effects on children is often based on subjective attitudes concerning the traditional family, on implied or explicit views of women's roles, and on assumptions about the requisites for healthy child development, and this subjective evaluation may help explain why day care is such a controversial issue.

Popular beliefs in the United States hold that development will suffer negative consequences if children are not raised (at least in the early years) by an exclusive caretaker. Since the first few years of life are the time when children usually develop the attachment relationships so crucial to social development, major concerns with day care have been that children will not form selective attachments, that those which do form may be insecure, or that attachments will form to day-care staff rather than to parents (Rutter, 1981).

Definitive evidence to support these concerns is not extensive, and many of the studies which have been conducted can be criticized on methodological grounds (cf. Belsky & Steinberg, 1978; Belsky, Steinberg, & Walker, 1982). It appears, however, that day care *need not* have adverse consequences for young children and infants. A review of literature on day care by Rutter (1981) reveals that the belief that day care may result in children's failures to form attachments, or to form them with day-care staff rather than parents, has been consistently negated by empirical research. Rather, the common finding, across different types of studies and means of assessment has been that day-care children usually develop primary bonds with their parents and that children form bonds in similar ways, at similar times, whether or not they experience day care. As one example, babies raised by nurses (*metaploth*) in kibbutzim in Israel develop attachments to their mothers, even though they spend relatively little time with them (Fox, 1977; Maccoby & Feldman, 1972).

Evidence supporting the concern that day-care children may form insecure attachments has been somewhat less consistent. Two studies, one involving infants (Vaughn, Gove, & Egeland, 1980), and one involving preschoolers (Blehar, 1974), have reported that children in substitute care are more likely to develop insecure attachments to their mothers than are home-reared children. Several other studies, however, some involving similar methods and others adapting very different strategies, have failed to replicate these findings (Brookhart & Hock, 1976; Caldwell, Wright, Honig, & Tannenbaum, 1970; Campbell & Ramey, 1977; Cochran, 1977; Doyle, 1975; Doyle & Somers, 1978; Feldman, 1974; Kagan, Kearsley, & Zelazo, 1978; Moskowitz, Schwarz, & Corsini, 1977; Portnoy & Simmons, 1978; Ragozin, 1980; Roopnarine & Lamb, 1978, 1980). Two possible reasons for the inconsistency have been advanced. First, Blanchard and Main (1979) report that the effects may be evident only in the period immediately following enrollment in out-of-home care and may then disappear; the inconsistent results may reflect differences in the time at which research was conducted. Second, Roopnarine and Lamb (1978, 1980) report that the differences between home-care and day-care groups may antedate enrollment in day care, because parents who *choose* to keep their children at home may differ in significant ways from parents who choose to enroll their children in day care. This possibility highlights a major methodological problem emphasized by Frye (1979): without random assignment to day-care and non-day-care groups, we cannot assess the effects of day care since observed differences may be a function of variables other than the use of day care itself. Similarly, indices of attachment used to assess the effects of day care would be more telling if they were compared to attachment behavior before day care began. Without such a comparison, factors which are assumed to be effects of day care might actually have been in existence before the day-care variable was introduced.

As is evident in a review by Rutter (1981), many variables besides the ones discussed above can make it difficult to interpret results of existing literature on day care as well as to carry out research yielding definitive results. The age of children studied, for example, may have an influence in several ways. The effects of day care may be different for younger children, in the process of forming initial attachments, than for older ones, who have already developed attachments. Age may also be involved in determining the extent to which children want, and are able to benefit from, contact with peers in day care. Additionally, age may differentiate children who have always experienced day care from those who had originally been cared for at home. This last variable is similar to one mentioned above: regardless of age, the length of time children have been in day care may influence the effect via the children's reactions to a novel versus a habitual experience. Children's prior experiences with separation or with peers, too, may affect their reactions to day care. Other potential influences which have not received much attention in the literature, include the number of children in a family and the child's ordinal position, and children's sex and temperament differences.

Another factor which may influence children's reactions to day care is parent involvement. Experience with the Head Start program suggests that children benefit from parents' involvement with the child-care center (Valentine & Stark, 1979). A recent study (Zigler & Turner, in prep.), however, finds extremely low parental involvement at a day-care center which encourages visitation and participation: an average of 7.4 minutes per day. Both the reasons for parents' lack of involvement and the effect of differing amounts of involvement need further examination. Certainly the quality of parents' interactions with their children can be expected to mediate the effects of day care, as can the degree of congruence between parents' values and those of supplementary caretakers and parents' reasons for utilizing day care.

Of course, characteristics of the day-care facility such as consistency and training of staff, staff/child ratios, and type of environment are crucial considerations in assessing the effects of day care. A major problem which limits the generalizability of findings is that all studies have been based on high-quality, center-based day care, often provided by university-affiliated centers. This focus is not at all representative, since most children are not enrolled in centers but in family day-care arrangements, and most of the rest are in centers of much poorer quality than those that have been studied. The variability is a problem, too, in the actual fact of day care. Children cared for by relatives or in other non-center-based arrangements may benefit from more personal attention from caretakers. On the other hand, the care they receive may be inferior, especially if caretakers are overburdened or uninformed about child development (and, of course, if the situation would be different in center-based day care). It is obvious that either kind of arrangement may be quite good or quite bad, and we cannot compare them unless we control for variance in the quality of both types. All we can say at present with any confidence, therefore, is that supplementary care outside the family *need not* have adverse consequences.

Research concerned with the effects of day care has tended to take the approach of looking at potential harmful consequences. Few studies have taken the opposite position and considered the potential benefits offered by day-care experiences, such as increased association with peers (Rubenstein & Howes, 1979) and attachments which may be formed to supplementary caretakers as well as to parents (Willis & Ricciuti, 1974). Although children's tendencies in interaction with peers seem to depend, in large part, on maturation and peer group experiences, some effects of group rearing may be seen. Children tend to exhibit apprehension in the face of interaction with an unfamiliar peer, followed (after approximately the age of 20 months) by an increase in reciprocal play; group-reared children tend to lose the initial apprehension more quickly or at an earlier age than family-reared children (Rutter, 1981).

Research on day care has also focused almost exclusively on the effects on mother-child relationships; only one study has considered the potential effects of day care on children's relationships with their fathers (Roopnarine & Lamb, 1980). In general, more studies are needed to assess the effects of different types of care settings and to consider the important interaction between the parents' attitudes and the values of the supplementary caretakers (e.g., Bloom-Feshbach, Bloom-Feshbach, & Gaughran, 1980). Instead of asking whether supplementary care affects children, we now need to ask, more specifically, how different types of children from different social backgrounds are affected by different types of supplementary care.

14

The Effects of Divorce

Over the last few decades there have been dramatic increases in the number of divorces and in the number of children who experience the divorce of their parents (Bronfenbrenner, 1975b; Glick, 1979). Recent projections indicate that just under 30% of the children under 18 in 1990 will have experienced the divorce of their parents (Glick, 1979). About 90% of these will be placed in the custody of their mothers and will thus spend some time in a fatherless family. Most early studies on the effects of divorce focused on status characteristics such as father absence and did not attempt to consider dynamic factors such as the nature of both pre- and postdivorce parent-child relationships. We will discuss the implications of these studies shortly but first will consider the results of investigations focused directly on divorce and its sequelae.

Studies by Hetherington, Cox, and Cox (1976, 1979), Wallerstein and Kelly (e.g., 1980), and Hess and Camara (1979) have been most revealing. In each case, participant families were recruited as early as possible in the divorce case: Wallerstein and Kelly first examined children just after separation (before the final divorce decree), while Hetherington et al. recruited families 2 months after the divorce decree was issued. Both studies showed that the divorce process was highly stressful for all concerned. Employing clinical methods (without a control group, unfortunately), Wallerstein and Kelly reported that most children of all ages from 3 to 18 were affected and that symptoms remained a year later in about half of the children of every age. Hetherington et al. studied preschoolers as well as their parents, and found stress and disorganization manifested by both parents and children. One year after the divorce, parents (both custodial and noncustodial) still experienced loneliness, incompetence, depression, difficulties in establishing meaningful relationships with adults, and problems managing the children. Observations revealed that the children were inadequately controlled and disciplined. Adjustment and behavior problems in the children were reported by both parents and teachers. Only 2 years after the divorce had things returned to normal for most of the divorced families, though of course some were still having problems at this stage too. Custodial mothers had special problems managing boys. This is consistent with the evidence reported below suggesting that father absence has clearer effects on boys than on girls.

In their study, Hess and Camara (1979) attempted to identify the factors associated with good and bad adjustment in the children of divorce. They found that the quality of parent-child and parent-parent relationships both before and after the divorce was critical. Adjustment was much easier when spousal hostility was less and the child was able to maintain good relationships with both the custodial and noncustodial parents.

As noted above, early work on divorce was concerned with status characteristics such as father absence. In fact, the reason for the fathers' absence was seldom considered (divorce, death, employment), but presumably most were absent because of marital dissolution. Many of the studies failed to obtain control groups of father-present children from comparable socioeconomic or ethnic backgrounds, and consequently much of this research is seriously flawed methodologically (Herzog & Sudia, 1973). Nevertheless some conclusions are possible based on the results of the more careful studies (see Biller, 1976, 1981; Lamb, 1976; Shinn, 1978, for reviews). First, boys whose fathers are absent tend to be less masculine in behavior and in cognitive style than those whose fathers are present. They also may be hypo- or hyper-aggressive, have lower IQ's, and achieve more poorly in school. Second, the time of the fathers' departure is also important: effects are most likely when fathers are absent from the first 3 years of the children's lives. Third, psychologically absent fathers (i.e., fathers who are nominally living with the children but seldom have any interaction with them) have qualitatively similar effects, though to a lesser degree, on the development of their children.

The effects of father absence on daughters' development have received much less attention than the effects on sons. In one interesting study, however, Hetherington (1972) found that the adolescent daughters of divorcees were unusually forward and brazen in their interactions with males, whereas the girls whose fathers had died were unusually timid and shy with males.

Most reviews of the literature on the effects of father absence emphasize the absence of an adult male model as the basis for the effects. In addition to this direct effect, there are also indirect effects mediated by the effects of divorce on the mothers' economic and socioemotional state. The studies on the immediate effects of divorce (e.g., Hess & Camara, 1979; Hetherington, 1982; Hetherington et al., 1979; Santrock, Warshak, & Elliott, 1982; Wallerstein & Kelly, 1980) promise to elucidate these indirect effects; at present, there is no way of assessing the relative importance of direct and indirect effects in mediating the effects of divorce/father absence.

One final qualification is in order. Even those studies which show clearly long-term effects attributable to divorce/father absence focus on group differences and seldom emphasize a crucially important point: namely, that adverse effects are not inevitable and that *most* children of divorce show no evidence of long-term effects. Further, if one is weighing the relative costs of divorce against the prolongation of marital hostility, it must be acknowledged that prolonged marital hostility is much more likely to have adverse effects on child development than is father absence/divorce (e.g., Rutter, 1971, 1973, 1979).

Most of the research on the long-term effects of divorce deals with father absence, since 90% of divorces involving children end in the award of custody to mothers (Glick, 1979). Little is known about the fate of those few children who are placed in the custody of their fathers. An excellent book by Levine (1976) indicated that most single fathers manage quite adequately—indeed, single fathers are usually much better off economically than are single mothers. In an ongoing comparison of single mothers and single fathers, Santrock and his colleagues (1979, 1982) report that male and female single parents tend to cope equivalently well. Single fathers are most likely to have problems with daughters, whereas single mothers are most likely to have problems with sons.

15

Intracultural Variation

Although there are many factors which might be used to distinguish groups within a given society, social class is the most thoroughly studied. Differences in behavior or personality between classes and, more importantly, the means by which such differences appear, is clearly a topic of relevance to the study of socialization. There are difficulties, however, with an examination of these topics. To begin with, the concept of *social class* is vague, emphasizing modal personalities within a group and variation between groups. Such an approach may have a certain plausibility when applied to discrete societies which have a clearly defined membership and can be distinguished from other groups in many obvious ways. It has much less plausibility when applied to subgroups of one society, because membership in these subgroups is uncertain, there is much interaction and mobility between groups, and the groups share a common core of history and values. Additionally, in emphasizing homogeneity of behavior within a class and heterogeneity across classes, there may be little attention given to variability within a class or to similarities across classes because these considerations are irrelevant to the main purpose. Furthermore, intracultural studies are by their nature correlational rather than experimental and so may be difficult to interpret in a useful and meaningful manner. With these difficulties in mind, we will examine both the explanations of social class differences which have been suggested and the actual differences in behavior which research has documented.

Explanations of Intracultural Variation: Differences in Child Rearing

One type of explanation of social class differences is a sociogenic one which holds that typical adult personality results from the requirements of the role of the class member; the characteristic adult is one who is able to perform a given role. In this view, child training practices are one part of the required behavior, but they are not necessarily of special importance. In contrast, a psychogenic explanation of social class differences relies heavily upon the importance of child-rearing practices in producing modal personality characteristics which then influence other behavior. The psychogenic approach makes several assumptions: that parents use particular child-rearing practices because of their class membership, that these practices lead to definite personality traits in the children, and that these traits make children effective members of the class as adults (at which point the sequence repeats itself). Research in support of this thesis is varied and somewhat fragmentary. Many scholars have investigated class differences in child rearing assuming (without evidence) that these differences must affect later behavior, or they have examined class differences in children's behavior and assumed them to be the result of differences in child-rearing practices. In either case, empirical relationships between social class and behavior may have many possible explanations.

Interest in intracultural (social class) differences was considerable during the 1940s and 1950s, and most of the research in this period was focused on social class differences in specific child-rearing practices such as weaning, toilet training, and discipline (Davis & Havighurst, 1946; Littman, Moore, & Pierce-Jones, 1957; Miller & Swanson, 1958, 1960; Sears, Maccoby, & Levin, 1957; White, 1957). Researchers felt that studies of this sort would help them to understand the antecedents of social class differences in personality, while at the same time elucidating general processes of personality development. Perhaps most importantly, it was hoped that these studies would reveal how important contrasting early experiences were. (A similar rationale prompted studies of socialization practices in other countries throughout the world, Whiting and Whiting's [1975] "six culture" study being a good representative example.)

Unfortunately, these studies yielded confusion rather than understanding, chiefly because the major results of each study seemed to contradict the results of the other studies (Zigler, 1970b). To illustrate, two early well-known studies found virtually opposite results. The first, conducted in Chicago by Davis and Havighurst (1946), found differences between middle- and lower-class parents in feeding, weaning, and discipline and generally concluded that the child-rearing practices of the lower class were more permissive. In contrast, a study conducted 9 years later in the Boston area (Maccoby & Gibbs, 1954; Sears, Maccoby, &

Levin, 1957) found differences in toilet training and discipline, but not in feeding or weaning practices, and concluded that middle-class parents were generally more permissive, gentler, and warmer toward their children. A third study, conducted in Eugene, Oregon (Littman, Moore, & Pierce-Jones, 1957), attempted to resolve the disagreement between these first findings, but while it agreed with the Boston one on some aspects of rearing practices, it found close similarity between the classes on others. Littman, Moore, and Pierce-Jones pointed out that the three studies together yield a relatively small number of statistically significant findings, many of which are inconsistent from one study to another, and concluded tht there are probably no general or profound differences between the classes in socialization practices. Another study done to resolve the original discrepancy was conducted in the San Francisco area (White, 1957). The author concluded that the study showed more agreement with the Boston one and suggested that the discrepancies with the findings of the Chicago study (conducted a decade earlier) were due to changes during the intervening years. In fact, however, only a small number of variables differentiated the classes in this last study, and as they did not correlate consistently with findings of the Boston study, the bulk of the agreement between the two really consists of finding that the social classes did not differ on a number of child-rearing practices.

In contrast to this line of research, another perspective was brought to the investigation of social class differences in child-rearing practices by Miller and Swanson (1958), who argued that social class membership no longer implies a certain set of values, attitudes, goals, and life-styles but that the differentiating factor is a family's economic or "integration setting." This factor cuts across class lines, and child rearing is expected to be directed toward developing a personality suited to success in the family's integration setting rather than toward inculcating class-typed values and behavior. An entrepreneurial setting, which was said to involve a relatively small economic organization, the possibility of income mobility through risk taking and competition, and situations tending to isolate people from one another, was expected to correlate with child-rearing practices stressing rationality, self-control, self-reliance, and an active, manipulative stance toward the environment. On the other hand, a bureaucratic setting, involving large organizations, incomes in the form of salary or wages, income mobility through specialized training, and continuous employment and income despite fluctuations in the business cycle, was expected to correlate with practices stressing that children be accommodative, express impulses spontaneously, and seek direction from the organizational programs in which they participate. Although Miller and Swanson presented some limited evidence that the integration setting influences child-rearing practices and that information about the integration setting might reduce some of the disagreement among studies of social class differences in child-rearing practices, the evidence does not seriously challenge Littman, Moore, and

Pierce-Jones's (1957) negative conclusion about general differences in socialization practices.

Some investigators of social class differences concentrated on broad dimensions of child rearing (such as restrictive versus permissive) rather than on specific infant and child-care practices, and trends (although generally not statistically significant) have been found suggesting that upper-middle-class mothers showed more optimal child-rearing practices (neither too rigid nor overpermissive), while lower-middle-class mothers were more likely to have rigid practices (Klatskin, Jackson, & Wilkin, 1956). A number of studies which combined broad and specific approaches have indicated that middle-class parents are generally more permissive than lower-class parents (Elder, 1962; Klatskin, 1952). On the other hand, some studies have found evidence of more permissiveness on aspects of child-rearing in the lower class (Psathas, 1957) or of similarities between the classes (Kohn, 1959a). In sum, then, it seems that findings about social class and child rearing are far from consistent, even on broad dimensions. In fact, questions have been raised about the meaningfulness of broad dimensions such as permissiveness (Kohn, 1959a) and about the conceptual difficulties of abstracting broad dimensions from specific child-rearing practices (Littman, Moore, & Pierce-Jones, 1957).

One explanation offered for the inconsistencies among studies of child rearing was that the survey technique on which they depended was inadequate. As we have seen, although there is evidence that the parent interview technique can sometimes provide accurate information (e.g., Klatskin, 1952), evidence on the social desirability factor in subjective reports (Christie & Lundauer, 1963; Edwards, 1957; Marlowe & Crowne, 1961; Taylor, 1961) has suggested that some of the inconsistencies—and some of the supposed class differences in child rearing—may actually reflect what parents believe to be socially desirable statements about child rearing.

Inconsistencies have also been attributed to the fact that various studies are based on data collected at different times. In this regard, Bronfenbrenner published an influential integration and review of the evidence on social class and child rearing in his "Socialization and Social Class Through Space and Time" (1958), which brought some resolution to the contradictory findings we have been discussing. Bronfenbrenner argued that the contradictory results could be attributed to the fact that the studies had been conducted at different times (e.g., early 1940s versus mid-1950s) and in different parts of the country. By searching for similarities, researchers were ignoring the dramatic changes that the culture had undergone during this era—changes which should (and apparently did) affect the socializing practices of middle- and lower-class families differently. Bronfenbrenner (1958) also demonstrated, particularly for the middle class, a high degree of correspondence between child-rearing practices reported and expert advice prevailing at the time. Stendler (1950) and Wolfenstein (1953) have documented that the advice experts give parents on how to raise their children has changed over the years.

The implication of the conclusion that child-rearing practices within the social classes change with time suggested that it was futile to search for timeless and universal differences between social classes, and as a result, research on social class differences in socialization fell from favor. Two notable exceptions, however, deserve mention. First, Hess and Shipman (1965) reported that lower-class mothers tend to guide or teach their children using directives and instructions, whereas middle-class mothers employ questions and hints that encourage children to discover the answers for themselves. This difference does appear to represent a reliable and fairly consistent difference between lower- and middle-class parents. Second, Kohn (1969, 1976, 1979), elaborating the distinction investigated and explained by Miller and Swanson (1958, 1960), has shown in a series of studies that the way parents behave toward their children is often shaped by the way they relate to authority in their jobs. Thus lower-class adults often work in subservient positions where they are expected to obey unexplained instructions from supervisors without question. As parents, Kohn suggests, these adults expect their children to obey parental instructions unquestioningly. By contrast, middle-class adults often hold jobs in which they participate in decision making and are given explanations for the instructions they receive. They thus adopt an analogously democratic mode of supervising their children. Notice that Kohn and Hess and Shipman point to similar differences between lower- and middle-class parents—differences that appear to have some validity since they have been reported by other researchers as well (see Hess, 1970, for a review).

Other Explanations of Intracultural Variation

In general, there does not seem to be a basis for considering social class differences in child rearing to be the major source of intracultural variation in adult behavior. It may be possible that child training is generally less important in these ways than is often supposed, or it may be that its most important influences in relation to social class operate in a more complicated way than we have been discussing. In any case, there have been several other approaches to the study of intracultural variation, in terms of both the theoretical frameworks used to explain variation and the times at which socializing influences are assumed to occur.

One alternative to the special stress on childhood socialization, possible regardless of theoretical orientation, is emphasis on the continuing nature of socialization or on its special importance at other stages of the life cycle. Erikson (1950), for example, views behavior as the outcome of a series of conflicts or crises which occur throughout the life span and, while continuing to regard the early years as specially important, argues that equally explicit attention should be given to all periods. Social learning theorists' (cf. Bandura & Walters, 1959) emphasis on the importance of models whose behavior is imitated suggests that in adulthood the behavior of models in an individual's present environment will be of prime importance. Instrumental learning theorists (cf. Bijou & Baer, 1961) emphasize reinforcement contingencies as the ultimate determinant of an individual's social behavior; here, the greatest importance would be given to the individual's relatively recent history of rewards and punishments accompanying the particular social behavior of interest. Finally, more sociological thinkers (cf. Brim & Wheeler, 1966) argue that an individual never ceases to adopt new social roles and that the socialization pertinent to these roles occurs around the time of adoption rather than decades earlier.

These views lead to a question about the levels of analysis used to explain socialization. Approaches which stress socialization in adulthood for the roles then assumed may be sociogenic rather than psychogenic, in which case behavior is understood to result from a person's assigned roles as a member of a group rather than from internal psychological factors. Actually, the social class variable is more conducive to a sociogenic approach, since the commonly employed indices of class membership such as amount of education, occupation, and type of dwelling refer to individuals' social status in broad terms and not to their psychological characteristics. Even so, each discipline tends to prefer its own level of analysis (although there may be no differences among them in inherent validity), and psychologists usually will not feel they have explained a relationship between a sociological variable (e.g., social class) and a psychological one (e.g., individual behavior) until they reduce the sociological variable to psychological terms. For psychologists, the discovery of a relationship between social class membership and some particular behavior is in itself empty or meaningless; social class must be understood, for example, as a set of psychological events that could cause the behavior being explained. There may, of course, be many possible explanations, and a given relationship is not in itself likely to direct psychologists to the particular social-psychological processes mediating it. The hypothesis that class differences in adult behavior are mediated by class differences in child-rearing practices illustrates the point: while this hypothesis seems to have captured the most interest, this seems to be due more to the history of psychology than to empirically established relationships.

Explanations of relationships established on a social level may range from environmental to genetic. The study of child rearing is an example of the environmental approach, but it is not always the main focus. For example, some researchers have been mainly concerned with economic influences on socialization and personality, seeing these as the primary determinants of personality (Barry,

Child, & Bacon, 1959; Miller & Swanson, 1960). In these cases, it is assumed that a society requires individuals who are capable of performing certain economic functions, and child rearing may be simply one device which helps guarantee that individuals will develop characteristics appropriate for their niches in the economy. Much of this type of research has been intersocietal rather than intrasocietal (and will be discussed in Section 16), but Miller and Swanson's (1958, 1960) concept of the integration setting (discussed above) is an effort to derive from *class* a psychologically more meaningful concept.

At the opposite extreme from the environmental position (and rare in American psychology) is the genetic interpretation of social class variation in behavior. In the 1960s and 1970s, a group of theorists argued that different socioeconomic groups represent populations with different gene pools and that group differences in behavior were manifestations of genetic influences (Burt, 1961; Gottesman, 1965; Herrnstein, 1971, 1973; Jensen, 1973). For example, Gottesman's (1965) argument is that social class differences are differences between populations rather than individuals and that whenever populations show a sizable degree of reproductive isolation, they vary in the frequency with which specific genes occur in their gene pools. Basing his views on the fact of assortative mating within social classes and the evidence of definite genetic influence on some aspects of personality (see Vandenberg, 1965), Gottesman argues that some social class differences in behavior rest partially on a genetic basis rather than on the wholly environmental basis often supposed. This view has been generally held among psychologists so far as intelligence is concerned, and Gottesman argues that it may apply to many other variables as well.

A third approach to social class differences in behavior, falling somewhere between the environmental and genetic interpretations, is the developmental viewpoint advanced by Zigler and his co-workers (cf. Katz & Zigler, 1967; Kohlberg & Zigler, 1967; Phillips & Zigler, 1961, 1964) and by Havighurst (1970). These investigators suggest that, for reasons which may be environmental, genetic, or both, the developmental progression of individuals in the lower class is (on average) slower than that of individuals in the middle class. Differences in behavior between social classes, therefore, may be explained by differences in developmental level rather than by particular socialization practices.

Following Piaget (1950, 1953, 1955, 1962), the developmental approach to social class differences has emphasized that an individual's formal cognitive characteristics, which change with development, are crucial as a mediating structure between the individual and the environment. This psychological structure directly determines behavior; consequently, if social classes differ greatly in the distribution of the developmental levels of their members' cognitive structures, the classes would be expected to differ behaviorally. In contrast to Piaget's strict focus on formal cognitive processes, American psychologists have tended to broaden the definition of developmental level to include a variety of personal styles, social values, and psychological orientations that also change with development (cf. Phillips & Zigler, 1964; Zigler & Phillips, 1960, 1962). A number of these are related to the prestige, power, and general culture of class groups.

Several of the class differences in behavior which have been found conform to expectations generated from developmental theory. One example is the tendency among members of the middle class toward greater guilt, self-derogation, self-punishment, and even suicide (Henry & Short, 1954; Miller & Swanson, 1960; Zigler & Phillips, 1960). This is predictable from the developmental theory that the introjection of social standards implied by such "turning against the self" is more characteristic of higher than of lower levels of development (Phillips & Rabinovitch, 1958) and that the capacity for guilt increases with cognitive growth and development (Katz & Zigler, 1967). Another is Kohn's finding (1959a, 1959b) that working-class parents tend to discipline children in terms of the immediate consequences of the child's act, while middle-class parents tend to respond in terms of the child's intent; as Kohn points out, this is in keeping with Piaget's (1962) suggested developmental trends in moral reasoning. Also, research suggests that members of the lower class are more likely to use physical punishment, to be in occupations demanding a good deal of physical activity, and to engage in physical types of antisocial behavior, while members of the middle class tend to be more obsessive and ideational (Henry & Short, 1954; Miller & Swanson, 1960; Phillips & Zigler, 1964; Zigler & Phillips, 1960), and that lower-class children are less influenced than middle-class children by abstract, symbolic rewards (Davis, 1941; Terrell, Durkin, & Wiesley, 1959; Zigler & deLabry, 1962). These beliefs go along with developmental theorists' suggestion that developmentally early behavior is characterized by immediate, direct, and unmodulated responses to external stimuli and internal needs and higher levels of development by the appearance of indirect, ideational, conceptual, and symbolic or verbal responses (Freud, 1952; Hartmann, 1952; Kris, 1950; Lewin, 1936; Piaget, 1951; Rapaport, 1951; Werner, 1948).

Intracultural Variation in Behavior

In our discussion so far, we have not given specific treatment to the differences in behavior which research has found to correlate with social class; as with research on the various explanations of these differences, many of these data are contradictory. There has been considerable evidence presented, however, to suggest that there are class differences on broad dimensions of behavior such as quality of family relationships, patterns of affection and authority, parents' conceptions of their roles and children's perceptions of parents, parents' expectations for children, general expressive styles, and typical reactions to stress (for comprehensive reviews of this literature, see Clausen & Williams, 1963, and Miller & Swanson, 1960). For example, in his early work, Kohn (1959b) found class differences in parental values: middle-class parents tended to emphasize self-direction, stressing standards such as honesty, self-control, consideration, and curiosity, while working-class parents emphasized conformity, stressing respectability, obedience, neatness, and cleanliness. Even values which were shared by parents of all social classes (wishing children to be honest, happy, considerate, obedient and dependable) differed in emphasis between the classes. Similarly, early research found that working-class mothers seemed to feel a direct responsibility for making their children obey commands in an immediate context, while middle-class mothers seemed to feel more strongly a long-term responsibility for their children's growth, development, affection, and satisfaction (Duvall, 1946). Working-class mothers have been found to expect their husbands to be more directive and to play a larger role in the imposition of constraints (Kohn & Carroll, 1960), although working-class fathers may sometimes be less accessible to their chidren than middle-class fathers (Bronfenbrenner, 1961; Havighurst & Davis, 1955). In general, middle-class parents may have more acceptant, egalitarian relationships with their children and to be more accessible to them (Maas, 1951).

In terms of children's conceptions of adult roles, Rosen (1964) found that middle-class boys perceive their parents as more competent, emotionally secure, accepting, and interested in their children's performance than do lower-class boys, especially concerning perceptions of fathers. More broadly, Millner (1951) found lower-class children more likely than middle-class children to perceive adults in general as predominantly hostile. Differences have also been found in children's general styles of life or approaches to problems; for example, based on a finger-painting test, middle-class children were found to be less tolerant of getting dirty, of staying dirty, and of the products they produced while dirty (Alper, Blane, & Abrams, 1955).

We have mentioned the finding that both children and adults of the middle as compared to the lower class tend to exhibit a greater readiness to experience guilt (Miller & Swanson, 1960; Zigler & Phillips, 1960). Clausen and Williams (1963) point out that studies of this type (Davis, 1944; Green, 1946) gave rise to the view that working-class children were "better adjusted" because they were free of the excessive guilt, repressed hostility, and driving anxiety of middle-class children. Several studies, however, have found "better adjustment" in middle-class children (Burchinal, Gardner, & Hawkes, 1958; Sewell & Haller, 1956). Additionally, some class differences have been found in defense mechanisms used by children—repression in the middle class and denial in the lower class (Miller & Swanson, 1960)—and in expressive style—conceptual in the middle class and motor in the lower class (Miller et al., 1956, 1958, 1960). These last-mentioned differences in physical expression have been found among adults as well, in the tendency of lower-class adults toward overt acts of aggression against others as opposed to that of middle-class adults toward inner-directed hostility (Gold, 1958; Henry & Short, 1954; Zigler & Phillips, 1960). Findings on children's aggression have been somewhat inconsistent: McKee and Leader (1955) found lower-class children to be both more competitive and more aggressive, but Maas (1954) did not find lower-class adolescent boys consistently more aggressive than middle-class boys, and Body (1955) found more aggressive behavior in a middle-class than a lower-class nursery school.

Social class differences in achievement, independence, and conformity suggest more emphasis on independence in early childhood, higher expectations for school performance, greater beliefs in the availability of success, and greater willingness to pursue activities that make achievement possible among middle-class children (Rosen, 1956). Internalization of achievement striving has been found to be greater among middle-class than working-class high school students (Hoffman, Mitsos, & Protz, 1958), although McKee and Leader's (1955) finding of greater competitiveness in the lower class suggests that this difference may not always exist.

Perhaps the most substantial correlate of social class is IQ; even here, however, the correlations are less than .30, suggesting that social class at best accounts for less than 10% of the variance in IQ. Explanations of the IQ-social class correlation have ranged from the environmental extreme to the genetic extreme, but the environmental position has been more associated with research. One type of environmental explanation assumes that the average level of intellectual functioning probably does not differ from one class to another and that the observed relation is an artifact of measurement, a product of the unfairness of intelligence tests for lower-class populations (Davis, 1954; Eells et al., 1951; Haggard, 1954; Isaacs, 1962). For example, the information items which appear on many intelligence tests tend to refer to realms of information to which middle- and upper-class children have been much more exposed than have lower-class children. Kagan (1971) has pointed out that vocabulary words used on current tests are often more likely to be heard in middle-class white homes and that the solutions to reasoning problems may assume a middle-class, urban environment. The issue of test bias is a volatile one because of its implications for explanations of group differences in intelligence: if no test bias exists, there are real differences to be explained either by genetic or environmental factors. Thus, advocates of either side in the argument over the existence of class differences in intelligence have a stake in the one over the existence of test bias. In a recent book, Jensen (1980), a major proponent of genetic explanations of group differences in intelligence, argues against the existence of test bias. As pointed out in a review of this book (Cole, 1980), however, the issues of test bias and heritability of intelligence are subtly linked by Jensen, and the result is an implicit support of the thesis of hereditary differences despite the fact that the book does not deal with this issue.

A second environmental position assumes that there are real class differences in intellectual functioning produced by class differences in environment. The environmental events that have been postulated to explain these differences range from very general and sociogenic ones to specific and psychogenic or cognitive ones. Research has found, for example, broad class attitudes toward intelligence and education (e.g., Toby, 1963); general child-rearing practices favoring one cognitive style rather than another (e.g., Witkin et al., 1962); and specific types of class-related interpersonal communications resulting in specific intellectual functioning (e.g., Bernstein, 1961; Hess & Shipman, 1965).

The final characteristic class difference which we will mention is *locus of control* (see reviews by Lefcourt, 1976; Phares, 1976). Studies in this area regularly show that middle-class children and adults are more likely than their lower-class peers to attribute their successes and failures to their own effort, abilities, and other factors within their control (internal locus of control). By contrast, members of the lower classes tend to attribute both successes and failures to uncontrollable factors such as luck (external locus of control). These differences may result from accurate perceptions of the power over their own lives exercised by middle- and lower-class individuals. Middle-class individuals do in fact have a greater potential to control their destinies: they have political and economic power, can afford college educations and books, and have personal contacts to help them get ahead. By contrast, members of the lower class often lack the resources and contacts needed to improve their own circumstances. If these differing life experiences are the cause of the social class differences in locus of control, they illustrate how the personalities of individuals are shaped by the characteristics of the social ecologies in which they live—not only by individual agents of socialization (Bronfenbrenner, 1979).

Although many early studies appeared to view the middle class as a norm, deviations from which constituted the lower class, this *deficit model* has now fallen from favor. Contemporary researchers are much more likely to view the middle and lower classes as different rather than better or worse. We have seen the inconsistency of research on intracultural variation; in many instances, where some studies find differences others do not. Moreover, it appears that differences between social classes are small, and there is usually substantial overlap between measures of the two groups. Although we must not ignore differences which reflect the disadvantaged status of lower-class families and children, especially when they point toward appropriate areas for social policy intervention, we must recognize that any social class status is associated with both strengths and weaknesses. A recent study by Yando, Seitz, and Zigler (1979) illustrated clearly the need to compare lower- and middle-class children on a variety of measures in order to compute a profile of their relative strengths and weaknesses. Even when undertaking such *profile analyses*, moreover, it is important to remember that the differences exist in the context of tremendous similarities between children and families from the middle- and lower-class populations. The attention paid to the special circumstances of black families, Jewish families, lower-class families, etc. implicitly exaggerates the differences between them and thus underrepresents their similarities.

Yando et al. also underscored a problem involved in studies comparing lower- and middle-class children which was highlighted in our discussion of the developmental approach to studying intracultural variation. Since lower-class children are often less advanced intellectually than middle-class children of the same age, any differences between groups of children of the same age may be attributable to differences in developmental level rather than to social class. (Locus of control provides another example of this, as it tends to be more external both in younger children and in children of the lower classes.) If one attempts to identify clearly one of these factors by selecting only children of the same mental and chronological age, however, the resulting sample of lower-class children is likely to be unrepresentative, making generalization of the findings difficult and perhaps misleading.

Another sampling problem may also invalidate some social class comparisons. As Pavenstedt (1965) has shown most strikingly, the lower class is not a homogeneous group. Rather, it contains at least two distinct groups. One group consists of people who have limited financial resources but have permanent homes, adequate food, and reasonably stable employment. The other, smaller group consists of extremely deprived individuals who are rarely employed, move frequently, and have unpredictable financial resources. The inclusion of children from this lower-lower class in samples of children from the lower class may lead to inaccurate generalizations about the characteristics of lower-class children.

We must also consider another variable that is often confounded with social class—ethnicity. In most Western cultures, including the United States, blacks are overrepresented in the lower class. Many comparisons of blacks and whites often involve comparisons of children from different socioeconomic backgrounds. In their recent study, Yando et al. reached a conclusion consistent with that of most other careful studies: once one controls for the effects of social class, there are few, if any, ethnic differences left to explain. If blacks and whites differ behaviorally, in other words, it is probably because they come from different socioeconomic backgrounds rather than because they differ genetically.

As Clausen (1978) points out, finally, since categorization by social class is in terms of educational achievement and occupation, the social class variable involves a great many differences in life experience (e.g., type of housing occupied, neighborhood of residence, role differentiation between parents, fluency of lan-

the lives of poor preschoolers just before they entered first grade that they would perform at least as well as their middle-class peers from that point on. Head Start programs varied throughout the nation, depending on local conditions, needs, and customs, but most programs involved efforts to provide health and dental care while improving social, motivational, and intellectual characteristics. Head Start has continued to provide services and to evaluate and modify its programs, and the lessons learned from experience with the program are important to a general consideration of intervention efforts. (Details about the program itself are discussed by Dittmann in Part 2, Chapter 17.)

There has been considerable controversy over the effects of Head Start (Bronfenbrenner, 1974; Jensen, 1969; Westinghouse, 1969; Valentine, Ross & Zigler, 1980), but much of it results from a focus on different means of evaluation. As Zigler (1978a, 1978b) notes, Head Start has been a misunderstood program, represented as a failure by some researchers and reported by the media as having ceased to exist—even as it continued to serve many children—and as 90 to 95% of the parents using Head Start considered it valuable and successful. Unfortunately, much of the rhetoric at the outset of the program focused on Head Start's capacity to raise the IQ of underprivileged children, and consequently most of the attempts at evaluation focused on this too. As long as children were enrolled in the program, it was found, IQs were indeed raised—often quite substantially. A report by the Westinghouse Learning Corporation (1969), however, found that the initial gains of Head Start children over non-Head Start children faded 2 to 3 years after the children entered elementary school; several years after graduation from Head Start, those children who had been in the program were indistinguishable from lower-class peers who had not. Although this finding may be more of an indictment of the schools than of Head Start, it fostered the belief that Head Start had failed. More recently, however, the Westinghouse study has been found to have numerous methodological flaws (Campbell & Erlebacher, 1970; Datta, 1976; Smith & Bissell, 1970) and, in fact, some investigators have reanalyzed the original Westinghouse data and concluded that Head Start does have long-lasting, positive effects on children's IQ scores (Palmer & Andersen, 1979). Initially, it would found that the fade-out effect was prevented or alleviated when the program had involved attempts to support and train the parents and when the children were enrolled in follow-up enrichment programs. Even without these supplementary efforts, however, recent researchers have found that differences favoring previous Head Start participants reemerged later in the school years. Using school performance rather than IQ scores as the primary measure of effectiveness, the Consortium for Longitudinal Studies (composed of 12 independent investigators) found evidence of long-lasting gains from Head Start or other preschool experience—gains lasting as long as 13 years. Most notable was the fact that children who had been in intervention programs were less likely to be placed in special education classes or to be held back one or more grades (Darlington, Royce, Snipper, Murray, & Lazar, 1980). Long-lasting effects of Head Start or preschool experience have also been found based on achievement test measures: Children who had been in intervention programs scored significantly higher on fourth-grade standardized tests in math and tended to score higher in reading (*Lasting Effects After Preschool*, 1978).

A broader issue relevant in considering the impact of intervention programs concerns the question of emphasis on cognitive development versus emphasis on the whole child—cognitive, physical, and emotional. Zigler (1978a) argues that a focus on cognitive development stems from the false hypothesis that the essential problem of economically disadvantaged children is a deficit in intellectual capacity. No longer adhering to this assumption, we can see that intellectual potential is not a function of economic standing, although the opportunity to realize that potential may well be. Since Head Start's goals are comprehensive ones, Zigler argues that its evaluation should be in terms of social competence, a measure of physical and mental health and emotional development in addition to formal cognitive ability. Such a measure would tap a broader range of potential program benefits. It could also address the fact that IQ scores are not pure measures of intellectual ability: children may not use intellectual capacities which they possess for various emotional and motivational reasons. This issue of evaluation will be discussed further in our readings section.

When viewed in broader perspective, benefits other than educational ones become apparent as results of Head Start, and these benefits have implications for the environmental contexts in which children develop. One example is Head Start's impact on the health of enrolled children. Head Start provides nutritious meals and has been found to contribute to better nutritional practice and to the reduction of the prevalence of anemia (Social Research Group, 1977). Through Head Start, many children have received medical and dental screening and treatment (National Institute for Advanced Studies, 1980), and Head Start children have received immunizations at a rate 20% higher than the national average for low-income children (Richmond, Stipek, & Zigler, 1979). The Center for Disease Control in Atlanta indicates that the inoculation rate in America is declining in general, and in extreme poverty areas some 70% of children may not be inoculated—despite the availability of free inoculation services. One explanation for this situation is that the institutions which generally provide health services so alienate low-income people that they are avoided, whereas Head Start programs are integrated into communities and have earned the trust of parents. This situation points to the fact that the means by which services are offered are crucial to their effectiveness.

Two primary factors mediating the effectiveness of intervention programs are parent involvement and recognition of the importance of continuity in a child's environment. Children are primarily raised by their parents, whether or not they attend intervention programs, and research has shown that preschool intervention can succeed only when parents are actively involved in the educational process (Bronfenbrenner, 1974; Valentine & Stark, 1979). Many Head Start parents become involved in their children's education and development by providing volunteer services (National Institute for Advanced Studies, 1980). In addition, Head Start appears to influence parental attitudes at home, in ways ranging from allowing children to help more with household tasks to reading to the children and showing interest in their reading and writing skills (O'Keefe, 1979). The best hypothesis attempting to explain the effectiveness of Head Start on children's academic performance, then, is that contact with Head Start increases parents' effectiveness in encouraging their children's motivation to learn.

It is also of great importance that intervention programs build, in integral fashion, on a child's family environment, for without continuity between various aspects of a child's life, gains derived from one source can be eradicated by harmful effects of another source. Thus, for example, it is necessary to have well-trained workers in intervention programs, because the quality of the relationship with a caregiver affects a child's emotional development and motivation to learn—whether that caregiver is a parent or supplementary individual. It is significant that the 15th Anniversary Head Start Committee, commissioned by the U.S. President to evaluate the Head Start program, regards the caregiver-child relationship as a crucial index of overall program quality (*Head Start in the 1980s: Review and Recommendations*). This belief led the committee to conclude that effective provision of services depends not on the imposition of a standard curriculum but on caregiver training and incentives to obtain the training. This point becomes even more dramatic with regard to providing care for special-need children—for example, bilingual or handicapped children—who require special kinds of attention.

In addition to direct benefits from intervention programs, children may receive indirect ones if involvement with the center increases their parents' happiness, since this would influence the quality of the family context, which is primary for child development. This effect on parents does, in fact, seem to occur. In one survey (Abt, 1979), most Head Start parents reported finding the program personally helpful. One important issue here may be reducing parents' feelings of isolation (a factor which we will discuss later in connection with child abuse), and many graduates' parents found opportunities to get together with other parents through the program. Other effects may involve increasing parents' educational or occupational opportunities, as in Head Start's career development component, which enables parents to earn college credit as well as to train as child-care workers in the Child Development Associate program. The impact of career development may be both financial (offering jobs or the education requisite to increase occupational opportunity) and emotional (increasing self-esteem). Head Start parents also have real decision-making power (as opposed to the advisory role allowed in other intervention programs), and this seems to improve parents' self-esteem by increasing their sense of control over their lives. This, in turn, appears to affect the self-esteem of their children (*Head Start in the 1980s: Review and Recommendations*).

Intervention will be effective, of course, only insofar as it meets the needs of a given family, and no program can be expected to be best for every family in a particular income bracket or for every community. The Head Start program illustrates one means of allowing diversity within a national program by leaving specifics of particular curricula to the discretion of people involved with a given center instead of basing them on a single standardized curriculum—although national standards should be used to provide guides and limits of minimum quality. Other ways to achieve diversity include facilitating access to services with information and advice, rather than offering set programs to all families, and providing services which support families in their homes. These and other possibilities for intervention programs will be discussed at greater length in our readings section (see Part 2, article 20).

It has been pointed out that Head Start's strengths are closely entwined with its weaknesses (Valentine, Ross, & Zigler, 1980), and these weaknesses are important to consider, too. For example, the program's comprehensive approach has led to confusion over the relative importance of various goals (such as IQ increase versus health improvement); parent involvement has resulted in questions about whether the program's intent is to aid children or to provide an adult welfare service; flexibility of programs has raised questions about quality control and presented the difficulty of evaluating Head Start as a whole. Head Start's effectiveness also depends on economic and administrative factors, which determine how many children are reached, what quality of services they receive, and what goals are held for the program.

In terms of an overall evaluation, it may be useful to consider the principles which the 15th Anniversary Committee uses to guide their recommendations for the future of Head Start. Briefly, the principles are as follows: (1) integral parental involvement should not be compromised; (2) Head Start should remain a comprehensive, multiservice program and not be reduced to one with more narrow educational goals; (3) the quality of a child-care program depends on that of the caregiver-child interaction; (4) Head Start's flexibility appears to depend on direct funding to respect racial/ethnic identities and strengths; and (6) Head Start should strive for cost effectiveness. These principles indicate some of the most crucial factors in any intervention program. In addition, the principle of continuity is a relevant one. As Zigler (1978a) argues, there is no singular magic period in development; special needs go along with every age, and programs which address these needs can help children at any age. Intervention programs which do not adhere to this principle run the risk of giving up on children who have outgrown the "magic period" in question.

Despite the early problems of evaluation based on IQ, it is the component of evaluation which has enabled Head Start to try programs and learn from the attempts, and to serve as a model for other early child development programs. With the benefit of hindsight, most intervention programs today incorporate broader evaluation procedures than did early ones and utilize procedures which are designed to provide extended support for families and children rather than the 3-month "inoculation" provided in the initial Head Start program. Further, efforts are now being made to avoid the implication of early interventions that all children should aspire to the standards and characteristics of middle-class America (i.e., the deficit assumption). Certainly, interventions can and do affect the enthusiasm, social skills, motivation, and personality of young children, but these effects are eliminated by the rigors of life outside the intervention centers unless special efforts are made to reinforce and maintain them. Several of the readings in Part 2 highlight this discussion of the problems and successes of intervention programs.

16

Intercultural Variation

Anthropologists have recorded the customs of hundreds of societies throughout the world. Many of these societies have been studied while they were still fairly isolated from the modern world, so that the set of customs recorded in any society represents a separate instance of how a people may solve life problems. Among the customs recorded, with varying degrees of fullness, are those of socialization.

The documentation of variation in socialization practices in different cultures may be of value in several ways. Information derived from the study of these variations contributes to our understanding of causes and consequences of various socialization practices as well as to the discovery and understanding of differences within one culture. The study of intercultural variation in socialization practices also lets us see our own practices in a broader human perspective. Sometimes we may feel that our society imposes especially rigid requirements on children and young people; familiarity with the customs of tribal societies suggests, on the contrary, that our society is unusual in the variety of options it leaves open and is low in the degree to which it imposes universal and rigid demands. For several aspects of socialization, systematic comparisons have been made among tribal societies, and practices common in our society—or practices of individual families—can be viewed against that background. For example, Whiting and Child (1953, pp. 70–73) found, on analyzing reports from various societies, that American middle-class families were rather extreme in the earliness of the age at which babies were weaned but about average in the severity with which weaning was imposed.

Perspectives on Society and the Individual in Socialization

The nature of a society may be expected to have much to do with determining the socialization practices within that society. Different conceptualizations of this relationship are possible, and each approach entails particular assumptions about both child development and societal functioning.

The fact that a society and its culture are in operation both before and after given individuals' lifetimes has led many social scientists to regard society as having an existence of its own, independent of the individuals who at any moment make up its membership. This view, referred to as *societalism*, has been described as the core of traditional sociological and anthropological thought (Spiro, 1951). Within such a framework, concern is almost exclusively with culturally determined aspects of behavior, and socialization may be seen simply as the necessary learning of the culture by each new generation. Definitions of socialization focus on the molding of children to make them acceptable people in a given society (Dunham, 1957, cited in Smelser & Smelser, 1963, p. 102–3) or on the learning of the ways of a given society or social group, which enables functioning within it (Elkin, 1960). In this perspective, a child is seen mainly as someone capable of learning these ways, rather than as someone seeking satisfaction of needs and drives (Elkin, 1960); socialization means learning social roles, and it is motivated by social expectancies and accomplished through social interaction. Taken to an extreme, personality can be seen as a collection of roles learned through social interaction: Brim (1960) contends that behavior is determined by situational factors which call forth a particular role, and he views individuals' inconsistency across situations as a product of faulty socialization rather than as a function of core characteristics or personality traits. A societalistic approach sees individuals as developing passively, their behavior determined by demands of their society.

This view of society as an omnipotent superorganism presents a number of difficulties. It allows the construction of abstractions such as national character or modal personality but, as has been noted (Devereux, 1961; Inkeles, 1961), it tends to construct them in a way which ignores the great variability of individuals' actual behavior within a society. It is also inadequate for explaining cultural change, since internal cultural changes appear to depend on an interplay between individuals and society (Norbeck & DeVos, 1961; Smelser & Smelser, 1963; Spiro, 1961).

In contrast to the societalistic approach, individuals can be seen as integrally related to society and as developing actively in relation to the demands of social life. Cultures or social systems may be seen as internalized, cognitively and affectively, in the personalities of society members. Even researchers who see personality as deriving mainly from social systems and culture have argued that it remains independent inasmuch as individuals' needs and life experiences are unique (Parsons, 1958). In this view, the relation between society and the individual in socialization is one of *interpenetration*, in which society and individuals make intricate adjustments to each other.

This second approach to socialization points to a common ground, in which social theories recognize the importance of individual psychological factors and psychological theories account for the social context in which individuals develop. Despite general agreement that the study of individual and societal development should be complementary, however, scholars have tended to remain within their areas of specialization. As with the nature-nurture controversy discussed earlier, although the existence of a complex interaction between factors in development has been acknowledged, one factor is often disproportionately stressed and the nature of the interaction not well articulated. Even the strongest exponents of the view that culture and personality represent truly reciprocal forces have argued that the disciplines of anthropology and psychology should remain separate in studying this area, each concentrating on its particular realm of expertise (Kluckhohn, 1954).

Although this approach has been widespread, there are examples in the literature of efforts to construct models of human behavior which include both individual and social forces. For example, Inkeles and Levinson (1954) made a theoretically important distinction between personality patterns which are typical of members of a society and "socially required" personality patterns which are considered necessary for optimal societal functioning, and Sears (1951) extended classical learning theory to encompass individuals' social behavior. A review by Whitting (1961) emphasized a model of the relationship between culture and personality in which child-training practices, seen to influence individuals' personalities, are influenced by societies' *maintenance systems* (defined as economic, political, and social customs), and in which typical personalities are expressed in projective aspects of culture. In any case, theoretical models must be examined in light of empirical data, and although the correlational methods used in intercultural research may yield evidence favoring one model over another, they cannot pinpoint the direction of cause and effect. Because of this, common conclusions from highly diverse studies carry more conviction than any study of a single kind can, but—just as with the intracultural studies we have discussed—the problem of generality must be treated with caution.

Intersocietal Differences in Socialization Practices

One advantage of studying intercultural variation is that it permits us to test, on a worldwide scale, some of the possible causes and consequences of socialization practices. We can take one of two perspectives, focusing either on the processes by which a culture influences socialization practices or on the influences which socialization practices have on personality and adult culture. Of course, these two sequences are not completely independent, but we will separate them for convenience in discussion. Although we have room in this chapter to consider only broad cultural differences, it is important to recognize that effects of a culture on socialization are often much more subtle than those which become conspicuous in comparisons of cultures vastly different from one another. Very similar cultures have been found to have differing attitudes toward the socialization process, as in an early finding that socialization of British children emphasized respect for parents and authority figures and control of antisocial impulses, while that of American children stressed adjustment to other children and aimed for a varied armament of social skills which would enable them to get ahead (Farber, 1953). As we will see, some of the considerations in this discussion parallel those in our consideration of intracultural variation.

In our discussion of social class differences, we mentioned an explanation which stresses economic influences on child rearing. A particularly striking example of this, from an intercultural perspective, is Barry, Child, and Bacon's (1959) comparison of socialization practices in societies whose economies depend on differing degrees of food accumulation. Societies with high accumulation of food (e.g., depending on animal husbandry) were found to put strong pressure on their children to be responsible, obedient, and compliant, while societies with low accumulation of food (e.g., fishing societies) emphasized achievement, self-reliance, independence, and assertiveness. The authors interpreted their findings as indicating that the nature of the economy leads to the selection (over the course of many generations) of child-rearing practices which provide training in motives and behavior necessary for the adult role. If members of a herding society, for example, encouraged individual assertion rather than compliance, the result might be conflicts which would interfere with the patient, cooperative, and compliant behavior required for successful agriculture and care of livestock. Barry (1969) concluded, in a discussion of this issue, that there is probably a process of cultural adjustment and evolution in which child-training practices and the subsistence economy mutually affect each other.

Anthropological research also suggests that a society's economy has much to do with determining postpartum sex taboos, which establish the length of time between pregnancies and which alter infants' social environments (for example, by encouraging the mother and child to sleep together) and socialization. From a practical point of view, Whiting and Whiting (1960) point out that in nomadic societies, since it is not feasible for a family to include two children who cannot walk, children are spaced by means of a postpartum sex taboo lasting 3 to 4 years. In order to avoid carrying extra food for the young in such societies, mothers tend to engage in prolonged nursing periods. The effect of the economy may also be on nutrition, as when societies whose economy provides a low-protein diet adopt a long postpartum sex taboo, since keeping babies on a milk diet for a long period increases the babies' chances of survival.

The basic structure of the family and household also has a great impact on child rearing. Children growing up in households composed of an extended family—including grandparents, cousins, uncles, and aunts, for example—are in immediate contact with a much larger set of people than children raised in nuclear family households composed of only parents and their children. A number of illustrations of how differences in family patterns and household composition affect socialization practices are offered by Whiting and Whiting (1960). One finding is that high infant indulgence is more likely in polygynous or extended family households than in nuclear or mother-child households (Whiting, 1961). Similarly, variations in kinship systems affect overall patterns of thought and action found within a society, including ones with a direct impact on children (Hsu, 1961).

It may be particularly interesting to consider the practices followed in rearing boys and girls, and societies vary greatly in the extent to which they have differing expectations of and impose distinct demands on the two genders. Barry, Bacon, and Child (1957) found that gender distinction in socialization was minimal in societies where each nuclear family generally lives alone and in societies not dependent for food on the typically male enterprise of hunting large animals. We may see a possible explanation of this if we consider the relative demands of different life-styles. When extended families live close together, traditionally male and female tasks can be divided between family members, and when an individual cannot fulfill a task for some reason, another of the same sex can step in. When nuclear families are isolated, however, a sexual division of labor may be more difficult to achieve. When a mother cannot care for a child, for example, a father will more likely do so (and so, engage in a "female" activity) when there is no grandmother or aunt available. Similarly, when social roles are not necessarily sex-specific, there is not so much need for gender distinction in socialization as in societies whose economies depend on a sexual division of labor (as has been argued for hunter-gatherer societies, among others). Explanations such as these help us understand why gender distinctions can be so greatly reduced in present-day American society, where increasing mobility separates kin networks and so entails a less rigid division of sex roles, and where social roles no longer provide a rational basis for distinction in performance between the sexes. Intercultural findings may also be of use in estimating how much further the contemporary reduction in gender distinction could go.

In contrast to the above perspective, we can consider how cross-cultural differences in child-rearing practices correlates with differences in personality or how projective systems of culture may be seen as expressions of personality. (For more thorough reviews of this literature, see Barry, 1969; Child, 1967; Dager, 1964; Hsu, 1961; Whiting, 1961; and Whiting & Whiting, 1960). For instance, an extensive study of child rearing in relation to projective systems of culture concluded that a society's child-rearing practices have a persisting effect on adult personality, which in turn affects the society's customs about the anxiety-provoking fact of serious illness (Whiting & Child, 1953). One example is that societies with low initial satisfaction of dependence needs tended to explain illness as being caused by soul loss or spirit possession. Indirect confirmation of some of the relationships which Whiting and Child postulated as underlying correlations such as this one has been suggested by research findings which are predictable from the same assumptions. In this case, a relevant finding is that societies with low initial satisfaction of dependence tend to believe that supernatural beings cannot be influenced to be nurturant by means of compulsive ritual (Spiro & D'Andrade, 1958). Relationships have also been found between independence training and achievement motivation, such that societies with early and severe socialization of independence, or those which punish achievement behavior in particular, have more achievement imagery in their folktales (Child, Storm, & Veroff, 1958; McClelland & Friedman, 1952). In both cases, the authors suggest that suppressed activities manifest themselves in fantasy.

Cross-cultural differences in child rearing have been found to be related to a variety of other cultural phenomena as well. Barry (1969) notes that most societies tend to be highly indulgent toward infants and that the ethnographies of the few societies rated very low in infancy indulgence suggest pathological features in adult personalities—for example, highly suspicious and fearful adult social relationships (Gladwin & Sarason, 1959; Kardiner, 1945; Linton, 1939). Societies with a high overall consumption of alcoholic beverages tend to be low on overall infancy indulgence (Bacon, Barry, & Child, 1965), and the frequency of different types of crime has been found to correlate with the degree of infant indulgence (Bacon, Child, & Barry, 1963). A tendency toward correlation with child training has also been found for aspects of culture suggesting good mental health or ego strength (Allen, 1967).

Finally, the study of intercultural variation can add to knowledge about variation within a single society. For example, Ember (1973) encountered a community in Kenya where families differed widely in whether they required a young boy to perform household tasks ordinarily thought of as feminine, and found that regular performance of such tasks led to increased display of other typically feminine behavior. This suggests that much of the effect of socialization may be mediated by accidental factors such as the tasks children are assigned to do or the amount of time they spend with adults. These factors have a shaping influence on the child's behavior, and this effect is generalized without anyone's having deliberately attempted to influence the children in that direction (Whiting, 1980).

Recent Developments in Intercultural Research

Research on intercultural variations in socialization and personality development has now progressed to a point where anyone who wishes to look into it further will find special handbooks devoted to its methods and findings (Munroe, Munroe, & Whiting, 1981; Triandis & Heron, 1981). Whereas much of the early work on intercultural variation was conducted from a psychoanalytic or social learning point of view, however, there has recently occurred a shift to a more cognitive perspective. Leaders in this reorientation have been Michael Cole and his colleagues at the Laboratory of Comparative Human Cognition (Laboratory of Comparative Human Cognition, 1979). In terms of cognitive development, examination of children in Western and non-Western cultures has indicated that children of any given age in Western cultures may exhibit similarities to each other but not to children of the same age in nonliterate cultures. When they have had comparable amounts of schooling, however, children from nonliterate cultures perform like Western children (e.g., Rogoff, 1981; Sharp, Cole, & Lave, 1979). Thus, Cole and his colleagues warn that many of the developmental trends identified and studied by Western psychologists may actually be attributable to age-correlated differences in educational experience.

Apart from the presence or absence of formal educational institutions (like schools), different cultures and ecological conditions make very different demands on individuals—including children—who live in them. Those abilities that are valued and practiced in a society are likely to become better developed than those abilities or skills that are irrelevant to success in that culture. Thus, for example, Moroccan rug dealers may readily remember patterns that Western adults find difficult to encode and recall (Wagner, 1978). Similarly, while Western children may remember isolated bits of information better than do children from nonliterature cultures, non-Westernized children perform better when they are asked to recall organized three-dimensional scenes. These differences reflect the relevance of the respective tasks to the everyday existence of each group of children (Rogoff & Waddell, 1981). In addition, memory test performance may be related to the different ways in which, say, Mayan-Mexican and American children are characteristically instructed (Rogoff, 1981). Rogoff notes that Mayan children learn a great deal through observation of others, whereas American children are likely to receive comparatively more verbal instruction and less demonstration, and these differences may result in different cognitive strategies. Such findings as these are in keeping with somewhat earlier reviews of literature on intercultural variation in cognitive abilities which have shown that differences in perception, conceptual processing, learning, and memory may all be related to demands and practices of a society (Cole & Scribner, 1974). To pick an arbitrary example, susceptibility to perceptual illusions has been hypothesized to vary according to the environment: people living in environments which do not stress geometric relationships or distance perception are less susceptible to illusions which draw on these types of cues (Segall, Campbell, & Herskovitz, 1966).

Problems in Intercultural Research

The first problem with intercultural research is that of interpreting correlational data. Although most of the correlations between socialization practices and culture discussed above have been obtained in research guided by hypotheses which assume that child training influences personality, the direction of causal relation cannot really be established by correlations. It may be possible that cultural values are acquired by children largely as a result of their cognitive exploration of the world around them, or that the shared values of adults and children are responsible for the adults' behavior as socializers and for the children's general personality without there being an important causal relation directly between these latter two. For example, in Javanese culture, pervasive status differentiations in adulthood are congruent with children's respect and deference toward their fathers (Clausen & Williams, 1963), and the collective child-rearing practices found in the Israeli kibbutzim or in modern Russia have been influenced by the ideology and values of the members of these societies.

By whatever route, though, dominant values of a culture may be conspicuous in children even at a fairly early age. Dennis (1957) found, for instance, that Near Eastern children expected more praise for academic achievements, for assisting disadvantaged people, and for being quiet, polite, and obedient, while American children expected more praise for giving and for sharing performance in sports and games, for creative activities, and for assisting people other than the disadvantaged. In some cases, child-rearing practices and their correlates can be seen simply as common products of the structure of a society. Whiting, Kluckhohn, and Anthony (1958) interpreted a number of cross-cultural correlations as confirming a tendency for father absence and bed sharing by mother and son to create, in the sons, uncertain sex identification which led, around the time of puberty, to their imitating other boys in order to confirm their masculine identity. On the other hand, alternate interpretations for the same correlations have been offered, and it is not easy to choose among them with confidence.

These are only examples of the general difficulty inherent in correlational methods of study and in the interpretation of studies which have to be confined to those methods. The difficulty has been repeatedly stated in early discussions of cross-cultural research (e.g., Barry, 1969; Campbell, 1961; Honigmann, 1961), and of course it applies to any correlational studies. A second problem in intercultural research concerns the reliability of the ethnographic accounts on which much cross-cultural research is based. This reliability may be expected to vary with the adequacy of the phenomena observed, the particular aspect of culture studied, and the relation between the two. Interobserver agreement is more easily achieved with some aspects of culture than with others; not surprisingly, the reliability of observation decreases as the palpability of the event to be observed decreases.

Both favorable and unfavorable comments about the reliability and, therefore, the value of ethnographic reports on child rearing have been made. As Barry (1969) points out, many ethnographers do not obtain such data because they are not primarily interested in child training and because it is not as easy to observe care of infants and children in the home as to observe more public cultural activities. Child rearing certainly is an area where fullness and reliability of information can be expected to vary from one fieldworker to another. Aiming to increase the standardization of field techniques applied to this aspect of culture, Whiting, Child, and Lambert (1966) prepared a manual which has been published (with research employing it), for example, in *Six Cultures* (Whiting, 1963) and *Mothers of Six Cultures* (Minturn & Lambert, 1964). Trends in applying a comprehensive and uniform set of concepts and interview questions to the study of different societies greatly improve ethnographic coverage of socialization, just as comparable standardization has done for other aspects of culture.

The processing of ethnographic reports for systematic cross-cultural comparisons also poses problems. Some anthropologists, like Margaret Mead (1949), prefer private processing by the single expert, but those trained in psychology and sociology are more likely to prefer the more public and more readily evaluated procedures of preparing rating manuals, having separate kinds of variables rated by different judges, reducing and controlling the amount of information available to the judge, and replicating judgments to assess reliability (Bacon et al., 1965;

Whiting & Child, 1953). There are advantages to both procedures, but only the more public one can eliminate the possibility that positive findings are an artifact of an investigator's bias.

A final important problem in cross-cultural research has to do with generality. A psychologist might like to conclude from a cross-cultural study that certain child-rearing practices universally give rise to particular personality characteristics. This conclusion may be much more justified than it could be by any evidence gathered entirely within one society, but we must still guard against overconfident generalization. Many of the societies included in cross-cultural studies have been relatively small and simple, and the relationships discovered there might not hold in more complex societies. Even for issues where this does not seem likely, we must remember that—just as in dealing with correlational studies of individuals—finding a correlation does not necessarily establish what process is responsible or that the same process is involved in every case entering into the correlation. In relation to studies of individual differences within a society, cross-cultural research provides an important check on the broader validity of conclusions, but it is not a substitute method of research.

17

Atypical Development

For the most part, we are concerned in this book with the normal course of development and the factors that influence social and personality development. As we have repeatedly intimated, however, there is great diversity in what constitutes normality, and there is a fine line between the range of normality and what we consider atypical or abnormal. Moreover, much of our knowledge about normal development actually comes from studying abnormal cases. In this section, we discuss atypical development, focusing on developmental psychopathology, mental retardation, giftedness, and child abuse.

Developmental Psychopathology

Developmental psychopathology is a rather new term coined by Achenbach (1974) to describe an approach to the study of atypical or disturbed children. In this approach, disturbed children are not viewed as miniature versions of mentally disordered adults but as a group whose incomplete developmental status must be taken into account in both diagnosis and treatment. In the research literature, this approach has not been common, and most of the theories that attempt to explain deviant development involve downward extensions of theories devised to explain psychopathology in adults. Indeed, most theories view adult psychopathology as the product of childhood experiences.

When one considers the mental disorders in children, it is necessary to make an initial distinction between psychotic and neurotic behavior problems. Psychotic disorders are much more severe and much less common than neurotic disturbances. Like psychotic adults, psychotic children appear out of touch with reality. Many different syndromes have been described, with the distinctions between them being based largely on differences in the presumed etiology or origins of the disorders. Most of these distinctions are not well established, and in Achenbach's (1974) opinion, only three clearly distinguishable syndromes have been described. These three disorders are childhood schizophrenia, early infantile autism, and symbiotic psychosis. Childhood schizophrenia involves a period of relatively normal social and language development followed by an arrest or decline in social relatedness and in the appreciation of reality. By contrast, early infantile autism involves self-isolation and deficiencies in social relationships from infancy onward, accompanied by an obsessive desire to preserve consistency in the environment, and fairly profound speech disorders—ranging from echolalia (the repetition of what others say to them) to mutism. Symbiotic psychosis involves a failure to develop an identity separate from the primary caretaker. This is an extremely rare and little understood disorder.

Most researchers agree that a biological predisposition affects the likelihood of a child's becoming schizophrenic or autistic. Since autism occurs so early in the child's life, it is hard to imagine experiential factors (other than pre- and perinatal influences) that might affect its incidence. Twin studies likewise suggest that genetic factors are very important in the etiology of autism (Rimland, 1964). Genetic factors also appear to be important in the etiology of schizophrenia, although most of the major studies have focused on adult rather than childhood schizophrenia, and it is not clear how related these two disorders are. It seems likely that childhood schizophrenia involves an extreme and earlier occurring form of schizophrenia than the adult disorder and that the two are influenced by the same gene pool. Variations of Meehl's (1962) diathesis-stress model agree that people may inherit a tendency to become schizophrenic: whether they do or not depends on their experiences and the traumatic stresses they undergo. Thus environmental and genetic factors interact to determine whether and when a psychotic breakdown will occur. Recently, Zigler and Levine (1980) concretized this notion by suggesting that the common emergence of frank adult psychoses around 17 years of age occurs because of the emotional and social stresses that are common in mid-adolescence. It is not known whether early infantile autism and childhood schizophrenia are influenced by the same gene pool.

Neurotic behavior disorders are much more common than psychoses. However, researchers face many similar problems when investigating them. In both cases, clear-cut, empirically defined critiera for distinguishing syndromes are lacking. Fortunately, efforts are now being made to remedy this. Achenbach and

Edelbrock (1978, 1980; Achenbach, 1966, 1981) have developed behaviorally specific criteria for distinguishing between different types of behavior disorders. At the broadest level, there is a distinction between internalizing and externalizing problems. Internalized disorders involve symptoms such as anxiety, nightmares, obsessions, phobic fears, withdrawal, and the like. The internalized symptom cluster can be broken down into several "narrow-band" differentiations, but the reliability of narrow-band differentiations has been questioned (Quay, 1979). Externalized problems involve conduct disorders such as disobedience, stealing, aggression, and destructiveness. Externalizing symptoms are much more common among boys than among girls. Achenbach is now engaged in research designed to determine whether specific symptom-determined syndromes are differentially susceptible to treatment methods.

Unlike psychoses, of which some trace is likely to remain permanently, neurotic behavior disorders often completely disappear spontaneously—that is, without any attempted intervention. Behavior modification, moreover, is often effective in promptly relieving neurotic symptoms that would otherwise persist. Behavior modification is especially effective in dealing with specific behavioral disorders such as bedwetting or compulsions. It is less effective in dealing with more diffuse problems such as anxiety. Contrary to the claims of psychodynamically oriented theorists, there is no evidence that symptom substitution occurs when behavior modification is employed. (Symptom substitution is said to occur because the symptom and the underlying problem are distinct; consequently, when a symptom alone is relieved by behavior modification, the underlying problem will become manifest in the form of another symptom.)

Mental Retardation

Mental retardation is considerably more common and considerably easier to identify than the various kinds of developmental psychopathology. Mental retardation is largely defined by performance on intelligence tests, but it is interesting to note the arbitrary nature of this definition. For many years, mental retardation was generally defined as indicated by an IQ score in the lowest 3% of the population. In 1959, the American Association on Mental Deficiency (AAMD) defined mental retardation as including people with IQ scores of less than 85, or one standard deviation below the mean, and by this definition, 16% of the population was retarded. In 1973, the definition of mental retardation was again changed by the AAMD, this time to the present criterion of an IQ score less than 70 (two standard deviations below the mean). As a result of different definitions, the portion of the population considered to be retarded has changed from 3% to 16% to 2.3%.

Within the segment of the population deemed mentally retarded, a differentiation is made on the basis of severity of retardation. A substantial number (15 to 16% of the total population) fall into the categories of mild to borderline retardation. Individuals with IQ scores between 68 and 85 are considered to show evidence of borderline retardation, and many of these people function adequately in society (Zigler & Seitz, 1982a). A somewhat smaller group, with IQs between 52 and 67, are described as mildly retarded; they may not necessarily be considered retarded unless faced with tasks requiring complex learning. Individuals whose IQ scores fall below 50 are classified as follows: those with scores between 36 and 49 are considered moderately retarded (6% of the retarded population); between 20 and 35, severely retarded (3.5%); and below 20, profoundly retarded (1.5%). The retarded differ from those of normal intellect both in their rate of cognitive development and in the final level attained. The changing criteria for mental retardation discussed above, however, should indicate that there is nothing inherent in the nature of mental retardation to determine precisely where the defining line between retarded and nonretarded should be drawn.

IQ alone is not a sufficient definition of mental retardation; an additional criterion set by the AAMD is a deficit in adaptive behavior which prevents an individual from dealing effectively and creatively with social, work, and environmental demands throughout the life span. This criterion reflects the fact that the most distinctive feature of mental retardation is an impairment in social competence; in fact, it was this criterion which identified mentally retarded individuals before intelligence was measured. A greater reliance has been placed on the IQ score as an indicator of retardation since the development of intelligence tests, but an individual's score on an IQ test is not a very good predictor of adaptability and social competence in real life (Windle, 1962).

One reason for the low correlation between intelligence and adaptive behavior is that current intelligence tests were not designed to assess intelligence as a broad range of abilities but to predict which children would benefit from regular school and which required remedial education. Consequently, the validation of the tests was against achievement in school subjects (primarily reading and arithmetic) which do not demand much of the resourcefulness needed for adult social competence, and a high IQ score need not necessarily imply a high degree of adaptive behavior. Also, as Balla and Zigler (1980) point out, IQ tests have been criticized as culturally biased. This conclusion is suggested by the preponderance of black and Mexican-American children in special education classes for the retarded and by the greater incidence of mental retardation in these groups—despite the fact that innate cultural differences in intelligence are not presumed to exist. Furthermore, Zigler, Abelson, and Seitz (1973) suggest that factors other than formal cognitive processes (e.g., achievement and motivation) influence the outcome of intelligence tests, as indicated by the finding that IQ rose by 10 points when economically disadvantaged children were retested by the same person and with the same instrument after 1 to 2 weeks. If, as this suggests, factors such as unfamiliarity with testing situations and wariness of strangers affect IQ scores, children may be found to differ on measures of intelligence when underlying competence is equivalent. In fact, there is evidence that the overrepresentation of minority group members drops when social competence is added to the definition of mental retardation (Balla & Zigler, 1980). It should be noted, however, that social competence is itself a vague concept which differs according to the situation, subculture standards, and so on, and agreement on a precise definition has not been reached (Zigler & Trickett, 1978). Finally, adaptive behavior must be seen in relation to developmental stage, so that failure to perform well on a particular task might be normal for a young child but abnormal for an older one.

Returning to the definition of mental retardation, neither a low IQ score without a deficit in adaptive behavior nor evidence of impaired competence with an average IQ score would be taken to indicate mental retardation. Additionally, the deficits which are used to define mental retardation must occur in the developmental period rather than, for example, as the result of an accident later in life.

Causes of Mental Retardation

Mental retardation may be caused by several factors. Almost all of those who are profoundly, severely, and moderately retarded have clear organic pathologies which account for the deficits. Two of the best-known causes of severe and profound mental retardation are phenylketonuria (PKU), a genetic disorder inherited by the recessive mode (both parents carry the abnormal gene), and Down's syndrome, which results from extra chromosomal material. The incidence of Down's syndrome increases with greater maternal age; ova have been dormant longer and have had greater exposure to potentially harmful environmental insults (Balla & Zigler 1980). PKU is the result of a failure to metabolize phenylalanine; the substance accumulates in the body and is converted into an acid which is toxic to the nervous system. PKU can be controlled, if diagnosed early (before obvious manifestation), by means of a phenylalanine-free diet.

Other forms of mental retardation caused by recessive gene disorders include Tay-Sachs disease (involving an abnormal or absent enzyme in the body), galactosemia (involving carbohydrate metabolism), and cretinism, which can also result from nongenetic causes and involves decreased levels of the hormone thyroxine. Mental retardation may also be caused by dominant gene disorders, though these are rare. Additionally, some abnormalities of sex chromosomes are sometimes—but not always—associated with mental retardation. These include Turner's syndrome, in which individuals are phenotypically female but have a XO genotype; Klinefelter's syndrome, characterized by an XXY genotype; and XYY syndrome.

Aside from genetics, Balla and Zigler (1980) note several environmental causes of mental retardation. These include prenatal factors associated with the mother, such as poor nutrition, exposure to toxins and drugs, and disease (e.g., syphilis). Prematurity, lack of oxygen at birth, and birth injuries are additional potential causes, as is head injury resulting from accidents or child abuse.

More than a million individuals in the United States today are retarded because of known organic pathology. This group thus constitutes a deviation from the normal distribution curve, in the lower portions of this curve, suggesting that they should be considered as rather different from those who are mildly retarded and seem to represent only the lower portions of the normal range in intelligence (Zigler, 1969). Cases of organic retardation occur in all strata of society, while nonorganic ones are generally found in the lower socioeconomic levels.

The majority of retarded people have IQs above 50 and have no known organic pathologies. Since many come from families in which other close relatives are also retarded, this is referred to as *cultural-familial retardation;* the assumption is that the environmental and/or genetic background predisposes some family members to retardation. It is likely that an interaction between genetic and environmental factors is involved in the etiology of this type of mental retardation. The explanation of cultural-familial retardation, however, is a controversial subject.

Although behavior geneticists have conducted a number of studies demonstrating that heritability is involved in the determination of individual IQ, there is disagreement about the magnitude of genetic and environmental influences (e.g., Achenbach, 1974; Jensen, 1969; Kamin, 1974; Scarr, 1976). At one extreme, some believe that the causes of cultural-familial retardation are solely environmental. One source of evidence for this view is the greater incidence of cultural-familial retardation in lower socioeconomic classes. Another is the finding that children raised for different amounts of time in an institution reached different levels of intelligence: children adopted before age 2 reached average intelligence levels, but greater deficits in intelligence occurred with increased age at adoption (Dennis, 1973). As Balla and Zigler (1980) point out, however, these arguments do not account for the occurrence of cultural-familial retardation among the many children who do not experience extreme social or economic deprivation.

At the other extreme, two genealogical studies have stressed the genetic determination of cultural-familial retardation. One notes the high incidence of mental retardation in successive generations of a family (the Jukes) and attributes it to both genetic factors and poor environmental conditions (Dugdale, 1877). The other, which stresses a more purely genetic cause, traces two lines of descendants from a man called Kallikak. One line, born of a mentally retarded woman, revealed prevalent mental retardation, poverty, and alcoholism, but the other, children of Kallikak's nonretarded wife, showed none of these characteristics (Goddard, 1912).

Recent thinking suggests that intelligence is too complex a trait to be passed on by the simplistic laws of genetics called on in the above examples; IQ is held to be determined by many genes in such a way that the influence of any given one is small. By either the extreme genetic or environmental arguments, all children of a given family should be retarded if any are, but this does not prove to be the case (Balla & Zigler, 1980), and a polygenic model appears to be more accurate than the others in predicting the incidence of mental retardation. Cultural-familial retardation, then, can be explained by the same factors as normal intelligence, representing the inevitable lower portion of the normal curve. According to this view, individuals with cultural-familial retardation would be expected to exhibit a cognitive progression like that of the nonretarded; although development would be slower and the final stage reached would not be as high, the sequence of stages would be the same. Individuals of the same mental age should be identical in cognitive terms (Balla & Zigler, 1980), and observed differences would be explained by experiential or motivational factors.

In contrast to this developmental position, some view cultural-familial retardation as a result of inherent physiological or cognitive differences. It has been argued, for example, that the retarded exhibit cognitive rigidity (Kounin, 1941; Lewin, 1936); that they have a deficiency in the ability to guide behavior by verbal means (Luria, 1963); that rehearsal in memory is not used effectively and short-term memory is impaired (Ellis, 1970); and that deficiencies exist in retarded individuals' attention abilities (Fisher & Zeamon, 1973; Zeamon & House, 1963) or in their information processing (Spitz, 1973).

Personality Characteristics of the Retarded

Several personality characteristics of the retarded—such as rigidity, low expectations of success, outer-directedness, overdependency, and cue dependency— are attributable to the distinctive experiences of the retarded and are not in any way inherent or necessary characteristics, as implied in the "difference" theories just mentioned (Kounin, 1941a, 1941b; cf. Zigler, 1969). Zigler and his colleagues have been most influential in researching these motivational factors in the performance of the retarded, in accordance with Zigler's (1971) appeal that we consider the retarded child as a whole person, identifying both primary intellectual deficits and secondary motivational ones (see Balla & Zigler, 1980, and Zigler & Balla, 1982, for recent reviews). As article 7 in Part 2 discusses these factors in more detail, we simply touch on them here.

According to Zigler and Harter (1969), the single most important factor preventing most retarded people from becoming self-sustaining members of society is overdependency. This trait can be seen as a result of social deprivation: because of the relative absence of rewarding social interactions in their experience, the mentally retarded are especially eager to obtain social approval—a situation which results in overdependency. At the same time that social deprivation yields this result, however, it also makes retarded children wary of strange adults (Balla, Butterfield, & Zigler, 1974). Wariness appears to result when children's previous experiences with adults have been negative, motivation toward social reinforcement when they have been positive.

Another factor affecting the performance and behavior of the retarded is an expectation of failure. This expectancy of failure appears to result from a lifetime of failure experiences due to frequent encounters with problems or tasks with which the retarded child cannot deal. In addition to expecting failure (Cromwell, 1963), the retarded are more likely to blame themselves and their own incapacities when they do fail than are people of average intellect. For example, when prevented from completing a task and then questioned as to why it had not been completed, retarded children (in contrast to nonretarded ones) consistently blamed themselves (MacMillan, 1969; MacMillan & Keogh, 1971).

Past experiences also make retarded children less responsive to intangible reinforcement (e.g., the information that the performance was correct or incorrect) than are nonretarded children of the same mental age (Zigler, 1962; Zigler & deLabry, 1962; Zigler & Unell, 1962). Zigler (1971) argues that the incidence of failure may be so high among the retarded that training focuses on doing one's best rather than on necessarily finding a correct answer, and this emphasis would be expected to lower the reinforcement value of being right. Additionally, retarded children appear less motivated to use their capacities to the fullest; stated differently, their intrinsic effectance motivation (believed by White, 1959, to be an inherent human trait) is lower than that of nonretarded children (Harter & Zigler, 1974). Past experiences of failure may result in retarded children's pairing of effectance motivation with anxiety, and this may explain the greater inclination of retarded children to avoid failure than to achieve success (Cromwell, 1963).

When involved in solving problems, retarded children manifest an outer-directed style which makes them more susceptible to influence by the tester's cues and concrete situational cues than are intellectually average children (Achenbach & Weisz, 1975; Achenbach & Zigler, 1968; Turnure & Zigler, 1964). Again, this characteristic seems to be determined by the relative frequencies of success and failure in the individual's history, as well as by the level of cognitive development and extent of attachment to adults. Evidence concerning the effects of retardation on self-concept are conflicting and inconclusive, but the retarded do not seem to have more negative self-concepts (see Balla & Zigler, 1982, for a review).

Environmental Contexts

Some 50 to 80% of those who have borderline or mild retardation become self-supporting, with very few being institutionalized. It is essential to recognize, however, that institutionalization seems to have profound effects on mentally retarded individuals (Balla & Zigler, 1982). This fact makes much research on retardation difficult to interpret, because comparisons of "retarded" and "nonretarded" individuals are also often comparisons of institutionalized and noninstutionalized individuals, and the effects of either variable (retardation or institutionalization) are not seen independently.

Reports on the effects of institutionalization are inconsistent. On the one hand, some show the institutionalized retarded as less developmentally advanced; institutionalization has been associated with decreased performance on cognitive tasks, and deleterious effects of institutionalization on the behavior of normal children have been reported. On the other hand, however, some reports show increased autonomy, language utility, and variability in behavior, as well as less verbal dependency and outer-directedness in institutionalized retarded children (Balla & Zigler, 1980). Effects of institutionalization may be beneficial, for example, if children are protected from numerous experiences of failure. It appears that both positive and negative effects may occur, depending on the type of institution, preinstitutionalization personality and experiences, age at institutionalization, and other factors of this sort. The type of institution favored in public and professional opinion has changed at different times in history, so that small community-based facilities are now preferred to the large custodial facilities which were the norm during the first half of the twentieth century. Since the empirical basis for assessing institutional adequacy is minimal (Balla & Zigler, 1982), it appears that these changes have been in accordance with ideologies and attitudes concerning the mentally retarded rather than with research on the effects of the different types of institutions.

Just as the overall effect of institutionalization makes it impossible to compare institutionalized retarded with nonretarded subjects, differences in the quality of institutions prevent clear comparisons even between institutionalized groups. Various studies of the effects of different types of institutions on personality have been conducted. Butterfield and Zigler (1965) found that the type of institution was related to the degree of motivation for social support: children in a small, homelike environment were less motivated by social reinforcement than were children in a larger, more sterile and depriving institution. In the latter case, it is presumed that social deprivation leads children to place a very high value on even minor social reinforcement because they experience so little in their daily lives. McCormick, Balla, and Zigler (1975) found smaller living unit size, which necessitates viewing each resident as an individual, to be correlated with resident-oriented (versus institution-oriented) care and with a less socially depriving environment.

Preinstitutional experience is another crucial mediator of the effects of institutionalization (Balla, Butterfield, & Zigler, 1974). Zigler and Williams (1963), for example, found overall increases in children's social motivation after 3 years of institutionalization, suggesting that the effects of social deprivation on institutional life are cumulative. Notably, however, these researchers found a much greater increase in children who came from less socially depriving homes. This indicates that institutionalization is more socially depriving for those whose home environments were supportive (Balla & Zigler, 1975; Zigler et al., 1968) than for those who came from depriving environments. Similarly, after an additional 3 years in the institution, while overall social motivation decreased (reflecting increased maturity), the drop for children from less socially depriving backgrounds was smaller than the drop for children from highly deprived backgrounds.

The length of institutionalization can also mediate its effects, as indicated by a smaller degree of wariness in children institutionalized at younger ages (Balla, McCarthy, & Zigler, 1971). Additionally, gender differences have been reported; for example, expectancy of failure was higher for males than for females (Ollendick et al., 1971).

As is suggested by the above mentioned effects of preinstitutionalization experience, the family contexts in which retarded children live affect their development. Balla and Zigler (1980) point out that while it is often assumed that grave troubles plague families with retarded children, these problems need not be seen as necessary consequences. Rather, these authors suggest that difficulties result from larger IQ discrepancies between children and their parents, such as those that occur especially with organic retardation; in the case of cultural-familial retardation, a child need not be viewed as particularly deviant. Several typical parental reactions to having a retarded child have been described by Roos (1963). For example, parents may blame themselves for the retardation (attributing it to a defect in themselves) and, so, experience a loss of self-esteem. Parents may also respond with increased ambivalence: the child's behavior or slow development may cause parents to be rejecting and then, through guilt, overprotective. Chronic sorrow is experienced by many parents, and some become self-sacrificing in their focus on the retarded child—perhaps to the detriment of other family members. With regard to siblings, Balla and Zigler note that some appear to benefit from the experience of having a retarded sibling while others seem to suffer, especially when they have unusual responsibilities for child care.

The means by which a family adapts to having a retarded child must affect the climate in which the child develops. As described by Farber (1975), an initial phase occurs in which the family labels the child as retarded and realizes that family roles may change, followed by a phase in which the family attempts to maintain normal roles and extrafamilial relationships. These attempts may be intensified in a mobilization phase and, if it is unsuccessful, age and sex standards for familial roles may change in a revisionist phase. In a polarization phase, the family tries at all costs to maintain coherence, even to the point of failing to confront pathological beliefs which may arise. Finally, an elimination phase may be reached wherein the retarded child is institutionalized or, sometimes, a different family member leaves (e.g., parents divorce). Obviously, families stop their progression through these stages at whatever point adaptation is reached.

Families' abilities to cope with a retarded child, as well as the retarded person's ability to cope with life, depends a great deal on support found in the social system—schools, institutional and health care services. The prevalent notion in regard to programs for the retarded currently stresses normalization, or the attempt to approximate as closely as possible behaviors and characteristics which fit cultural norms. Accordingly, educational practice has increasingly emphasized mainstreaming, programs in which retarded children are placed in regular classes either for all subjects or for nonacademic ones. One initial incentive for mainstreaming was the belief that special education classes, which prevent association of retarded children with nonretarded peers, lead to a stigmatizing of the retarded and consequent feelings of inferiority. Empirical evidence on this point is inconclusive: studies of elementary school students suggest that mainstreamed children are less well accepted than those in special education classes, but in one study of high school students (Sheare, 1974), exposure to educable mentally retarded students in classes led to a more favorable view on the part of other students. In terms of academic performance, mainstreamed children do as well as those in special education classes, though there is little evidence to support the original idea that they would do better (that education in the special classes was inferior). In one study, mainstreamed children were found to have higher expectancies of failure than special education students (Gruen, Ottinger, & Ollendick, 1974).

As with children, the development of retarded children is affected by governmental policies and public attitudes. Recent litigation regarding the rights of the retarded has concerned the right to treatment in residential facilities, the right to state-funded education for all retarded children, and procedures for identifying and placing mildly retarded children in special education classes. For example, as a result of a law passed by the United States Congress (PL94-142), education of all children, including the severely and profoundly retarded, is now the responsibility of the public school system. Litigation in these areas must affect both the quality of life for the retarded and the support offered to their families.

Giftedness

In contrast to the previous two sections, we will discuss here a form of atypical development involving exceptionally high levels of intelligence. Gifted individuals have IQs which fall at the upper end of the distribution of intelligence, just as the IQs of the cultural-familial retarded fall at the lower end; each group is composed of the small percentage of the population we expect at the extremes of a normally distributed trait. In fact, lessons learned from studying the retarded are of use in considering the gifted as well, although it may seem ironic to consider similarities between two groups which, at first glance, appear to be complete opposites. Like the mentally retarded, however, the gifted may be considered "abnormal" in the sense that they differ significantly from the average person, exhibiting extreme deviations in intelligence. This difference from the rest of the population creates some similar types of problems in both cases.

The discussion of definitions of mental retardation is equally relevant here. In terms of IQ scores, giftedness has been variously considered as indicated by scores over 125, over 140, over 180, in the top 3% of the population, or in the top 2–4%. Although intelligence has never been disputed as a fundamental determinant of giftedness, controversy emerges over precisely which components of intelligence should be considered: intelligence may be regarded only in terms of g (general) or s (specific) abilities as well. Some workers in the field would argue that intellect is comprised of several distinct abilities and that the term *gifted* should be applied to children who reason extremely well mathematically or who demonstrate superior verbal skills even if they do not attain above-average IQ scores. In addition, creativity may be considered as a dimension of giftedness, as may productivity or demonstrated achievement, although these last factors seem more appropriate criteria for adults than for identifying gifted children. Finally, a small subgroup within the gifted are held to be geniuses, individuals whose accomplishments are not only judged outstanding and creative but stand the test of time; certainly more than IQ is necessary to differentiate this group.

As with mental retardation, a major theoretical question in the study of giftedness is whether intellectual differences represent differences in degree or in kind from the general population. On the one hand, the superior capabilities of gifted children may be seen as the result of having quantitatively more of something like g; on the other hand, they may be regarded as having some qualitatively different cognitive process. A related question is whether or not gifted individuals represent a homogeneous group; this is particularly important if the intellectual range for giftedness is rather broad, such as when the defining line is set at IQ 130 and the range is from IQ 130 to over 180. In view of the fact that mentally retarded people can be divided into disparate groups on the basis of etiology, we might expect to find that the gifted are also a heterogeneous group. Although there is no evidence for differentiating the gifted on the basis of etiology of their giftedness, differentiation may be made on some other basis, such as neuropsychological functioning, creativity, or cognitive style. Evidence exists, for example, that cognitive style may actually change with higher IQ. Spitz (1982) found that intellectually superior and retarded children of the same mental age who achieved the same composite scores on a number of cognitive tasks displayed significantly qualitative differences in their performance on the various tasks. It is possible that within the broad range of IQ that is regarded as indicating the gifted, similar qualitative differences in cognitive functioning may exist.

Heterogeneity among high-ability individuals is also suggested by inconsistencies concerning the psychological adjustment of geniuses and the gifted. Genius has often been associated with mental instability; the first systematic study of this relationship was carried out during the second half of the last century by Lombroso (1891), who concluded that genius is often a "degenerative psychosis of the epileptic group." Lombroso and others after him (Grant, 1968; Lange-Eichbaum, 1932; Tsanoff, 1949) noted the pathological behavior of hundreds of gifted artists, musicians, novelists, poets, and scientists. The examples of serious psychological disturbance are numerous: Franz Kafka, for one, has been described as suicidally depressed and probably schizophrenic; Vincent van Gogh as a neurotic-hysteric with impulsive and unreasoning rages; Edgar Allen Poe as psychopathic, paranoid, and megalomaniacal; Arthur Schopenhauer as bipolar manic-depressive.

In contrast to the evidence of mental instability among geniuses, Terman's longitudinal study of the gifted demonstrated that the great majority of individuals with IQs over 140 made good life adjustments (Termin & Oden, 1947, 1959). In fact, the incidence of minor or serious maladjustments and of suicides was lower in this group than in the general population, and those gifted individuals who encountered serious maladjustment made remarkably quick recoveries. Terman concluded that "superior intelligence does not appear to be a causal factor in mental disorders as found in this group but seems, rather, to have helped those affected to overcome their difficulties" (Terman & Oden, 1947, p. 108).

The contradictory findings of mad geniuses and well-adjusted, gifted individuals might be reconciled by Hollingworth's (1942) notion that there is an "optimum intelligence," between 125 and 155 IQ, but that too much of an intellectual "gift" may pose a serious obstacle to normal psychological development. If further evidence corroborates this relationship, it may be possible to differentiate at least two groups of gifted individuals. The first, with relatively lower IQ scores, would be continuous with the rest of the population and would not exhibit qualitatively distinguishable cognitive or neurological functioning. Members of the second group, with higher IQ scores, might be those who become true geniuses and make original contributions of unusually great value to society. In contrast to the first group, this one might be characterized by unusual neuropsychological functioning and, whether due to distinctive hereditary, metabolic, or developmental conditions, the qualitatively different factor or group of factors responsible for the much higher IQs would also make this group more susceptible to psychological maladjustment.

Creativity

We have used the term *creative* frequently in this discussion of giftedness, but the concept of creativity is itself not a clearly defined one. Definitions of creativity range from simple problem solving to actualization of the self, but most refer to creativity as a psychological process by which novel and valuable products are created, an ability to place things in new perspective and see previously unsuspected connections. Two of the most important criteria of creativity are originality and adaptiveness. An idea or product must also be appropriate to its context and make sense in light of the demands of the situation. For example, although the thinking of individuals who are mentally ill, especially schizophrenic, is unique and original, it would not be considered creative. Other criteria of creativity include elegance—esthetic quality—and transcendance—the power to transform the constraints of reality, to defy tradition and yield a new perspective (Mc-Kinnon, 1968).

Guilford (1968) postulated a number of intellectual factors that may account for individual differences in creativity, including associational fluency, ideational fluency, originality, adaptive flexibility, spontaneous flexibility, redefinition, and sensitivity to problems. Guilford's work is responsible for the notions of convergent and divergent thinking. *Convergent thinking* reflects analytical and reasoning processes; it is the ability to search for the most appropriate or most conventional solution to a problem and is the type of thinking typically assessed by most standard IQ tests. *Divergent thinking*, on the other hand, involves the ability to produce a variety of ideas or solutions to a given problem and is generally considered characteristic of creativity.

Another suggestion is that the significant factor in creativity is the ability to utilize cognitive processes at varying developmental levels (Werner, 1957). In this view, creativity is seen to require first a regression to earlier cognitive levels and then a progression to higher ones. In regressing, previously existing patterns are broken into simpler elements, and during the progression phase they are reorganized into previously nonexisting patterns. In an experimental analysis of this hypothesis, creative artists were found to give more of both mature and primitive responses in a Rorschach test than people who had not distinguished themselves for creativity in any of the culturally ascribed forms (Hersch, 1962). This finding indicates that creative individuals have available, and demonstrate more flexible use of, both more mature responses, reflecting differentiation and articulation, and more primitive responses indicative of synthesis and diffuseness.

Creativity has been associated with certain personality characteristics, although it must be emphasized that there is no single personality mold into which all creative people fit (McKinnon, 1968). Creative individuals have been described as dominant, poised, spontaneous, and self-confident in social interaction, although they may not be particularly sociable; as outspoken, sharp-witted, demanding, aggressive, self-centered, persuasive, and verbally fluent, and relatively uninhibited in expressing worries and complaints; and as comparatively free from conventional inhibitions, not preoccupied with impressions made on others, capable of independence and autonomy, and relatively ready to recognize and admit views that are unusual and unconventional.

It is generally assumed that creativity is one aspect of giftedness, but the bulk of evidence indicates that intelligence and creativity are not highly correlated (Getzels & Jackson, 1962; Hollingworth, 1942; Terman & Oden, 1947, 1959; Torrance, 1962). As discussed in regard to the intelligence/social competence issue in mental retardation, this situation may be attributed to the nature of intelligence tests and to the fact that these tests were not intended to assess creative ability. On the other hand, McNemar (1964) argued that creativity is an inherent aspect of intelligence and suggested that the low correlations found are primarily due to faulty experimental design, in which correlations are computed on restricted ranges of intelligence and creativity; the studies in which the low correlations were found were based on individuals who had either distinguished themselves in creative performance (and were likely to have IQs over 120) or in intellectual ability. Experimental support for this view is provided by Barron's (1961) finding that the correlation between intelligence and creativity over the whole range of ability is approximately .40, but the correlation between intelligence and creativity among individuals with IQs over 120 is only .10. Taken together, these findings support the notion that a moderately high level of intelligence is necessary for creative work but that beyond that point, being more or less intelligent does not determine the level of a person's creative ability (McKinnon, 1968).

Another issue in the relationship between intelligence and creativity concerns adult success. Because intelligence tests are validated against school performance, of which creativity is a small component, it has been argued that intelligence and academic performance have become equated, to the exclusion of creativity (Gold, 1965). Academic performance, however, has been found to have a low association with adult success (Heath, 1977). Wallach and Wing (1969) found that intelligence scores related to grades in college but not to success in extracurricular activities; outside of the classroom, what seemed to matter most was the person's "ideational resourcefulness" (the ability to generate ideas), a factor believed by these researchers to be an aspect of creativity.

Thus, it appears that creativity may be a factor in giftedness, much as social competence is in mental retardation. Neither is predicted well by IQ scores, yet each is characteristic of the respective group of people. It might, then, be beneficial to the field of giftedness to make creativity an explicit dimension of giftedness, just as adaptive behavior was made an explicit criterion of mental retardation.

Training of the Gifted and the Price of Giftedness

The very high IQ of gifted children tends to cause an emphasis on their studying, learning, and achievement in school, and the focus of most training programs for the gifted is on producing more and more intellectual growth. There is little agreement, however, on what type of education is best for gifted children: some suggest special attention in regular school classrooms, others suggest teaching groups of gifted children together, and still others suggest promoting gifted children to a grade which offers appropriate intellectual stimulation. This last option, especially, may entail emotional and social problems because the gifted children will be much younger than their classmates. In any case, the fact that some type of special attention is needed is suggested by Goertzel and Goertzel's (1962) finding that three-fifths of 400 of the most eminent men and women of our century remembered feeling dissatisfied with schools and teachers when they were children. It seems likely that if assigned work was not sufficient to interest these gifted children, they would become bored, frustrated, and uninterested. Nevertheless, the United States government does not appear to do very well in fostering the abilities of the gifted: according to a report from the U.S. Office of Education (1971), only a small percentage receive special services, and gifted children in minority and economically disadvantaged groups are especially neglected. While intellectually oriented programs are critical in providing the needed stimulation to gifted students, however, they should not be emphasized at the expense of social and emotional development. As discussed above, intelligence alone is a relatively poor predictor of significant achievement or competence. In his sample of gifted people, Terman found that what distinguished the successful from the unsuccessful group was motivation and emotional adjustment. Concern with the development of gifted children—as with any children—must recognize the whole person and not just cognitive systems.

One of the most important but, until recently, relatively neglected ways of fostering the development of the whole person is through play. In play, children not only have fun but learn about their environment and develop cognitively, socially, and emotionally. Singer and Singer (1977) suggest several major benefits of play: development of greater self-awareness and a sense of control over the environment; development of imagery skill; development of verbal skills; development of emotional awareness, sensitivity, and roles for new social situations; increase in the ability to explore new contexts and try out new situations in odd combinations. Experiences such as these may lay the groundwork for the development of creativity. The open-ended quality of play, for example, may foster the development of the divergent type of thinking that is a characteristic of creativity (Fein & Clarke-Stewart, 1973; Sutton-Smith, 1971). The earliest symbolic play involves deleting or ignoring some attributes of objects; later, children violate the functional aspects of objects and attribute outrageous possibilities to objects whose actual functions may be vague. Singer and Singer (1977) show that people who have demonstrated creative achievements early in their lives engaged in a good deal of fantasy as children, such as developing imaginary companions, hearing storytelling, and playing pantomime games with their parents. All this suggests that academic acceleration efforts for gifted children, with their focus on facts, skills, and experiences that will develop logical, deductive, and analytical cognitive processes, may deprive gifted children of the complete development of their full intellectual potential. Without opportunities for play, gifted children may not develop the synthetic, divergent thought processes characteristic of creativity.

Another consideration is that the gifted, like the retarded, generally have different types of social and cognitive experiences from other children, and these make them more vulnerable to personality difficulties. High IQs and achieving well in school do not necessarily result in feelings of self-worth and esteem. A recent study (Phillips, 1981) found that 20% of over 100 high-achieving fifth-grade children had low self-concepts. Similarly, Katz and Zigler (1967) found that bright high school students had lower self-concept scores than low-IQ students. It may be that the disparity between high aspirations and low self-assessment makes some gifted children feel considerable self-derogation, guilt, and anxiety. Further, the high expectations imposed on these children may convey the message that they are failures for not living up to their potential, leading to a decrease in the motivation to try. Thus, in Phillips' study, the children with low self-concepts also set lower achievement standards for themselves and had lower expectations for success in school. These conclusions may account partly for the finding of a study in the Midwest that gifted children drop out of school at a rate three to five times that of the rest of the population.

Another frequent emotional and social consequence of a very high IQ is social isolation. A child whose IQ is so much higher than those of any of his peers or even of many adults may have difficulty finding people with whom to share confidences and receive emotional support, and may tune out others, therefore not using adult and peer models for learning social behavior. The result may be the development of further difficulties in interacting with others. Of course, these are not necessary results: by the same fact of their brilliance, gifted children may use their intellectual resources to solve such problems in a way which results in better rather than worse personal adjustments.

Child Abuse

Child abuse differs from the other topics discussed in this section in that the problem is defined not by the child's behavior or characteristics but by the behavior of the parents or caretakers. Child abuse is a phenomenon that has recently become a major concern in most Western countries, including the United States, partly because statistics indicate that the incidence of child abuse is increasing. Actually, this is not at all clear, since the increased reporting may have more to do with community awareness, the changing definition of abuse, and recent legislative mandates requiring the reporting of suspected abuse than with any changes in actual frequency. As it is, we still do not know just how common child abuse is: statistics for the United States range from an estimated incidence of less than 400,000 cases per year to estimates of more than 2 million.

One difficulty in addressing the problem of child abuse is that no universally agreed upon definition exists, so the term *child abuse* may mean different things to different people. As we will see, the various explanations of child abuse and approaches to its prevention utilize different definitions. In terms of research and assessment, this lack of a standardized definition means that different phenomena are labeled with the same term, yielding misleading results and statistics which differ according to precisely what is measured in a given study. Some definitions of child abuse are narrow, emphasizing only extreme physical abuse; others are broad, considering emotional damage and lesser degree of physical abuse as well. In terms of combating abuse, definitions determine which actions will be tolerated by the legal system and which will be deterred. For example, the definition of where on the punishment continuum discipline becomes abusive (Alvy, 1975;

Hurt, 1975; Maurer, 1974) determines the point at which federal or state intervention into families is considered warranted.

Child abuse is also a difficult issue to approach because it is an emotionally laden one. Partially for this reason, the question of how much attention it deserves is controversial. Zigler (1980) argues that one explanation of the controversy may be a widespread occurrence of the psychological mechanism of denial: people refuse to believe that child abuse can happen because the idea of parents' being violent with their children causes such revulsion. This revulsion may be due to the fact that the idea of parental violence is threatening: the thought of being helpless and not receiving proper care touches people's deepest dependency needs. For adults who find great satisfaction in relationships with their children, child abuse may seem horribly perverse. Also, the revulsion may be strengthened by the belief, based on an outmoded and misguided approach to human behavior, that abuse results from a lack of maternal instinct. In any case, child abuse is a subject which is difficult to approach objectively.

Another reason for the argument over the extent of the problem of child abuse is the tendency to evaluate issues on the basis of absolute numbers. By this standard, abuse is a lesser danger than childhood accidents, for example, which are the major causes of death for children under 16 years of age (Furrow, Gruendel, & Zigler, 1979).

Child abuse in our society is evident not only in parental maltreatment but also in abuses occurring in schools and federal or state institutions. For example, legalized abuse of retarded children has been documented by Blatt (1980), and physical abuse of children in hospitals for the emotionally disturbed and schools for delinquents was shown in the television documentary "This Child Is Labelled X." Abuse and neglect in day-care settings have been documented by Keyserling (1972). Additionally, cases of extreme abuse in schools appear, not too rarely, in the media (Zigler & Andersen, in press). The occurrence of child abuse in these contexts is harmful not only in itself but also because of the example it provides for parents—an example which is supported by the United States government's sanction of physical means of discipline, highlighted by the 1975 Supreme Court decision upholding the right to use corporal punishment in schools. This sanction is in contrast, for example, to the Swedish government's ban of parents'—as well as institutional—use of corporal punishment, which implies a conception of abuse as including physical punishment.

The implications of attitudes toward corporal punishment are important because of the potential relationship between physical punishment and child abuse. When corporal punishment is accepted, a distinction must be made between (accepted) discipline and (unaccepted) abuse, but at least some forms of physical discipline are condoned. Since the distinction between punishment and abuse is a subjective one, this attitude sets the stage for abuse to continue. Zigler (1980) argues that the use of corporal punishment, even in mild forms, may increase the potential for abuse because parents may unintentionally hurt a child if they misjudge their strength and the child's vulnerability, or if they cannot control their anger. He suggests, moreover, that the fault in such a situation lies in the societal approval of corporal punishment as a means to discipline children which establishes this potential for abuse. The use of corporal punishment in schools may be particularly significant in perpetuating the use of physical means of discipline because of the crucial role which schools play in children's lives. The effect of corporal punishment in schools may be direct, in that punishment or abuse which is experienced at school may be traumatic, like abuse experienced at home. The effect may also be indirect, in influencing home experiences through the schools' roles as models for family practices.

Moreover, the premises underlying the use of corporal punishment are questionable aside from any connection with abuse. It is often argued that unruly children can be controlled only by physical means, especially in light of the prevalence of aggressive acts by children in classrooms. According to research, however, corporal punishment tends to be ineffective in the long run: unless it is administered continually, at levels which even its advocates would not approve, it will not be a dependable way of eliminating behavior (Zigler & Alexander, in press). Additionally, constant punishment may eventually be ignored as routine, and physical punishment may only increase levels of aggression, create stress, and interefere with learning. On the other hand, rewarding positive behavior may produce more lasting effects and enhance learning (Dorow, 1973; Firestone & Brody, 1975; Raffel, O'Leary, & Armel, 1974; Rosenshine & Furst, 1971; Solomon & Kendall, 1976; Tikunoff, Berliner, & Rist, 1975).

Definitions and Explanations of Child Abuse

Although child maltreatment has occurred since ancient times (Ross, 1980), it was not formally defined until the early 1960s. The attempt to define child abuse may be seen in relation to the modern professionalization of certain social functions: as conflicts which were once dealt with by religion or folk custom have come into the domain of law and social services, it has become necessary to delineate rules determining appropriate cases for an institution's attention (Aber & Zigler, 1981). At present, definitions of child abuse vary according to needs and theoretical perspectives: the legal definition of abuse is necessarily different from definitions which guide research, and the latter vary with different theoretical approaches. Three types of explanation for child abuse may be distinguished:

the psychiatric, or medical, the sociological, and the social-situational. Each of these is based on particular assumptions which influence all levels of research, from the types of questions asked and methodologies used to the interpretation of data.

The *medical model* attributes child abuse to the pathological personality of the abusive parent. This model was developed in the early 1960s as a result of the discovery by radiologists of repeated fractures on children's x-rays which could not be explained by their parents (Kempe, Silverman, Steele, Droegemueller, & Silver, 1962). The term applied was *battered child syndrome*, and the conception of the problem stressed parents' abusive tendencies. One result of this model was a two-category classification system which discriminated between parents who abused their children and those who did not. The definition of child abuse used was a diagnostic one aimed at identifying an underlying pathology (characteristics of the abuser) so as to allow therapeutic intervention (Aber & Zigler, 1981).

Research which focused on individual characteristics was common in the early 1960s, and many different personality characteristics have been reported to be typical of abusive parents. Unfortunately, it is rare for findings of this sort to be replicated, and for every report that a given trait is typical, there are several which fail to find differences between abusive and nonabusive parents on the dimension in question. Reviews of the literature have concluded that there is little evidence of common pathology in abusive parents (Parke & Collmer, 1975; Spinetta & Rigler, 1972). There is some, albeit tentative, evidence that abusive parents often have poor self-esteem or self-concepts (Steele & Pollock, 1974) and that alcoholism or drug abuse is associated with child maltreatment (Kempe & Kempe, 1978). Also, there is suggestive evidence that abusive parents are more likely to have been abused themselves as children than are nonabusive parents (Curtis, 1963; Kempe, Silverman, Steele, Droegemueller, & Silver, 1962; Steele & Pollock, 1974), perhaps because these parents have grown up without adequate models of effective, nonabusive parenting. Of course, this does not mean that abused children will necessarily become abusing parents; while some may, it is equally clear that others will not (Zigler, 1980).

The medical model of child abuse has several limitations. First, the original definition focused on extreme physical abuse, excluding both the less extreme and cases of neglect (Zigler, 1980). The inclusion of these other categories creates a much broader definition which emphasizes not strictly physical abuse but over-all lack of fulfillment of a child's developmental needs. The medical model also entailed a classification system based solely on parental actions. Perhaps more important than overt actions, however, are parents' intentions and less obvious ways of hindering children's development. Piaget pointed out the fact that in early development children's moral perceptions change from an awareness of consequences of parents' behavior to an awareness of intentions. The medical model is not able to account for the fact that children may suffer more serious damage from repeated emotional rejection than from isolated instances of physical abuse. In this regard, Zigler (1980) suggests that child abuse be considered on a continuum of behaviors ranging from affectionate interaction to extreme abuse. In contrast to the classification system inherent in the medical model, this implies that all parents are potential abusers and that abusive and nonabusive acts are different in degree but not in kind. Thus, we can imagine parents who begin with a mild punishment and find, in horror, that they have seriously injured their child. While the dichotomous classification in the medical model allows a dismissal of child abusers as psychopathic, a continuum approach forces parents to confront their own potential abusiveness. In so doing, it may enable nonabusers to see abusers as similar to themselves rather than as deviant and allow nonabusers to feel more empathy and to have a greater tendency to help instead of punish abusers.

The approach to child abuse most at odds with the medical model is the *sociological model*, which argues that abuse occurs when parents are subjected to intolerable amounts of emotional, social, and economic stress. It implicitly assumes, as above, that any parents could become abusive depending upon the circumstances and their ability to tolerate stress and frustration. The means to control abuse, according to this view, would lie in changing social attitudes and conditions.

There is substantial evidence to support the view that stress increases the likelihood of abuse, just as there is good evidence for the broader principle of which it is a special case—that frustration increases aggression (e.g., Berkowitz, 1968, 1974). Particularly impressive are the epidemiological studies conducted by Garbarino and his associates (Garbarino, 1976, 1977, Garbarino & Sherman, 1980). Garbarino and Sherman (1980) compared two census tracts that were highly similar on most demographic characteristics (income, education levels, density, family size, etc.) but that reported child abuse in very different frequencies. Garbarino and Sherman found that abuse was higher in the neighborhood with the highest incidence of social isolation, few ties with extended family members, etc.—presumably because parents in this neighborhood lacked the emotional support which would facilitate their ability to tolerate social stresses. This hypothesis must remain speculative, however, because since the research is correlational, it cannot be conclusively determined whether isolation leads to abusiveness or abusive parents become isolated from the community (Zigler, 1980). In any case, several researchers have found that abusing parents tend not to have close ties with neighbors or to participate in community organizations (Giovannoni & Billingsley, 1970; Kempe & Kempe, 1970; Parke and Collmer, 1975). In light of these findings, it may be surprising that abuse is often found in homes with a single (female) working parent (Elmer, 1967; Garbarino, 1976; Gil, 1970), as these mothers often experience stress and isolation.

Stress may also be implicated in the finding that abuse is more common in working-class and lower socioeconomic (SES) groups (Gil, 1969; Newberger et al., 1975). Zigler (1980) argues, on the basis of literature on social class and child rearing, that this relation cannot be explained only in terms of differing rearing practices, but that the stressful conditions facing many low-income families lead to the expectation of a higher incidence of child abuse. Significantly, this role of stress in mediating abuse suggests that low-income families are not inherently more abusive (Zigler, 1980). One model which could help explain a correlation between SES and abuse emphasizes cumulative stress, based on findings that only 19% of separate "risk factors" (in terms of parent, child, or situational characteristics) differentiate abusive families from nonabusive ones but that the cumulative difference between them is significant (Rohner & Rohner, 1978). If the correlation between SES and abuse is substantiated, however, we must be careful not to take it to disparage the poor, as has been done, for example, in past programs which offer "help" but do not change the stressful circumstances which lead to abuse (Zigler, 1980).

One problem with the sociological model of child abuse, discussed by Aber and Zigler (1981), is that it defines abuse by the act rather than by its effect on a child; it assumes that a social judgment of maltreatment corresponds to a child's subjective experience. For example, these authors cite the fact that sexual abuse is considered by professionals to be the second most serious type of maltreatment and emotional maltreatment the fifth. In a child's experience, sexual abuse might be infrequent and emotional maltreatment continuous, but this definition necessarily ranks the least harmful sexual abuse more serious than the most harmful emotional rejection. Aber and Zigler argue that the sociological approach cannot treat child abuse as an empirical issue to see that damage to a child (social, emotional, cognitive, or physical) does not depend on society's definition of harmful acts.

Another problem is that the sociological model, like the medical one, fails to consider the role of the child in abuse. Although using different perspectives, these approaches both view abuse in a unidirectional manner rather than as a result of interactions among parent, child, and environmental conditions. Thus, neither the medical nor the sociological approach can readily explain one puzzling fact concerning the incidence of abuse: often only one child in the family is abused. If the parents were pathologically disturbed or were simply responding to intolerable stresses, all children in the family would be equally liable to abuse. The fact that one child is often selected to be the repeated victim of abuse has prompted the development of a third explanatory approach—the social-situational.

Within the framework of the *social-situational model*, the abuser is seen not in isolation but in the context of a family which is itself embedded in a larger social, economic, and political community. Proponents of this approach (Burgess, 1979; Frodi & Lamb, 1980; Parke & Collmer, 1975) argue that the occurrence of abuse depends jointly on the characteristics of parent, child, and environment, so that while characteristics of the environment affect stressfulness, characteristics of the parent affect parenting capacities and frustration tolerance. Research literature provides neither a set of personality traits typical of abusive parents nor a means of determining causality, and the characteristics which have been noted as common among these parents must be seen as inseparable from the sociological environment. As has been discussed, abuse is frequently found in single-parent homes, when parents are isolated from social support, and (tentatively) in lower SES groups. Additionally, abuse may occur if power and responsibility for rearing are concentrated in one parent or if they shift too often between parents (Gelles, 1980; Parke & Collmer, 1975). Some researchers have found parents with little or no secondary school education most likely to act aggressively toward their children (Garbarino, 1976; Gil, 1970) and others that parents with only a high school diploma are overrepresented in statistics on child abuse (Gelles, 1980). Notably, abusive parents may have unrealistic expectations about their children's capacities, leading them to interpret behaviors such as crying or soiling diapers as intentional attempts to misbehave (Zimbardo & Ruch, 1975).

Characteristics of the child also affect abuse, although again, the direction of causality is unclear. Premature and low birthweight babies are often victims of abuse. Some explanations of this might be that unusual circumstances surrounding the birth may make acceptance into the family difficult (Zigler, 1980); that separation of premature infants from their mothers at birth may interfere with the formation of attachment bonds (Klaus & Kennell, 1976); that premature babies' slow development entails extra demands and frustration for parents; or that premature birth causes family stress and anxiety (Newberger & Hyde, 1975; Parke & Collmer, 1975; Stern, 1973). Also, theories of premature and "difficult" infants are perceived to be more aversive and irritating than those of normal infants (Frodi, Lamb, Leavitt, & Donovan, 1978; Frodi, Lamb, Leavitt, Donovan, Neff, & Sherry, 1978). That characteristics of the parents are integrally related, however, is indicated by the fact that abusive parents regard all social bids from children—both positive and negative—as equivalently aversive (Disbrow, Doerr, & Caufield, 1977; Frodi & Lamb, 1980). It is not clear whether this situation is a cause or consequence of pathological parent-child interactions.

In the area of child abuse, the premises and objectives of research, clinical treatment, and legal practices are very different, and a useful definition of child abuse must suit the purpose to which it will be applied. Despite the problems posed by the lack of a single definition, those used in the theoretical models we have been discussing prove inadequate as guidelines for legal intervention; consequently, a separate legal definition has been necessary (Aber & Zigler, 1981). Interestingly, the legal definition, developed for the Juvenile Justice Standards Project (1977), was the first one to focus on harm to the child rather than on the actual act of abuse, considering the existence or risk of physical or emotional damage to a child. Aber and Zigler note several advances of this definition over the medical or sociological ones. First, the legal definition differentiates between objectives, defining abuse as including emotional damage for the purpose of determining cause for intervention but limiting it to physical injury for the purpose of mandatory reporting of abuse. Second, the definition makes explicit the underlying values on which it is based (preserving family autonomy and cultural differences in child rearing and providing intervention reflecting children's developmental differences and needs for continuous, stable environments) as well as the overt objectives. Third, it accounts for parental intention by excluding cases in which an injury can be proved accidental in origin. Finally, it insists on evidence of both physical damage (e.g., disfigurement) and emotional damage (e.g., withdrawal).

A major issue which is reflected in the legal definition, but which has a bearing on all of the theoretical approaches we have considered, is the developmental context of child abuse (Aber & Zigler, 1981). A developmental framework emphasizes that the factors involved in child abuse are not static but are each continually developing and changing. The role of children's developmental level is perhaps most obvious: for example, the misguided parental expectations which correlate with abuse depend on developmental considerations, on the recognition (or lack thereof) of children's different capabilities at different ages. As Aber and Zigler note, the provocation of abuse may also depend on a child's developmental level: some parents may feel extreme rage at helpless, inconsolable infants, while others find toddlers' increasing locomotion and disruptions most frustrating, and still others are most prone to abuse when their children are considered old enough to reason and the children's actions are construed as intentional. Aber and Zigler point out the importance of developmental considerations in the legal definition of abuse, since vulnerability to different types of abuse may change with age, and what causes harm at one age may not at another. Also, the manifestation of emotional damage will take different forms at different ages, and the symptoms on which a legal interpretation of harm are based must be evaluated with this in mind. Developmental factors—the issues salient at a given age—may also be used to operationalize various indices of emotional damage and so aid in identifying abused children.

A developmental approach may also be applied to conceptualizations of parents' potential for abuse. Aber and Zigler suggest viewing some of the major risk factors (characteristics associated with abuse) as deviations in parents' development rather than as static traits. For example, instead of simply identifying a single parent or teenage mother as potentially abusive, Aber and Zigler suggest considering a parent's marital and social status as a reflection of the development of adult attachment relationships and social support systems. The static model may be both simplistic and dangerous in identifying potentially abusive parents because they fit into a particular category; within a developmental framework, parents can be seen in relation to factors which are changeable and changing. Similarly, static risk factors such as unemployment or financial stress may be related to the development of adult social competence and self-esteem, and age-inappropriate expectations of children may derive from parents' immature social, cognitive, and moral development. Finally, parent-child relations take place in a cultural context which undergoes perpetual change. Not only do social, economic, and political developments in a society affect the incidence of child abuse, but these factors inform the attitudes by which the society evaluates parental acts and their effects.

Several strategies for reducing the incidence of child abuse are generated by the social-situational approach (cf. Gerbner, Ross, & Zigler, 1980), but we will mention them only briefly here since they are the subject of article 16 in Part 2. One of these strategies is to combat the widespread assumption that adults are entitled to use physical means of punishing and controlling children. Another is to make available shelters and 24-hour nurseries where parents can bring their children when they feel unable to cope. Still another is to make available to lonely parents nonjudgmental professionals who can provide them with counsel and comfort. The availability of supplementary child-care services for single parents (who are responsible for a large proportion of abusive incidents) and of guaranteed income levels would also help eliminate the stresses that threaten to overwhelm isolated, inexperienced, and poor parents. Effective governmental efforts in these directions could make an enormous contribution to safeguarding the health and safety of young children.

18

Conclusion

More than any other area of psychology, the study of socialization has obvious and immediate practical implications. Many empirical findings or theoretical predictions are translated into advice for parents and others responsible for the care of children. By the same token, those who study and theorize about personality development are liable to influence by changing popular attitudes and values. Wolfenstein (1953) traced the changes during the preceding 40 years in the types of advice provided to parents, while the nature of Benjamin Spock's advice to parents has varied in tone across successive editions of his famous *Baby and Child Care* (e.g., 1976) in accordance with the prevailing sentiments about permissiveness, breast feeding, parental authority, and maternal employment. The ready willingness of parents to buy "how-to" books written by self-proclaimed experts ensures many opportunities for exploitation. Unfortunately, few lay readers are able to evaluate such popularized accounts or to determine the extent to which responsible research findings have been distorted or ignored.

On the other hand, it is the duty of developmental psychologists to clarify the implications of their theories and findings for parents and for those who make social policy that is likely to affect children and families (whether or not the effects are intentional). We believe that the dangers of exploitation discussed above would be lessened if this duty were taken seriously by responsible researchers. As our discussions of social class differences, intervention programs, and atypical development have indicated, many of the topics of interest to developmental psychologists have direct implications for social policy. For many years, developmental psychologists distinguished between basic and applied research, with an unwritten implication that applied research is of lower quality and status. Fortunately, this misperception is changing.

One reason for the lack of utilization of social science knowledge in social policy may be the conception that social science research is free of subjective values, while policy is made in a value-laden context (Zigler & Heller, 1980). As we saw in our discussion of child abuse, however, social science research is clearly influenced by the values of those carrying it out. Zigler and Heller suggest that social science research is commonly perceived to be irrelevant to social problems because it is meant to be basic rather than applied. To the contrary, Zigler and Heller note evidence that the federal government is looking for answers from social science research in the increase, over the last decade, in funding for applied research. Another problem discussed by these authors is that policy makers and social scientists do not provide each other with information to support effective collaboration. Rather, scientists find that the questions asked by policy makers do not facilitate valid and reliable research, while policy makers do not feel that social science provides clear, unambiguous answers to appropriate questions. Although single studies may be unlikely to have a great effect of social policy, and even accumulated research may add complications rather than provide definite answers, this research can help to clarify differences and perspectives. Most importantly, principles drawn from social science research play a role in sensitizing policy makers to new ideas, clarifying alternatives, and turning research questions into policy issues.

As Zigler (1980) points out, the distinction between applied and basic effort forces a false dichotomy. Good research can advance understanding while also having applied implications. Social policy implications of basic research relating to mental retardation, intelligence, and intervention have been discussed in some detail by Zigler and Seitz (1982a, 1982b). Other discussions of the interface between developmental research and social policy are also contained in the readings in Part 2.

It should be clear from the account we have provided that the determinants of personality development are complex indeed. Every aspect of personality appears to be multiply determined and overdetermined (Lamb, 1978b). Parental influences are supplemented by the intentional and unwitting effects of teachers, the print and electronic media, peers, and genetic influences. All agents of socialization affect development by administering reinforcements and punishments, by modeling modes of behavior that can be imitated, and by behaving in ways that affect the child's eagerness to conform to or be like the person concerned. We are increasingly aware, furthermore, that self-socialization is extremely important, as children choose which models to emulate and which behaviors to add to their repertoire in order to become more competent. These processes all complement one another over time. This makes it impossible to define *the* event or aspect of parental behavior that has a crucial effect. In the face of such extensive overdetermination, it is often hard to identify factors that necessarily make a difference, let alone satisfy factors that can be proven the necessary conditions for influences of one sort or another.

Because of the complexity of socialization, psychologists have progressed slowly in their understanding of it, but the progress is tangible. In the preceding pages, as well as in the readings that follow, we have tried to describe what we currently know about the processes involved in shaping personality as well as about the socialization agents associated with each of these processes. To illustrate the complementary and supplementary action of diverse agents and processes, we also focused on specific products of the socialization process. Clear gaps in our knowledge were evident quite often: these gaps constitute the agenda for future work in this area. Unfortunately, the complexity of socialization not only makes work in this area exciting and challenging, but also makes meaningful work difficult and progress slow.

References

Abelson, R. P. The psychological status of the script concept. *American Psychologist*, 1981, *36*, 715–29.

Aber, L. & Zigler, E. Developmental considerations in the definition of child maltreatment. In D. Cicchetti & R. Rizley, (Eds.), *New directions for child development*, San Francisco, Jossey Bass, 1981.

Aberle, D. F. Culture and socialization. In F. L. K. Hsu (Ed.), *Psychological anthropology: Approaches to culture and personality*. Homewood, Ill.: Dorsey, 1961.

Aberle, D. F. & Naegele, K. D. Middle-class fathers' occupational role and attitudes toward children. *American Journal of Orthopsychiatry*, 1952, *22*, 366–378.

Abt Associates. *Final report of the national day care study: Children at the center*. Washington, D.C.: U.S. Government Printing Office, 1979.

Achenbach, T. M. The classification of children's psychiatric symptoms: A factor-analytic study. *Psychological Monographs*, 1966, *80* (whole number 615).

Achenbach, T. M. *Developmental psychopathology*. New York: Ronald, 1974.

Achenbach, T. M. The role of taxonomy in developmental psychopathology. In M. E. Lamb & A. L. Brown (Eds.), *Advances in developmental psychology*, Vol. 1. Hillsdale, N.J.: Erlbaum, 1981.

Achenbach, T. M. & Edelbrock, C. A. The classification of child psychopathology: A review and analysis of empirical efforts. *Psychological Bulletin*, 1978, *85*, 1275–1301.

Achenbach, T. M. & Edelbrock, C. S. Behavioral problems and competencies reported by parents of normal and disturbed children aged 4–16. *Monographs of the Society for Research in Child Development*, 1980, *44* (whole number 185).

Achenbach, T. M. & Weisz, J. R. A longitudinal study of relations between outer-directedness and IQ changes in preschoolers. *Child Development*, 1975, *46*, 650–657.

Achenbach, T. M. & Zigler, E. F. Social competence and self-image disparity in psychiatric and nonpsychiatric patients. *Journal of Abnormal and Social Psychology*, 1963, *67*, 197–205.

Achenbach, T. M. & Zigler, E. F. Cue-learning and problem learning strategies in normal and retarded children. *Child Development*, 1968, *39*, 827–848.

Adams, D. Parent involvement, parent development. Berkeley, California, Center for the Study of Parent Involvement, 1976.

Ainsworth, M. D. S. *Infancy in Uganda*. Baltimore: Johns Hopkins University Press, 1967.

Ainsworth, M. D. S. The development of infant-mother attachment. In B. M. Caldwell,

& H. N. Ricciuti (Eds.), *Review of child development research*, Vol. 3. Chicago: University of Chicago Press, 1973.

Ainsworth, M. D. S., Bell, S. M., & Stayton, D. J. Infant-mother attachment and social development: 'Socialisation' as a product of reciprocal responsiveness to signals. In M. P. M. Richards (Ed.), *The integration of the child into a social world*. Cambridge, England: Cambridge University Press, 1974.

Ainsworth, M. D. S., Blehar, M., Waters, E., & Wall, S. N. *Patterns of attachment*. Hillsdale, N.J.: Erlbaum, 1978.

Ainsworth, M. D. S. & Wittig, B. A. Attachment and exploratory behavior of one-year-olds in a strange situation. In B. M. Foss (Ed.), *Determinants of infant behaviour*, Vol. 4. London: Methuen, 1969.

Allen, M. G. Childhood experience and adult personality: A cross-cultural study using the concept of ego strength. *Journal of Social Psychology*, 1967, *71*, 53–68.

Allport, G. W. *Becoming*. New Haven: Yale University Press, 1955.

Alper, T. G., Blane, H. T., & Abrams, B. K. Reactions of middle and lower class children to finger paints. *Journal of Abnormal and Social Psychology*, 1955, *51*, 439–448.

Alvy, K. T. Preventing child abuse. *American Psychologist*, 1975, *30*, 921–928.

Anastasi, A. Heredity, environment, and the question "how?" *Psychological Review*, 1958, *65*, 197–208.

Anderson, J. W. On the psychological attachment of infants to their mothers. *Journal of Biosocial Science*, 1972, *4*, 197–225.

Ardrey, R. *The territorial imperative*. New York: Atheneum, 1967.

Arend, R., Gove, F. L., & Sroufe, L. A. Continuity of individual adaptation from infancy to kindergarten: A predictive study of ego-resiliency and curiosity in preschoolers. *Child Development*, 1979, *50*, 950–959.

Armsby, R. E. A reexamination of the development of moral judgments in children. *Child Development*, 1971, *42*, 1242–1248.

Aronfreed, J. *Conduct and conscience*. New York: Academic, 1968.

Aronfreed, J. The concept of internalization. In D. A. Goslin (Ed.), *Handbook of socialization theory and research*. New York: Rand McNally, 1969.

Asher, S. R., Oden, S. L., & Gottman, J. M. Children's friendships in school settings. In L. G. Katz (Ed.), *Current topics in early childhood education*, Vol. 1. Norwood, N.J.: Ablex, 1977.

Bacon, M. K., Barry, H., III, & Child, I. L. A cross-cultural study of drinking: II. Relations to other features of culture. *Quarterly Journal of Studies on Alcohol*, 1965, *26*, Suppl. No. 3, 29–48.

Bacon, M. K., Child, I. L., & Barry, H., III. A cross-cultural study of correlates of crime. *Journal of Abnormal and Social Psychology*, 1963, *66*, 291–300.

Baker, J. P. & Christ, J. L. Teachers expectancies: A review of the literature. In J. D. Elashoff & R. E. Snow (Eds.), *Pygmalion reconsidered*. Worthington, Ohio: Charles A. Jones, 1971.

Baldwin, C. P. & Baldwin, A. L. Children's judgments of kindness. *Child Development*, 1970, *41*, 29–47.

Ball, S. & Bogatz, G. A. *The first year of Sesame Street: An evaluation*. Princeton, N.J.: Educational Testing Service, 1970.

Balla, D., Butterfield, E. C., & Zigler, E. F. Effects of institutionalization on retarded children: A longitudinal cross-institutional investigation. *American Journal of Mental Deficiency*, 1974, *78*, 530–549.

Balla, D., McCarthy, E., & Zigler, E. F. Some correlates of negative reaction tendencies in institutionalized retarded children. *Journal of Psychology*, 1971, *79*, 77–84.

Balla, D. & Zigler, E. F. Preinstitutional social deprivation and responsiveness to social reinforcement in institutionalized retarded individuals: A six-year follow-up study. *American Journal of Mental Deficiency*, 1975, *80*, 228–230.

Balla, D. & Zigler, E. F. Mental retardation. In A. E. Kazdin, A. S. Bellack, & M. Herzen (Eds.), *New perspectives in abnormal psychology*. New York: Oxford University Press, 1980.

Balla, D. & Zigler, E. F. Impact of institutional experience on the behavior and development of retarded persons. In E. F. Zigler & D. Balla, *Mental retardation: The developmental-difference controversy*. Hillsdale, N.J.: Erlbaum, 1982.

Bandura, A. Social learning through imitation. In M. R. Jones (Ed.), *Nebraska symposium on motivation*. Lincoln: University of Nebraska Press, 1962.

Bandura, A. Social learning theory of identificatory processes. In D. A. Goslin (Ed.), *Handbook of socialization theory and research.* Chicago: Rand McNally, 1969.

Bandura, A. *Aggression: A social learning analysis.* Englewood Cliffs, N.J.: Prentice-Hall, 1973.

Bandura, A. *Social learning theory.* Englewood Cliffs, N.J.: Prentice-Hall, 1977.

Bandura, A. & Huston, A. C. Identification as a process of incidental learning. *Journal of Abnormal and Social Psychology*, 1961, *63*, 311–318.

Bandura, A., Ross, D., & Ross, S. Transmission of aggression through imitation of aggressive models. *Journal of Abnormal and Social Psychology*, 1961, *63*, 575–582.

Bandura, A., Ross, D., & Ross, S. Imitation of film-mediated aggressive models. *Journal of Abnormal and Social Psychology*, 1963, *66*, 3–11.

Bandura, A. & Walters, R. H. *Adolescent aggression.* New York: Ronald, 1959.

Bandura, A. & Walters, R. H. *Social learning and personality development.* New York: Holt, Rinehart and Winston, 1963. (a)

Bandura, A. & Walters, R. H. *The social learning of deviant behavior: A behavioristic approach to socialization.* New York: Holt, Rinehart and Winston, 1963. (b)

Barash, D. P. *Sociobiology and behavior.* New York: Elsevier/North Holland, 1977.

Barber, T. X. Pitfalls in research: Nine investigator and experimenter effects. In R. M. W. Travers (Ed.), *Handbook of research on teaching* (2nd ed.). Chicago: Rand McNally, 1974.

Barber, T. X. & Silver, M. J. Fact, fiction, and the experimenter bias effect. *Psychological Bulletin*, 1968, *70*, 1–29.

Barron, F. Creative vision and expression in writing and painting. In *The creative person.* Berkeley Institute of Personality Assessment and Research, University of California, 1961.

Barry, H. III. Cultural variations in development of mental illness. In S. C. Plog & R. B. Edgerton (Eds.), *Changing perspectives in mental illness.* New York: Holt, Rinehart, and Winston, 1969.

Barry, H. III, Bacon, M. K., & Child, I. L. A cross-cultural survey of some sex differences in socialization. *Journal of Abnormal and Social Psychology*, 1957, *55*, 327–332.

Barry, H. III, Child, I. L., & Bacon, M. K. Relation of child training to subsistence economy. *American Anthropologist*, 1959, *61*, 51–63.

Baruch, G. K. & Barnett, R. *The competent woman.* New York: Irvington, 1978.

Baumrind, D. Current patterns of parental authority. *Developmental Psychology Monographs*, 1971, *1* (whole number 2).

Baumrind, D. *Early socialization and the discipline controversy.* Morristown, N.J.: General Learning Press, 1975.

Becker, W. C. Consequences of different kinds of parental discipline. In M. L. Hoffman & L. W. Hoffman (Eds.), *Review of child development research*, Vol. 1. New York: Russell Sage Foundation, 1964.

Bell, R. Q. A reinterpretation of the direction of effects in studies of socialization. *Psychological Review*, 1968, *75*, 81–95.

Bell, R. Q. & Harper, L. V. *Child effects on adults.* Hillsdale, N.J.: Erlbaum, 1977.

Bell, R. Q., Weller, G. M., & Waldrop, M. F. Newborn and preschooler: Organization of behavior and relations between periods. *Monographs of the Society for Research in Child Development*, 1971, *36* (whole number 142).

Bell, S. M. & Ainsworth, M. D. S. Infant crying and maternal responsiveness. *Child Development*, 1972, *43*, 1171–1190.

Belsky, J. Early human experience: A family perspective. *Developmental Psychology*, 1981, *17*, 3–28.

Belsky, J. & Steinberg, L. The effects of day care: A critical review. *Child Development*, 1978, *49*, 929–949.

Belsky, J., Steinberg, L., & Walker, A. The ecology of day care. In M. E. Lamb (Ed.), *Nontraditional families: Parenting and child development.* Hillsdale, N.J.: Erlbaum, 1982.

Berkowitz, L. Impulse, aggression, and the gun. *Psychology Today*, 1968, *2*, 18–22.

Berkowitz, L. Some determinants of impulsive aggression: Role of mediated associations with reinforcements for aggression. *Psychological Review*, 1974, *81*, 165–176.

Berkowitz, L. & Frodi, A. M. Reactions to a child's mistakes as affected by her/his looks and speech. *Social Psychology Quarterly*, 1979, *42*, 420–425.

Berkowitz, L. & LePage, A. Weapons as aggression-eliciting stimuli. *Journal of Personality and Social Psychology*, 1967, *7*, 202–207.

Berlyne, D. E. *Conflict, arousal, and curiosity.* New York: McGraw-Hill, 1960.

Berndt, T. J. The effect of reciprocity norms on

moral judgment and causal attribution. *Child Development*, 1977, *48*, 1322–1330.

Bernstein, B. Social class and linguistic development: A theory of social learning. In A. H. Halsey, J. Floud, & C. A. Anderson (Eds.), *Education, economy and society.* Glencoe, Ill.: Free Press, 1961.

Bijou, S. W. & Baer, D. M. *Child development,* Vol. 1. *A systematic and empirical theory.* New York: Appleton-Century-Crofts, 1961.

Bijou, S. W. & Baer, D. M. *Child development,* Vol. 2. *Universal stage of infancy.* New York: Appleton-Century-Crofts, 1963.

Biller, H. B. *Paternal deprivation: Family, school, sexuality and society.* Lexington, Mass.: Heath, 1974.

Biller, H. B. The father and personality development: Parental identification and sex-role development. In M. E. Lamb (Ed.), *The role of the father in child development.* New York: Wiley, 1976.

Biller, H. B. Father absence, divorce, and personality development. In M. E. Lamb (Ed.), *The role of the father in child development* (2d ed.). New York: Wiley, 1981.

Birns, B. The emergence and socialization of sex differences in the earliest years. *Merrill-Palmer Quarterly*, 1976, *22*, 229–254.

Birren, J. E. & Schaie, K. W. (Eds.). *Handbook of the psychology of aging.* New York: Van Nostrand-Reinhold, 1977.

Blanchard, M. & Main, M. Avoidance of the attachment figure and social-emotional adjustment in day-care infants. *Developmental Psychology*, 1979, *15*, 445–446.

Blatt, B. The Pariah industry: A diary from purgatory and other places. In G. Gerbner, C. Ross, & E. Zigler (Eds.), *Child abuse: An agenda for action.* New York: Oxford University Press, 1980.

Blehar, M. C. Anxious attachment and defensive reactions associated with day care. *Child Development*, 1974, *45*, 683–692.

Blehar, M. C., Lieberman, A. F., & Ainsworth, M. D. S. Early face-to-face interaction and its relation to later infant-mother attachment. *Child Development*, 1977, *48*, 182–194.

Block, J. H. Issues, problems, and pitfalls in assessing sex differences: A critical review of *The psychology of sex differences. Merrill-Palmer Quarterly*, 1976, *22*, 283–308.

Block, J. H. Another look at sex differentiation in the socialization behaviors of mothers and fathers. In F. Denmark (Ed.), *Psychology of women: Future directions for research.* New York: Psychological Dimensions, 1979.

Block, J. H. & Block, J. The role of ego-control and ego-resiliency in the organization of behavior. In W. A. Collins (Ed.), *Minnesota symposia on child psychology*, Vol. 11. Hillsdale, N. J.: Erlbaum, 1980.

Bloom, B. *Stability and change in human characteristics.* New York: Wiley, 1964.

Bloom-Feshbach, J. *The beginnings of fatherhood.* Unpublished doctoral dissertation. Yale University, 1979.

Bloom-Feshbach, S., Bloom-Feshbach, J., & Gaughran, J. The child's tie to both parents: Separation and nursery school adjustment. *American Journal of Orthopsychiatry*, 1980, *50*, 505–521.

Body, M. K. Patterns of aggression in the nursery school. *Child Development*, 1955, *26*, 3–12.

Borke, H. Interpersonal perception of young children: Egocentrism or empathy? *Developmental Psychology*, 1971, *5*, 263–269.

Borke, H. The development of empathy in Chinese and American children between three and six years of age: A cross-cultural study. *Developmental Psychology*, 1973, *9*, 102–108.

Bowers, K. S. Situationism in psychology: an analysis and critique. *Psychological Review*, 1973, *80*, 307–336.

Bowlby, J. *Maternal care and mental health.* Geneva: World Health Organization, 1951.

Bowlby, J. The nature of the child's tie to his mother. *International Journal of Psychoanalysis*, 1958, *39*, 350–373.

Bowlby, J. *Attachment and loss,* vol. 1. *Attachment.* New York: Basic Books, 1969.

Brim, O. G., Jr. Personality development as role-learning. In I. Iscoe, & H. W. Stevenson (Eds.), *Personality development in children.* Austin: University of Texas Press, 1960.

Brim, O. G., Jr. & Kagan, J. *Constancy and change in human development.* Cambridge, Mass.: Harvard University Press, 1980.

Brim, O. G., Jr. & Wheeler, S. *Socialization after childhood: Two essays.* New York: Wiley, 1966.

Bronfenbrenner, U. Socialization and social class through time and space. In E. Maccoby, T. Newcomb, & R. E. Hartley (Eds.), *Read-*

ings in social psychology (3d ed.). New York: Holt, 1958.

Bronfenbrenner, U. Freudian theories of identification and their derivatives. *Child Development*, 1960, *31*, 15–40.

Bronfenbrenner, U. The changing American child—a speculative analysis. *Journal of Social Issues*, 1961, *17*, 6–18.

Bronfenbrenner, U. *Is early intervention effective?* Washington, D.C.: U.S. Government Printing Office, 1974.

Bronfenbrenner, U. Research on the effects of day care. Unpublished manuscript, Cornell University, 1975. (a)

Bronfenbrenner, U. Social change: The challenge to research and policy. Paper presented to the Society for Research in Child Development, Denver, April, 1975. (b)

Bronfenbrenner, U. Toward an experimental ecology of human development. *American Psychology*, 1977, *32*, 513–531.

Bronfenbrenner, U. *The ecology of human development*. Cambridge, Mass.: Harvard University Press, 1979.

Brookhart, J. & Hock, E. The effects of experimental context and experiential background on infants' behavior toward their mothers and a stranger. *Child Development*, 1976, *47*, 333–340.

Bryan, J. H. Children's cooperation and helping behaviors. In E. M. Hetherington (Ed.), *Review of child development research*, Vol. 5. Chicago: University of Chicago Press, 1975.

Burchinal, L. G., Gardner, B., & Hawkes, G. R. Children's personality adjustment and the socioeconomic status in their families. *Journal of General Psychology*, 1958, *92*, 149–159.

Burgess, R. L. Child abuse: A social interactional analysis. In B. B. Lahey & A. E. Kazdin (Eds.), *Advances in clinical child psychology*, Vol. 2. New York: Plenum, 1979.

Burt, C. Intelligence and social mobility. *British Journal of Statistical Psychology*, 1961, *14*, 3–24.

Burton, R. W. Generality of honesty reconsidered. *Psychological Review*, 1963, *70*, 481–499.

Butterfield, E. C. & Zigler, E. F. The influence of differing institutional social climates on the effectiveness of social reinforcement in the mentally retarded. *American Journal of Mental Deficiency*, 1965, *70*, 48–56.

Caldwell, B. M. The effects of infant care. In

M. L. Hoffman & L. W. Hoffman (Eds.), *Review of child development research*, Vol. 1. New York: Russell Sage Foundation, 1964.

Caldwell, B. M., Wright, C. M., Honig, A. S., & Tannenbaum, J. Infant day care and attachment. *American Journal of Orthopsychiatry*, 1970, *40*, 397–412.

Campbell, D. T. The mutual methodological relevance of anthropology and psychology. In F. L. K. Hsu (Ed.), *Psychological anthropology: Approaches to culture and personality*. Homewood, Ill.: Dorsey, 1961.

Campbell, D. T., & Erlebacher, A. How regression artifacts in quasi-experimental evaluations can mistakenly make compensatory education look harmful. In J. Hellmuth (Ed.), *Disadvantaged child: III. Compensatory education: A national debate*. New York: Brunner/Mazel, 1970.

Campbell, F. & Ramey, C. T. The effects of early intervention on intellectual development. Paper presented to the Society for Research in Child Development, New Orleans, March 1977.

Caparulo, B. K. Mainstreaming and teachers' attitudes toward mainstreaming. Their influence on the behavior of mildly retarded children. Unpublished manuscript, 1980.

Chandler, M. J. & Greenspan, S. Ersatz egocentrism: A reply to H. Borke. *Developmental Psychology*, 1972, *7*, 104–106.

Chess, S., Thomas, A., & Birch, H. G. *Your child is a person*. New York: Viking, 1965.

Child, I. L. Socialization. In G. Lindzey (Ed.), *Handbook of social psychology*. Reading, Mass.: Addison-Wesley, 1954.

Child, I. L. Personality in culture. In W. W. Lambert & E. Borgatta (Eds.), *Handbook of personality theory and research*. Chicago: Rand McNally, 1967.

Christie, R. & Lindauer, F. Personality structure. *Annual Review of Psychology*, 1963, *14*, 201–207.

Clarke, A. M. & Clarke, A. D. B. *Early experience: Myth and evidence*. London: Open Books, 1976.

Clausen, J. A. American research on the family and socialization. *Children Today*, March–April, 1978, 7–10, 46.

Clausen, J. A. & Williams, J. R. Sociological correlates of child behavior. In *Child psychology*. Part 1. Chicago: National Society for the Study of Education, 1963.

Coates, B. & Pusser, H. E. Positive reinforcement and punishment in "Sesame Street" and "Mister Rogers' Neighborhood." *Journal of Broadcasting*, 1975, *19*, 143–151.

Coates, B., Pusser, H. E., & Goodman, I. The influence of "Sesame Street" and "Mister Rogers' Neighborhood" on children's social behavior in the preschool. *Child Development*, 1976, *47*, 138–144.

Cochran, M. A comparison of group day and family child-rearing patterns in Sweden. *Child Development*, 1977, *48*, 702–707.

Cohen, D. J. & Zigler, E. F. Federal day care standards: Rationale and recommendations. *American Journal of Orthopsychiatry*, 1977, *47*, 456–465.

Cole, M. & Bruner, J. S. Cultural differences and inferences about psychological processes. *American Psychologist*, 1971, *26*, 867–876.

Cole, M., Gay, J., Glick, J. A., & Sharp, D. W. *The cultural context of learning and thinking: An exploration in experimental anthropology.* New York: Basic Books, 1971.

Cole, M. & Scribner, S. *Culture and thought.* New York: Wiley, 1974.

Cole, N. S. Can we be neutral about bias. *Contemporary Psychology*, 1980, *25*, 868–871.

Coleman, J. S. et al. *Equality of educational opportunity.* Washington, D.C.: U.S. Government Printing Office, 1966.

Comstock, G. A. & Rubinstein, E. A. (Eds.), *Television and social behavior*, Vol. 1. *Media content and control.* Washington, D.C.: U.S. Government Printing Office, 1972. (a)

Comstock, G. A. & Rubinstein, E. A. (Eds.), *Television and social behavior*, Vol. 3. *Television and adolescent aggressiveness.* Washington, D.C.: U.S. Government Printing Office, 1972. (b)

Comstock, G. A., Rubinstein, E. A., & Murray, J. P. *Television and social behavior*, Vol. 5. *Television's effects: Further explorations.* Washington, D.C.: U.S. Government Printing Office, 1972.

Condry, J. G. & Condry, S. Sex differences: A study of the eye of the beholder. *Child Development*, 1976, *47*, 812–819.

Conger, J. J. *Adolescence and youth: Psychological development in a changing world* (2nd ed.). New York: Harper, 1977.

Conger, J. J. Adolescence: A time for becoming. In M. E. Lamb (Ed.), *Social and personality development.* New York: Holt, Rinehart and Winston, 1978.

Cromwell, R. L. A social learning approach to mental retardation. In N. R. Ellis (Ed.), *Handbook of mental deficiency.* New York: McGraw-Hill, 1963.

Curtis, G. Violence breeds violence. *American Journal of Psychiatry*, 1963, *120*, 386–387.

Dager, E. Z. Socialization and personality development in the child. In H. T. Christensen (Ed.), *Handbook of marriage and the family.* Chicago: Rand McNally, 1964.

Darlington, R. B., Royce, J. M., Snipper, A. S., Murray, W. H., & Lazar, I. Preschool programs and later school competence of children from low income families. *Science*, 1980, *208*, 202–204.

Datta, L. The impact of the Westinghouse/Ohio evaluation on the development of Project Head Start: An examination of the immediate and longer-term effects and how they came about. In C. C. Abt (Ed.), *The evaluation of social programs.* Beverly Hills, California: Sage, 1976.

Davies, D. *An overview of the status of citizen participation in educational decision making.* Washington Institute for Responsive Education and the Educator and Human Resources Development Division of Optimum Computer Systems, Inc., 1978.

Davis, A. American status systems and the socialization of the child. *American Sociological Review*, 1941, *6*, 234–254.

Davis, A. Socialization and adolescent personality. In *Adolescence.* Part 1. Chicago: National Society for the Study of Education, 1944.

Davis, A. Social-class influences upon mental problem-solving. In W. E. Martin & C. B. Stendler (Eds.), *Readings in child development.* New York: Harcourt, Brace, 1954.

Davis, A. & Havighurst, R. J. Social class and color differences in child-rearing. *American Sociological Review*, 1946, *11*, 698–710.

Dennis, W. A cross-cultural study of the reinforcement of child behavior. *Child Development*, 1957, *28*, 431–438.

Dennis, W. *Children of the creche.* New York: Appleton-Century-Crofts, 1973.

DePalma, D. J. & Foley, J. M. (Eds.), *Moral development: Current theory and research.* Hillsdale, N.J.: Erlbaum, 1975.

Deutsch, H. *The psychology of women*, Vol. 1. New York: Grune & Stratton, 1944.

Devereux, G. Two types of modal personality models. In B. Kaplan (Ed.), *Studying person-*

ality cross-culturally. Elmsford, N.Y.: Row, Peterson, 1961.

Disbrow, M., Doerr, H., & Caufield, C. *Measures to predict child abuse* (Project Report). Seattle: University of Washington, 1977.

Dollard, J., Doob, L. W., Miller, N. E., Mowrer, O. H., & Sears, R. R. *Frustration and aggression.* New Haven: Yale University Press, 1939.

Dollard, J. & Miller, N. *Social learning and imitation.* New Haven: Yale University Press, 1941.

Dollard, J. & Miller, N. E. *Personality and psychotherapy.* New York: McGraw-Hill, 1950.

Dominick, J. R. & Greenberg, B. S. Attitudes toward violence: The interaction of television exposure, family attitudes, and social class. In G. A. Comstock & E. A. Rubinstein (Eds.), *Television and social behavior,* Vol. 3: *Television and adolescent aggressiveness.* Washington, D.C.: U.S. Government Printing Office, 1972.

Dorow, L. G. The effects of teacher approval/disapproval ratios on student music selection behavior and concert attentiveness (Doctoral dissertation, Columbia University, 1973). *Dissertation Abstracts International,* 1973, *34,* 2157A–2158A (University Microfilms No. 73-25, 157).

Doyle, A. B. Infant development in day care. *Developmental Psychology,* 1975, *11,* 655–656.

Doyle, A. B. & Somers, K. The effects of group and family day care on infant attachment. *Canadian Journal of Behavioral Science,* 1978, *10,* 38–45.

Dugdale, R. *The Jukes: A study in crime, pauperism, disease, and heredity.* New York: Putnam, 1877.

Dunham, H. W. Methodology of sociological investigations of mental disorders. *International Journal of Social Psychiatry,* 1957, *3,* 7–17.

Duvall, E. M. Conceptions of parenthood. *American Journal of Sociology,* 1946, *52,* 193–203.

Dweck, C. S. The role of expectations and attributions in the alleviation of learned helplessness. *Journal of Personality and Social Psychology,* 1975, *31,* 674–685.

Dweck, C. S. Achievement. In M. E. Lamb (Ed.), *Social and personality development.* New York: Holt, Rinehart and Winston, 1978.

Dweck, C. S. & Bush, E. S. Sex differences in learned helplessness: I. Differential debilita-

tion with peer and adult evaluators. *Developmental Psychology,* 1976, *12,* 147–156.

Dweck, C. S., Davidson, W., Nelson, S., & Enna, B. Sex differences in learned helplessness: II. The contingencies of evaluative feedback in the classroom and III. An experimental analysis. *Developmental Psychology,* 1978, *14,* 268–276.

Dweck, C. S. & Gilliard, D. Expectancy statements as determinants of reactions to failure: Sex differences in persistence and expectancy change. *Journal of Personality and Social Psychology,* 1975, *32,* 1077–1084.

Dweck, C. S. & Reppucci, N. D. Learned helplessness and reinforcement responsibility in children. *Journal of Personality and Social Psychology,* 1973, *25,* 109–116.

Easterbrooks, M. A. & Lamb, M. E. The relationship between quality of infant-mother attachment and infant competence in initial encounters with peers. *Child Development,* 1979, *50,* 380–387.

Edwards, A. *The social desirability variable in personality assessment and research.* New York: Dryden, 1957.

Eells, K., Davis, A., Havighurst, R. J., Herrick, V. E., & Tyler, R. W. *Intelligence and cultural differences.* Chicago: University of Chicago Press, 1951.

Eisdorfer, C. & Lawton, M. P. (Eds.), *Psychology of adult development and aging.* Washington, D.C.: American Psychological Association, 1973.

Elashoff, J. D. & Snow, R. E. *Pygmalion reconsidered.* Worthington, Ohio: Charles A. Jones, 1971.

Elder, G. H., Jr. Structural variations in the child rearing relationship. *Sociometry,* 1962, *25,* 241–262.

Elkin, F. *The child and society.* New York: Random House, 1960.

Ellis, N. R. Memory processes in retardates and normals. In N. R. Ellis (Ed.), *International review of research in mental retardation,* Vol. 4. New York: Academic, 1970.

Elmer, E. *Children in jeopardy.* Pittsburgh: University of Pittsburgh Press, 1967.

Ember, C. R. Feminine task assignment and the social behavior of boys. *Ethos,* 1973, *1,* 424–439.

Endsley, R. C., Garner, A. R., Odom, A. H. & Martin, M. J. Interrelationships among selected maternal behaviors and preschool children's verbal and nonverbal curiosity behavior. Paper presented to the Society for Research in Child Development, Denver, April, 1975.

Erickson, E. H. *Childhood and society*. New York: Norton, 1950.

Erikson, E. H. *Childhood and society*. New York: Norton, 1963.

Eron, L. D., Huesmann, L. P., Lefkowitz, M. M., & Walder, L. O. Does television violence cause aggression? *American Psychologist*, 1972, *27*, 253–263.

Escalona, S. K. *The roots of individuality*. Chicago: Aldine, 1968.

Eysenck, H. J. *Race, intelligence, and education*. London: Temple Smith, 1971.

Fagot, B. I. Sex differences in toddlers' behavior and parental reaction. *Developmental Psychology*, 1974, *10*, 554–558.

Fagot, B. I. Teacher reinforcement of feminine-preferred behavior revisted. Paper presented to the Society for Research in Child Development, Denver, April, 1975.

Fagot, B. I. Consequences of moderate cross-gender behavior in pre-school children. *Child Development*, 1977, *48*, 902–907.

Fagot, B. I. & Patterson, G. R. An in vivo analysis of reinforcing contingencies for sex-role behavior in the preschool child. *Developmental Psychology*, 1969, *1*, 563–568.

Farber, I. E. Sane and insane: Constructions and misconstructions. *Journal of Abrnomal Psychology*, 1975, *84*, 589–620.

Farber, M. L. English and Americans: Values in the socialization process. *Journal of Psychology*, 1953, *36*, 243–250.

Farran, D. C. & Ramey, C. T. Infant day care and attachment behaviors toward mothers and teachers. *Child Development*, 1977, *48*, 1112–1116.

Fein, G. G. & Clarke-Stewart, K. A. *Day care in context*. New York: Wiley, 1973.

Feld, S. Need achievement and test anxiety in children and maternal attitudes and behaviors toward independent accomplishments: A longitudinal study. Paper presented to the American Psychological Association, Cincinnati, August, 1959.

Feldman, S. S. The impact of day care on one aspect of children's social-emotional behavior. Paper presented to the American Association for the Advancement of Science, San Francisco, February, 1974.

Feldman, S. S. & Nash, S. C. Interest in babies during young adulthood. *Child Development*, 1978, *49*, 617–622.

Feldman, S. S. & Nash, S. C. Understanding sex differences in responsiveness to babies among mature adults. *Developmental Psychology*, 1979, *15*, 430–435. (a)

Feldman, S. S. & Nash, S. C. Changes in responsiveness to babies during adolescence. *Child Development*, 1979, *50*, 942–949. (b)

Feldman, S. S., Nash, S. C., & Cutrona, C. The influence of age and sex on responsiveness to babies. *Developmental Psychology*, 1977, *13*, 675–676.

Feshbach, S. & Singer, R. D. *Television and aggression: An experimental field study*. San Francisco: Jossey-Bass, 1971.

Firestone, G. & Brody, N. Longitudinal investigation of teacher-student interactions and their relationship to academic performance. *Journal of Educational Psychology*, 1975, *67*, 544–550.

Fisher, M. A. & Zeamon, D. An attention-retention theory of retardate discrimination learning. In N. R. Ellis (Ed.), *International review of research in mental retardation*, Vol. 6. New York: Academic, 1973.

Flapan, D. *Children's understanding of social interaction*. New York: Teachers College Press, 1968.

Ford, M. The construct validity of egocentrism. *Psychological Bulletin*, 1979, *86*, 1169–1188.

Fossey, D. More years with mountain gorillas. *National Geographic*, 1971, *140*, 574–586.

Fox, N. Attachment of kibbutz infants to mother and metapelet. *Child Development*, 1977, *48*, 1228–1239.

Freedman, D. G. *Human infancy: An evolutionary perspective*. Hillsdale, N.J.: Erlbaum, 1974.

Freud, A. The mutual influences in the development of ego and id: Introduction to the discussion. *Psychoanalytic Study of the Child*, 1952, *7*, 42–50.

Freud, S. *An outline of psychoanalysis* (1940). New York: Norton, 1948.

Freud, S. Some psychological consequences of the anatomical distinction between the sexes. In *Collected papers*, Vol. 5. London: Hogarth, 1950.

Freud, S. Group psychology and the analysis of the ego (1921). In *The standard edition of the complete psychological works of Sigmund Freud*, Vol. 18. London: Hogarth, 1955.

Freud, S. *Three essays on the theory of sexuality* (1905). New York: Avon, 1962.

Frodi, A. M. & Lamb, M. E. Sex differences in responsiveness to infants: A developmental study of psychophysiological and behavioral responses. *Child Development*, 1978, *49*, 1182–1188.

Frodi, A. M. & Lamb, M. E. Child abusers' responses to infant smiles and cries. *Child Development*, 1980, *51*, 238–241.

Frodi, A. M., Lamb, M. E., Leavitt, L. A., & Donovan, W. L. Fathers' and mothers' responses to infant smiles and cries. *Infant Behavior and Development*, 1978, *1*, 187–198.

Frodi, A. M., Lamb, M. E., Leavitt, L. A., Donovan, W. L., Neff, C., & Sherry, D. Fathers' and mothers' responses to the faces and cries of normal and premature infants. *Developmental Psychology*, 1978, *14*, 490–498.

Frodi, A. M., Macauley, J., & Thome, P. R. Are women always less aggressive than men? A review of the experimental literature. *Psychological Bulletin*, 1977, *84*, 334–360.

Frye, D. The problem of infant day care. Unpublished manuscript, Bush Center for Social Policy Studies, Yale University, 1979.

Furrow, D., Gruendel, J., & Zigler, E. F. Protecting America's children from accidental injury and death: An overview of the problem and an agenda for action. Unpublished manuscript, 1979.

Gagnon, J. H. Scripts and the coordination of sexual conduct. *Nebraska Symposium on Motivation*, 1973, *21*, 27–81.

Garbarino, J. A. A preliminary study of some ecological correlates of child abuse: The impact of socioeconomic stress on mothers. *Child Development*, 1976, *47*, 178–185.

Garbarino, J. A. The human ecology of child maltreatment: A conceptual model for research. *Journal of Marriage and the Family*, 1977, *39*, 721–727.

Garbarino, J. & Sherman, D. High-risk neighborhoods and high risk families: The human ecology of child maltreatment. *Child Development*, 1980, *51*, 188–198.

Garvey, C. & Hogan, R. Social speech and social interaction. *Child Development*, 1973, *44*, 562–268.

Geertz, C. *The interpretation of cultures.* New York: Basic Books, 1973.

Gelles, R. A profile of violence toward children

in the United States. In G. Gerbner, C. Ross, & E. F. Zigler (Eds.), *Child abuse: An agenda for action.* New York: Oxford University Press, 1980.

Gerbner, G., Ross, C., & Zigler, E. F. (Eds.), *Child abuse: An agenda for action.* New York: Oxford University Press, 1980.

Gesell, A. *Infancy and human growth.* New York: Macmillan, 1928.

Gesell, A. Early evidences of individuality in the human infant. *Scientific Monthly*, 1937, *45*, 217–225.

Gesell, A. & Ilg, F. L. *Infant and child in the culture of today.* New York: Harper and Row, 1943.

Getzels, J. W. & Jackson, P. W. *Creativity and intelligence.* New York: Wiley, 1962.

Gewirtz, J. L. & Stingle, K. G. Learning of generalized imitation as the basis for identification. *Psychological Review*, 1968, *75*, 374–397.

Gil, D. G. Physical abuse of children: Findings and implications of a nationwide survey. *Pediatrics*, 1969, *44*, 857–864.

Gil, D. G. *Violence against children: Physical child abuse in the United States.* Cambridge, Mass.: Harvard University Press, 1970.

Gladwin, T. & Sarason, S. B. Culture and individual personality integration on Truk. In M. K. Opler (Ed.), *Culture and mental health.* New York: Macmillan, 1959.

Glick, P. C. Children of divorced parents in demographic perspective. *Journal of Social Issues*, 1979, *35*, 170–182.

Goddard, H. H. *The Kallikak family: A study in the heredity of feeblemindedness.* New York: Macmillan, 1912.

Goertzel, V. & Goertzel, M. G. *Cradles of eminence.* Boston: Little, Brown, 1962.

Gold, M. Suicide, homicide, and the socialization of aggression. *American Journal of Sociology*, 1958, *63*, 651–661.

Gold, M. J. *Education of the intellectually gifted.* Columbus: Merrill, 1965.

Goodall, J. Chimpanzees of the Gombe Stream Reserve. In I. DeVore (Ed.), *Primate behavior: Field studies of monkeys and apes.* New York: Holt, Rinehart, and Winston, 1965.

Goodenough, E. W. Interest in persons as an aspect of sex differences in the early years. *Genetic Psychology Monographs*, 1957, *55*, 287–323.

Gottesman, I. I. Personality and natural selection. In S. G. Vandenberg (Ed.), *Methods and goals in human behavior genetics*. New York: Academic, 1965.

Gottesman, I. I. & Shields, J. *Schizophrenia and genetics*. New York: Academic, 1972.

Goulet, L. R. & Baltes, P. B. (Eds.), *Life-span developmental psychology: Research and theory*. New York: Academic, 1970.

Graham, R. & Rutter, M. Psychiatric disorder in the young adolescent: A follow-up study. *Proceedings of the Royal Society of Medicine*, 1973, *66*, 1226–1229.

Grant, V. W. *Great abnormals*. New York: Hawthorn, 1968.

Green, A. W. Middle-class male child and neurosis. *American Sociological Review*, 1946, *11*, 31–41.

Greif, E. B. The father's role in moral development. In M. E. Lamb (Ed.), *The role of the father in child development*. New York: Wiley, 1976.

Gruen, G., Ottinger, D., & Ollendick, T. Probability learning in retarded children with differing histories of success and failure in school. *American Journal of Mental Deficiency*, 1974, *79*, 417–423.

Gruen, G. & Zigler, E. F. Expectancy of success and the probability learning of middle-class, lower-class, and retarded children. *Journal of Abnormal Psychology*, 1968, *73*, 343–352.

Guilford, J. P. *Intelligence, creativity, and their educational implications*. San Diego: Knapp, 1968.

Haggard, E. A. Social-status and intelligence: An experimental study of certain cultural determinants of measured intelligence. *Genetic Psychology Monographs*, 1954, *49*, 141–186.

Hall, C. S. & Lindsay, G. *Theories of personality* (3rd ed.), New York: Wiley, 1978.

Harlow, H. F. Mice, monkeys, men, and motives. *Psychological Review*, 1953, *60*, 23–32.

Harlow, H. F. & Mears, C. The nature of complex, unlearned responses. In M. Lewis & L. A. Rosenblum (Eds.), *The development of affect*. New York: Plenum, 1978.

Harlow, H. F. & Zimmerman, R. R. Affectional responses in the infant monkey. *Science*, 1959, *130*, 421.

Harter, S. & Zigler, E. F. The assessment of effectance motivation in normal and retarded children. *Developmental Psychology*, 1974, *10*, 169–180.

Hartmann, H. Mutual influences in the development of ego and id. *Psychoanalytic Study of the Child*, 1952, *7*, 9–30.

Hartmann, H. Ego psychology and the problem of adaptation (tr. D. Rapaport). New York: International Universities Press, 1958.

Hartshorne, H. & May, M. A. *Studies in the nature of character*, Vol. 1. *Studies in deceit*. New York: Macmillan, 1928.

Hartshorne, H., May, M. A., & Maller, J. B. *Studies in the nature of character*, Vol. 2. *Studies in self-control*. New York: Macmillan, 1930.

Hartup, W. W. Peer interaction and social organization. In P. H. Mussen (Ed.), *Carmichael's manual of child psychology*, Vol. 2 (3d ed.). New York: Wiley, 1970.

Hartup, W. W. Peer interaction and the behavioral development of the individual child. In E. Schopler & R. J. Reichler (Eds.), *Psychopathology and child development*. New York: Plenum, 1976.

Hartup, W. W. Peer interaction and the processes of socialization. In M. J. Guralnick (Ed.), *Early intervention and the integration of handicapped and nonhandicapped children*. Baltimore: University Park Press, 1977.

Hartup, W. W. Two social worlds: family relations and peer relations. In M. Rutter (Ed.), *Scientific foundations of developmental psychiatry*. London: Heinemann, 1980.

Havighurst, R. J. Minority subcultures and the law of effect. *American Psychologist*, 1970, *25*, 313–322.

Havighurst, R. J. & Davis, A. A comparison of the Chicago and Harvard studies of social class differences in child rearing. *American Sociological Review*, 1955, *20*, 438–442.

Head Start in the 1980s: Review and Recommendations. Report requested by the President of the United States. September, 1980.

Heath, D. H. High undergraduate achievers found less competent as adults. *Behavior Today*, 1977, *8*, 5.

Heider, F. *The psychology of interpersonal relations*. New York: Wiley, 1958.

Heilbrun, A. B. An empirical test of the modelling theory of sex-role learning. *Child Development*, 1965, *36*, 789–799.

Henry, A. F. & Short, J. F. *Suicide and homicide: Some economic, sociological and psychological aspects of aggression*. New York: Free Press, 1954.

Herrnstein, R. J. IQ. *Atlantic Monthly*, 1971, *228*, 43–64.

Herrnstein, R. J. *IQ in the meritocracy*. Boston: Little-Brown, 1973.

Hersch, C. The cognitive functioning of the creative person: A developmental analysis. *Journal of Projective Techniques*, 1962, *20*, 193–200.

Herzog, E. & Sudia, C. Children in fatherless families. In B. M. Caldwell & H. N. Ricciuti (Eds.), *Review of child development research*, Vol. 3. Chicago: University of Chicago Press, 1973.

Hess, R. D. Social class and ethnic influences upon socialization. In P. H. Mussen (Ed.), *Carmichael's manual of child psychology*, Vol. 2, (3d ed.). New York: Wiley, 1970.

Hess, R. D. & Camara, K. A. Post-divorce family relationships as mediating factors in the consequences of divorce for children. *Journal of Social Issues*, 1979, *35*, 79–96.

Hess, R. D. & Shipman, V. C. Early experience and the socialization of cognitive modes in children. *Child Development*, 1965, *34*, 869–886.

Hetherington, EM. M. A developmental study of the effects of sex of the dominant parent on sex-role preference, identification, and imitation in children. *Journal of Personality and Social Psychology*, 1965, *2*, 188–194.

Hetherington, E. M. Effects of father-absence on personality development in adolescent daughters. *Developmental Psychology*, 1972, *7*, 313–326.

Hetherington, E. M., Cox, M., & Cox, R. Divorced fathers. *Family Coordinator*, 1976, *25*, 417–428.

Hetherington, E. M., Cox, M., & Cox, R. Family interactions and the social, emotional, and cognitive development of children following divorce. In V. C. Vaughn & T. B. Brazelton (Eds.), *The family: setting priorities*. New York: Science and Medicine Publishers, 1979.

Hetherington, E. M., Cox, M., & Cox, R. The effects of divorce. In M. E. Lamb (Ed.), *Nontraditional families: Parenting and child development*. Hillsdale, N.J.: Erlbaum, 1982.

Hetherington, E. M. & Deur, J. L. The effects of father absence on child development. *Young Children*, 1971, *26*, 233–248.

Hetherington, E. M. & Frankie, G. Effects of parental dominance, warmth, and conflict on imitation in children. *Journal of Personality and Social Psychology*, 1967, *6*, 119–125.

Hinde, R. A. *Biological bases of human social behavior*. New York: McGraw-Hill, 1974.

Hinde, R. A. & Stevenson-Hinde, J. (Eds.), *Constraints on learning*. New York: Academic, 1973.

Hoffman, L. W. Effects of maternal employment on the child: A review of the research. *Developmental Psychology*, 1974, *10*, 204–228.

Hoffman, L. W. Changes in family roles, socialization, and sex differences. *American Psychologist*, 1977, *32*, 644–657.

Hoffman, L. W. Maternal employment: 1979. *American Psychologist*, 1979, *34*, 859–865.

Hoffman, M. L. Power assertion by the parent and its impact on the child. *Child Development*, 1960, *31*, 129–143.

Hoffman, M. L. Conscience, personality, and socialization techniques. *Human Development*, 1970, *13*, 90–126. (a)

Hoffman, M. L. Moral development. In P. H. Mussen (Ed.), *Carmichael's manual of child psychology*, Vol. 2 (3d ed.). New York: Wiley, 1970 (b).

Hoffman, M. L. The role of the father in moral internalization. In M. E. Lamb (Ed.), *The role of the father in child development* (2d ed.). New York: Wiley, 1981.

Hoffman, M. L., Mitsos, S. B., & Protz, R. E. Achievement striving, social class and test anxiety. *Journal of Abnormal and Social Psychology*, 1958, *56*, 401–403.

Hoffman, M. L. & Saltzstein, H. D. Parent discipline and the child's moral development. *Journal of Personality and Social Psychology*, 1967, *5*, 45–57.

Hollingworth, L. S. *Children above 180 IQ*. New York: Harcourt, Brace and World, 1942.

Honigmann, J. J. *Culture and personality*. New York: Harper, 1954.

Honigmann, J. J. North America. In F. L. K. Hsu (Ed.), *Psychological anthropology: Approaches to culture and personality*. Homewood, Ill.: Dorsey, 1961.

Hsu, F. L. K. Psychological anthropology in the behavioral sciences. In F. L. K. Hsu (Ed.), *Psychological anthropology: Approaches to culture and personality*. Homewood, Ill.: Dorsey, 1961.

Hull, C. L. *Principles of behavior*. New York: Appleton-Century-Crofts, 1943.

Hull, C. L. *Essentials of behavior*. New Haven: Yale University Press, 1951.

Hull, C. L. *A behavior system: An introduction to behavior theory concerning the individual organism.* New Haven: Yale University Press, 1952.

Hurt, M., Jr. *Child abuse and neglect: A report on the status of the research.* Washington, D.C.: U.S. Government Printing Office, 1975. U.S. Dept. of Health, Education, and Welfare Pub. No. (OHD), 74-20.

Hymes, J. Child care problems of the night shift mother. *Journal of Consulting Psychology,* 1944, 225–228.

Inkeles, A. National character and modern political systems. In F. L. K. Hsu (Ed.), *Psychological anthropology: Approaches to culture and personality.* Homewood, Ill.: Dorsey, 1961.

Inkeles, A. & Levinson, D. J. National character: The study of modal personality and socio-cultural systems. In G. Lindzey (Ed.), *Handbook of social psychology.* Reading, Mass.: Addison-Wesley, 1954.

Irwin, D. M. & Ambron, S. R. Moral judgement and role-taking in children aged three to seven. Paper presented to the Society for Research in Child Development, Philadelphia, March, 1973.

Isaacs, J. T. Frequency curves and the ability of nations. British *Journal of Statistical Psychology,* 1962, *15,* 76–79.

Jencks, C. et al. *Inequality: A reassessment of the effect of family and schooling in America.* New York: Basic Books, 1972.

Jensen, A. R. How much can we boost IQ and scholastic achievement? *Harvard Educational Review,* 1969, *39,* 1–123.

Jensen, A. R. *Educability and group differences.* New York: Harper and Row, 1973.

Jensen, A. R. *Bias in mental testing.* New York: Free Press, 1980.

Johnson, M. M. Sex role learning in the nuclear family. *Child Development,* 1963, *34,* 315–333.

Jolly, A. The study of primate infancy. In K. J. Connolly & J. S. Bruner (Eds.), *The growth of competence.* New York: Academic, 1973.

Jones, M. C. The elimination of children's fears. *Journal of Experimental Psychology,* 1924, *7,* 382–390.

Jones, M. C. The later careers of boys who were early- or late maturing. *Child Development,* 1957, *28,* 113–128.

Jones, M. C. Psychological correlates of somatic development. *Child Development,* 1965, *36,* 899–916.

Jones, M. C., Bayley, N., MacFarlane, J. W., & Honzik, M. P. (Eds.), *The course of human development.* Waltham, Mass.: Xerox Publishing, 1971.

Jones, M. C. & Mussen, P. H. Self-conceptions, motivations, and interpersonal attitudes of early- and late-maturing girls. *Child Development,* 1958, *29,* 491–502.

Juvenile Justice Standards Project. *Standards relating to abuse and neglect.* Cambridge, Mass.: Ballinger, 1977.

Kagan, J. The beneficiaries of change. Paper presented at Symposium on Crises on Our Conscience, Washington, D.C.: October, 1971.

Kagan, J., Kearsley, R. B., & Zelazo, P. R. *Infancy: Its place in human development.* Cambridge, Mass.: Harvard University Press, 1978.

Kagan, J. & Klein, R. E. Cross-cultural perspectives on early development. *American Psychologist,* 1973, *28,* 947–961.

Kagan, J. & Moss, H. A. *Birth to maturity.* New York: Wiley, 1962.

Kamerman, S. & Kahn, A. (Eds.), *Family policy: Government and families in 14 countries.* New York: Columbia University Press, 1978.

Kamin, L. J. *The science and politics of IQ.* Hillsdale, N.J.: Erlbaum, 1974.

Kardiner, A. *The individual and his society.* New York: Columbia University Press, 1939.

Kardiner, A. *The psychological frontiers of society.* New York: Columbia University Press, 1945.

Katz, P. & Zigler, E. F. Self-image disparity: A developmental approach. *Journal of Personality and Social Psychology,* 1967, *5,* 186–195.

Kelley, H. H. The process of causal attribution. *American Psychologist,* 1973, *28,* 107–128.

Kempe, C. H., Silverman, F. N., Steele, B. B., Droegemueller, W., & Silver, H. K. The battered-child syndrome. *Journal of the American Medical Association,* 1962, *181,* 17–24.

Keniston, K. & The Carnegie Council on Children. *All our children.* New York: Harcourt, Brace, Jovanovitch, 1977.

Kessen, W. Research in the psychological development of infants: An overview. *Merrill-Palmer Quarterly,* 1963, *9,* 83–94.

Kessen, W. *The child.* New York: Wiley, 1965.

Keyserling, M. D. *Windows on day care.* New York: National Council of Jewish Women, 1972.

King, M. The development of some intention

concepts in young children. *Child Development*, 1971, *42*, 1145–1152.

Klatskin, E. H. Shifts in child care practices in three social classes: Under an infant care program of flexible methodology. *American Journal of Orthopsychiatry*, 1952, *22*, 52–61.

Klatskin, E. H., Jackson, E. B., & Wilkin, L. C. The influence of degree of flexibility in maternal child care practices on early child behavior. *American Journal of Orthopsychiatry*, 1956, *26*, 79–93.

Klaus, M., Jerauld, R., Kreger, N. C., McAlpine, W., Steffa, M., & Kennell, J. H. Maternal attachment: Importance of the first postpartum days. *New England Journal of Medicine*, 1972, *286*, 460–463.

Klaus, M. & Kennell, J. *Maternal-infant bonding*. St. Louis: Mosby, 1976.

Kluckhohn, C. Culture and behavior. In G. Lindzey (Ed.), *Handbook of social psychology*. Reading, Mass.: Addison-Wesley, 1954.

Kohlberg, L. The development of modes of moral thinking and choice in the years 10 to 16. Unpublished doctoral dissertation, University of Chicago, 1958.

Kohlberg, L. Moral development and identification. In H. W. Stevenson (Ed.), *Child psychology: 62nd yearbook of the National Society for the Study of Education*. Chicago: University of Chicago Press, 1963.

Kohlberg, L. Sex differences in morality. In E. E. Maccoby (Ed.), *The development of sex differences*. Stanford: Stanford University Press, 1966.

Kohlberg, L. Stage and sequence: The cognitive-developmental approach to socialization. In D. A. Goslin (Ed.), *Handbook of socialization theory and research*. Chicago: Rand McNally, 1969.

Kohlberg, L. Moral stages and moralization: The cognitive developmental approach. In T. Lickona (Ed.), *Moral development and behavior: Theory, research, and social issues*. New York: Holt, Rinehart and Winston, 1976.

Kohlberg, L. & Zigler, E. F. The impact of cognitive maturity on the development of sex-role attitudes in the years four to eight. *Genetic Psychology Monographs*, 1967, *75*, 89–165.

Kohn, M. L. Social class and the exercise of parental authority. *American Sociological Review*, 1959, *24*, 352–366. (a)

Kohn, M. L. Social class and parental values. *American Journal of Sociology*, 1959, *64*, 337–351. (b)

Kohn, M. L. *Class and conformity: A study in values*. Homewood, Ill.: Dorsey, 1969.

Kohn, M. L. Social class and parental values: Another confirmation of the relationship. *American Sociological Review*, 1976, *41*, 538–545.

Kohn, M. L. The effects of social class on parental values and practices. In D. Reiss & H. A. Hoffman (Eds.), *The American family: Dying or developing?* New York: Plenum, 1979.

Kohn, M. L. & Carroll, E. E. Social class and the allocation of parental responsibilities. *Sociometry*, 1960, *23*, 372–392.

Korner, A. F. & Thoman, E. B. Visual alertness in neonates as evoked by maternal care. *Journal of Experimental Child Psychology*, 1970, *10*, 67–78.

Korner, A. F. & Thoman, E. B. The relative efficacy of contact and vestibular-proprioceptive stimulation in soothing neonates. *Child Development*, 1972, *43*, 443–453.

Kounin, J. Experimental studies of rigidity. I. The measurement of rigidity in normal and feeble minded persons. *Character and Personality*, 1941, *9*, 251–272. (a)

Kounin, J. Experimental studies of rigidity. II. The explanatory power of the concept of rigidity as applied to feeble mindedness. *Character and Personality*, 1941, *9*, 273–282. (b)

Kris, E. Notes on development and on some current problems of psychoanalytic child psychology. *Psychoanalytic Study of the Child*, 1950, *5*, 34–62.

Kurtines, W. & Greif, E. B. The development of moral thought: Review and evaluation of Kohlberg's approach. *Psychological Bulletin*, 1974, *81*, 453–470.

Laboratory of Comparative Human Cognition. Cross-cultural psychology's challenges to our ideas of children and development. *American Psychologist*, 1979, *34*, 827–833.

Lamb, M. E. The role of the father: An overview. In M. E. Lamb (Ed.), *The role of the father in child development*. New York: Wiley, 1976.

Lamb, M. E. The development of mother-infant and father-infant attachments in the second year of life. *Developmental Psychology*, 1977, *13*, 637–648. (a)

Lamb, M. E. Father-infant and mother-infant interaction in the first year of life. *Child Development*, 1977, *48*, 167–181. (b)

Lamb, M. E. The influence of the child on marital quality and family interaction during the prenatal, paranatal, and infancy periods. In R. M. Lerner & G. B. Spanier (Eds.), *Child influences on marital and family interaction: A lifespan perspective.* New York: Academic, 1978. (a)

Lamb, M. E. Psychosocial development: A theoretical overview and a look into the future. In M. E. Lamb (Eds.), *Social and personality development.* New York: Holt, Rinehart and Winston, 1978. (b)

Lamb, M. E. Paternal influences and the father's role: A personal perspective. *American Psychologist*, 1979, *34*, 938–943.

Lamb, M. E. The development of parent-infant attachments in the first two years of life. In F. A. Pedersen (Ed.), *The father-infant-relationship: Observational studies in a family setting.* New York: Praeger, 1980.

Lamb, M. E. The development of social expectations in the first year of life. In M. E. Lamb & L. R. Sherrod (Eds.), *Infant social cognition: Empirical and theoretical considerations.* Hillsdale, N.J.: Erlbaum, 1981. (a)

Lamb, M. E. Developing trust and perceived effectance in infancy. In L. P. Lipsitt (Ed.), *Advances in infancy research*, Vol. 1. Norwood, N.J.: Ablex, 1981. (b)

Lamb, M. E. Paternal influence on child development: An overview. In M. E. Lamb (Ed.), *The role of the father in child development* (2d ed.). New York: Wiley, 1981. (c)

Lamb, M. E. On the familial origins of personality and social style. In L. Laosa & I. Sigel (Eds.), *The family as a learning environment.* New York: Plenum, 1982. (a)

Lamb, M. E. The origins of individual differences in infant sociability and their implications for cognitive development. In H. W. Reese & L. R. Lipsitt (Eds.), *Advances in child development and behavior*, Vol. 16. New York: Academic, 1982. (b)

Lamb, M. E. & Baumrind, D. Socialization and personality development in the preschool years. In M. E. Lamb (Ed.), *Social and personality development.* New York: Holt, Rinehart and Winston, 1978.

Lamb, M. E. & Campos, J. J. *Development in infancy: An introduction.* New York: Random House, 1982.

Lamb, M. E. & Easterbrooks, M. A. Individual differences in parental sensitivity: Origins, components, and consequences. In M. E. Lamb & L. R. Sherrod (Eds.), *Infant social cognition: Empirical and theoretical considerations.* Hillsdale, N.J.: Erlbaum, 1981.

Lamb, M. E., Easterbrooks, M. A., & Holden, G. W. Reinforcement and punishment among preschoolers: Characteristics, effects, and correlates. *Child Development*, 1980, *51*, 1230–1236.

Lamb, M. E., & Hwang, C.-P. Maternal attachment and mother-infant bonding: A critical review. In M. E. Lamb & A. L. Brown (Eds.), *Advances in developmental psychology*, Vol. 2. Hillsdale, N.J.: Erlbaum, 1982.

Lamb, M. E. & Lamb, J. E. The nature and importance of the father-infant relationship. *Family Coordinator*, 1976, *25*, 379–385.

Lamb, M. E. & Roopnarine, J. L. Peer influences on sex-role development in preschoolers. *Child Development*, 1979, *50*, 1219–1222.

Lamb, M. E. & Urberg, K. A. The development of gender role and gender identity. In M. E. Lamb (Ed.), *Social and personality development.* New York: Holt, Rinehart and Winston, 1978.

Lange-Eichbaum, W. *The problem of genius* (E. & C. Paul, trans.). New York: Macmillan, 1932.

Langlois, J. H. & Downs, A. C. Mothers, fathers, and peers as socialization agent of sex-typed play behaviors in young children. *Child Development*, 1980, *51*, 1237–1247.

Lasting effects after preschool. A report of the Consortium for Longitudinal Studies under the supervision of Irving Lazar and Richard B. Darlington, October, 1978. DHEW Publication No. (OHDS) 79-30178.

Lefcourt, H. *Locus of control: Current trends in theory and research.* Hillsdale, N.J.: Erlbaum, 1976.

Lefkowitz, M., Eron, L., Walder, L., & Huesmann, L. R. *Growing up to be violent.* New York: Pergamon, 1977.

Leiderman, P. H. The critical period hypothesis revisited. In F. D. Horowitz (Ed.), *Early developmental hazards: Prediction and precautions.* Boulder: Westview Press, 1978.

Lesser, G. *Children and television: Lessons from*

"Sesame Street." New York: Vintage Books, 1974.

Levine, J. *And who will raise the children?* Philadelphia: Lippincott, 1976.

Lewin, K. *A dynamic theory of personality.* New York: McGraw-Hill, 1936.

Lewis, M. Parents and children: Sex role development. *School Review,* 1972, *80,* 229–240. (a)

Lewis, M. State as an infant-environment interaction: An analysis of mother-infant interaction as a function of sex. *Merrill-Palmer Quarterly,* 1972, *18,* 95–121. (b)

Lewis, M. Early sex differences in the human: Studies of socioemotional development. *Archives of Sexual Behavior,* 1975, *4,* 329–335.

Lewis, M. & Rosenblum, L. A. (Eds.), *The effect of the infant on its caregiver.* New York: Wiley, 1974.

Ley, R. G. & Koepke, J. E. Sex and age differences in the departures of young children from their mothers. Paper presented to the Society for Research in Child Development, Denver, April, 1975.

Lickona, T. (Ed.), *Moral development and behavior: Theory, research, and social issues.* New York: Holt, Rinehart and Winston, 1976.

Lightfoot, S. L. *Worlds apart relationships between families and schools.* New York: Basic Books, 1978.

Linton, R. Marquesan culture. In A. Kardiner (Ed.), *The individual and his society.* New York: Columbia University Press, 1939.

Littman, R. A., Moore, R. C. A., & Pierce-Jones, J. Social class differences in child-rearing: A third community for comparison with Chicago and Newton. *American Sociological Review,* 1957, *22,* 694–704.

Livesley, W. J. & Bromley, D. B. *Person perception in childhood and adolescence.* London: Wiley, 1973.

Locke, J. *Some thoughts concerning education.* London: Churchill, 1693.

Lombroso, C. *The man of genius.* London: Walter Scott, 1891.

Lopate, C., Flaxman, E., Bynum, E., & Gordon, E. *Some effects of parent and community participation on public education.* New York: E.R.I.C. Clearinghouse of the Urban Disadvantaged, Teachers College, Columbia University, 1969.

Lorenz, K. *On aggression.* New York: Harcourt, Brace, 1966.

Luria, A. R. Psychological studies of mental deficiency in the Soviet Union. In N. R. Ellis (Ed.), *Handbook of mental deficiency.* New York: McGraw-Hill, 1963.

Lyle, J. & Hoffman, H. R. Children's use of television and other media. In E. A. Rubinstein, G. A. Comstock, & J. P. Murray (Eds.), *Television and social behavior,* Vol. 4. *Television in day-to-day life: Patterns of use.* Washington, D.C.: U.S. Government Printing Office, 1972.

Maas, H. S. Some social class differences in the family systems and group relations of pre- and early adolescents. *Child Development,* 1951, *22,* 145–152.

Maas, H. S. The role of member in clubs of lower-class and middle-class adolescents. *Child Development,* 1954, *25,* 241–252.

Maccoby, E. E. & Feldman, S. S. Mother-attachment and stranger-reactions in the third year of life. *Monographs of the Society for Research in Child Development,* 1972, *37* (whole number 146).

Maccoby, E. E. & Gibbs, P. K. Methods of child rearing in two social classes. In W. E. Martin & C. B. Stendler (Eds.), *Readings in child development.* New York: Harcourt, 1954.

Maccoby, E. E. & Jacklin, C. N. *The psychology of sex differences.* Stanford: Stanford University Press, 1974.

Maccoby, E. E. & Wilson, W. C. Identification and observational learning from films. *Journal of Abnormal and Social Psychology,* 1958, *55,* 76–87.

MacMillan, D. L. Motivational differences: Cultural-familial retardates vs normal subjects on expectancy for failure. *American Journal of Mental Deficiency,* 1969, *74,* 254–258.

MacMillan, D. L. & Keogh, B. K. Normal and retarded children's expectancy for failure. *Developmental Psychology,* 1971, *4,* 343–348.

Mahler, M. *On human symbiosis and the vicissitudes of individuation.* New York: International Universities Press, 1969.

Main, M. Exploration, play and cognitive functioning as related to child-mother attachment. Unpublished doctoral dissertation, Johns Hopkins University, 1973.

Mann, D. *Ten years of decentralization: A review of the urban communities in school decision making.* New York: Institute for Urban and Minority Education, Columbia University, 1975.

Marlowe, D. & Crowne, D. Social desirability and response to perceived situational demands. *Journal of Consulting Psychology*, 1961, *25*, 109–115.

Martin, B. Parent-child relations. In F. D. Horowitz (Ed.), *Review of child development research*, Vol. 4. Chicago: University of Chicago Press, 1975.

Maslow, A. H. *Motivation and personality*. New York: Harper, 1954.

Matas, L., Arend, R. A., & Sroufe, L. A. Continuity of adaptation in the second year: The relationship between quality of attachment and later competence. *Child Development*, 1978, *49*, 547–556.

Matheny, A. P. Bayley's Infant Behavior Record: Behavioral components and twin analyses. *Child Development*, 1980, *51*, 1157–1167.

Matteson, D. *Adolescence today*. Homewood, Ill.: Dorsey, 1975.

Maurer, A. Corporal punishment. *American Psychologist*, 1974, *29*, 614–626.

McClelland, D. C., Atkinson, J. W., Clark, R. A., & Lowell, E. L. *The achievement motive*. New York: Appleton-Century-Crofts, 1953.

McClelland, D. C. & Friedman, G. A. A cross-cultural study of the relationship between child-training practices and achievement motivation appearing in folk tales. In G. E. Swanson, T. M. Newcomb, & E. H. Hartley (Eds.), *Readings in social psychology*. New York: Holt, 1952.

McCormick, M., Balla, D., & Zigler, E. F. Resident-care practices in institutions for retarded persons: A cross-institutional, cross-cultural study. *American Journal of Mental Deficiency*, 1975, 80, 1–17.

McKee, J. P. & Leader, F. The relationship of socioeconomic status and aggression to the competitive behavior of preschool children. *Child Development*, 1955, *26*, 135–142.

McKinnon, D. W. Creativity. In *The international encyclopedia of the social sciences*, Vol. 3. New York: Macmillan and The Free Press, 1968.

McNemar, W. Lost: Our intelligence? Why? *American Psychologist*, 1964, *19*, 871–882.

Mead, M. *Male and female*. New York: Morrow, 1949.

Medinnus, G. R. & Johnson, R. C. *Child and adolescent psychology: Behavior and development*. New York: Wiley, 1969.

Meehl, P. E. Schizotaxia, schizotypy, schizophrenia. *American Psychologist*, 1962, *17*, 827–838.

Miller, D. R. & Swanson, G. E. The study of conflict. In M. R. Jones (Ed.), *Nebraska symposium on motivation*, 1956. Lincoln: University of Nebraska Press, 1956.

Miller, D. R. & Swanson, G. E. *The changing American parent*. New York: Wiley, 1958.

Miller, D. R. & Swanson, G. E. *Inner conflict and defense*. New York: Holt, 1960.

Miller, E. A. A study of the relationships between reading readiness in grade one school children and patterns of parent-child interaction. *Child Development*, 1951, *22*, 95–112.

Miller, N. E. & Dollard, J. *Social learning and imitation*. New Haven: Yale University Press, 1941.

Minturn, L. & Lambert, W. W. *Mothers of six cultures*. New York: Wiley, 1964.

Mischel, W. Continuity and change in personality. *American Psychologist*, 1969, *24*, 1012–1018.

Mischel, W. Toward a cognitive social learning reconceptualization of personality. *Psychological Review*, 1973, *80*, 252–283.

Money, J. & Ehrhardt, E. E. *Man and woman, boy and girl*. Baltimore: Johns Hopkins University Press, 1972.

Money, J., Hampson, J. G., & Hampson, J. L. Imprinting and the establishment of gender role. *Archives of Neurology and Psychiatry*, 1957, *77*, 333–336.

Money, J. & Tucker, P. *Sexual signatures*. Boston: Little, Brown, 1975.

Montagu, M. F. A. *Man and aggression*. New York: Oxford University Press, 1968.

Mood, D., Johnson, J., & Shantz, C. U. Affective and cognitive components of empathy in young children. Paper presented to the Southeastern Conference on Human Development, Chapel Hill, N.C., March, 1974.

Morris, D. *The naked ape*. New York: Dell, 1967.

Moskowitz, D., Schwarz, C., & Corsini, D. Initiating day care at three years of age: Effects on attachment. *Child Development*, 1977, *48*, 1271–1276.

Moss, H. A. Sex, age, and state as determinants of mother-infant interaction. *Merrill-Palmer Quarterly*, 1967, *13*, 19–36.

Mossler, D. G., Marvin, R. S., & Greenberg, M. T. Conceptual perspective taking in 2- to 6-year-old children. *Developmental Psychology*, 1976, *12*, 85–86.

Mueller, E. & Vandell, D. Infant-infant inter-actions. In J. D. Osofsky (Ed.), *Handbook of infant development*. New York: Wiley, 1979.

Mullahy, P. *Oedipus: Myth and complex*. New York: Hermitage, 1948.

Munroe, R. H., Munroe, R. L., & Whiting, B. B. (Eds.), *Handbook of cross-cultural human development*. New York: Garland STPM Press, 1981.

Murray, A. D. Infant crying as an elicitor of parental behavior: An examination of two models. *Psychological Bulletin*, 1979, *86*, 191–225.

Murray, J. P. *Television and youth*. Boys Town, Neb.: Boys Town Center for the Study of Youth Development, 1980.

Murray, J. P. & Kippax, S. From the early window to the last night show: International trends in the study of television's impact on children and adults. In L. L. Berkowitz (Ed.), *Advances in experimental social psychology*, Vol. 12. New York: Academic, 1979.

Murray, J. P., Rubinstein, E. A., & Comstock, G. A. (Eds.), *Television and social behavior*, Vol. 2. *Television and social learning*. Washington, D.C.: U.S. Government Printing Office, 1972.

Mussen, P. H. Early socialization: Learning and identification. In T. M. Newcomb (Ed.), *New directions in psychology III*. New York: Holt, Rinehart and Winston, 1967.

Mussen, P. H. & Eisenberg-Berg, N. *Roots of caring, sharing, and helping: The development of prosocial behavior in children*. San Francisco: Freeman, 1977.

Mussen, P. H. & Jones, M. C. Self-conceptions, motivations, and interpersonal attitudes of late and early maturing boys. *Child Development*, 1957, *28*, 243–256.

Nash, S. C. & Feldman, S. S. Sex role and sex-related attributions: Constancy or change across the family life cycle? In M. E. Lamb & A. L. Brown (Eds.), *Advances in developmental psychology*, Vol. 1. Hillsdale, N.J.: Erlbaum, 1981.

National Institute for Advanced Studies. *Summary report: An analysis of 1978–79 Head Start performance indicators*, February 29, 1980 (DHEW Contract No. 105-79-1000).

Nelson, K. & Gruendel, J. Generalized event representations: Basic building blocks of cognitive development. In M. E. Lamb & A. L.

Brown (Eds.), *Advances in developmental psychology*, Vol. 1. Hillsdale, N.J.: Erlbaum, 1981.

Newberger, E. H. & Hyde, J. N. Child abuse: Principles and implications of current pediatric practice. *Pediatric Clinics of North America*, 1975, *22*, 695–715.

Newberger, E. H., Reed, R., Daniel, J., Hyde, J., & Kotelchuck, M. Toward an etiologic classification of pediatric social illness: A descriptive epidemiology of child abuse and neglect, failure to thrive, accidents, and poisonings in children under four years of age. Paper presented at the biennial meeting of the Society for Research in Child Development, Denver, April, 1975.

Norbeck, E. & DeVos, G. Japan. In F. L. K. Hsu (Ed.), *Psychological anthropology: Approaches to culture and personality*. Homewood, Ill.: Dorsey, 1961.

Oden, S. & Asher, S. R. Coaching children in social skills for friendship making. *Child Development*, 1977, *48*, 495–506.

O'Keefe, A. *What Head Start means to families*. Washington, D.C.: U.S. Government Printing Office, 1979. DHEW Publication No. (OHDS) 79-31129.

Ollendick, T., Balla, D., & Zigler, E. F. Expectancy of success and the probability learning of retarded children. *Journal of Abnormal Psychology*, 1971, *77*, 275–281.

Palmer, F. H. & Anderson, L. W. Long-term gains from early intervention: Findings from longitudinal studies: In E. F. Zigler & J. Valentine (Eds.), *Project Head Start: A legacy of the war on poverty*. New York: Free Press, 1979.

Parke, R. D. Parent-infant interaction: Progress, paradigms and problems. In G. P. Sackett (Ed.), *Observing behavior*, Vol. 1: *Theory and applications in mental retardation*. Baltimore: University Park Press, 1978.

Parke, R. D. & Collmer, C. W. Child abuse: An interdisciplinary analysis. In E. M. Hetherington (Ed.), *Review of child development research*, Vol. 5. Chicago: University of Chicago Press, 1975.

Parsons, T. The father symbol: An appraisal in the light of psychoanalytic and sociological theory. In L. Bryson, L. Kinkelstein, R. M. MacIver, & R. McKeon (Eds.), *Symbols and values*. New York: Harper and Row, 1954.

Parsons, T. Social structure and the development of personality: Freud's contribution to the integration of psychology and sociology. *Psychiatry*, 1958, *21*, 321–340.

Parsons, T. & Bales, R. F. *Family, socialization, and interaction process*. Glencoe, Ill.: Free Press, 1955.

Pastor, D. L. The quality of mother-infant attachment and its relationship to toddlers' initial sociability with peers. Paper presented to the International Conference on Infant Studies, New Haven, April, 1980.

Patterson, G. R. The aggressive child: Victim and architect of a coercive system. In L. A. Hammerlynck, L. C. Handy, & E. J. Mash (Eds.), *Behavior modification and families*. New York: Brunner/Mazell, 1976.

Patterson, G. R. & Cobb, J. A. A dyadic analysis of "aggressive" behaviors. In J. P. Hill (Ed.), *Minnesota symposia on child psychology*, Vol. 5. Minneapolis: University of Minnesota Press, 1971.

Patterson, G. R., Littman, R. A., & Bricker, W. Assertive behavior in children: A step toward a theory of aggression. *Monographs of the Society for Research in Child Development*, 1967, *32* (whole number 113).

Patterson, G. R. & Moore, D. R. Interactive patterns as units. In M. E. Lamb, S. J. Suomi, & G. R. Stephenson (Eds.), *Social interaction analysis: Methodological issues*. Madison: University of Wisconsin Press, 1979.

Patterson, G. R. & Reid, J. B. Reciprocity and coercion: Two facets of social systems. In C. Neuringer & J. L. Michael (Eds.), *Behavior modification in clinical psychology*. New York: Appleton-Century-Crofts, 1970.

Pavenstedt, E. A comparison of the child-rearing environment of upper-lower and very low-lower class families. *American Journal of Orthopsychiatry*, 1965, *35*, 89–98.

Pederson, F. A. Mother, father, and infant as an interaction system. Paper presented at the meeting of the American Psychological Association, Washington, D.C., September, 1976.

Pederson, F. A., Anderson, B. J., & Cain, R. L. An approach to understanding linkages between the parent-infant and spouse relationships. In F. A. Pederson (Ed.), *The father-infant relationship: Observational studies in a family context*. New York: Praeger, 1980.

Peevers, B. H. & Secord, P. F. Developmental changes in attribution of descriptive concepts to persons. *Journal of Personality and Social Psychology*, 1973, *27*, 120–128.

Peterson, D. R., Becker, W. C., Hellmer, L. A., Shoemaker, D. J., & Quay, H. C. Parental attitudes and child adjustment. *Child Development*, 1959, *30*, 119–30.

Phares, J. *Locus of control in personality*. Morristown, N.J.: General Learning Press, 1976.

Phillips, D. A. High-achieving students with low academic self-concepts: Achievement motives and orientations. Unpublished doctoral dissertation, Yale University, 1981.

Phillips, D. A. & Zigler, E. F. Children's self image disparity. Effects of age, socioeconomic status, ethnicity and gender. *Journal of Personality and Social Psychology*, 1980, *39*, 689–700.

Phillips, L. & Rabinovitch, M. S. Social role and patterns of symptomatic behaviors. *Journal of Abnormal and Social Psychology*, 1958, *57*, 181–186.

Phillips, L. & Zigler, E. F. Social competence: The action-thought parameter and vicariousness in normal and pathological behaviors. *Journal of Abnormal and Social Psychology*, 1961, *63*, 137–146.

Phillips, L. & Zigler, E. F. Role orientation, the action-thought dimension, and outcome in psychiatric disorder. *Journal of Abnormal and Social Psychology*, 1964, *68*, 381–389.

Phoenix, C. H., Goy, R. W., & Young, W. C. Sexual behavior: General aspects. In L. Martini & W. F. Ganong (Eds.), *Neuroendocrinology*, Vol. 2. New York: Academic, 1967.

Piaget, J. *The language and thought of the child*. New York: Harcourt, Brace, 1926.

Piaget, J. *The moral judgment of the child*. London: Kegan Paul, 1932.

Piaget, J. *The psychology of intelligence*. New York: Harcourt, Brace, 1950.

Piaget, J. Principal factors in determining evolution from childhood to adult life. In D. Rapaport (Ed.), *Organization and pathology of thought*. New York: Columbia University Press, 1951.

Piaget, J. *The origin of intelligence in the child*. London: Routledge, 1953.

Piaget, J. *The origins of intelligence in children*. New York: Basic Books, 1954.

Piaget, J. *The child's construction of reality*. London: Routledge, 1955.

Piaget, J. *Play, dreams, and imitation in childhood.* New York: Norton, 1962.

Piaget, J. Piaget's theory. In P. H. Mussen (Ed.), *Carmichael's manual of child psychology*, Vol. 1. New York: Wiley, 1970.

Piaget, J. & Inhelder, B. *The child's conception of space.* London: Routledge & Kegan Paul, 1956.

Piaget, J. & Inhelder, B. *The child's construction of quantities.* New York: Basic Books, 1974.

Portnoy, F. & Simmons, C. Day care and attachment. *Child Development*, 1978, *49*, 239–242.

Power, M. J., Ash, P. M., Schoenberg, E., & Sorey, E. C. Delinquency and the family. *British Journal of Social Work*, 1974, *4*, 13–38.

Powers, E. & Witmer, H. *An experiment in the prevention of delinquency.* New York: Columbia University Press, 1951.

Psathas, G. Ethnicity, social class, and adolescent independence from parental control. *American Sociologicl Review*, 1957, *22*, 415–423.

Quay, H. C. Classification. In H. C. Quay & J. S. Werry (Eds.), *Psychopathological disorders of childhood* (2d ed.). New York: Wiley, 1979.

Ragozin, A. S. Attachment behavior of day-care children: Naturalistic and laboratory observations. *Child Development*, 1980, *51*, 409–415.

Rajecki, D. W., Lamb, M. E., & Obmascher, P. Toward a general theory of infantile attachment: A comparative review of aspects of the social bond. *Behavioral and Brain Sciences*, 1978, *1*, 417–464.

Rapaport, D. Toward a theory of thinking. In D. Rapaport (Ed.), *Organization and pathology of thought.* New York: Columbia University Press, 1951.

Rest, J. Longitudinal study of the Defining Issues Test: A strategy for analyzing developmental change. *Developmental Psychology*, 1975, *11*, 738–748.

Rest, J. New approaches in the assessment of moral judgment. In T. Lickona (Ed.), *Moral development and behavior.* New York: Holt, Rinehart and Winston, 1976.

Rheingold, H. L. & Cook, K. W. The contents of boys' and girls' rooms as an index of parents' behavior. *Child Development*, 1975, *46*, 459–463.

Rheingold, H. L. & Eckerman, C. O. The infant separates himself from his mother. *Science*, 1970, *168*, 78–83.

Richards, M. P. M., Bernal, J. F., & Brackbill, Y. Early behavioral differences: Sex or circumcision? Unpublished manuscript, Cambridge University, 1977.

Richmond, J. B., Stipek, D. J., & Zigler, E. F. A decade of Head Start. In E. Zigler & J. Valentine (Eds.), *Project Head Start: A legacy of the war on poverty.* New York: Free Press, 1979.

Rimland, B. *Infantile autism.* New York: Appleton-Century-Crofts, 1964.

Roby, P. *Child care—who cares?* New York: Basic Books, 1973.

Rogers, C. *Client-centered therapy.* Boston: Houghton Mifflin, 1951.

Rogers, C. & Dymond, R. *Psychotherapy and personality change.* Chicago: University of Chicago Press, 1954.

Rogoff, B. Schooling and the development of cognitive skills. In H. C. Triandis & A. Heron (Eds.), *Handbook of cross-cultural psychology*, Vol. 4. Boston: Allyn and Bacon, 1981.

Rogoff, B. Mode of instruction and memory test performance. Unpublished manuscript, 1982.

Rogoff, B. & Waddell, K. J. Memory for an organized scene: A cross-cultural comparison. *Developmental Psychology*, 1982, *18*, in press.

Rohner, R. P. & Rohner, E. C. A multivariate model for the study of parental acceptance-rejection and child abuse. University of Connecticut at Storrs. Published in ERIC/ECE, 1978.

Roopnarine, J. L. & Lamb, M. E. The effects of day care on attachment and exploratory behavior in a strange situation. *Merrill-Palmer Quarterly*, 1978, *24*, 85–95.

Roopnarine, J. L. & Lamb, M. E. Peer and parent-child interaction before and after enrollment in nursery school. *Journal of Applied Developmental Psychology*, 1980, *1*, 77–81.

Roos, P. Psychological counseling with parents of retarded children. *Mental Retardation*, 1963, *1*, 345–350.

Rosen, B. C. The achievement syndrome: A psycho-cultural dimension of social stratification. *American Sociological Review*, 1956, *21*, 203–211.

Rosen, B. C. Social class and the child's perception of the parent. *Child Development*, 1964, *35*, 1147–1153.

Rosen, B. C. & D'Andrade, R. The psychosocial origins of achievement motivation. *Sociometry*, 1959, *22*, 185–218.

Rosenshein, B. & Furst, N. Research in teacher

performance criteria. In B. O. Smith (Ed.), *Research in teacher education*. Englewood Cliffs, N.J.: Prentice-Hall, 1971.

Rosenthal, D. *Genetics of psychopathology*. New York: McGraw-Hill, 1971.

Rosenthal, R. *Experimenter effects in behavioral research*. New York: Appleton-Century-Crofts, 1966.

Rosenthal, R. & Jacobson, L. *Pygmalion in the classroom: Teacher expectations and pupils' intellectual development*. New York: Holt, Rinehart and Winston, 1968.

Ross, C. The lessons of the past: Defining and controlling child abuse in the United States. In G. Gerbner, C. Ross, & E. F. Zigler (Eds.), *Child abuse: An agenda for action*. New York: Oxford University Press, 1980.

Rousseau, J-J. *Emile.* (1762) London: Dent, 1911.

Rubenstein, J. L. & Howes, C. Caregiving and infant behavior in day care and in homes. *Developmental Psychology*, 1979, *15*, 1–24.

Rubin, J. Z., Provenzano, F. J., & Luria, Z. The eye of the beholder: Parents' views on sex of newborns. *American Journal of Orthopsychiatry*, 1974, *44*, 512–519.

Rubin, K. H. Egocentrism in childhood: A unitary construct? *Child Development*, 1973, *44*, 102–110.

Rubinstein, E. A., Comstock, G. A., & Murray, J. P. (eds.), *Television and social behavior*, Vol. 4. *Television in day-to-day life: Patterns of use*. Washington, D.C.: U.S. Government Printing Office, 1972.

Rushton, J. P. *Altruism, socialization, and society*. Englewood Cliffs, N.J.: Prentice-Hall, 1980.

Rutter, M. Parent-child separation: Psychological effects on the children. *Journal of Child Psychology and Psychiatry*, 1971, *12*, 233–260.

Rutter, M. *Maternal deprivation reassessed*. Harmondsworth, England: Penguin, 1972.

Rutter, M. Why are London children so disturbed? *Proceedings of the Royal Society of Medicine*, 1973, *66*, 1221–1225.

Rutter, M. Epidemiological strategies and psychiatric concepts in research on the vulnerable child. In E. J. Anthony & C. Koupernik (Eds.), *The child in his family: Children at psychiatric risk*, Vol. 3. New York: Wiley, 1974.

Rutter, M. Maternal deprivation, 1972–1978: New findings, new concepts, new approaches. *Child Development*, 1979, *50*, 283–305.

Rutter, M. Social/emotional consequences of day care for pre-school children. *American Journal of Orthopsychiatry*, 1981, *50*, 505–521.

Rutter, M., Cox, A., Tupling, C., Berger, M., & Yule, W. Attainment and adjustment in two geographical areas, I: The prevalence of psychiatric disorder. *British Journal of Psychiatry*, 1975, *126*, 493–509.

Rutter, M., Maugham, B., Mortimer, P., Ouston, J., & Smith, A. *Secondary schools and their effects on children: 15,000 hours*. London: Open Books, 1979.

Sameroff, A. J. & Chandler, M. Reproductive risk and the continuum of caretaking casuality. In F. D. Horowitz (Ed.), *Review of child development research*, Vol. 4. Chicago: University of Chicago Press, 1975.

Sameroff, A. J. & Harris, A. E. Dialectical approaches to early thought and language. In M. H. Bornstein & W. Kessen (Eds.), *Psychological development from infancy*. Hillsdale, N.J.: Erlbaum, 1979.

Sanders, B., Zigler, E. F., & Butterfield, E. C. Outerdirectedness in the discrimination learning of normal and mentally retarded children. *Journal of Abnormal Psychology*, 1968, *73*, 368–375.

Sanders, L. W. Issues in early mother-child interaction. *Journal of the American Academy of Child Psychiatry*, 1962, *1*, 141–166.

Santrock, J. W. & Warshak, R. A. Father custody and social development in boys and girls. *Journal of Social Issues*, 1979, *35*, 112–125.

Santrock, J. W., Warshak, R. A., & Elliott, G. L. Social development and parent-child interaction in father-custody and stepmother families. In M. E. Lamb (Ed.), *Nontraditional families: Parenting and child development*. Hillsdale, N.J.: Erlbaum, 1982.

Scarr, S. Social introversion-extraversion as a heritable response. *Child Development*, 1969, *40*, 823–832.

Scarr, S. An evolutionary perspective on infant intelligence: Species patterns and individual variations. In M. Lewis (Ed.), *Infant intelligence*. New York: Plenum, 1976.

Schaffer, H. R. & Emerson, P. E. The development of social attachments in infancy. *Monographs of the Society for Research in Child Development*, 1964, *29*(3), Serial no. 94.

Sears, R. R. A theoretical framework for personality and social behavior. *American Psychologist*, 1951, *6*, 476–483.

Sears, R. R. The relation of early socialization

experiences to aggression in middle childhood. *Journal of Abnormal and Social Psychology*, 1961, *63*, 466–492.

Sears, R. R., Maccoby, E. E., & Levin, H. *Patterns of child-rearing.* Evanston, Ill.: Row, Peterson, 1957.

Sears, R. R., Rau, L., & Alpert, R. *Identification and child-rearing.* Stanford: Stanford University Press, 1965.

Segall, M. H., Campbell, D. T., & Herskovitz, M. J. *The influence of culture on visual perception.* Chicago: Bobbs-Merrill, 1966.

Seligman, M. E. P. *Helplessness.* San Francisco: Freeman, 1975.

Selman, R. L. *The growth of interpersonal understanding.* New York: Academic, 1980.

Selman, R. L. & Byrne, D. F. A structural-developmental analysis of levels of role-taking in middle childhood. *Child Development*, 1974, *45*, 803–806.

Serbin, L. A., Tonick, L. J., & Sternglanz, S. H. Shaping cooperative cross-sex play. *Child Development*, 1977, *48*, 924–929.

Sewall, W. M. & Haller, A. O. Social status and the personality adjustment of the child. *Sociometry*, 1956, *9*, 114–125.

Shantz, C. U. The development of social cognition. In E. M. Hetherington (Ed.), *Review of child development research*, Vol. 5. Chicago: University of Chicago Press, 1975.

Sharpe, D., Cole, M., & Lave, C. Education and cognitive development: The evidence from experimental research. *Monographs of the Society for Research in Child Development*, 1979, *44* (whole number 178).

Shatz, M. & Gelman, R. The development of communication skills: Modifications in the speech of young children as a function of listener. *Monographs of the Society for Research in Child Development*, 1973, *38* (serial number 152).

Sheare, J. B. Social acceptance of EMR adolescents in integrated programs. *American Journal of Mental Deficiency*, 1974, *78*, 678–682.

Sherrod, L. R. Issues in cognitive-perceptual development: The special case of social stimuli. In M. E. Lamb & L. R. Sherrod (Eds.), *Infant social cognition: Empirical and theoretical considerations.* Hillsdale, N.J.: Erlbaum, 1981.

Shinn, M. Father absence and children's cognitive development. *Psychological Bulletin*, 1978, *85*, 295–324.

Siegal, M. Kohlberg versus Piaget: To what extent has one theory eclipsed the other? *Merrill-Palmer Quarterly*, 1980, *26*, 285–297.

Singer, D. G. & Singer, J. L. *Partners in play.* New York: Harper and Row, 1977.

Singer, J. L. & Singer, D. G. Can TV stimulate imaginative play? *Journal of Communication*, 1976, *26*, 74–80.

Skinner, B. F. *The behavior of organisms.* New York: Appleton-Century-Crofts, 1938.

Skinner, B. F. *About behaviorism.* New York: Appleton-Century-Crofts, 1974.

Skinner, B. F. *Reflections of behaviorism and society.* Englewood Cliffs, N.J.: Prentice-Hall, 1978.

Slaby, R. G. & Frey, K. S. Development of gender constancy and selective attention to same sex models. *Child Development*, 1975, *46*, 849–856.

Smelser, N. J. & Smelser, W. T. Analyzing personality and social systems. In N. J. Smelser & W. T. Smelser (Eds.), *Personality and social systems.* New York: Wiley, 1963.

Smith, M. & Bissell, J. S. Report analysis: The impact of Head Start. *Harvard Educational Review*, 1970, *40*, 51–104.

Snow, C. Mothers' speech to children learning language. *Child Development*, 1972, *43*, 549–565.

Social Research Group, The George Washington University. *A review of Head Start research since 1969 and an annotated bibliography.* Washington, D.C.: May, 1977 (Contract No. HEW 105-76-1120).

Soloman, D. & Kendall, A. J. *Final report of individual characteristics and children's performance in varied educational settings.* Chicago: Spencer Foundation Project Report, May, 1976.

Spinetta, J. J. & Rigler, D. The child-abusing parent: A psychological review. *Psychological Bulletin*, 1972, *77*, 296–304.

Spiro, M. E. Culture and personality: The natural history of a false dichotomy. *Psychiatry*, 1951, *14*, 19–46.

Spiro, M. E. An overview and a suggested reorientation. In F. L. K. Hsu (Ed.), *Psychological anthropology: Approaches to culture and personality.* Homewood, Ill.: Dorsey, 1961.

Spiro, M. E. & D'Andrade, R. G. A cross-cultural study of some supernatural beliefs. *American Anthropologist*, 1958, *60*, 456–466.

Spitz, H. H. The channel capacity of educable mental retardates. In D. K. Routh (Ed.), *The experimental psychology of mental retardation.* Chicago, Ill.: Aldine, 1973.

Spitz, H. H. Intellectual extremes, mental age and the nature of human intelligence. In E. F. Zigler & D. Balla (Eds.), *Mental retardation: The developmental-difference controversy.* Hillsdale, N.J.: Erlbaum, 1982.

Spock, B. *Baby and child care* (rev. ed.). New York: Pocket Books, 1976.

Staub, E. *Positive social behavior and morality,* Vol. 1. *Social and personal influences.* New York: Academic, 1978.

Staub, E. *Positive social behavior and morality,* Vol. 2. *Socialization and development.* New York: Academic, 1979.

Steele, B. F. & Pollock, D. A psychiatric study of parents who abuse infants and small children. In R. E. Helfer & C. H. Kempe (Eds.), *The battered child,* (2nd ed.). Chicago: University of Chicago Press, 1974.

Stein, A. H. & Friedrich, L. K. Impact of television on children and youth. In E. M. Hetherington (Ed.), *Review of child development research,* Vol. 5. Chicago: University of Chicago Press, 1975.

Steiner, C. *Scripts people live: Transactional analysis of life scripts.* New York: Group, 1974.

Stendler, C. Sixty years of child training practices. *Journal of Pediatrics,* 1950, *36,* 122–134.

Stern, L. Prematurity as a factor in child abuse. *Hospital Practice,* 1973, *8,* 117–123.

Suomi, S. J. & Harlow, H. F. The role and reason of peer friendship in rhesus monkeys. In M. Lewis & L. A. Rosenblum (Eds.), *Friendship and peer relations.* New York: Wiley, 1975.

Suomi, S. J. & Harlow, H. F. Early experience and social development in rhesus monkeys. In M. E. Lamb (Ed.), *Social and personality development.* New York: Holt, 1978.

Sutton-Smith, B. The role of play in cognitive development. In R. E. Herron & B. Sutton-Smith (Ed.), *Child's play.* New York: Wiley, 1971.

Taffel, S. J., O'Leary, K. D., & Armel, S. Reasoning and praise: Their effects on academic behavior. *Journal of Educational Psychology,* 1974, *66,* 291–295.

Tasch, R. J. Interpersonal perceptions of fathers and mothers. *Journal of Genetic Psychology,* 1955, *87,* 59–65.

Taylor, J. What do attitude scales measure: The problem of social desirability. *Journal of Abnormal and Social Psychology,* 1961, *62,* 386–390.

Terman, L. M. *Psychological factors in marital happiness.* New York: McGraw-Hill, 1938.

Terman, L. M. & Oden, M. H. *The gifted child grow up.* Vol. IV, *Genetic studies of genius.* Stanford: Stanford University Press, 1947.

Terman, L. M. & Oden, M. H. *The gifted group at midlife.* Vol. V, *Genetic studies of genius.* Stanford: Stanford University Press, 1959.

Terrell, G., Jr., Durkin, K., & Wiesley, M. Social class and the nature of the incentive in discrimination learning. *Journal of Abnormal and Social Psychology,* 1959, *59,* 270–272.

Thomas, A., Birch, H. G., Chess, S., Hertzig, M. E., & Korn, S. *Behavioral individuality in early childhood.* New York: New York University Press, 1963.

Thomas, A. & Chess, S. *Temperament and development.* New York: Brunner/Mazel, 1977.

Thomas, A. & Chess, S. *The dynamics of psychological development.* New York: Brunner/Mazel, 1979.

Thomas, A., Chess, S., & Birch, H. G. *Temperament and behavior disorders in children.* New York: New York University Press, 1968.

Thompson, R. A. & Lamb, M. E. Infants, mothers, families, and strangers. In M. Lewis & L. A. Rosenblum (Eds.), *Beyond the dyad.* New York: Plenum, in press.

Thompson, S. K. Gender labels and early sex-role development. *Child Development,* 1975, *46,* 339–347.

Tikunoff, W., Berliner, D. C., & Rist, R. C. *An ethnographic study of the forty classrooms of the beginning teacher evaluation study known sample.* Technical Report No. 75-10-5. San Francisco: Far West Laboratory for Educational Research and Development, October, 1975.

Toby, J. Orientation to education as a factor in the school maladjustment of lower-class children. In N. J. Smelser & W. T. Smelser (Eds.), *Personality and social systems.* New York: Wiley, 1963.

Tomkins, S. S. Script theory: Differential magnification of affects. *Nebraska Symposium on Motivation.* Lincoln, Neb.: University of Nebraska Press, 1981.

Torrance, E. P. *Guiding creative talent.* Englewood Cliffs, N.J.: Prentice-Hall, 1962.

Triandis, H. C. & Heron, A. (Eds.), *Handbook of cross-cultural psychology,* Vol. 4. Boston: Allyn and Bacon, 1981.

Tsanoff, R. A. *The ways of genius.* New York: Harper, 1949.

Tulkin, S. R. & Konner, M. J. Alternative conceptions of intellectual functioning. *Human Development,* 1973, *16,* 33–52.

Turnbull, C. M. *The mountain people.* New York: Simon and Schuster, 1973.

Turnure, J. & Zigler, E. F. Outer-directedness in the problem solving of normal and retarded children. *Journal of Abnormal and Social Psychology,* 1964, *69,* 427–436.

U.S. Office of Education. *Education of the gifted and talented,* Vol. 1. Report to the Congress of the U.S. by the U.S. Commissioner of Education. Washington, D.C.: Government Printing Office, 1971.

Vandenberg, S. G. (Ed.), *Methods and goals in human behavior genetics.* New York: Academic, 1965.

Valentine, J., Ross, C., & Zigler, E. F. Project Head Start. *Children Today,* 1980, *9*(3), 22–23.

Valentine, J. & Stark, E. The social context of parent involvement in Head Start. In E. F. Zigler & J. Valentine (Eds.), *Project Head Start: A legacy of the war on poverty.* New York: The Free Press, 1979.

Vaughn, B. E., Gove, F. L., & Egeland, B. The relationship between out-of-home care and the quality of infant-mother attachment in an economically disadvantaged population. *Child Development,* 1980, *51,* 1203–1214.

Wagner, D. A. Memories of Morocco: The influence of age, schooling, and environment on memory. *Cognitive Psychology,* 1978, *10,* 1–28.

Wald, K. *Children of Che: Child care and education in Cuba.* Palo Alto, Cal.: Ramparts Press, 1978.

Wallach, M. A. & Wing, C. W. *The talented student.* New York: Holt, 1969.

Wallerstein, J. S. & Kelly, J. B. *Surviving the breakup.* New York: Basic Books, 1980.

Waters, E., Wippman, J., & Sroufe, L. A. Attachment, positive affect, and competence in the peer group: Two studies in construct validation. *Child Development,* 1979, *50,* 821–829.

Watson, J. B. Psychology as the behaviorist views it. *Psychological Review,* 1913, *20,* 158–177.

Watson, J. B. *Psychological care of infant and child.* London: Allen and Unwin, 1928.

Watson, J. B. & Raynor, R. Conditioned emotional reactions. *Journal of Experimental Psychology,* 1920, *3,* 1–14.

Weiner, B. *Theories of motivation.* Chicago: Markham, 1972.

Weiner, B. *Achievement motivation and attribution theory.* Morristown, N.J.: General Learning Press, 1974.

Weisz, J. R. Transcontextual validity in developmental research. *Child Development,* 1978, *49,* 1–12.

Werner, H. *Comparative psychology of mental development* (2d ed.). Chicago: Follet, 1948.

Werner, H. The concept of development from a comparative and organismic point of view. In D. B. Harris (Ed.), *The concept of development: An issue in the study of human behavior.* Minneapolis: University of Minnesota Press, 1957.

West, D. J. & Farrington, D. P. *Who becomes a delinquent?* London: Heinemann, 1973.

West, D. J. & Farrington, D. P. *The delinquent way of life.* London: Heinemann, 1977.

Westinghouse Learning Corporation. *The impact of Head Start.* Ohio State University report to the Office of Educational Opportunity, Clearinghouse for Federal, Scientific, and Technical Information, Washington, D.C., 1969.

White, B. L. *The first three years of life.* Englewood Cliffs, N.J.: Prentice-Hall, 1975.

White, M. Social class, child rearing practices, and child behavior. *American Sociological Review,* 1957, *22,* 704–712.

White, R. Motivation reconsidered: The concept of competence. *Psychological Review,* 1959, *66,* 297–333.

White, R. Competence and the psychosexual stages of development. *Nebraska Symposium on Motivation.* Lincoln, Neb.: University of Nebraska Press, 1960.

Whiting, B. B. (Ed.), *Six cultures: Studies of child rearing.* New York: Wiley, 1963.

Whiting, B. B. Culture and social behavior: A model for the development of social behavior. Manuscript in preparation, 1980.

Whiting, B. B. & Whiting, J. W. M. *Children of six cultures: A psychocultural analysis.* Cambridge, Mass.: Harvard University Press, 1975.

Whiting, J. W. M. *Becoming a Kwoma.* New Haven: Yale University Press, 1941.

Whiting, J. W. M. Socialization process and personality. In F. L. K. Hsu (Ed.), *Psychological anthropology: Approaches to culture and personality.* Homewood, Ill.: Dorsey, 1961.

Whiting, J. W. M. Methods and problems in cross-cultural research. In G. Lindzey & E. Aronson (Eds.), *The handbook of social psychology*, Vol. 2, (2d ed.). Reading, Mass.: Addison-Wesley, 1968.

Whiting, J. W. M. & Child, I. L. *Child training and personality: A cross-cultural study*. New Haven: Yale University Press, 1953.

Whiting, J. W. M., Child, I. L., Lambert, W., et al. *Field guide for a study of socialization*. New York: Wiley, 1966.

Whiting, J. W. M., Kluckhohn, R., & Anthony, A. The function of male initiation ceremonies at puberty. In E. Maccoby, T. M. Newcomb, & E. L. Hartley (Eds.), *Readings in social psychology* (3d ed.). New York: Holt, Rinehart, and Winston, 1958.

Whiting, J. W. M. & Whiting, B. B. Contributions of anthropology to the methods of studying child-rearing. In P. L. Mussen (Ed.), *Handbook of research methods in child development*. New York: Wiley, 1960.

Willis, A. & Ricciuti, H. Longitudinal observations of infant's daily arrivals at a day care. Unpublished manuscript, Cornell University, 1974.

Wilson, E. O. *Sociobiology: The new synthesis*. Cambridge, Mass.: Harvard University Press, 1975.

Wilson, E. O. *On human nature*. Cambridge, Mass.: Harvard University Press, 1978.

Windle, C. Prognosis of mental subnormals. *American Journal of Mental Deficiency*, 1962, *66*, Monograph Supplement 5.

Winterbottom, M. The relation of need for achievement in learning experiences in independence and mastery. In J. Atkinson (Ed.), *Motives in fantasy, action, and society*. Princeton, N.J.: Van Nostrand, 1958.

Witkin, H. A., Dyk, R. B., Faterson, H. F., Goodenough, D. R., & Karp, S. A. *Psychological differentiation*. New York: Wiley, 1962.

Wolfenstein, M. Trends in infant care. *American Journal of Orthopsychiatry*, 1953, *23*, 120–130.

Yando, R., Seitz, V., & Zigler, E. F. *Imitation: A developmental perspective*. Hillsdale, N.J.: Erlbaum, 1978.

Yando, R., Seitz, V., & Zigler, E. F. *Intellectual and personality characteristics of children: Social class and ethnic group differences*. Hillsdale, N.J.: Erlbaum, 1979.

Yando, R. & Zigler, E. F. Outerdirectedness in the problem-solving of institutionalized and noninstitutionalized normal and retarded children. *Developmental Psychology*, 1971, *4*, 277–288.

Yarrow, M. R., Campbell, J. D., & Burton, R. V. *Childrearing*. San Francisco: Jossey-Bass, 1968.

Zeamon, D. & House, B. J. The role of attention in retardate discrimination learning. In N. R. Ellis (Ed.), *Handbook of mental deficiency*. New York: McGraw-Hill, 1963.

Zigler, E. F. Rigidity in the feebleminded. In E. Trapp & P. Himelstein (Eds.), *Readings on the exceptional child*. New York: Appleton-Century-Crofts, 1962.

Zigler, E. F. Metatheoretical issues in developmental psychology. In M. Marx (Ed.), *Psychological theory* (2d ed.). New York: Macmillan, 1963. (a)

Zigler, E. F. Social reinforcement, environment, and the child. *American Journal of Orthopsychiatry*, 1963, *33*, 614–623. (b)

Zigler, E. F. Developmental versus difference theories of mental retardation and the problem of motivation. *American Journal of Mental Deficiency*, 1969, *73*, 536–556.

Zigler, E. F. The nature-nurture issue reconsidered. In H. C. Haywood (Ed.), *Social-cultural aspects of mental retardation*. New York: Appleton-Century-Crofts, 1970. (a)

Zigler, E. F. Social class and the socialization process. *Review of Educational Research*, 1970, *40*, 87–110. (b)

Zigler, E. F. The retarded child as a whole person. In H. E. Adams & W. K. Boardman III (Eds.), *Advances in experimental clinical psychology*, Vol. 1. New York: Pergamon, 1971.

Zigler, E. F. Controlling child abuse in America: An effort doomed to failure? In D. Adamovicz (Ed.), *Proceedings of the First National Conference on Child Abuse and Neglect*. Pittsburgh: Brandegee Associates, 1976.

Zigler, E. F. America's Head Start Program: An agenda for its second decade. *Young Children*, July, 1978, 4–11. (a)

Zigler, E. F. The effectiveness of Head Start: Another look. *Educational Psychologist*, 1978, *13*, 71–77. (b)

Zigler, E. Controlling child abuse: Do we have the knowledge and/or the will? In G. Gerbner, C. Ross, & E. Zigler (Eds.), *Child abuse: An agenda for action*. New York: Oxford University Press, 1980.

Zigler, E. F. Welcoming a new journal. *Journal of Applied Developmental Psychology*, 1980, *1*, 1–6.

Zigler, E. F., Abelson, W., & Seitz, V. Motivational factors in the performance of disadvantaged children on the Peabody Picture Vocabulary Test. *Child Development*, 1973, *44*, 294–303.

Zigler, E. F. & Anderson, E. Abuse of our children: The sociopolitical context. *UCLA Educator*, in press.

Zigler, E. F. & Balla, D. Motivational and personality factors in the performance of the retarded. In E. F. Zigler & D. Balla (Eds.), *Mental retardation: The developmental difference controversy*. Hillsdale, N.J.: Erlbaum, 1982.

Zigler, E. F., Balla, D., & Butterfield, E. C. A longitudinal investigation of the relationship between preinstitutional social deprivation and social motivation in institutionalized retardates. *Journal of Personality and Social Psychology*, 1968, *10*, 437–445.

Zigler, E. F. & Cascione, R. *On being a parent*. ERIC Clearinghouse on Elementary and Early Childhood Education, 1981.

Zigler, E. F. & Child, I. L. *Socialization and personality development*. Reading, Mass.: Addison-Wesley, 1968.

Zigler, E. F. & deLabry, J. Concept-switching in middle-class, lower-class, and retarded children. *Journal of Abnormal and Social Psychology*, 1962, *65*, 267–273.

Zigler, E. F. & Goodman, J. On day care standards—again! *Networker*, Fall, 1980, *2*, 1, 7.

Zigler, E. F. & Goodman, J. The recent history of our nation's battle over day care: A view from the trenches. *American Journal of Orthopsychiatry*, 1982, in press.

Zigler, E. F. & Harter, S. Socialization of the mentally retarded. In D. A. Goslin & D. C. Glass (Eds.), *Handbook of socialization theory and research*. New York: Rand McNally, 1969.

Zigler, E. F. & Heller, K. Child welfare: The policy-research rift. *New York University Quarterly* 1980, *xi*(4) 11–18.

Zigler, E. F. & Hunsinger-Muenchow, S. Principles and social policy implications of a whole-child psychology. In S. Salzinger, J. Antrobus, & J. Glick (Eds.), *The ecosystem of the "sick" kid*. New York: Academic Press, in press.

Zigler, E. F., Kagan, S. L., & Muenchow, S. Preventive intervention in schools. In C. R.

Reynolds & T. B. Gutkin (Eds.), *Handbook of school psychology*. New York: Wiley, 1982.

Zigler, E. F. & Kanzer, P. The effectiveness of two classes of verbal reinforcers on the performance of middle- and lower-class children. *Journal of Personality*, 1962, *30*, 157–163.

Zigler, E. F. & Levine, J. Age on first hospitalization of schizophrenics: A developmental approach. Manuscript submitted for publication, 1980.

Zigler, E. F., Levine, J., & Gould, L. Cognitive challenge as a factor in children's humor appreciation. *Journal of Personality and Social Psychology*, 1967, *6*, 332–336.

Zigler, E. F. & Phillips, L. Social effectiveness and symptomatic behaviors. *Journal of Abnormal and Social Psychology*, 1960, *61*, 231–238.

Zigler, E. F. & Phillips, L. Social competence and the process-reactive distinction in psychopathology. *Journal of Abnormal and Social Psychology*, 1962, *65*, 215–222.

Zigler, E. F. & Seitz, V. Changing trends in socialization theory and research. *American Behavioral Scientist*, 1978, *21*, 731–756.

Zigler, E. F. & Seitz, V. Social policy implications of research on intelligence. In R. J. Steinberg (Ed.), *Handbook of human intelligence*. New York: Cambridge University Press, 1982. (a)

Zigler, E. F. & Seitz, V. Status of research relating to children. In *Status of research on children and families*. Washington, D.C.: U.S. Administration for Children, Youth, & Families, 1982. (b)

Zigler, E. F. & Trickett, P. K. IQ, social competence, and evaluation of early childhood intervention programs. *American Psychologist*, 1978, *33*, 789–798.

Zigler, E. F. & Turner, P. Parent involvement in day care. Manuscript in preparation.

Zigler, E. F. & Unell, E. Concept-switching in normal and feebleminded children as a function of reinforcement. *American Journal of Mental Deficiency*, 1962, *66*, 651–657.

Zigler, E. F. & Williams, J. Institutionalization and the effectiveness of social reinforcement: A three-year follow up study. *Journal of Abnormal and Social Psychology*, 1963, *66*, 197–205.

Zigler, E. F. & Yando, R. Outerdirectedness and imitative behavior of institutionalized and noninstitutionalized younger and older children. *Child Development*, 1972, *43*, 413–425.

Zimbardo, P. G. & Ruch, F. *Psychology and life* (9th ed.). Glenview, Ill.: Scott, Foresman, 1975.

Zimiles, H. Preventive aspects of school experience. In E. Cowen, E. Gardner, & M. Zax (Eds.), *Emergent approaches to mental health problems.* New York: Appleton-Century-Crofts, 1967.

Part Two

Determinants of Development

1. FUTURE RESEARCH ON SOCIALIZATION AND PERSONALITY DEVELOPMENT

Edward Zigler

Victoria Seitz

The study of human development is inevitably double-edged. On the one side, there is the scientific, scholarly component. The change from the tiny, prelinguistic, physically clumsy infant to the large, verbal, gracefully coordinated adult is one of the most challenging phenomena a scientist can explore. For the past half century, researchers have been responding to this challenge, studying the basic events in development—perception, cognition, learning, physical growth, socialization—and research in these areas is flourishing as never before. Much of this research could be labeled "basic" research, as it is motivated broadly by the desire to expand human knowledge about ourselves and our environment.

But the study of development has another, "applied" aspect, as it can often be undertaken in order to help meet a society's perceived needs. Just as physiology and anatomy are the basic sciences for medicine, developmental psychology is the basic science for child rearing and for social policy planning in areas related to children and families. In principle, one purpose of the scientific study of human development must always be to have practical application. Because the subject matter is children, rather than rocks, stars, or fishes, the potential applicability to society's problems of any facts discovered by developmental psychologists is almost inevitable.

One of the most important developments in recent research relating to children has been an increased recognition that there is no real gap between basic and applied approaches (Zigler, 1979). In this review, it will be evident that much current research—on issues such as day care, child abuse, mainstreaming, and the effects of schooling—reveals a synergistic interplay between the worlds of the ivory tower and the real settings in which children spend their lives. As will be seen, the presumed chasm between basic and applied research has been bridged many times, and we believe that researchers will and must bridge it with increasing frequency. Society will benefit the most from social science when it represents a dialectic between basic and applied research, or, as one commentator has so aptly put it, when it is "in a state of creative tension—be-

A version of this article appeared under the title "Status of Research on Children" in Grotberg, Edith H. (ed.), *The Status of Children, Youth and Families 1979*, Washington, D.C.: U.S. Administration for Children, Youth and Families, 1979, pp. 153–170.

Edward Zigler is Sterling Professor of Psychology and Victoria Seitz is Assistant Professor of Psychology at Yale University.

tween the pursuit of answers to contemporary social questions and the quest for firm scientific principles" (Weisz, 1978, p. 1). In this article we will examine first several trends that have characterized recent research relating to children. Then we shall examine research in several key areas.

CHANGING TRENDS IN RESEARCH ON CHILDREN

Recent research on children shows evidence of three clear trends. One such trend is an increasing emphasis on *biological determinants* of development. A second is an increasing emphasis on the concept of *interaction* within families. Finally, there is increasing concern with the larger *context* within which families must function. We discuss each of these trends below.

Biological Influences on Development

With only occasional exceptions, such as the maturational approach of Gesell and his colleagues (Gesell, 1937; Gesell & Ilg, 1943), American psychology historically has been characterized by a strong commitment to environmentalism. This commitment reached a peak in the 1960s with many psychologists believing that young children were so malleable that rather minimal interventions in their early years would have major, lasting impacts (Bloom, 1964; Hunt, 1961). The 1970s have witnessed a diminution of this environmentalist ardor and an increased interest in the importance of biological factors in development. One sign of this trend is in a reemergence of a maturational approach in the cross-cultural work of Kagan and his colleagues (Kagan & Klein, 1973; Kagan, Klein, Finley, Rogoff, & Nolan, 1979), who argued that certain aspects of children's cognitive functioning may emerge regardless of environmental influences such as schooling.

The biologically oriented approach of ethology is also having a widening impact on developmental theory. Ethological concepts such as imprinting and critical periods have importance for research on human social attachments (Ainsworth, 1979; Bowlby, 1969; Klaus, Jerauld, Kreger, McAlpine, Steffa, & Kennell, 1972) and on sex-role identity (Money, Hampson, & Hampson, 1957), and, in general, there is an increased interchange of theory and research methods between those who study animals and those who study humans. Researchers who have examined the social behavior of animals in their natural habitats, for example, have provided evidence of possible genetic bases for certain maternal and other social behaviors in humans (Fossey, 1971; Goodall, 1965). Human behavior has, in turn, begun to be used as a source of hypotheses about what to study in animals. Researchers are attempting to determine, for example, whether any primates other than humans display the sequence of sensorimotor cognitive stages that Piaget has described (Jolly, 1974). There is current interest as well in whether any nonhuman animals might show other cognitive abilities long believed to be exclusively human, such as linguistic ability and self-awareness. Language research with chimpanzees has aroused so much interest that the names of the highly tutored chimps—"Lana," "Sarah," and "Washoe"—have almost become household words.

The role of specifically genetic factors is also receiving increased attention. There has been an attempt by sociobiologists, for example, to incorporate most of human social behavior into a comprehensive explanatory framework based upon genetic factors (Wilson, 1975, 1978). Within psychology, the major impact has come from the field of behavior genetics, which has become an active area in the 1970s. Currently, research is being conducted on genetic factors in a wide variety of traits including alcoholism (Goodwin, Schulsinger, Hermanson, Guze, & Winokur, 1973), schizophrenia (for reviews see Gottesman & Shields, 1972; Heston, 1970; and Rosenthal & Kety, 1968), intelligence (Gottesman, 1963; Scarr & Weinberg, 1976), and stuttering (Kidd, 1977). Behavior-genetic research obviously has altered the emphasis on environmental factors prevalent 25 years ago. At that time, explanations for stuttering, for example, would have stressed psychodynamic factors such as the child's relationship with his mother.

While the behavior-genetic approach appears very promising, it has often been the subject of controversy. This has been the case particularly for behavior-genetic investigations of IQ test performance. A paper by Jensen titled "How much can we boost IQ and scholastic achievement?" (1969) ignited a storm of reaction that has persisted now for almost a decade. There are some psychologists who take the position that we should not study possible genetic factors for this trait at all (Kamin, 1974). It appears to us that such a reaction is too extreme. The discovery of genetic determinants of behavior does not rule out the importance of environmental determinants as well. Behavior geneticists have pointed out that with most traits one will find a "range of reaction"—a range of possible outcomes that may arise from a given genetic endowment depending upon the environments encountered. (See Hirsch, 1970, for a particularly thoughtful treatment of this controversial issue.)

As Anastasi (1958) has pointed out, the question of greatest interest in the nature-nurture issue is "how?": How does a genetic potential become translated into an actual physical or psychological characteristic through the organism's interaction with the environment? We have not yet answered Anastasi's question, but the fact

that research on biological factors is becoming active is a promising step in the right direction.

Interaction within Families

Another important conceptual advance in the past few years has been the recognition that the family is more complex than the mother-child dyad. Researchers have, for example, discovered the father. The nature of his role in the family is now an active topic for investigation (Biller, 1971; Clarke-Stewart, 1978; Hoffman, 1971; Lamb, 1976; Lynn, 1974). In keeping with Bronfenbrenner's (1977) recommendations, a great deal remains to be done to explore the role of other family members, such as siblings and grandparents, in socialization. Variations of family structure, such as communes and the single-parent family, are also receiving much more attention (Hetherington, Cox, & Cox, 1976; Johnston & Deisher, 1973; Rabin, 1971). The present research focus much more adequately reflects the fact that children are reared within diverse family structures than did the earlier preoccupation with the mother-child relationship in the intact nuclear family.

Awareness of the complexity of the family has been accompanied by interest in the quality of interactions among family members and in the active role that children themselves may play in their own socialization. It is now considered a truism that if parents are to some degree molders of children, children are at least equally molders of parents. A number of researchers now have shown that caretakers are responsive to individual differences in infants, and, conversely, that the tactics employed by socializing agents have different results depending upon the nature of the child to whom they are applied (see Bell, 1971; Bell & Harper, 1977; Clarke-Stewart, 1979; Freedman, 1974; Lewis & Rosenblum, 1974). For example, some neonates are more physically energetic than average, and such babies rarely if ever become slow-moving, quiet children, no matter how motivated their parents are to change them (Thomas & Chess, 1977).

The shift from viewing children as passive to viewing them as active has had consequences for the kinds of behaviors that are investigated. Research based on the passive infant view assumed a unidirectional influence in parent-child relationships, with the parent controlling what the child experienced. Psychologists focused on caretaking practices, such as how children were fed, or talked to, or disciplined, and tried to determine the effects of such practics on children. The active child point of view has generated a different kind of research focusing on how infants influence parents, and especially how stable patterns of interaction become established (Bell, 1968; Brazelton, 1969; Clarke-Stewart, 1979; Freedman, 1974; Thomas & Chess, 1977). Two theoretical models that have been advanced to deal with these complex interactions are the *transactional* model of Sameroff and Chandler (1975) and the *canalization* model described by Scarr-Salapatek (1976).

The active-child view has also influenced opinions concerning the nature of effective parenting. Many theorists now suggest that the effective parent is not someone stamped from a mold, responding in the same way to all children, but rather is one who has empathic understanding of the idiosyncratic style of his or her child (Ainsworth, Bell, & Stayton, 1974; Baumrind, 1975; Blehar, Lieberman, & Ainsworth, 1977; Schaffer & Emerson, 1964; Thomas, Chess, & Birch, 1968). The concept that some children are inherently more difficult to rear than others, but that such children nevertheless can be socialized effectively, is another important contribution (Thomas & Chess, 1977). It is now widely accepted that the responsibility for the outcome of socialization rests neither on the parents nor on the child alone.

The Family in Context

For many years, the socialization of the child was viewed as a very lonely kind of interaction between parents and their children. The emerging view is that neither the developing child nor the family exists in isolation but rather that they are affected by virtually every institution in a society (Keniston & The Carnegie Council on Children, 1977). Children are influenced by the media, by the state of the economy, by the length of the work day, and by an industry's decision about whether its employees must move from city to city every few years. Children are influenced by the availability or unavailability of satisfactory day-care arrangements. And they are affected by whether they live in high-rise urban apartments an elevator's ride from the playground or in suburban housing with fenced back yards. The family is still seen as the primary agent of a child's socialization, but it is seen no longer as the sole agent. This recognition has changed greatly the nature of developmental research.

One manifestation of this trend is an increased interest in cross-cultural studies. The principal problem with such evidence is the fact that the data are usually correlational. It is difficult to determine the causal factors in cultural differences. Nevertheless, anthropological and cross-cultural data provide a window onto very different circumstances in how children and families exist elsewhere, and such data are valued particularly as providing "natural experiments" for examining the factors that influence development. In the study of the effects of cultural change, for example, the extreme case of one African tribe, the Ik, has demonstrated that the external destruction of traditional societal practices can result in a total breakdown of family structure, a near abandonment of care for children, and the disappearance of such basic human qualities as affection and concern for others (Turnbull, 1973). Other provocative insights have come from the more recent reports of childrearing and family support systems in China (Kessen, 1975).

RECENT RESEARCH ON CHILDREN: SOME KEY ISSUES OF CURRENT INTEREST

Having considered how research on children has been changing in recent years, we will now examine in greater detail several topics of active current research.

Child Abuse

Child abuse is one of the most visible and pressing problems confronting developmental psychologists today. (See Gerbner, Ross, & Zigler, 1980, for a more complete overview of this complex research area.) It is also an issue in which the relationship between basic and applied research is very visible. Most people would agree that research seeking explanations for the development of inappropriate interactions between abusing parents and abused children has great social relevance. In contrast, most people would probably categorize studies on the behavior of infant monkeys toward terrycloth-covered surrogate "mothers" as basic research having no obvious social application. Ainsworth, however, has been studying the anomalous development of attachment bonds in families in which abuse occurs (1980) and has found important connections between what occurs in these families and the results from Harlow's research with monkeys. Several particularly provocative findings are that infant rhesus monkeys will cling to surrogate mothers if they behave in a frightening manner by emitting air blasts (1961), and that the infant monkeys will even cling to their own mothers who physically abuse them (1963). These findings have important implications for detection and prevention of child abuse in that they support clinical evidence that abused children may still seek to be with abusive parents (Ainsworth, 1980).

Harlow's basic studies have also contributed toward Ainsworth's theories that abuse occurs only where insecure attachment develops, that identifiable characteristics of the parent and/or of the child foster "anxious attachment," and that these anxiously attached parents and children harbor more frustrations and angers than do other parents and children. Ainsworth further suggested that instruments that could measure attachment of parents and children could be used to help identify families at risk of abuse, and that programs aimed at promoting secure parent-child bonds would probably help to alleviate the child abuse problem. While Ainsworth has drawn upon other researchers' results in addition to Harlow's (e.g., Bowlby, 1969, 1973; DeLozier, 1978; George & Main, 1979), Harlow's particular contribution clearly illustrates how basic research can form a foundation for applied work.

Although there are few firm conclusions in the child abuse area, some tentative information does emerge. There is, for example, evidence that possessing certain characteristics may make a child more prone to being abused (Alvy, 1975; Gelles, 1973; Gil, 1969; Hurt, 1975; Newberger, Reed, Daniel, Hyde, & Kotelchuck, 1975; Zimbardo & Ruch, 1975). The characteristics of abused children that have been investigated include age, gender, birth order, temperament, physical development, and congenital features.

One relationship found most repeatedly is that premature children experience a heightened incidence of child abuse (Caplan, Mason, & Kaplan, 1965; Hurt, 1975; Kaplan, Smith, Grobstein, & Fischman, 1973; Newberger & Hyde, 1975; Stern, 1973). Because the characteristics of abused children are often highly interrelated, however, the interpretation of findings is somewhat speculative. For example, there is a suggestion that children small for their age are more likely to be abused. But body size is sometimes related to prematurity. Another suggestive finding is that children with deviant congenital characteristics are more likely to be abused than are children without such defects (Gil, 1969; Milowe & Lourie, 1964). Congenital defects may be related not only to body size and prematurity but also to mental retardation, another child characteristic found to be associated with child abuse (Hurt, 1975).

A considerable amount of work in the child abuse area has focused also on the psychodynamic and sociocultural characteristics of abusing parents (Alvy, 1975; Bronfenbrenner, 1974; Daniel & Hyde, 1975; Garbarino, 1976; Hurt, 1975; Newberger & Hyde, 1975; Newberger et al., 1975). At a psychodynamic and somewhat tentative level, it has been reported that abusing and neglectful parents have poor self-concepts or poor self-esteem (Daniel & Hyde, 1975). Alcoholism and drug usage also have been found to be associated with being an abusing parent (Newberger, 1973; Newberger & Hyde, 1975). While it is often presumed that children who are abused grow into abusing parents, there has been only minor support for this expectation in the research findings (e.g., Silver, Dublin, & Lourie, 1969). In one review, Gelles (1973) noted Gil's finding that 11% of abusing parents were abused as children. In Gil's (1969) survey data, this amounted to only 14% of abusing mothers and 7% of abusing fathers having been abused during childhood.

In terms of implications for effective intervention, one of the potentially most important research findings is that abusing parents often have unrealistic expectations about what behaviors their children are capable of and/or a general lack of knowledge concerning the development of children (Alvy, 1975; Daniel & Hyde, 1975; Elmer, 1967; Gelles, 1973; Hurt, 1975; Newberger & Hyde, 1975). They are, for example, more likely to interpret crying, soiling of diapers, or breaking a toy as a deliberate attempt to misbehave or to be spiteful and cause trouble. It thus appears that anything we can do to teach the general population about child care and the normal course of the development of children would be helpful in reducing the incidence of child abuse. We therefore endorse the suggestion of many workers that our nation commit itself to teaching parents how to be parents, with courses in parenthood becoming part of the curriculum of every high school in America. A model for such an effort is the Education for Parenthood Program mounted jointly by the Administration for Children, Youth, and Families and the Office of Education.

Day Care

The need for adequate day care increasingly is being brought to the attention of both scientists and the public (Fraiberg, 1977). This need is pressing. In the United States, more than half of all women with school-age children now work, and over 30% of women with children under 6 do so. These figures have risen markedly since 1952, when they were 35% and 16%, respectively (White House Conference on Children, 1970). While preschool children traditionally have been the recipients of alternative child-care arrangements and the focus of research interest, there is increasing interest in infant day care, since there is proportionately an especially rapid rise in mothers of infants returning to work; and in school-age day care, since two-thirds of day-care needs are now for school-age children. The sheer number of children involved is staggering. Nearly 2,000,000 school-age children are "latch-key children," who return home to an empty house each day (U.S. Department of Commerce, Bureau of the Census, 1970).

As with the child abuse issue, day care is an area in which the reciprocal nature of basic and applied research is evident. Much of the theoretical underpinning for research on day care has come and will continue to come from research on parent/child attachments (Ainsworth, 1979; Ainsworth & Bell, 1970, 1973; Blehar, 1974; Bowlby, 1969, 1973). Another important area of research is the investigation of peer group socialization (Bryan, 1975; Hartup, 1975, in press; Lewis & Rosenblum, 1975).

From the more applied approach, a valuable source of information has been the work of Israeli researchers who have studied children reared in the group-care arrangements of the Israeli kibbutzim. These researchers have examined, for example, relationships between kibbutz child-rearing practices and kibbutz-reared children's later effectiveness as soldiers (Amir, 1969), their personality development (Kaffman, 1965; Nevo, in press), their sex-role development (Rabin, 1970), and their moral attitudes (Rettig, 1966). This research is applied because it is motivated in part by the need to know whether the kibbutz is producing healthy, useful members of its society. This research, however, has also added to our basic knowledge of child development. The kibbutz studies are providing valuable information not only on the aforementioned topics but on development of self-concept (Handel, 1961), of mental and motor faculties (Kohen-Raz, 1968), and of relationships with parents and peers (Devereux, Shouval, Bronfenbrenner, Rodgers, Kav-Venaki, Kiely, & Karson, 1974; Rabin & Goldman, 1966; Sharabany, 1974) under different child-rearing systems.

While there are no simple conclusions yet to be drawn from the kibbutz studies (Beit-Hallahmi and Rabin [1977] provide an excellent review of this literature), it is evident that the effects of this rather extreme form of day care have not been catastrophic for the children or society. The kibbutz results also support the conclusion of American researchers that we must expect much greater complexity than finding simply that day care does or does not harm children.

There has been considerable American research on the effects of working mothers and/or substitute caretakers (e.g., Blehar, 1974; Etaugh, 1974; Fein & Clarke-Stewart, 1973; Fraiberg, 1977; Provence, Naylor, & Patterson, 1977; Rubenstein & Howes, 1979; Webb, 1977). While this research has yielded many valuable findings, however, it is still very incomplete. Much research on day care has examined only possible negative consequences, such as damage to the parent-child attachment bonds, and only more recently has there been more interest in possible positive effects, such as increased cooperativeness and altruism, which might result from children's attending group day-care centers (e.g., Rubenstein & Howes, 1979). Most research has also focused on high-quality, expensive day-care centers. Since only a small percentage of children who receive day care attend licensed day-care centers, much more information is needed on the effects of other kinds of day care, such as care in the child's home by an adult other than the mother, or care in someone else's home.

The School as a Socializing Agent

It is widely recognized that the school is an important socializing agent, but research has focused often on cognitive rather than social effects of schooling. In recent years, this emphasis has begun to change. One issue that has been the focus of much recent research is school segregation. Placing children in homogeneous groups from their earliest days in school has implications for how they will adjust to a heterogeneous society. The Clarks' research in the 1940s and 1950s (Clark, 1955; Clark & Clark, 1947) showed the power of segregated schooling to overcome the efforts of even the most dedicated black families to make their children feel valued by society. The issue remains important with many unanswered questions. For example, while results of studies of school integration are not consistent, one disturbing trend is for black children's educational and occupational aspirations to be lower when they are in integrated rather than in segregated schools (St. John, 1975). For many reasons it has been difficult to study the effects of large and sudden social changes, such as desegregation and busing. (For reviews of research on effects of school desegregation and busing, see Armor, 1972; Coleman, Campbell, Hobson, McPartland, Mood, Weinfeld, & York, 1966; St. John, 1975.) Researchers studying the effects of racial mix in schools or the effects of busing, therefore, generally have treated these as unitary phenomena. There are signs, however, that future research will address the psychological variables more directly, as in attempting to determine those conditions that lead to high-quality desegregation (St. John, 1975).

In the broader sense, school integration should refer to mixture across many lines, not just ethnic or socioeconomic ones. Recent efforts to mainstream handicapped children into regular classrooms are an example. Although many states now have laws requiring that handicapped children be integrated with nonhandicapped children in the classroom, as yet we have little knowledge as to how this can be accomplished best or the consequences for the children. As has been the case in studies of preschool intervention programs, the danger exists that IQ or achievement scores alone may be taken as indicators of the success or failure of mainstreaming efforts. As for other intervention programs, we would argue that social competence should be the ultimate criterion for monitoring the effectiveness of mainstreaming (Zigler & Muenchow, 1979). In academic areas,

mainstreamed retarded children appear to do as well as children in special classes, although there is little evidence that mainstreaming is more effective (Gruen, Ottinger, & Ollendick, 1974). But the expectation that mainstreamed retarded children would be less stigmatized than children in special classes has not been borne out (Goodman, Gottlieb, & Harrison, 1972; Gottlieb & Budoff, 1973). Clearly, more research is needed to determine which children, and which handicaps, are most likely to benefit from mainstreaming, and how best to promote their acceptance by normal peers.

Intervention and "Compensatory Education"

A related area in which there now has been considerable productive interplay between basic and applied research has been in the planning and evaluation of preschool intervention programs. Several areas of research gave rise in the 1960s to an expectation that society could prepare economically disadvantaged children to profit from schooling by providing appropriate preschool intervention. For example, research with animals raised in barren or in stimulating environments had shown that impoverished environments often had adverse effects on the animals' learning ability. Much animal research had suggested also the existence of critical periods in development—periods of time, usually early in life, when a small amount of environmental input was particularly effective in producing significant changes in subsequent development. Some psychologists argued eloquently that similar critical periods probably existed for children's intellectual growth (Bloom, 1964; Hunt, 1961). These and other factors gave rise to a number of intervention programs, including Project Head Start.

Early evaluations of intervention programs were encouraging. For example, a common finding was that Head Start children showed a 10-point increase in their

IQs. However, enthusiasm for intervention programs waned in 1969 with the publication of a study known as the Westinghouse Report. This report, based on the comparison of Head Start graduates and children who had not attended Head Start, concluded that Head Start children's IQ advantage disappeared soon after the children entered school, and that Head Start graduates showed little difference from non-Head Start graduates in the early grades. This document, plus an influential article by Arthur Jensen in the *Harvard Educational Review* (Jensen, 1969), gave rise to a wave of pessimism about the value of preschool intervention.

For several reasons, however, it is now clear that the notion that intervention programs are ineffective is a myth that deserves to be dispelled. One of these reasons is the existence of evidence that programs such as Head Start have resulted in gains in children's social competence (Zigler, 1973; Zigler & Trickett, 1978). The mere fact of the existence of Head Start in a community appears to be associated with an improvement of health and educational services available to children and families (Kirschner, 1970). There also has been evidence that intervention results in changes in children's motivation to use their intellectual abilities. One of the first benefits of applied research in intervention was to contribute to basic knowledge about the determinants of children's performance on IQ tests. Research in which children's motives during testing have been influenced directly has shown that disadvantaged children often bring a number of negative motives into a test situation. If these motivational problems, such as fear of the examiner and fear of being tested, are alleviated, the children's IQs have been found to increase by as much as 10 points (Jacobson, Berger, Bergman, Millham, & Greeson, 1971; Seitz, Abelson, Levine, & Zigler, 1975; Thomas, Hertzig, Dryman, & Hernandez, 1971; Zigler, Abelson, & Seitz, 1973; Zigler & Butterfield, 1968). The results of this research, thus, suggest that the initial 10-point IQ gains found in early studies of Head Start were not illusory, but neither were they indicative of any real intellectual changes in children. Rather, these results suggest that intervention programs may have their greatest benefit in helping to reduce negative motivational factors and thus permit children to perform at levels more commensurate with their actual abilities. In short, it was social competence, revealed by children's willingness to display their intellectual abilities, and not the abilities themselves, that a brief Head Start program had affected.

Another cause for optimism has been the results of long-term, longitudinal studies of intervention. The Westinghouse Study, as a cross-sectional study with known sampling problems, has been widely criticized (Campbell & Erlebacher, 1970; Smith & Bissell, 1970), and the significance of these methodological criticisms has been borne out by the fact that more appropriately conducted studies have generally shown that effects of intervention often do not "fade out." For example, in an unusually careful study, Miller and Dyer (1975) assigned children randomly to different kinds of preschool interventions, and found that there were significant differences several years later in ways meaningfully related to the kinds of programs the children had attended. The results of several longitudinal studies of preschool interventions also suggest long-term positive effects of intervention. Especially important is the result that fewer intervention group children than control children have needed to be placed in classes below their grade level or in special training classes (Lazar, Hubbell, Murray, Rosche, & Royce, 1977).

The chief implication of the intervention studies of the 1970s is that the result of an intervention appears to be commensurate with the effort that is invested in the intervention. Intensive programs begun in infancy, providing a broad array of services, and involving the entire family have had lasting and measurable benefits for intervention relative to control children long after the programs have ceased (Garber & Heber, 1977; Ramey, Collier, Sparling, Loda, Campbell, Ingram, & Finkelstein, 1976; Trickett, 1979). Preschool programs that have been followed by several years of additional intervention in elementary school have also had lasting positive effects, albeit less dramatic effects than those from the infant intervention studies (Seitz, Apfel, & Efron, 1978; Seitz, Apfel, & Rosenbaum, 1979).

The experience of the past two decades has taught us the folly of searching for any single "magic age" or "magic program" for children. The preschool years are important, but so are a child's school years and adolescence. Similarly, while any given program may have merit, there is greater value in providing an intervention center that has a group of programs—almost a cafeteria style approach letting families decide for themselves what they most need, whether it be day care, toddler care, inoculations, preschools, and so forth. The notion of such a "Child and Family Resource Program" is spelled out in a recent governmental report (Comptroller General, 1979), and existing evidence on the effects of such a comprehensive program is thus far highly favorable.

In summary, one may well ask whether, in intervention research, one should view the glass as being half full or half empty (Richmond, 1975). There now appears to be much evidence to support the optimistic response that it is half full and that we are likely to continue to add to its contents in the next decade.

ideal for some scientists remains Pasteur's advice to work serenely in the quiet of the laboratory, but others now believe that a scientist's responsibilities must include a willingness to direct his or her research toward assuaging society's problems. Developmental psychologists are prone to take the latter position simply because it is difficult to study children without producing some kind of potentially useful information.

The breadth of research is evident clearly in the present overview. The focus is now on children in context—that is, not on children alone but on children living in a complex world of family interactions and societal forces. The significance of food stamps, unemployment, and television commercials as forces to be reckoned with in understanding how children develop is recognized increasingly by psychologists. There is also an increased appreciation for the role of biology, and a willingness of theoreticians to consider both nature and nurture within a realistic balance. And finally, there is a healthy interplay of researchers from many areas attempting to come to grips with some of society's most challenging problems. Such problems as child abuse, how to meet the nation's needs for day care, how best to educate children, and when, how, and whether society should intervene in the lives of economically disadvantaged children are weighty issues that have drawn the talents of many dedicated researchers. Because of the growing concern of developmental psychologists for the social policy implications of research, the present status of research relating to children is much richer than was true only a decade ago and shows promise of even greater benefits to come.

CONCLUSION

Research relating to children has broadened considerably in recent years. The

REFERENCES

Ainsworth, M. D. S. Attachment as related to mother-infant interaction. In J. S. Rosen-blatt, R. A. Hinde, C. Beer, & M. C. Busnel (Eds.), *Advances in the study of behavior*, Vol. 9. New York: Academic Press, 1979.

Ainsworth, M. D. S. Attachment and child abuse. In G. Gerbner, C. Ross, & E. Zigler (Eds.), *Child abuse reconsidered: An analysis and agenda for action.* New York: Oxford University Press, 1980.

Ainsworth, M. D. S. & Bell, S. M. Attachment, exploration, and separation: Illustrated by the behavior of one-year-olds in a strange situation. *Child Development*, 1970, *41*, 49–67.

Ainsworth, M. D. S. & Bell, S. M. Mother-infant interaction and the development of competence. In K. J. Connolly & J. S. Bruner (Eds.), *The growth of competence.* New York: Academic Press, 1974.

Ainsworth, M. D. S., Bell, S. M., & Stayton, D. J. Infant-mother attachment and social development: "Socialization" as a product of reciprocal responsiveness to signals. In M. P. M. Richards (Ed.), *The integration of a child into a social world.* Cambridge, Massachusetts: Cambridge University Press, 1974.

Alvy, K. T. Preventing child abuse. *American Psychologist*, 1975, *30*, 921–928.

Amir, Y. The effectiveness of the kibbutz-born soldier in the Israel Defense Forces. *Human Relations*, 1969, *22*, 333–344.

Anastassi, A. Heredity, environment, and the question "how?" *Psychological Review*, 1958, *65*, 197–208.

Armor, D. J. The evidence on busing. *The Public Interest*, 1972 (Serial No. 28), 90–126.

Baumrind, D. M. *Early socialization and the discipline controversy.* Morristown, New Jersey: General Learning Press, 1975.

Beit-Hallahmi, B. & Rabin, A. I. The kibbutz as a social experiment and as a child-rearing laboratory. *American Psychologist*, 1977, *32*, 532–541.

Bell, R. Q. A reinterpretation of the direction of effects in studies of socialization. *Psychological Review*, 1968, *75*, 81–95.

Bell, R. Q. Stimulus control of parent or caretaker behavior by offspring. *Developmental Psychology*, 1971, *4*, 63–72.

Bell, R. Q., & Harper, L. V. *The effects of children on adults.* Hillsdale, New Jersey: Lawrence Erlbaum Associates, 1977.

Biller, H. B. *Father, child, and sex role.* Lexington, Massachusetts: D.C. Heath, 1971.

Blehar, M. C. Anxious attachment and defensive reactions associated with day care. *Child Development*, 1974, *45*, 683–692.

Belhar, M. C., Lieberman, A. F., & Ainsworth, M. D. S. Early face-to-face interaction and its relation to later infant-mother attachment. *Child Development*, 1977, *48*, 182–194.

Bloom, B. *Stability and change in human characteristics.* New York: Wiley, Inc., 1964.

Bowlby, J. *Attachment and loss*, Vol. 1. *Attachment.* New York: Basic Books, Publishers, 1969.

Bowlby, J. *Attachment and loss*, Vol. 2. *Separation: Anxiety and anger.* New York: Basic Books, 1973.

Brazelton, T. B. *Infants and mothers: Differences in development.* New York: Dell Publishing Co., Inc., 1969.

Bronfenbrenner, U. The origins of alienation. *Scientific American*, 1974, *231*, 53–61.

Bronfenbrenner, U. Toward an experimental ecology of human development. *American Psychologist*, 1977, *32*, 513–531.

Bryan, J. H. Children's cooperation and helping behaviors. In E. M. Hetherington (Ed.), *Review of child development research*, Vol. 5. Chicago: University of Chicago Press, 1975.

Campbell, D. T. & Erlebacher, A. How regression artifacts in quasi-experimental evaluations can mistakenly make compensatory education look harmful. In J. Hellmuth (Ed.), *Compensatory education: A national debate*, Vol. III of *The disadvantaged child.* New York: Brunner/Mazel, 1970.

Caplan, G., Mason, E. A., & Kaplan, D. M. Four studies of crisis in parents of prematures. *Community Mental Health Journal*, 1965, *1*, 149–161.

Clark, K. B. *Prejudice and your child.* Boston: Beacon Press, 1955.

Clark, K. B. & Clark, M. P. Racial identification and preference in Negro children. In T. M. Newcomb & E. L. Hartley (Eds.), *Readings in social psychology.* New York: Henry Holt, 1947.

Clarke-Stewart, K. A. And daddy makes three: The father's impact on mother and child. *Child Development*, 1978, *49*, 466–478.

Clarke-Stewart, K. A. Evaluating parental effects on child development. In L. S. Shulman (Ed.), *Review of research in education*, Vol. 6, 1978. Itasca, Illinois: F. E. Peacock, 1979.

Coleman, J. S., Campbell, E., Hobson, C., McPartland, J., Mood, A., Weinfeld, F., &

York, R. *Equality of educational opportunity.* Washington, D.C.: U.S. Government Printing Office, 1966.

Comptroller General of the United States. *Early childhood and family development programs improve the quality of life for low-income families.* Report to the Congress of the United States, United States General Accounting Office, Report HRD-79-40, February 6, 1979.

Daniel, J. H. & Hyde, J. N. Working with high-risk families. *Children Today,* 1975, *4,* 23–25, 36.

DeLozier, P. An application of attachment theory to the study of child abuse. Unpublished doctoral dissertation, California School of Professional Psychology, Los Angeles, 1978.

Devereux, E. C., Shouval, R., Bronfenbrenner, U., Rodgers, R. R., Kav-Venaki, S., Kiely, E., & Karson, E. Socialization practices of parents, teachers and peers in Israel: The kibbutz versus the city. *Child Development,* 1974, *45,* 269–281.

Elmer, E. *Children in jeopardy.* Pittsburgh, Pennsylvania: University of Pittsburgh Press, 1967.

Etaugh, C. Effects of maternal employment on children: A review of recent research. *Merrill-Palmer Quarterly,* 1974, *20,* 71–98.

Fein, G. G., & Clarke-Stewart, K. A. *Day care in context.* New York: John Wiley & Sons, Inc., 1973.

Fossey, D. More years with mountain gorillas. *National Geographic,* 1971, *140,* 574–586.

Fraiberg, S. *Every child's birthright.* New York: Basic Books, 1977.

Freedman, D. G. *Human infancy: An evolutionary perspective.* Hillsdale, N.J.: Erlbaum, 1974.

Garbarino, J. A preliminary study of some ecological correlates of child abuse: The impact of socioeconomic stress on mothers. *Child Development,* 1976, *47,* 178–185.

Garber, H. & Heber, F. R. The Milwaukee Project: Indications of the effectiveness of early intervention in preventing mental retardation. In P. Mittler (Ed.), *Research to practice in mental retardation,* Vol. 1. Baltimore, Md.: University Park Press, 1977.

Gelles, R. J. Child abuse as psychopathology: A sociological critique and reformulation. *American Journal of Orthopsychiatry,* 1973, *43,* 611–621.

George, C. & Main, M. Social interactions of young abused children: Approach, avoidance and aggression. *Child Development,* 1979, *50,* 306–318.

Gerbner, G., Ross, C., & Zigler, E. *Child abuse: An agenda for action.* New York: Oxford University Press, 1980.

Gesell, A. Early evidence of individuality in the human infant. *Scientific Monthly,* 1937, *45,* 217–225.

Gesell, A. & Ilg, F. L. *Infant and child in the culture of today.* New York: Harper & Row, 1943.

Gil, D. G. Physical abuse of children. Findings and implications of a nation-wide survey. *Pediatrics,* 1969, *44,* No. 5, Part 2 (Supplement), 857–864.

Goodall, J. Chimpanzees of the Gombe Stream Reserve. In I. DeVore (Ed.), *Primate behavior: Field studies of monkeys and apes.* New York: Holt, Rinehart & Winston, 1965.

Goodman, H., Gottlieb, J., & Harrison, R. H. Social acceptance of EMRs integrated into a nongraded elementary school. *American Journal of Mental Deficiency,* 1972, *76,* 412–417.

Goodwin, D. W., Schulsinger, F., Hermanson, L., Guze, S. B., & Winokur, G. Alcohol problems in adoptees raised apart from alcoholic biological parents. *Archives of General Psychiatry,* 1973, *28,* 238–243.

Gottesman, I. I. Genetic aspects of intelligent behavior. In N. Ellis (Ed.), *Handbook of mental deficiency.* New York: McGraw-Hill, 1963.

Gottesman, I. I., & Shields, J. *Schizophrenia and genetics—a twin study vantage point.* New York: Academic Press, 1972.

Gottlieb, J. & Budoff, M. Social acceptability of retarded children in nongraded schools differing in architecture. *American Journal of Mental Deficiency,* 1973, *78,* 15–19.

Gruen, G., Ottinger, D., & Ollendick, T. Probability learning in retarded children with differing histories of success and failure in school. *American Journal of Mental Deficiency,* 1974, *79,* 417–423.

Handel, A. [Self-concept of the kibbutz adolescent.] *Megamot,* 1961, *11,* 142–159.

Harlow, H. F. The development of affectional patterns in infant monkeys. In B. M. Foss (Ed.), *Determinants of Infant behaviour,* Vol. 1. New York: Wiley, 1961.

Harlow, H. F. The maternal affectional system. In B. M. Foss (Ed.), *Determinants of infant behaviour,* Vol. 3. New York: Wiley, 1963.

Hartup, W. W. Origins of friendship. In M. Lewis & L. Rosenblum (Eds.), *Friendship and peer relations.* New York: Wiley, 1975.

Hartup, W. W. Two social worlds: Family relations and peer relations. In M. Rutter (Ed.), *Scientific foundations of developmental psychiatry.* London: Heinemann, in press.

Heston, L. L. The genetics of schizophrenic and schizoid disease. *Science,* 1970, *167,* 249–256.

Hetherington, E. M., Cox, M., & Cox, R. The aftermath of divorce. Paper presented at the 84th Annual Convention of the American Psychological Association, Washington, D.C., September 3, 1976.

Hirsch, J. Behavior-genetic analysis and its biosocial consequences. *Seminars in Psychiatry,* 1970, *2,* 89–105.

Hoffman, M. L. Father absence and conscience development. *Developmental Psychology,* 1971, *4,* 400–406.

Hunt, J. McV. *Intelligence and experience.* New York: Ronald, 1961.

Hurt, M., Jr. *Child abuse and neglect: A report on the status of the research.* Washington, D.C.: U.S. Government Printing Office, Department of Health, Education, and Welfare Publication No. (OHD) 74-20, 1975.

Jacobson, L. I., Berger, S. E., Bergman, R. L., Millham, J., & Greeson, L. E. Effects of age, sex, systematic conceptual learning, acquisition of learning sets, and programmed social interaction on the intellectual and conceptual development of preschool children from poverty backgrounds. *Child Development,* 1971, *42,* 1399–1415.

Jensen, A. R. How much can we boost IQ and scholastic achievement? *Harvard Educational Review,* 1969, *39,* 1–123.

Johnston, C. M., & Deisher, R. W. Contemporary communal child rearing: A first analysis. *Pediatrics,* 1973, *52,* 319–326.

Jolly, A. The study of primate infancy. In K. J. Connolly & J. S. Bruner (Eds.), *The growth of competence.* New York: Academic Press, 1974.

Kaffman, M. A comparison of psychopathology: Israeli children from kibbutz and from urban surroundings. *American Journal of Orthopsychiatry,* 1965, *35,* 509–520.

Kagan, J., & Klein, R. E. Cross-cultural perspectives on early development. *American Psychologist,* 1973, *28,* 947–961.

Kagan, J., Klein, R. E., Finley, G. E., Rogoff, B., & Nolan, E. A cross-cultural study of cognitive development. *Monographs of the Society for Research in Child Development,* 1979, *44* (5, Serial No. 180).

Kamin, L. J. *Science and politics of I.Q.* Potomac, Md.: Erlbaum, 1974.

Kaplan, D. M., Smith, A., Grobstein, R., & Fischman, S. E. Family mediation of stress. *Social Work,* 1973, *18,* 60–69.

Kaye, E. *The family guide to children's television: What to watch, what to miss, what to change, and how to do it.* New York: Pantheon Books, 1974.

Keniston, K., & The Carnegie Council on Children. *All our children: The American family under pressure.* New York: Harcourt Brace Jovanovich, 1977.

Kessen, W. (Ed.). *Childhood in China.* New Haven, Conn.: Yale University Press, 1975.

Kidd, K. K. A genetic perspective on stuttering. *Journal of Fluency Disorders,* 1977, *2,* 259–269.

Kirschner Associates. A national survey of the impacts of Head Start centers on community institutions. Report prepared for the U.S. Office of Child Development, May 1970.

Klaus, M. H., Jerauld, R., Kreger, N. C., McAlpine, W., Steffa, M., & Kennell, J. H. Maternal attachment: Importance of the first post-partum days. *The New England Journal of Medicine,* 1972, *286,* 460–463.

Kohen-Raz, R. Mental and motor development of kibbutz, institutionalized, and home-reared infants in Israel. *Child Development,* 1968, *39,* 489–504.

Lamb, M. E. The role of the father: An overview. In M. E. Lamb (Ed.), *The role of the father in child development.* New York: Wiley, 1976.

Lazar, I., Hubbell, V. R., Murray, H., Rosche, M., & Royce, J. The persistence of preschool effects: A long-term follow-up of 14 infant and preschool experiments. Final report to the Administration on Children, Youth and Families, U.S. Department of Health, Education, and Welfare, Grant No. 18-76-07843, 1977.

Lewis, M., & Rosenblum, L. (Eds.). *Friendship and peer relations.* New York: Wiley, 1975.

Lynn, D. B. *The father: His role in child development.* Monterey, Calif.: Brooks/Cole Publishing Co., 1974.

Miller, L. B., & Dyer, J. L. Four preschool programs: Their dimensions and effects. *Monographs of the Society for Research in Child Development*, 1975 (Serial No. 162).

Milowe, I. D., & Lourie, R. S. The child's role in the battered child syndrome. *Abstracts of the Society for Pediatric Research*, 1964, *25*, 1079.

Money, J., Hampson, J. G., & Hampson, J. L. Imprinting and the establishment of gender role. *Archives of Neurology and Psychiatry*, 1957, *77*, 333–336.

Nevo, B. Personality differences between kibbutz born and city born adults. *American Journal of Psychology*, in press.

Newberger, E. H. The myth of the battered child syndrome. *Current Medical Dialog*, 1973, *40*, 327–334. Reprinted in S. Chess & A. Thomas (Eds.), *Annual progress in child psychiatry and child development, 1974*. New York: Brunner/Mazel, 1975.

Newberger, E. H., & Hyde, J. N. Child abuse. Principles and implications of current pediatric practice. *Pediatric Clinics of North America*, 1975, *22*, 695–715.

Newberger, E. H., Reed, R., Daniel, J., Hyde, J., & Kotelchuck, M. Toward an etiologic classification of pediatric social illness: A descriptive epidemiology of child abuse and neglect, failure to thrive, accidents and poisonings in children under four years of age. Paper presented at the Biennial Meeting of the Society for Research in Child Development, Denver, Colorado, April 11, 1975.

Provence, S., Naylor, A., & Patterson, J. *The challenge of daycare*. New Haven, Conn.: Yale University Press, 1977.

Rabin, A. I. The sexes: Ideology and reality in the Israeli kibbutz. In G. M. Seward & L. C. Williamson (Eds.), *Sex roles in a changing society*. New York: Random House, 1970.

Rabin, A. I. *Kibbutz studies*. East Lansing, Michigan: Michigan State University Press, 1971.

Rabin, A. I., & Goldman, H. The relationship of severity of guilt to intensity of identification in kibbutz and non-kibbutz children. *Journal of Social Psychology*, 1966, *69*, 159–163.

Ramey, C. T., Collier, A. M., Sparling, J. J., Loda, R. A., Campbell, F. A., Ingram, D. L., & Finkelstein, N. W. The Carolina Abecedarian Project: A longitudinal and multidisciplinary approach to the prevention of developmental retardation. In T. Tjossem (Ed.), *Intervention strategies for high-risk infants and young children*. Baltimore, Md.: University Park Press, 1976.

Rettig, K. S. Relation of social systems to intergenerational changes in moral attitudes. *Journal of Personality and Social Psychology*, 1966, *4*, 400–414.

Richmond, J. B. The state of the child: Is the glass half-empty or half-full? *American Journal of Orthopsychiatry*, 1974, *44*, 484–490.

Rosenthal, D., & Kety, S. S. (Eds.). *The transmission of schizophrenia*. London: Pergamon Press, 1968.

Rubenstein, J. L., & Howes, C. Caregiving and infant behavior in day care and in homes. *Developmental Psychology*, 1979, *15*, 1–24.

St. John, N. H. *School desegregation: Outcomes for children*. New York: Wiley, 1975.

Sameroff, A. J., & Chandler, M. J. Reproductive risk and the continuum of caretaking casualty. In F. D. Horowitz, E. M. Hetherington, S. Scarr-Salapatek, & G. Siegel (Eds.), *Review of child development research*, Vol. 4. Chicago: University of Chicago Press, 1975.

Scarr, S., & Weinberg, R. A. IQ test performance of black children adopted by white families. *American Psychologist*, 1976, *31*, 726–739.

Scarr-Salapatek, S. Genetic determinants of infant development: An overstated case. In L. P. Lipsitt (Ed.), *Developmental psychobiology: The significance of infancy*. Hillsdale, N.J.: Erlbaum, 1976.

Schaffer, H. R., & Emerson, P. E. The development of social attachments in infancy. *Monographs of the Society for Research in Child Development*, 1964, *29*, (3, Serial No. 94).

Seitz, V., Abelson, W. D., Levine, E., & Zigler, E. Effects of place of testing on the Peabody Picture Vocabulary Test scores of disadvantaged Head Start and non-Head Start children. *Child Development*, 1975, *46*, 481–486.

Seitz, V., Apfel, N. H., & Efron, C. Long-term effects of early intervention: The New Haven Project. In B. Brown (Ed.), *Found: Long-term gains from early intervention*. *AAAS 1977 Selected Symposium 8*. Boulder, Colo.: Westview Press, 1978.

Seitz, V. R., Apfel, N. H., & Rosenbaum, L. Projects Head Start and Follow Through: A longitudinal evaluation of adolescents. In M. J. Begab, H. Garber, & H. C. Haywood (Eds.), *Proceedings of the NICHD Conference on the Prevention of Retarded Development in Psychosocially*

Disadvantaged Children, Madison, Wisconsin, July 25, 1978. Madison, Wis.: University of Wisconsin Press, in press.

Sharabany, R. Intimate friendship among kibbutz and city children and its measurement. Unpublished doctoral dissertation, Cornell University, 1974.

Silver, L. B., Dublin, C. C., & Lourie, R. S. Does violence breed violence? Contributions from a study of the child abuse syndrome. *American Journal of Psychiatry*, 1969, *126*, 404–407.

Smith, M. S., & Bissell, J. S. Report analysis: The impact of Head Start. *Harvard Educational Review*, 1970, *40*, 51–104.

Stern, L. Prematurity as a factor in child abuse. *Hospital Practice*, 1973, *8*, 117–123.

Thomas, A., & Chess, S. *Temperament and development.* New York: Brunner/Mazel, 1977.

Thomas, A., Chess, S., & Birch, H. G. *Temperament and behavior disorders in children.* New York: New York University Press, 1968.

Thomas, A., Hertzig, M. E., Dryman, I., & Fernandez, P. Examiner effect in IQ testing of Puerto Rican working-class children. *American Journal of Orthopsychiatry*, 1971, *41*, 809–821.

Trickett, P. K. Yale Child Welfare Research Program: An independent follow-up five years later. Paper presented at the 1979 Biennial Meeting of the Society for Research in Child Development, San Francisco, March 1979.

Turnbull, C. M. *The mountain people.* New York: Simon & Schuster, 1973.

U.S. Department of commerce. *Bureau of the Census*, 1970.

Webb, R. (Ed.). *Social development in daycare.* Baltimore, Md.: Johns Hopkins Press, 1977.

Weisz, J. R. Transcontextual validity in developmental research. *Child Development*, 1948, *49*, 1–12.

White House Conference on Children. *Profiles on children.* Washington, D.C.: U.S. Government Printing Office, 1970.

Wilson, E. O. *Sociobiology: The new synthesis.* Cambridge, Mass.: Harvard University Press, 1975.

Wilson, E. O. *On human nature.* Cambridge, Mass.: Harvard University Press, 1978.

Zigler, E. Project Head Start: Success or failure? *Learning*, 1973, *1*, 43–47.

Zigler, E. Welcoming a new journal. *Journal of Applied Developmental Psychology*, 1980. *1*(1), 1–6.

Zigler, E., Abelson, W. D., & Seitz, V. Motivational factors in the performance of economically disadvantaged children on the Peabody Picture Vocabulary Test. *Child Development*, 1973, *44*, 294–303.

Zigler, E., & Butterfield, E. C. Motivational aspects of changes in IQ test performance of culturally deprived nursery school children. *Child Development*, 1968, *39*, 1–14.

Zigler, E., & Muenchow, S. Mainstreaming: The proof is in the implementation. *American Psychologist*, 1979, *34*(10), 993–995.

Zigler, E., & Trickett, P. K. IQ, social competence, and evaluation of early childhood intervention programs. *American Psychologist*, 1978, *33*, 789–798.

Zimbardo, P. G., & Ruch, F. L. *Psychology and life* (9th ed.). Glenview, Ill.: Scott, Foresman, 1975.

2. PRINCIPLES OF PSYCHOLOGICAL DEVELOPMENT AND RESPONSE TO ART

Irvin L. Child

"Everyone to his own taste." As this old saying suggests, preferences in art are highly varied, and they often seem completely arbitrary. But psychologists, looking for order underlying diversity in human experience and behavior, find much regularity even in matters of taste.

For one thing, there really is a lot of agreement among people in what they like. Seeking to understand how the agreement arises, psychologists began long ago by stressing one of two sources, according to what kinds of agreement they were considering.

1. Heredity. This source has been stressed in confronting some regularities that seem to run through all of humankind. Preferences among simple colors, for instance—not works of art, but one of the elements used in visual art. Wherever people have been sampled, they always seem—on the average, despite individual differences—to like blue-green better than orange-red, to prefer cool colors over warm. It is easy to ascribe this to inborn human nature (though that doesn't carry us very far, and leaves us still without any explanation for the many individuals who have the opposite preference).

2. Environment. This source has been stressed in confronting the great differences between people in one society and people in another society. A preference for Japanese art is common in Japan, and a preference for Italian art is common in Italy. It is natural to attribute this to socialization in the simplest sense: pressure on individuals, exerted in a variety of ways, to conform to the preferences traditional in their society. This source, too, cannot easily be appealed to all by itself to explain the origin of unusual preferences in art.

Each of these views has its value in understanding human response to art and its elements. Each of them has in the past had its advocates as a comprehensive psychological theory of artistic taste. But today they seem overly simple, and a developmental view, with its recognition of greater complexity, is widespread. What sort of research does a developmental view guide us to, and what are some of the outcomes? Let's focus just on visual art, though we may hope that some of what we learn will apply to the other arts as well.

A developmental view would suggest that a person's liking for a work of art, or his or her judgment of how good a work of art it is, emerges from genuine interaction with it—that the person perceives, understands, and reacts to the work of art in a way determined by what he or she is and what the work is. It would suggest, moreover, that a person's preferences or judgments would develop slowly through the years, as the cumulative result at any time of the person's relevant experiences and reactions up to then.

This article was adapted from one entitled "Aesthetic Judgment in Children." Published by permission of Transaction, Inc. from *Transaction*, Vol. 7, No. 7. Copyright © 1970 by Transaction, Inc.

But what aspect of preferences or judgments would be most useful to select for initial study? I started with the assumption that people greatly interested and widely knowledgeable in the fine arts are likely to respond to a painting or sculpture in especially illuminating ways. So, as a reference point in studying responses to visual art, I sought the judgments of such people, whom I call experts; in my study, the experts were mostly graduate students in art or art history. The material apparatus I used in the study consisted of many pairs of specially prepared slides. Each pair shows two works of art similar in subject matter and usually similar in style, but very different in esthetic quality; that is, the experts agreed in considering one work to be much better than the other it was paired with. I then looked to see how other people would react to these same pairs.

PERSONALITY AND JUDGMENT

If it is true, as a developmental view suggests, that an individual's evaluation of a work of art emerges largely from his own real interaction with it, then different people, having followed somewhat different paths of development and interacting differently with the work of art, should arrive at differing evaluations. Perhaps we have much to learn about specific personal characteristics that encourage a preference for various features of art. The fact of special interest at the beginning of research here, though, should be what personal characteristics encourage development of preferences that resemble those of the experts. The preferences of experts—of artists and of those who especially value what artists produce—may be taken to define what we mean by esthetic interest or esthetic sensitivity. If we can describe the personality characteristics of people who have those interests, we may be able to infer what

kinds of satisfaction are to be found in an esthetic approach to art.

I began by comparing Yale undergraduates' judgments of the paired slides with those of the experts who had provided the initial point of reference. The resulting scores ranged, for different individuals, from high agreement with experts down to a random relation, and even further to a slight tendency toward systematic disagreement with the preferences of the experts. The scores for these individuals were then correlated with a number of measures of their personality characteristics. The results indicate that agreement with experts tends to go with an independent cognitive approach to the world. What I mean by this is that an individual with this kind of stance vis-à-vis the world searches for complex and novel experience, which he understands and evaluates in a process of relatively autonomous interaction between himself and the objects that provide him with that kind of experience.

We found that three personality characteristics regularly correlated with the extent to which a person's art preferences agreed with expert judgment: independence of judgment, awareness of impulsive emotion and of childish tendencies, and a tolerance of complexity, unrealistic experience, ambiguity, and ambivalence. A colleague, Sumiko Iwao, later translated into Japanese the questionnaires used to determine these characteristics, and she found that male undergraduates in Japan yielded similar correlations. Other colleagues in Pakistan (Mah Pervin Anwar, later Mah Pervin Hassan) and in Greece (M. Haritos-Fatouros) confirmed the same correlations within their own countries. Moreover, secondary-school students of both sexes in the United States showed many of the same correlations. It's interesting to note, also, that these personality characteristics are similar to those that other researchers have found to be related to creativity in the professions, including architecture and writing. The indication is that the satisfactions obtained by artistic creation and artistic appreciation are to a considerable extent the same; that is, both offer the pleasure of independent mastery over challenges posed by complex stimulation from without and complex memories, images, and impulses from within.

Another implication is that some agreement might be expected among people who have, within different cultural traditions, developed an interest in art. To hereditarians this should come as no surprise at all. Indeed, the pure hereditarian view would suggest a high degree of agreement extending to everyone, not just to people with a developed interest in art. Ethnographic studies indicate that similar esthetic interest appears in some highly diverse societies. But negative cases are found as well. There are, of course, societies whose artistic productions are not often considered by Westerners to have a high degree of esthetic interest. In addition, there seem to be societies in which Western observers cannot find much sign of esthetic response to anything. How do the hereditarians account for this jarring contradiction? If universal human nature is responsible for esthetic response, why isn't a work of art recognized as such in different cultural settings and capable of similar appeal in all those settings? The answer that our research suggests is that agreement about a given work would not necessarily be expected when we compare broadly representative samples of different societies; it might appear only when we compare samples of people who have a specialized interest in art, who have perhaps been led to it, in part, by such personality characteristics as I have described.

Several studies have now compared preferences (or judgments) by artistically knowledgeable people in other societies with esthetic judgments by American experts, using in each instance pictures that seem to require little special cultural background in order to be fairly well understood. The results so far suggest that in a number of diverse societies people interested in art do have preferences showing a small but dependable tendency to agree in their evaluation of esthetic worth.

CHILDREN'S EVALUATIONS OF PICTURES

Now let us turn to a directly developmental study of response to visual art—that is, to the study of children's art-related response to pictures. Here, too, we compared the children's responses to those of the experts, and here, too, we used pairs of slides.

Rosaline Schwartz and I showed the slides to school children without telling them how or why the pairs had been assembled, and asked them to indicate their personal preference for one or the other picture in each pair. The children were responding, of course, like our earlier adult subjects, to pairs in which the two pictures were alike or closely similar in many features likely to influence personal preference. The children were never asked to choose between an abstract and a representational painting, for example; if one picture was abstract, so was the other. Moreover, if one was a geometrical abstract, the other was also. If one portrayed a man, so did the other. We did this, of course, to reduce irrelevant kinds of variation among pictures, so that whatever kinds of differences may be associated with expert judgment of esthetic value would emerge more clearly. Irrelevant variations could not be entirely eliminated, naturally, but they were greatly reduced.

I would not argue that this method is ideal for studying the early development of esthetic sensitivity. It may be that young children do exhibit something closely akin to the esthetic sensitivity of art experts, but only in response to stimuli that would have no esthetic interest for adults. In the early 1930s Norman Meier's students tested preferences of very young children for symmetry versus asymmetry, unity versus disunity, etc., using simple materials appropriate to the children's interests. He wrote in 1933 that the results indicated the presence of some forms of esthetic sensitivity as early as "the second or third year in certain individuals and by the fifth year in significant group averages." Similarly, recent work by various experimental psychologists on the preferences of babies and young children for geometrical shapes and other patterns of varying complexity shows that we need to remain alert to the possibility that some forerunner of esthetic response may be present even at an age when the child cannot understand such complicated stimuli as ours.

We used very complex stimuli, however, slides reproducing real works of art. We have shown various school children, from first grade through twelfth, about 900 pairs of slides, asking each child to indicate which picture in a pair he or she liked better.

To what extent do the children at each age level prefer that work in each pair which the experts consider to be esthetically better? In elementary schools, at ages about 6 through 11, the agreement with experts averages about 40%, indicating a definite tendency to prefer the work the experts consider poorer. Through the 6 years of elementary school there is no consistent change in this percentage. In the six grades of secondary school, however, we do find regular changes from year to year. The percentage of agreement rises year by year until it finally approaches but does not quite reach 50%.

What changes in the maturing individuals underlie this increase in agreement with experts? One relevant change in some individuals, I am sure, is the accumulation of knowledge about what kind of art experts in our culture or people of higher rather than lower status consider to be fine—the influence that environmentalists stress. There is no easy way of assessing the exact importance of this source of change. Even if it plays the indispensable role I believe it does, we may be sure it interacts with other influences, and the interaction is partly by way of how it enters into the general development of the individual child. I would like to present evidence from two sources about what some of the other influences may be.

One kind of evidence comes from asking children to explain why they prefer one picture over the other. We interviewed 124 children, carefully selected to include at each grade level children who strongly tend to prefer what experts consider better and children who tend to prefer what experts consider poorer—"high scorers" and "low scorers" on esthetic preference.

The second kind of evidence does not depend upon the children's statements. It starts from the observation that the proportion of a given group of children whose preference agrees with expert judgment varies, from one pair of slides to another, all the way from a small minority to a large majority. We can analyze the contrast presented by each pair by asking to what extent the particular work experts consider better stands higher than its mate on a scale of brightness, a scale of saturation, a scale of judged happiness, and so on. We can then correlate the two kinds of information about the population of pairs: the magnitude of contrast on a perceptual dimension and the strength of preferential response of a group of children. In similar fashion, we can relate the perceptual contrasts to changes in the responses from one age group to another, to the differences in responses between boys and girls, and so on. Of special interest is the relation between these stimulus dimensions and the response of selected children—selected, like those we interviewed, to represent either high scorers or low scorers.

WHY EVALUATIONS CHANGE WITH AGE

I would organize changes in children's reactions to art around three progressive changes in development. The first is increased objectivity. Pavel Machotka has identified this change in the child's increasing recognition of affect located in the symbolism of the picture itself and in decreasing reference to his or her own idiosyncratic emotional responses. Our perceptual correlates of preference are not refined enough to capture this change. But some of the reasons our children gave for their choices do seem to change in ways that indicate increasing objectivity. One is a reason we called the *evocativeness* of a picture; here the choice of one work is justified by its more strongly suggesting a story or bringing to the child's mind a place or person he knows, as when a child explained his choosing a Hals portrait over a Rembrandt by saying, with little close relevance to the picture, "Because he's like a fighter—a famous sword-fighter on a horse. He's wearing a black hat so the enemy won't recognize him." Such obviously subjective reasons decrease with increasing age.

Another relevant category is reference to subject matter. Despite our effort to make the paired slides similar in subject, children often cited differences in explaining their preferences. We found such reasons to decline with age. The connection with objectivity may not be obvious in this case; but it is justified if we consider that the older child has relatively less concern with subject matter because he has come to have more concern with the objective characteristics of the sculpture or painting, with its status as a physical object, and with the separate symbols making it up, rather than just with the overall message of what it represents.

A second progressive change is increased cognitive differentiation. Younger children respond most to simple, quantitative aspects of a work of art. Asked to explain their preferences, they often mention colorfulness—high saturation and great variety of colors. Older children mention color in a way suggesting a complicated consideration of its relation to other features of the picture—its appropriateness, for example.

Young children also mention other quantitative considerations—liking a picture because it has more things in it, or because it looks complete rather than fragmentary, or because it looks as though it must have taken someone a very long time to make. Older children give these quantitative reasons less often. Qualitative and varied references to a great many other characteristics of the art—texture or shape, for example, activity or style—replace the younger child's reference to simple dimensions of stimulation value or abundance.

A third progressive change with development seems to be an increased tolerance for arousal or upset. Here I suggest that we are dealing with a cognitive consequence of general increase in ego strength. The more a person feels able to cope with his world on his own, the less he needs to defend against the possibility that the need to cope might arise. Young children are more likely to justify their preferences for one work or another by reasoning we would call sentimental—a liking for what is pleasant, pretty, or unthreatening to emotional equilibrium. Older children are more likely to give reasons that seem to assert a liking for deep and genuine feeling, whether pleasant or not, and a dislike for shallow or unacknowledged feeling.

We find, then, that children's preferences and the reasons they give for them do change with age in some uniform ways that can be understood by appealing to general principles of human development. At the same time, I would also stress that our findings indicate that we need to recognize that there are alternative paths of cognitive development and that there are great differences among them. I have described some of the general differences between younger and older children. These tend to hold true regardless of whether the children show any tendency to agree with experts' judgments. But I could equally well describe general differences between high scorers and low scorers, between children who do and do not tend to agree with experts. These differences are of the same general character regardless of whether we are considering children in grade school or in secondary school.

When we compare differences between scoring groups with differences between age groups, it does not look as though high scorers are simply developing faster. Some of the differences between high and low scorers are indeed the same as those between older and younger children. But some other differences between scoring groups are not close parallels to those for age. The low scorers say they like clarity and detail, for instance, where the high scorers instead indicate a liking for lack of detail and order. The high scorers like activity, roughness, depth, and challenges to understanding. Here, the reasons they give for their preference confirm what was suggested by the personality correlates I mentioned earlier: that esthetic orientation has to do with a liking for challenge to cognitive mastery of the environment. We seem to have evidence that, at least as early as grade-school age, children who lack an esthetic approach like clarity and detail, whereas children who have an esthetic approach like disorder, lack of detail, and various complexities of form and emotion which pose a challenge to understanding. Perhaps these two groups of children differ importantly in the general path of development. If so, the children with personalities that may lead them to esthetic interest are those whose specific path of development we need to trace to understand more adequately the internal processes out of which esthetic responsiveness arises.

3. MY BROTHER, MY SELF

Donald Dale Jackson

This is the tale of two Jims, identical twins who were separated in infancy, raised by adopted parents, and reunited only last year when they were 39. The startling parallels in their lives and behavior have made them a living laboratory in the study of heredity and environment, nature and nurture.

Jim Lewis was jittery. To shore up his courage for the encounter to come, he had brought along his fiancee, his younger brother, and his sister-in-law, but as he drove past the little white house just inside the Dayton city limits, he still wasn't sure that he wanted to go in. The man who waited inside had told him on the telephone that he was the identical twin who had dropped out of his life only a few weeks after they were born 39 years earlier, but Lewis couldn't help wondering. Was it possible? Could this, this *stranger*, really be the brother his adoptive mother had told him about so long ago, or was this some kind of cruel hoax? And what if it were his lost twin and he turned out to be crippled, or drunk, or hard up for money? A hundred uncomfortable questions raced through his mind. They were early anyway, he told the others; there was time for a beer at the Pizza Hut—a few more minutes couldn't hurt—before this confrontation he simultaneously craved and dreaded.

Inside the house at 1159 Chelsea Avenue, Jim Springer smoked one cigarette after another and tried to suppress a similar rush of apprehension: did he need a kidney transplant, this twin who had suddenly materialized? Had he been in the war? Was he bald? What if he wanted

money? Springer knew he was born a twin, but his adoptive parents had been told that his brother had died in infancy. He thought to himself that this was almost like meeting a ghost. And where the hell was he?

When the knock on the front door finally came, Springer and his wife, Betty, opened it to find Lewis's fiancee, Sandy, at the head of a nervous procession. Behind her was Lewis's adoptive brother, Larry, and his sister-in-law, Marie. Lagging in the rear, still wavering, was Lewis himself. As Springer recalled the moment, "Jim and I shook hands and then we all just looked at each other for a few seconds. Then we broke out laughing."

It was the superficial differences that struck all of them first: Springer wore glasses and Lewis didn't (they learned later that Lewis had worn glasses at one time and that their vision was identical); Springer combed his long brown hair forward, over his forehead, while Lewis's hair was shorter and neatly brushed back. But when Springer removed his glasses, the final phantom doubts vanished: there was no question in anyone's mind that they were identical twins. "They were so much alike it was ridiculous," says Betty Springer, not only in size and coloring and features but "in the way they stood, the way they held

This article is reprinted with permission from *Smithsonian Magazine*, October 1980.

their hands." When the Jims were left to share what they knew about their natural parents and the circumstances of their adoptions, their deep and drawling voices were so similar that the others couldn't tell who was speaking. A few minutes later the two men, both brimming over with emotion, got up and awkwardly embraced. "We just sort of let everything go," Jim Lewis says.

As they look back now on their reunion after 39 years apart, both twins see it as an almost mystical turning point in their lives. "Right off the bat I felt close, it wasn't like meeting a stranger," Lewis says. "I wish every family could experience that feeling," says Springer. "It was like we'd known each other all our lives and we'd just been gone a hell of a long time. God, every time I think about it"—his voice breaks—"it just gets to me."

When they had first talked on the phone, the brothers had discovered a mutual taste for Miller's *Lite* beer. "I asked him what kind he drank," Springer recalls, "and when he said Miller's, I said, 'Damn, so do I!' " But an occasion this festive clearly demanded something more. The Lewises and Springers toasted each other with champagne, often and ardently enough that the snapshots they took reveal a dewy-eyed reverie only partially attributable to the emotions of the moment. When Lewis was persuaded to brush his hair forward, the brothers looked like a matched set of slightly out-of-focus figurines.

Amid the euphoria of their rediscovery of each other, the brothers stumbled upon the first of a series of startling parallels in their lives and behavior, parallels that would almost instantly transform them into a kind of living laboratory for behavioral scientists, while at the same time turning them into quasi-celebrities. The first revelation was the names: not only had both been named James by their adoptive families, but they discovered that both had been married twice, that both of their first wives

were named Linda and both of their second wives Betty. Lewis had three sons, one of whom was named James Allan; Springer had three daughters and a son, James Allan; both had at one time owned dogs named Toy. The eerie pattern of the repetitious names ("We both just thought it was weird, that's all," Lewis says) would turn out to be merely the first of a series of similarities which would eventually go to the heart of one of science's oldest and most profound enigmas, the relative influence on human behavior of heredity and environment, genes and life experience—nature and nurture. The dramatic reunion of the brothers Jim, the story of a bond arbitrarily sundered only to be joyfully restored four decades later, was something else as well—a clue, perhaps, to the eternally intriguing mysteries of personality and behavior.

When the twins met again 2 weeks later at Jim Lewis's home in Elida, Ohio, some 80 miles north of Dayton, a local reporter wrote an article about them that was picked up by the Associated Press. Reading this story in the *Minneapolis Tribune*, a lanky University of Minnesota psychologist named Thomas Bouchard immediately recognized a once-in-a-lifetime scientific opportunity. The study of identical twins reared apart, Bouchard knew, was one of the purest and most definitive methods of separating the influences of heredity and environment; in the simplest terms, any differences between them—in behavior, personality, interests, values, even physiology—would have to be due to the differences in their environments.

"I was trained as an environmentalist," Bouchard says, "but in recent years the evidence that genetics has a greater effect on behavior than we previously thought has been mounting. For me, the chance to study identical twins reared apart was irresistible. It's the ultimate experiment in behavioral genetics." In less than an hour after he read the story, Bouchard had secured a preliminary grant from the university to fund a clinical look at the Jim twins that would include dozens of personality and aptitude tests in addition to extensive medical and psychiatric examinations. The Jims had met each other on February 9, 1979; on March 11 they reported to Bouchard's office in Minneapolis for an all-expense-paid week under scientific scrutiny.

"Dr. Bouchard said he wanted to get us before we were—what was that word he used?—'contaminated' by being around each other too much," Springer remembers. "I didn't believe him when he first called. It sounded, you know, too good to be true." It sounded even better when Bouchard told them that the invitation included their wives. Lewis and Sandy, his third wife, had been married only a few days before, with Springer standing beside his brother as best man.

The personality and attitude profiles that emerged from the Jim twins' tests stunned Bouchard and his colleagues. "We couldn't get over it," he declares. "I was expecting to find all kinds of differences because of their different backgrounds, but what leaped out at us were the striking similarities between the twins. I wasn't prepared for it. Nothing prepares you for it."

In one test, which measured such personality variables as tolerance, conformity, flexibility, self-control, and sociability, the twins' scores were so close that they approximated the totals that result when the same person takes the test twice. "In intelligence, in mental abilities, in their likes and dislikes and their interests, they were remarkably similar," Bouchard says. "The pattern carried through in the little things that go together to form a personality," he points out, "the way you sit or gesture, the pace of your voice, your body language. They were like bookends."

Between the tests and their after-hours conversations, the Jims found that each of them enjoyed working with wood, making

frames and furniture at their basement workbenches. Both had been indifferent students, Lewis dropping out in the tenth grade and Springer barely graduating from high school. Both had served as sheriff's deputies in nearby Ohio counties. Both drove Chevrolets, chain-smoked Salems, gnawed their fingernails, enjoyed stock-car racing, and disliked baseball. They were amazed to discover that they both had vacationed at the same three-block-long beach on the Florida Gulf Coast.

The parallels in their medical histories were equally stunning. Both had slightly high blood pressure and both had experienced what they thought were heart attacks, with no heart disease diagnosed. Both had gained weight at about the same time and leveled off, again at about the same time. Both had undergone vasectomies. Most striking of all, both suffered severe headaches that began when they were teenagers and continued sporadically afterward. In both cases the headaches had been diagnosed as migraines; they generally persisted for about 12 hours and were not relieved by aspirin or other drugs. "What struck me," says Dr. Leonard Heston, a psychiatrist who participated in Bouchard's study, "is that they used almost exactly the same words to describe the headaches." "It feels like somebody's hitting you in the back of the neck with a two-by-four," Springer told me. "It's centered in the back of the neck, and it damn near knocks me out sometimes," Lewis said. "I can always tell when my brother's got a headache," he went on, "by the way he acts—sort of sluggish. I know the feeling." Their brain-wave tests, which produce skyline-like graphs illustrating their responses to various stimuli, look like two views of the same city.

For Springer and Lewis, the weeks after their visit to Minneapolis were a whirl of head-turning celebrity-style activity. They appeared on Johnny Carson's show ("We stayed through three segments," Springer marvels), chatted with Mike Douglas, and met fellow Ohioan Jonathan Winters at a Beverly Hills coffee shop ("He's a nut," Lewis alleges). Articles appeared in *People*, *Newsweek*, and other magazines. A writer began work on a book, and a film company expressed interest. They acquired—but later got rid of—an agent. Springer, the more gregarious of the two, did most of the talking, but neither man succumbed to delusions of stardom. Both are essentially small-town Midwesterners who have struggled—often working at two jobs—all their lives; Lewis is now a steelworker, Springer a records clerk for a power company. One of Lewis's fellow workers might nickname him "Hollywood," but the two Jims know better.

The real beneficiaries of the Jims' season in the sun were Bouchard and his cohorts in Minnesota. Several other sets of identical twins who had been raised separately and later reunited got in touch with Bouchard after they saw or read about the Jim-and-Jim show. Two by two they arrived in the Twin Cities—an electronics expert whose brother was a fisherman in Florida, a pair of middle-aged British housewives, 16-year-old Nigerian boys who had both emigrated to the United States, two women who had lived much of their lives in St. Louis without knowing each other. By the summer of 1980, Bouchard had burdened his computer with data on 15 pairs and ferreted out leads on 34 more.

The pattern of behavioral and medical similarities which the Jim twins had exhibited recurred time and again. Not always, to be sure—and Bouchard is careful to point out that the findings at this stage are still tentative and suggestive, not conclusive—but often enough to indicate that "the genetic effect," in Bouchard's words, "pervades the entire structure of personality. If someone had come to me with results like this, I wouldn't have believed him. I was aghast."

When a British pair named Bridget and Dorothy got off the plane in Minneapolis, they were each wearing seven rings. One had named her son Richard Andrew; the other had a son called Andrew Richard. Another pair of women shared the same phobias—both were uncomfortable in the water, in closed-in places, and at high elevations. Two other British women had the same rare thyroid disease, while four sets of twins struggled with the same speech defects. In one case, both twins—young men—were homosexuals, though in another instance one was homosexual and the other heterosexual.

The twins who caused the biggest sensation were Oskar Stöhr of Germany and Jack Yufe of California. Separated soon after their birth in Trinidad, they had grown up in starkly different cultural surroundings: Oskar raised by his grandmother in occupied Czechoslovakia, went to a Nazi-run school; Yufe was brought up a Jew by their Jewish father in Trinidad. Though differences in their attitudes persist, Bouchard saw arresting similarities in "temperament, tempo, the way they do things," as well as in their idiosyncrasies—both wore neatly clipped moustaches, stored rubber bands around their wrists, and read magazines back to front. Both also shared the peculiar habit of sneezing loudly in public to get a reaction, a trait that baffles scientists and passers-by alike. "With some of these things," Bouchard smiles, "you can only shrug and say, 'It's in someone else's hands.' "

Does all this mean that there is a gene for public sneezing, another for jewelry preference, and a third governing the choice of vacation resorts? Not quite. But while repeatedly emphasizing the danger of springing to conclusions before all the data are collected and analyzed, Bouchard observes that some characteristics thought to be environmental—phobias, for instance—may well have a genetic component.

Bouchard also suspects that twins raised apart may actually be more similar than those reared together, since pairs brought up together often emphasize and elaborate the differences between them. Critics contend that the twins' different environments have been inadequately studied and that adopted twins may not be a fair sample because the specific circumstances of the adoption may affect subsequent behavior. But Bouchard believes that most scientists are awaiting his conclusions with open minds. "In a sense we're tempering the idea of the importance of the family in child rearing," he says. "Our findings suggest that the subtle differences between and within families are not as important as people have thought in determining interests, abilities, and personalities." He may be threatening an entire profession dealing with guidance and family counseling. The tree may not grow as the twig is bent after all.

The Minnesota academics also worry about the political and moral implications of their work, which could conceivably be misused to support theories of inherent racial superiority and such proposals as the high-IQ "sperm bank" promoted by Nobel laureate William Shockley. "People will try to bend our findings to support their own values," Bouchard fears. "Social judgments are not related to our findings, and shouldn't be. True science can be a two-edged sword, but I believe that new knowledge, when properly used, will always have a beneficial effect."

"My house is near the end of the block," Jim Lewis told me on the telephone. "It's the only one with a white bench around a tree in the front yard."

Lewis greeted me at the door of his comfortable three-bedroom house and led me into the kitchen, where we sat down at a table. He lit a cigarette, poured a cup of coffee, and began talking in a slow, even drawl about his boyhood and his search for his brother.

"My father worked as a boilerman for the school board in Lima," he said. "In his spare time he remodeled houses. When I got big enough, I helped him. Neither of my parents had much education, and Dad wasn't home too much—he was always working. There were times when we were poor, when my dad was sick. I can remember eating powdered eggs. I got into trouble some at school, fights and stuff. Once I ran off to Cincinnati and my mom left me in a juvenile home there for fourteen days, to teach me a lesson."

There was a controlled intensity about Lewis and a sense of somber strength. His gaze was level but not altogether open—something seemed held in reserve. His manner was courteous and somewhat grave. He smoked constantly.

"My mother told me I had a twin when I was about six, but I wasn't that interested. The only way she found out was when she went to the courthouse to get the final papers and told 'em my name was Jim and they said, 'His twin's named Jim, too.' I got a little more curious about it as I got older, but I didn't do anything about it. I dropped out of school and went into the Marines when I was seventeen." His chin rested on his fist as he talked. "When I got out—I wish now that I'd stayed in—I worked in a bakery, drove a gas truck awhile, then got a job at the steel mill.

"I always kinda felt I wanted to have somebody close to me. I felt alone, I guess. When I was about five my mother adopted twin boys—Larry and Gary—and we'd fight all the time. After I grew up, I started thinking about having a twin, but then I'd put it out of my mind. I was working at the mill. Once, about five years ago, I took off for Bradford—that's where we were born—to see if I could find him. I didn't really know what I was looking for, just hoping to run into him, I guess.

"Then about two years ago I got to talking to my mother about it and I decided to see what I could find out. I don't know why I did it then—maybe it wasn't meant to happen before. I went to the courthouse and they had his name. They got in touch with Jim's mother to see if it was O.K., and she called Jim and Jim tried to call me, but I had an unlisted number on account of my police work. So he finally left a message with my brother Larry, and I called him. I just right out asked him, 'Are you my brother?' and he said yes. I think we were both nervous wrecks on the phone. We didn't say much else, just arranged to meet at his place."

Getting up to show me his basement workshop and some of his woodwork— frames, a miniature picnic table, block letters spelling out "I LOVE YOU" in the bedroom—Lewis walked with a slight hitch. It was a tough-guy walk. "I gotta go talk to the loan companies tomorrow, tell'em I'm gonna be late," he said. He smiled a slow, careful smile that gentled his rugged face. "I s'pose it could be worse."

He told me that his tastes in music ran to classical and country-and-western, in movies he liked comedies and good dramas but "not X-rated stuff," and that he cared little for politics, voting for Nixon twice and for Carter in 1976. "You know, Jim and me, we don't think too much about the similarities and all, we just accept it like it is," he said. "We're mainly just tickled to death to have each other"—the phrase sounded strangely soft, somehow out of character, but it was obviously genuine— "and we're enjoying it. I kinda like the publicity and all, too, but I know I'm no big wheel, I'm just riding the wave."

I asked him if his friends ever told him that he resembled anyone in particular. "Yeah, you know that guy that was in *Cheyenne*, Clint Walker, they say I look like him." I could see the resemblance.

Two days later, I met the other Jim in the yard outside his five-room rented duplex in Dayton. "Hi there," he said in the manner of a comic master of ceremonies, "I'm Jim Springer." My first reaction was surprise at their different styles; they were obviously not carbon copies of each other. Springer wore a T shirt inscribed "I'm only here for the beer" and carried a cocktail. His manner was animated and outgoing; he joked constantly, almost compulsively, and sprinkled his conversation with such modish expressions as "far out" and "it blows my mind." He spoke in his brother's voice, but the words came in rambling paragraphs instead of unadorned sentences. He seemed at once more vulnerable and less melancholy than his twin. I remembered a comment that Bouchard had made: however tantalizing the similarities, he had said, the differences between separated twins might ultimately be even more significant. I asked the same question that I had asked Lewis—did his friends say he looked like anyone in particular? "Dick Van Dyke," he replied without hesitation. I was startled to find myself in agreement.

Settling into a chair in his tiny living room, Springer turned down the volume on a record player blaring rock music and lit a cigarette. He told me that his father had worked as a lineman for a power company. "He drank a lot," he said, "but he was never mean. We always had enough to get by." They lived in Piqua, about 45 miles from the town Jim Lewis grew up in. "My mother was very religious. I worked in a grocery store when I was a kid, and later I fixed up used cars. I got out of the draft because I was married and had a baby. I became a meter reader in Troy and then got this job I have now. It's boring work, but I've been doing it too long to change."

He frequently replied to my questions with one-liners. "How did you do in school?" "I was there." "What subject did you like?" "Sex." "How far back can you remember?" "About six months." But the more we talked, the more the resemblances to his brother began to intrude on the differences. Like his brother, he is demonstrative and affectionate with his family—both scatter love notes around the house. Both spend their weekends doing household chores and yard work. Like Lewis, Springer considers himself apolitical; he said he voted for Carter, Nixon, and Humphrey in three presidential elections. Both men dwell in the present and worry little about the past or future. "I saw the loan company yesterday," Springer told me. "I didn't have to tell them I'd be late, they just take it for granted.

"The differences between Jim and me may be the differences between living in the city and the country," he said. "Maybe it was just wishing or maybe it was this bond that twins are supposed to have, but I always figured he was alive; it was like I had this secret playmate somewhere. I went chasing up to a bowling alley in Troy one time after some guy told me that he saw me there. I was looking for him. Then I went to Bradford where we were born and looked there."

The Jims were most alike, it seemed to me, in ways that the scientists can't quantify; they are, in the fullest sense of the phrase, kindred spirits. "If I know something will tick him off I don't do it, because I know it would tick me off," Springer said. "God, we're just enjoying each other. Nobody can imagine what it feels like." Jim Lewis had expressed the same thought in almost precisely the same words. "A couple of months ago we built a picnic table together, it was the first thing we ever made together." Springer rubbed his eyes. "Jim said he'd been waiting all his life to do something like that. And so had I. I just feel lucky as hell. I'm me and he's him, but at the same time he's me and I'm him. Do you understand?" He went into another room and came back with a framed scroll that his brother had made and given to him. "February 9, 1979, was the most important day of my life," the inscription read. "On that day we started a lifetime relationship together and we will never be apart again."

And that, it seemed to me, was the final truth of the Jims' reunion, not the genetic similarities or the environmental differences but the joyous consummation of a bond restored, of love regained—the triumph of family. Both Jims recognized that truth intuitively and reacted to it identically—with gratitude. The scientists can't prove it, but maybe their souls are identical, too.

As I walked through the Springers' yard to my car, I noticed something that I hadn't seen before—a white bench built around a tree, like the one on Jim Lewis's lawn. It was the only one on the block.

4. CONCEPTION, PREGNANCY, AND BIRTH: THE POLITICS OF INFANCY

Freda Rebelsky

Carollee Howes

Joanne Krakow

It is important to remember that infants are born into a world, a political world, a world of people and institutions. We suggest that infant researchers need to be continually aware of this social-political reality. "Infancy" comes from the word *infans*, which means without language. This chapter addresses the question, who speaks for the infant?—this creature who cannot speak for itself. The answer is that no one does: There are few data available on many important issues related to infancy. Our goal is to point out some social issues on which research and action are needed.

The popular press has recently recognized that infants are born into a political system. A review of a recent book on the history of contraception (Reed, 1978) concluded: "Pregnancy has not been simply a personal matter or even a subjective question of vice and virtue. It has always belonged to politics, economics and technology" (Filene, 1978, p. 11). We propose to raise issues related to pregnancy, primarily in the United States. We address two sets of questions: First, who gets pregnant and bears children? Second, what political factors affect fetal development and relate to producing healthy, active infants? Although we subtitled our article "The Politics of Infancy," the political issues of concern here affect the infant before birth and even before conception.

WHO GETS PREGNANT AND BEARS CHILDREN?

Approximately 5 million women in the United States become pregnant each year. Of these pregnancies, 800,000 end in miscarriages, 1 million in abortions, 36,000 in stillbirths, and 3,120,000 in live births. One-fifth of the women who become pregnant are adolescents (*Eleven Million Teenagers*, 1976); that is, 1 of every 10 adolescent girls gets pregnant annually. Of the 1 million teenagers who become pregnant each year, approximately one-fourth are married at the time of conception. Another 10% marry before giving birth, 20% bear children out of wedlock, 27% obtain abortions, and 14% abort spontaneously (*Eleven Million Teenagers*, 1976). These statistics are sobering indeed. Three-quarters of a million fetuses are conceived out of wedlock to adolescents every year in this country.

That 20 to 27% of all pregnancies end in abortion suggests that a great many pregnancies in this country are unplanned and unwanted. Zill (1977), asking mothers after the birth of their babies, found that one out of every seven American children was initially unwanted.

The obvious question raised by these statistics is: Why do so many unwanted pregnancies occur? The answer is related to sex and parenthood education and to the availability of contraception and contraceptive information.

SEX AND PARENTHOOD EDUCATION: HOW DO YOUNG PEOPLE LEARN ABOUT SEX, CONCEPTION, AND PARENTHOOD?

Sex education is mandated in six states in the United States, and health education is mandated in 28 (*Eleven Million Teenagers*, 1976). Health education does not necessarily include sex education, however, nor does it necessarily include realistic information about sex, about conception, or about what it is like to be a parent.

Most young people do not know what birth is about or how babies are conceived. They know about sex in the same way that many lay people know about electricity: They know the vocabulary and can use the words but do not really understand the process. They are unable to use their knowledge in relation to decisions or to other facts.

Teenagers also lack basic information about their bodies and their sexuality. Thorbeck (1976), in a study of changes in body concept with the onset of menarche, interviewed 205 teenage girls. At the end of the interview, she told each subject to leave an anonymous note if there were any questions she would like answered. Of the 205 14-year-old girls, 187 (91%) left notes with questions such as, "Why doesn't anyone teach us about LIFE?" or "Nobody talks to me about sex—I have to learn it in the streets." or "Why are my parents so afraid?" or "What happens when you kiss somebody? Can you get pregnant?"

Many parents and teachers are uncomfortable talking to young people about sex. This is true among the privileged as well as the underprivileged: A survey by high school students in a prosperous suburban community (Denebola, 1978) found that only 14% of the students considered the school sex education informative.

As important as what specific information to provide about sex is the issue of how to teach it to young people. Developmentalists are well aware that adolescents are very different from full-grown people. They are different cognitively, socially, and emotionally.

The two most frequent death factors in adolescence are suicides and accidents (Massachusetts Department of Public Health, 1975; Puffer & Griffith, 1967). In both instances it is possible that some adolescents feel that death cannot happen to them, and then get into situations where by luck or chance it does. This suggests that adolescents lack the ability to think about consequences of acts in an abstract and realistic way. They lack formal operations (to use Piaget's term), the ability to reason abstractly especially about their own lives. At issue is how to embed a relevant educational program in a high school when students do not really know how to think about their futures and do not yet know how to perceive themselves as people with a future. It is a difficult question and one that developmentalists must address.

Another issue for education concerns parenting. In general, most people in our society, including adolescents and childless adults, have very little experience with children. Many teenage girls babysit; few teenage boys do. When high schools or junior high schools do offer courses in child development or child care, they tend to offer them to girls only. And nowhere do future parents systematically learn about how to take care of children, to parent, or to fit parenting into other demands in their lives, demands such as work, recreation, and being a spouse. When Rebelsky teaches child psychology, she mentions that babies do not sleep through the night until they are approximately 3 months old, and that many babies do not sleep in the quiet way that adults expect. (Babies, in fact, seldom sleep predictably, unless one is trying to measure something in a lab!) She also tells her classes that babies are very intrusive on parents' free time, and that sooner or later most people resent their babies for intruding. Years later, students write to tell her how useful that knowledge was in preparing them for the realities of parenthood. As with sex education, developmentalists can make important contributions to planning parent education programs for young people which fit their cognitive and socioemotional levels.

CONTRACEPTION: WHO LEARNS ABOUT HOW TO AVOID UNWANTED PREGNANCY?

Even the most effective education programs for adolescents will only provide partial solutions to the problems of unwanted pregnancies. Contraception can be wanted but unavailable. Historically, birth control has been a political issue rather than a personal-choice issue. In the nineteenth century the middle classes were exhorted to have children in order to compete with the "lesser" classes (Reed, 1978). More recently, the other side of the same coin appeared with the "discovery" of the population explosion in the Third World. Rapid expansion of the population, it was reasoned, threatened rapid economic development. By 1965 the Rockefeller Foundation Population Council claimed that population control was a relatively noncontroversial part of economic wisdom (Reed, 1978). The council may have been surprised to hear its policies emotionally opposed as "forced genocide." Although, to paraphrase Mark Twain, the reports of the death of the controversy are premature, one clear political issue in the United States concerns open access to contraception.

In the early 1980s contraception continues to be a political issue in the United States in at least two major ways: in uneven delivery of information, services, and methods and in responsibility for contraception. Today good contraceptives are often unavailable to the young, the poor, and men.

Despite the sexual activity of teenagers (11 million people between the ages of 15 and 19 are estimated to have had sexual intercourse [*Eleven Million Teenagers*, 1976]), it is still illegal in several states to provide contraception to minors without parental consent. In fact, only 26 states specifically affirm the right of minors to consent to their own contraceptive care (*Eleven Million Teenagers*, 1976). One-half of all the sexually active teenagers in this country have no access to birth control information (O'Reilly, 1978). This is a political issue. Legislators must consider the effect of voting in favor of enabling teenagers access to birth control. They must weigh the effects of such a vote against their record for future political campaigns.

We know that voluntary childlessness is also related to income and education. Low- and marginal-income women are faced with involuntary pregnancies and involuntary sterilization. When poor or uneducated women are given contraceptive information, they are likely to be encouraged to use the pill or IUD method and not be told of the potentially harmful side effects (Boston Women's Health Book Collective, 1975).

Also, poor nonwhite women are more likely than other women in this society to be sterilized. In Puerto Rico, 35% of the females of childbearing age are sterilized. It is estimated that 16% of white women, 20% of all black adult women, and even a higher percentage of American Indians are sterilized (U.S. Department of Health, Education and Welfare, 1978).

The U.S. Department of Health, Education and Welfare has been pressured, by litigation by various groups, such as the American Civil Liberties Union, and by studies documenting sterilization abuses using HEW money, to formulate new guidelines for sterilization. There are presently interim guidelines in Washington which provide for a 72-hour waiting period between consent and actual operation and that do not allow sterilization of anyone under 18 years of age. Many groups are now fighting for a 30-day waiting period and a minimum age of 21 for sterilization. The reason for the former is that women have frequently been approached about sterilization at the time of childbirth, a time when few will be able to give much thought to the long-term consequences. For relatively illiterate women, intimidated by the public health system, a 30-day waiting period will allow for a balanced decision separated from the stress of childbirth and delivery. Middle-class, well-educated women in the private health system are not usually approached at such a time unless there is a medical need. The new regulations will apply only to elective operations and not those ordered by doctors for medical reasons, although many groups (e.g., women's groups and Planned Parenthood) advocate no distinction between elective and necessary sterilization. The intent is to give women time to consider the consequences when they are sufficiently mature and sufficiently unstressed to decide well. Any new regulations, however, as they "protect" the poor more, also reduce the ability of the poor to make a decision about sterilization as easily as a more wealthy woman with a private doctor. Again, it is not easy to say what is the "best" guideline, but it is clear from this discussion that guidelines are political gestures.

A final issue related to contraception concerns responsibility. All of the effective means of preventing pregnancy (e.g., the Pill, IUD, diaphragm) require the woman to take the responsibility. In a culture where the majority of our doctors and medical researchers are male, one wonders why no adequate contraceptive methods for males have been developed. At a minimum, we should ask how the focus of new research is selected and how funding for research is allocated.

ABORTION

An alternative to contraception is pregnancy plus abortion. This is another political issue. The idea that abortion is wrong and should be illegal did not become widespread in the United States until the late nineteenth century. In fact, even Pope Pius IX formally proscribed it as immoral only in 1869 (Rich, 1976). As with the issue of contraception, there is a disparity between high- and low-income women in access to abortions under medically safe conditions. Essentially, women who can pay may have them, whereas those who cannot pay may not. In state after state, legislatures have withdrawn funds for abortions as part of medical assistance programs for poor people. At this writing, only seven states fund all abortions as part of Medicaid. The remaining 43 states fund abortions only under certain conditions (such as when the woman's life is in danger or when the pregnancy resulted from rape or incest [Kschinka, 1978]).

In short, we have seen that political issues are involved in who learns about planning for wanted and preventing unwanted pregnancies. Access to information varies by income, by age, and by education. We end this section with a final word about adolescent pregnancy. Aside from questions about the adequacy of adolescent parenting, we are concerned about the social and economic consequences when an adolescent female leaves the educational system. Pregnancy is the most common cause of school dropout (*Eleven Million Teenagers*, 1976). Leaving school means leaving the milieu of socialization and for many entering a life of isolation and poverty.

Preparation for parenting includes both education about parenting and experience as an adult in society. Current political practices prevent such preparation.

The remainder of this chapter is directly concerned with fetal development: assuming that one wants to have a child, what social-political factors are related to producing a healthy, active infant?

PRENATAL CARE AND EDUCATION

Prenatal care has many facets: nutritional counseling, screening for diseases such as rubella, testing for maternal infections, instruction about drugs to avoid, and maintenance of good general health throughout the pregnancy. Lack of prenatal care is a predictive factor for many postnatal problems, among them mental retardation and low birth weight (Sameroff & Chandler, 1975). Low birth weight itself constitutes a major problem: it is related to a wide variety of sequelae including death, learning problems, and poor health.

As with contraception, access to prenatal care depends on social class and race (Tulkin, 1972). Again, poor and nonwhite women are those who are least likely to receive prenatal care.

Another issue concerns when prenatal care begins. We know that the fetus is most vulnerable to insult during the first trimester. We now have means to determine whether a woman is pregnant within 10 days of conception. However, most women of all socioeconomic groups do not see an obstetrician until the second or third prenatal month. By then it is too late to benefit from counsel against potentially harmful over-the-counter drugs (such as aspirin and cold remedies [Wilson, 1973]). And by then, the woman has already missed 2 months of supplemental vitamins. Teen-

agers present a special case of late prenatal care. A study of teenage parenting found them to delay confirming their pregnancies until well into the second trimester (Cannon-Bonventre, Kahn, & Engellman, 1977). Seventy percent of pregnant adolescents get no prenatal care until the second or third trimester.

ENVIRONMENTAL POLLUTANTS

One of the things we now know is that there is "pollution of the fetus." According to traditional wisdom, the placenta is a semipermeable membrane. The newer data suggest that it is a *very* permeable membrane. Our old notions that a mother could give up her own health for the health of her baby are simply not true. For example, we used to think that the mother's teeth would fall out if she were malnourished, but that the baby would be okay. "It just ain't so." Many things in our society seem to be going through the mother to the baby.

For example, alcohol, drug addiction, and cigarette smoking have some effect on the fetus. Although we do not understand the specific mechanisms that operate to affect the fetus, we cannot ignore the data. Women who smoke tend to have premature babies, to have smaller babies, and to have a higher incidence of perinatal mortality. We do not *know* that smoking *causes* these results. Women who smoke may be different emotionally, may be more or less active, or may eat less or differently from women who do not smoke. Any number of factors may covary with maternal smoking. Nonetheless, maternal smoking is associated with increased prenatal risk.

We do have easily interpretable data about alcohol: high alcohol intake on the part of the mother is linked to fetal alcohol syndrome and to high activity at birth (Winsmore, 1977). Even without substantive political interference, political empire building blocks action on this issue. The

Bureau of Alcohol, Tobacco, and Firearms in the Treasury Department began proceedings to require labels on alcoholic beverages warning women that drinking during pregnancy may cause birth defects. As reported in *Science* on February 17, 1978, these hearings continued for a long time due to a jurisdictional dispute between the Food and Drug Administration and the Bureau of Alcohol, Tobacco, and Firearms in the Treasury Department. The debate had nothing to do with whether or not alcohol is good for a baby, or whether it is good for a mother, or whether labeling should occur. The question was who should do it. And, as part of this lengthy process, on November 6, 1981, *Science* reported that the issue is still alive. An educational campaign of NIAAA (National Institute of Alcohol Abuse and Alcoholism) has a simple message for women: "For baby's sake . . . and yours, don't drink during pregnancy" (p. 642). But, as the NIAAA director says, "The message is certainly controversial." And now the debate is over what to say.

What goes through to the fetus seems to be practically anything that anybody looks at. The long-range results are not always something we can predict. But we can look at short-range consequences and potential long-range ones. Babies born near airports seem to be smaller, have more birth defects, and to be less responsive to noise than babies born far from airports (Ando & Hattori, 1973). In the Los Angeles Basin, the air pollution levels are related to significant variances in baby birth weights—11 ounces lower in the most polluted areas compared to the least polluted areas, controlling for social class (Williams, Spence & Tideman, 1977). Industrial pollutants are getting through the placenta.

Unfortunately, there are many harmful substances that individual pregnant women cannot avoid (see, for example, Howes & Krakow, 1977). Women must breathe air, drink water, and eat something during pregnancy.

In addition, 9 out of 10 women will work outside of the home sometime during their lives, and most work during the childbearing years. What is the work environment like? If it has x-rays, kepone gases, or lead, then women workers as well as the wives of male workers risk an increase in sterility, spontaneous abortion, and birth defects when they work in such establishments (Howes & Krakow, 1977).

In our society, we drug mothers. A study in Houston, Texas, found that middle-class and upper-class women with private doctors took between 3 and 29 different drugs during pregnancy: 41% of them took antibiotics, 35% took antacids, and almost all of them smoked or drank alcohol. We must begin to provide women with information about the potential fetal effects of such pollutants. And we must press the medical profession to recognize these effects and to advise patients accordingly.

Some environmental pollutants cause structural malformation in babies, some retard growth, and some cause changes in the genetic material. The main point is that we know very little about the mechanisms and long-term results. Control of environmental pollutants and control of drug availability are political issues. How much should we interfere with the right of a company to make and to advertise products? How much should we interfere to make a company stop spewing gases into the air? There is a tradeoff between limiting pollution and other considerations. For example, increased cleanliness of the air may mean limitation of industry or a decrease in employment. It becomes a big political issue.

Another way in which economics impact on pregnancy outcome is through maternal nutrition. Malnutrition (especially protein deficiency) has been linked directly to low birth weight, to prematurity, to perinatal death, and to congenital malformations (Lester, 1977). And of course, malnutrition is directly related to income level (Kaplan, 1972). Thus, babies of poor women who do not get enough to eat are at risk for many problems.

One way in which this is a political issue is in varying federal and state policies regarding pregnant women. For instance, not all states take advantage of the federal program providing supplemental food and money benefits to pregnant women.

Delivery of prenatal care, control of environmental pollution, prevention of alcohol and drug abuse, provision of adequate diet: these are political issues that affect the developing fetus. Continued research is essential.

THE BIRTH PROCESS

Two generations ago, babies were delivered at home, either by a doctor or by a midwife. Infant mortality was not uncommon, nor was maternal death. The development of modern medical procedures has had an enormous impact on both perinatal mortality rates and maternal mortality rates. In 1940, the infant mortality rate was 47 per 1000 live births. By 1976, it had dropped to 15.2 (U.S. Bureau of the Census, 1978). Similarly, the maternal mortality rate dropped from 670 per 100,000 live births in 1930 (Guttmacher, 1973) to 12.3 in 1976 (U.S. Bureau of the Census, 1978). "This achievement in obstetrics has few, if any, parallels in the whole field of modern medicine" (Guttmacher, 1973, p. 107).

Despite this progress, important psychological issues remain; and as a result of it, new issues have arisen. These positive changes in infant and maternal survival rates have been accompanied by a questionable "medicalization" of pregnancy and birth. Today's baby is born in a hospital with an attending physician and medical environment. In 1978, 95% of U.S. births included some maternal anesthetic or analgesic (Brackbill, 1978). Estimates indicate that up to 25% of births annually are by caesarian section.

Some of the political questions raised by the medicalization of pregnancy and birth are: How much medical intervention is necessary to insure safe births? When does medical intervention interfere with important developmental processes (e.g., social bonding between parent and child)?

Why do we use drugs with delivery? Many people say that we use drugs because we think they are going to make delivery somewhat easier. Of course, the question is: for whom? The answer is: for the attending personnel and for the mother. From the infant's point of view, maternal medication has deleterious short- and long-term effects. A review of 35 studies (Brackbill, 1978) indicates that there are "significant behavioral effects of obstetric medication" (p. 3). The direction of effect was uniformly negative, toward behavioral degradation. These effects were not only present immediately after birth but persisted for up to 7 years (Brackbill, 1978).

Moreover, the use of drugs at birth appears to be related to social class. Prepared natural childbirth with classes is a welcome phenomenon. Young, poor, and poorly educated women are not usually enrolled in such classes, however, and are not given information that would help them decide how much labor pain to tolerate for the future benefit of their babies. In fact, medical recommendations about drugs often emphasize the lack of physical effects and ignore behavioral effects (see, for example, *The Stork Manual*, 1978).

We are concerned about medications whose sole purpose is comfort, not those that might be medically necessary. Given the evidence cited in the foregoing, why do we allow the development and use of drugs? Is it because they provide profits for the drug companies and enable the medical community to control and organize pregnancy and birth?

The medicalization of the birth process is not limited to routine administration of maternal drugs. The lithotomy position (on back, knees up) is standard for many U.S. hospital deliveries. The position cuts off oxygen to the baby, decreases blood return, detracts from the mother's ability to work with her contractions, and works against gravity (Danforth, 1977, p. 591). Nonetheless, it is convenient for the doctor. We quote from a 1977 obstetrics text: "Use of the lithotomy position has two purposes: it makes maintenance of asepsis easier and it contributes greatly to the convenience of the obstetrician. These advantages more than compensate for the somewhat unphysiologic posture and the discomfort of the position itself" (Keefer, 1977). Careful exploration of the continuing hazards of infection is needed in light of the availability of antibiotics. And attention is needed to balance the doctor's ability to function safely and efficiently against the risk of decreased oxygen and blood supplies to the baby and the mother's inability to push the baby through the birth canal.

Caesarian delivery is another facet of medicalization. Necessary for some births (e.g., ecphalopelvic disproportion), its occurrence has increased dramatically in the past 5 years. This increase coincides with the development of fetal monitors. Electronic monitoring of low-risk normal births may actually increase the chances of such a birth becoming an emergency caesarian section delivery. Fetal monitors require the woman to remain immobile, which in many cases slows down the course of labor.

A recent study at Brown University revealed a greater maternal mortality rate with caesarian births than those by vaginal delivery (Evrard & Gold, 1977). It is well known in the medical community that some doctors schedule caesarian sections at their own convenience. Moreover, fear of lawsuits, generated by insurance industry-induced hysteria, has led many doctors to operate sooner than reasonable medical judgment would require.

We need studies on the effects and correlates of the increased number of caesarian sections. Do these procedures mean more maternal drugging? Longer separation between mother and baby after birth? A necessary repeat caesarian section in subsequent births? What are the long-range effects of caesarian sections and other medical responses to labor and delivery on individual development? On families?

CONCLUSION

This article has raised political questions about who conceives, about the quality of the prenatal environment, and about the process of birth. As psychologists, we know that these are important issues. For instance, infants who act unresponsive at birth do not elicit social stimulation, nor do they act on the environment to promote their own development (Howes & Krakow, 1977). A very weak baby or a tired baby after a long delivery, a poorly nourished baby, a baby shaking from alcohol or drug addiction cannot make eye contact with parents and cannot sustain important social interaction.

As psychologists, we would all like to provide the best chance for life. We would like to provide that for infants. That means we should have *wanted* babies. We should have good prenatal care and a healthful prenatal environment. We also need to have adults around who can act adult, who can make choices, and who can think about the future. To do so, people must have adequate income for food, and for clothing, and for shelter. Such economic opportunity in the United States is a political issue.

Providing infants with the best chance

for life also means that we have to have adults who know how to sacrifice for the long-term good of the next generation. We need people who are critical, thoughtful, differentiated, who can think using high-level formal operations, because thinking about the consequences of having a child is an important issue. Infant researchers and psychologists are interested in infants. But all of us are also citizens, and the quality of infancy is of more concern to all of us than just having an adequate population pool for our studies. And if we are interested in the human organism, we have to be concerned with its beginnings: the fetus and the infant. We have tried to point out that the fate of infants depends very much on the politics of infancy. As George Miller said when he was president of the American Psychological Association:

The most urgent problems of our world today are the problems we have made for ourselves. They have not been caused by some heedless or malicious inanimate Nature; nor have they been imposed on us as punishment by the will of God. They are human problems whose solutions will require us to change our behavior and our social institutions.

As a science directly concerned with behavioral and social processes, psychology might be expected to provide intellectual leadership in the search for new and better personal and social arrangements. . . .

This is the social challenge that psychologists face. In the years immediately ahead we must not only extend and deepen our understanding of mental and behavioral phenomena, but we must somehow incorporate our hard-won knowledge more effectively into the vast social changes that we all know are coming. (1969, p. 1063)

REFERENCES

Ando, Y. & Hattori, H. Statistical studies on the effects of intense noise during human fetal life. *Journal of Sound and Vibration*, 1973, *27*, 101–110.

Boston Women's Health Book Collective. *Our bodies, ourselves.* New York: Simon and Schuster, 1975.

Brackbill, Y. *Lasting behavioral effects of obstetric medication on children; Research findings and public implications.* Statement before the Senate Subcommittee on Health and Scientific Research, April 17, 1978.

Cannon-Bonventure, K., Kahn, J., & Engelman, E. *Educational methodologies to reduce the relative incidence of second trimester abortions.* Unpublished manuscript, AIR, Cambridge, Mass.: 1977.

Danforth, D. N. (Ed.). *Obstetrics and gynecology* (3d ed.). Hagerstown, Md.: Harper and Row, 1977.

Denebola, Newton, Mass. South High School, *17*, No. 7. March 1, 1978.

Eleven million teenagers: What can be done about the epidemic of adolescent pregnancies in the United States. New York: Alan Guttmacher Institute, 1976.

Evrard, J. R. & Gold, E. M. Ceasarean section and maternal mortality in Rhode Island: Incidence and risk factors, 1965–1975. *Obstetrics and Gynecology*, 1977, *50*, 594–597.

Filene, P. From birth to birth control. *New York Times Book Review*, February 26, 1978, p. 11.

Guttmacher, A. F. *Pregnancy, birth and family planning.* New York: Signet, 1973.

Howes, C. & Krakow, J. Effects of inevitable environmental pollutants. In F. Rebelsky, *Pollution of the fetus.* Symposium presented at the 85th Annual Convention of the American Psychological Association, San Francisco, August 1977.

Kaplan, B. Malnutrition and mental deficiency. *Psychological Bulletin*, 1972, *78*, 321–334.

Keefer, G. Delivery experience. In F. Rebelsky, *Pollution of the fetus.* Symposium presented at the 85th Annual Convention of the American Psychological Association, San Francisco, August 1977.

Kschinka, J. Public funding in the states: An overview. *National Abortion Rights Action League Newsletter*, October 1978, 6.

Lester, B. Maternal malnutrition and fetal outcome. In F. Rebelsky, *Pollution of the fetus.* Symposium presented at the 85th Annual Convention of the American Psychological Association, San Francisco, August 1977.

Massachusetts Department of Public Health. *Annual report of vital statistics, 1975.*

Miller, G. Psychology as a means of promoting human welfare. *American Psychologist,* 1969, *24,* 1063–1075.

O'Reilly, J. Abortion: The hidden agenda. *The Nation,* April 15, 1978, 437–439.

Promoting the health of mothers and children: FY 1972. Rockville, Md.: U.S. Department of Health, Education and Welfare, 1972.

Puffer, R. & Griffith, G. *Patterns of urban mortality.* Washington, D.C.: Pan American Health Organization, 1967.

Reed, J. *From private vice to public virtue: The birth control movement and American society since 1830.* New York: Basic Books, 1978.

Rich, A. *Of women born: Motherhood as experience and institution.* New York: Norton, 1976.

Sameroff, A. & Chandler, M. Reproductive risk and the continuum of caretaking casuality. In F. P. Horowitz, M. Hetherington, S. Scarr-Salapatek, & G. Siegel (Eds.), *Review of child development research.* Chicago: University of Chicago Press, 1975.

Science, 6 November 1981, *214,* 642–644.

Smith, R. Jeffrey. Agency drags its feet on warning to pregnant women. *Science,* 17 February 1978, *199,* 748–749.

The stork manual: Handbook for prospective parents. Kaiser Permanente Medical Center, 1978.

Thorbeck, J. *Onset of menarche and body image in adolescent females.* Unpublished doctoral dissertation, Boston University, 1976.

Tulkin, S. An analysis of the concept of cultural deprivation. *Developmental Psychology,* 1972, *6,* 326–339.

United States Bureau of the Census. *Statistical abstract of the United States, 1978* (99th ed.). Washington, D.C., 1978.

United States Department of Health Education and Welfare. Hearings on sterilization, February 1978.

Williams, L., Spence, M. A., & Tideman, S. Implications of the observed effect of air pollution on birth weight. *Social Biology,* 1977, *24,* 1–9.

Wilson, J. G. *Environment and birth defects.* New York: Academic Press, 1973.

Winsmore, G. Alcoholism and drug addiction. In F. Rebelsky, *Pollution of the fetus.* Symposium presented at the 85th Annual Convention of the American Psychological Association, San Francisco, August 1977.

Zill, N. Summary of preliminary results, National Survey of Children. Unpublished manuscript. New York: Foundation for Child Development, 1977.

5. DIVORCE, A CHILD'S PERSPECTIVE

E. Mavis Hetherington

The rate of divorce in the United States, particularly of divorce involving those who have children, has increased dramatically since 1965. It is estimated that 40% of the current marriages of young adults will end in divorce and that 40%–50% of children born in the 1970s will spend some time living in a single-parent family. The average length of time spent by children in a single-parent home as a result of marital disruption is about 6 years. The majority of these children reside with their mothers, with only 10% living with their fathers, even though this proportion has tripled since 1960. Living with the father is most likely to occur with school-aged rather than preschool children (Glick & Norton, 1978).

This article first presents an overview of the course of divorce and its potential impact on children and then uses research findings as a basis for describing the process of divorce as it is experienced by the child. Since the research on single-parent families headed by fathers is meager and since after divorce most children live in a single-parent family headed by the mother, the article focuses primarily on children in this family situation.

THE COURSE OF DIVORCE

In studying the impact of divorce on children, much confusion has resulted from viewing divorce as a single event rather than a sequence of experiences involving a transition in the lives of children. This transition involves a shift from the family situation before divorce to the disequilibrium and disorganization associated with separation and divorce, through a period when family members are experimenting with a variety of coping mechanisms, some successful and some unsuccessful, for dealing with their new situation. This is followed by the reorganization and eventual attainment of a new pattern of equilibrium in a single-parent household. For most children, within 5 years of the divorce there is also a later period of reentry into a two-parent family involving a stepparent, which necessitates further alterations in family functioning. The point at which we tap into the sequence of events and changing processes associated with divorce will modify our view of the adjustment of the child and the factors which influence that adjustment. Although divorce may be the best solution to a destructive family relationship and may offer the child an escape from one set of stresses and the opportunity for personal growth, almost all children experience the transition of divorce as painful. Even children who later are able to recognize that the divorce had constructive outcomes initially undergo considerable emotional distress with family dissolution. The children's most common early responses to divorce are anger, fear, depression, and guilt. It is usually not until after the first

Reprinted with permission from *American Psychologist*, Vol. 34, No. 10, 851–858. Copyright 1979 by the American Psychological Association, Inc.

year following divorce that tension reduction and an increased sense of well-being begin to emerge.

A crisis model of divorce may be most appropriate in conceptualizing the short-term effects of divorce on children. In the period during and immediately following divorce, the child may be responding to changes in his or her life situation—the loss of a parent, the marital discord and family disorganization that usually precede and accompany separation, the alterations in parent-child relations that may be associated with temporary distress and emotional neediness of family members, and other real or fantasized threats to the well-being of the child that are elicited by the uncertainty of the situation. In this period, therefore, stresses associated with conflict, loss, change, and uncertainty may be the critical factors.

The research evidence suggests that most children can cope with and adapt to the short-term crisis of divorce within a few years. However, if the crisis is compounded by multiple stresses and continued adversity, developmental disruptions may occur. The longer-term adjustment of the child is related to more sustained or concurrent conditions associated with the quality of life in a household headed by a single parent—alterations in support systems, the increased salience of the custodial parent, the lack of availability of the noncustodial parent, the presence of one less significant adult in the household to participate in decision making, to serve as a model or disciplinarian, or to assume responsibility for household tasks and child care, and finally, changes in family functioning related to continued stresses associated with practical problems of living, such as altered economic resources.

VARIABILITY IN RESPONSE TO DIVORCE

In considering how the child experiences and responds to divorce and to life in a single-parent household, investigators are beginning to examine the interplay among situational factors, stresses, and support systems. However, even when these factors are comparable, wide variability in the quality and intensity of responses and the adaptation of children to divorce remains. Some children exhibit severe or sustained disruptions in development, others seem to sail through a turbulent divorce and stressful aftermath and emerge as competent, well-functioning individuals. Although there is increasing interest in the relative vulnerability or invulnerability of children to psychosocial stress (Garmezy, 1975; Rutter, 1979b), this issue has not been systematically explored in relation to divorce. It seems likely that temperamental variables, the past experience of the child, and the child's developmental status all contribute to individual differences in coping with divorce. There also have been some provocative findings suggesting that boys are more vulnerable to the adverse effects of divorce than are girls, although the reasons for this difference have yet to be clarified.

Temperament and the Response to Divorce
Temperamentally difficult children have been found to be less adaptable to change and more vulnerable to adversity (Chess, Thomas, & Birch, 1968; Graham, Rutter, & George, 1973; Rutter, 1979a) than are temperamentally easy children. The difficult child is more likely to be the elicitor and the target of aversive responses by the parent, whereas the temperamentally easy child is not only less likely to be the recipient of criticism, displaced anger, and anxiety but also is more able to cope with it when it hits. Children who have histories of maladjustment preceding the divorce are

more likely to respond with long-lasting emotional disturbance following divorce (Kelly, Note 1). This, of course, could be attributable either to temperamental factors or to a history of pathogenic environmental factors.

Cumulative Stress and the Response to Divorce
Rutter (1979b) reported that when children experience only a single stress it carries no appreciable psychiatric risk. However, when children who have been exposed to chronic stress or several concurrent stresses must deal with family discord, the adverse effects increase multiplicatively. The effects of stresses in the family also are compounded by those in the larger social milieu. Extrafamilial factors such as stresses and supports in other social institutions or networks, the quality of housing, neighborhoods, child care, the need for the mother to work, economic status, and geographic mobility will moderate or potentiate stresses associated with divorce (Colletta, 1978; Hodges, Wechsler, & Ballantine, Note 2). Finally, transactional effects may occur in cases where divorce may actually increase the probability of occurrence of another stressor. This is most apparent in the stresses associated with the downward economic movement that frequently follows divorce and makes raising children and maintaining a household more difficult (Bane, 1976; Brandwein, Brown, & Fox, 1974; Kriesberg, 1970; Winston & Forsher, 1971).

Developmental Status and the Response to Divorce
The adaptation of the child will also vary with his or her developmental status. The limited cognitive and social competencies of the young child, the young child's dependency on parents and more exclusive restriction to the home will be associated with different responses and coping strategies from those of the more mature and self-sufficient older child or adolescent who operates in a variety of social milieus. Note that I am saying the experience of divorce will differ qualitatively for children of varying ages rather than that the trauma will be more or less intense. The young child is less able accurately to appraise the divorce situation, the motives and feelings of his or her parents, his or her own role in the divorce, and the array of possible outcomes. Thus the young child is likely to be more self-blaming in interpreting the cause of divorce and to distort grossly perceptions of the parents' emotions, needs, and behavior, as well as the prospects of reconciliation or total abandonment (Tessman, 1978; Wallerstein & Kelly, 1974, 1975). Although most adolescents experience considerable initial pain and anger when their parents divorce, when the immediate trauma of divorce is over, they are more able accurately to assign responsibility for the divorce, to resolve loyalty conflicts, and to assess and cope with economic and other practical exigencies (Wallerstein & Kelly, 1974, 1975). It should be noted that this is often accompanied by premature, sometimes destructive disengagement from the family and an increased future orientation. However, if the home situation is particularly painful adolescents more than younger children do have the option to disengage and seek gratification elsewhere, such as in the neighborhood, peer group, or school.

Sex Differences in Responses to Divorce
The impact of marital discord and divorce is more pervasive and enduring for boys than for girls (Hetherington, Cox, & Cox, 1978, in press; Porter & O'Leary, 1980; Rutter, 1979a; Tuckman & Regan, 1966; Hetherington et al., Note 3; Wallerstein, Note 4). Disturbances in social and emotional development in girls have largely disappeared two years after the divorce, although they may reemerge at adolescence in the form of disruptions in heterosexual relations (Hetherington, 1972). Al-

though boys improve markedly in coping and adjustment in the two years after divorce, many continue to show developmental deviations. Boys from divorced families, in contrast with girls from divorced families and children from nuclear families, show a higher rate of behavior disorders and problems in interpersonal relations in the home and in the school with teachers and peers. Although especially in young children both boys and girls show an increase in dependent help-seeking and affection-seeking overtures following divorce, boys are more likely also to show more sustained noncompliant, aggressive behavior in the home (Hetherington et al., 1978, in press, Note 3).

Why should this be the case? It has been suggested that loss of a father is more stressful for boys than for girls. It also may be that the greater aggressiveness frequently observed in boys and the greater assertiveness in the culturally prescribed male role necessitates the use of firmer, more consistent discipline practices in the control of boys than of girls. Boys in both nuclear and divorced families are less compliant than girls, and children are less compliant to mothers than fathers (Hetherington et al., 1978). It also could be argued that it is more essential for boys to have a male model to imitate who exhibits mature self-controlled ethical behavior or that the image of greater power and authority vested in the father is more critical in controlling boys, who are culturally predisposed to be more aggressive. Although these factors may all be important, recent divorce studies suggest that these sex differences may involve a more complex set of mediators. Boys are more likely to be exposed to parental battles (Wallerstein, Note 4) and to confront inconsistency, negative sanctions, and opposition from parents, particularly from mothers, following divorce. In addition, boys receive less positive support and nurturance and are viewed more negatively by mothers,

teachers, and peers in the period immediately following divorce than are girls (Hetherington et al., 1978, in press; Santrock, 1975; Santrock & Trace, 1978; Hetherington et al., Note 3). Divorced mothers of boys report feeling more stress and depression than do divorced mothers of girls (Colletta, 1978; Hetherington et al., 1978). Boys thus may be exposed to more stress, frustration, and aggression and have fewer available supports.

THE CHILD'S CHANGED LIFE EXPERIENCES FOLLOWING DIVORCE

Keeping in mind the many factors that contribute to the wide variability in the responses of children to divorce, let us examine the changes in the child's experiences associated with divorce. Some of these changes are related to alterations in economic status and practical problems of living, others involve changes in family functioning, and still others are associated with social networks external to the family.

Economic Changes and Practical Problems of Living

Some of the most prevalent stresses confronting children of divorce are those associated with downward economic mobility. Poor parents and those with unstable incomes are more likely to divorce (Brandwein et al., 1974; Ross & Sawhill, 1975), and divorce is associated with a marked drop in income. This is in part attributable to the fact that less than one third of ex-husbands contribute to the support of their families (Kriesberg, 1970; Winston & Forsher, 1971). Moreover, many divorced women do not have the education, job skills, or experience to permit them to obtain a well-paying position or to pay for high-quality child care. Divorced mothers are more likely to have low-paying part-time jobs or positions of short duration. For the child this results in erratic, sometimes inadequate provisions for child care and, if the mother feels forced to work, in a dissatisfied, resentful mother.

If the divorced mother wishes to work and adequate provisions are made for child care and household management, maternal employment may have positive effects on the mother and no adverse effects on the children. However, if the mother begins to work at the time of divorce or shortly thereafter, the preschool child seems to experience the double loss of both parents, which is reflected in a higher rate of behavior disorders (Hetherington et al., 1978). In addition, maternal employment may add to the task overload experienced when a single parent is attempting to cope with the tasks ordinarily performed by two parents in a nuclear family. It has been suggested that as the divorced mother struggles to distribute her energies across the many demands placed on her, the child may be maternally deprived rather than paternally deprived (Brandwein et al., 1974). This is sometimes associated with what one mother termed a "chaotic life-style," where family roles and responsibilities are not well delineated and many routine chores do not get accomplished. Children of many divorced parents receive less adult attention and are more likely to have erratic meals and bedtimes and to be late for school (Hetherington et al., 1978).

The downward economic mobility of families headed by a divorced mother also involves a lower standard of living and relocation. Following divorce, families are likely to shift to more modest housing in poorer neighborhoods, and their greater social isolation may be exacerbated by moving (Marsden, 1969; Pearlin & Johnson, 1977). For the child, such moves not only involve losses of friends, neighbors, and a familiar educational system, but also may be associated with living in an area with high delinquency rates, risks to per-

sonal safety, few recreational facilities, and inadequate schools. For children involved in family dissolution, such moves represent further unraveling of the skein of their lives at a time when continuity of support systems and the environment can play an ameliorative role (Tessman, 1978).

Changes in Parent-Child Relations
Many changes in family interaction are associated with divorce and living in a single-parent family. In early studies the role of the loss or relative unavailability of the father was emphasized. More recently, family conflict, the increased salience of the custodial mother, changes in mother-child interaction and in the life circumstances of the single-parent family have been the focus of attention.

CONFLICT
A high degree of discord characterizes family relations in the period surrounding divorce. The conflict between parents often enmeshes the child in controversy. Children are exposed to parental quarreling, mutual denigration and recrimination, and are placed in a situation of conflicting loyalties, with one parent frequently attempting to coerce or persuade children to form hostile alliances against the other parent. This results in demands for a decision to reject one parent which children are unprepared or unable to make. The vast majority of children wish to maintain relations with both parents. Conflict also gives children the opportunity to play one parent against the other and in some children develops exploitative manipulative skills (Tessman, 1978; Wallerstein, Note 4). The behavior of some children actively escalates conflict between divorced parents and between parents and stepparents following remarriage.

The frequent mutual demeaning and criticism of divorcing parents leads to dissonance, questioning, and often precipitous revision and deidealization of children's perceptions of their parents (Hetherington, 1972; Tessman, 1978; Wallerstein, Note 4). When the mother is hostile and critical of the father, the child begins to view the father in a more ambivalent or negative manner and as a less acceptable role model. For young boys this is associated with disruption in sex typing (Hetherington et al., Note 3). For girls it may be associated with disruptions in heterosexual relations at adolescence (Hetherington, 1972). Elementary-school-aged children and adolescents in particular are concerned with their parents' morality and competence. Perhaps because of their own awakening sexuality, preadolescents and adolescents are particularly distressed by an increased awareness of their parents as sex objects, first when both parents are dating and then when parents remarry (Wallerstein & Kelly, 1974). Younger children are most anxious about the mother's ability to cope with family conflicts and stresses and her emotional condition following divorce, because of their precarious dependence on the single parent (Wallerstein, Note 4).

Research findings are consistent in showing that children in single-parent families function more adequately than children in conflict-ridden nuclear families (Rutter, 1979b; Hetherington et al., Note 3). The eventual escape from conflict may be one of the most positive outcomes of divorce for children. However, family conflict does not decline but escalates in the year following divorce (Hetherington et al., 1978; Kelly, Note 1; Hetherington et al., Note 3; Wallerstein, Note 4). During this period children in divorced families, particularly boys, show more problems than do children in discordant nuclear families.

FATHER ABSENCE

In the current eagerness to demonstrate that single-parent families headed by mothers can provide a salutary environment for raising children and that the presence of fathers is not essential for normal development in children, there has been a tendency to overlook the contribution of fathers to family functioning. In trying to escape from the earlier narrowly biased view emphasizing father absence as the cause of any obtained developmental differences between children from single-parent and nuclear families, the pendulum may have swung too far in the other direction. Fathers may have a relatively unique contribution to make to family functioning and the development of the child. In the single-parent home some of the father's functions may be taken over by the mother or by other people, social institutions, relatives, siblings, a stepfather, friends, neighbors, a housekeeper, day-care centers, and schools. However, the roles the alternative support systems play may be qualitatively different from those of an involved accessible father (Pederson, Rubenstein, & Yarrow, 1979).

Some of the roles fathers play in parenting are indirect and serve to support the mother in her parenting role; others impact more directly on the child. The father in a nuclear family indirectly supports the mother in her maternal role in a number of ways—with economic aid, with assistance and relief in household tasks and child rearing, and with emotional support and encouragement and appreciation of her performance as a mother. In addition, an intimate relation in which the mother is valued and cherished contributes to her feelings of self-esteem, happiness, and competence which influence her relationship with her children (Hetherington et al., 1978).

The father also may play a more direct and active role in shaping the child's behavior as an agent of socialization, by discipline, direct tuition, or acting as a model. In a single-parent family there is only one parent to serve those functions. The single parent or even two adults of the same sex offer the child a more restricted array of positive characteristics to model than do two parents (Pederson et al., in press). A mother and father are likely to exhibit wider ranging interests, skills, and attributes than a single parent. In addition, the father with his image of greater power and authority may be more effective in controlling children's behavior and in serving as backup authority for the mother's discipline.

Finally, one parent can serve as a protective buffer between the other parent and the child in a nuclear family. In a nuclear family a loving, competent, or well-adjusted parent can help counteract the effects of a rejecting, incompetent, emotionally unstable parent. In a single-parent family headed by a mother, the family is not present to mitigate any deleterious behaviors of the custodial parent in day-to-day living experiences (Hetherington et al., Note 3). Thus, the constructive and pathogenic behaviors of the mother are funneled more directly onto the child, and the quality of the mother-child relationship will be more directly reflected in the adjustment of the child than it is in a nuclear family.

DIVORCED FATHERS AND THEIR CHILDREN

A finding that should be of some concern to those making custody recommendations is that there is little continuity between the quality of a pre- and postseparation parent-child interaction, particularly for fathers (Hetherington et al., 1976; Kelly, Note 1). This discontinuity is another factor contributing to the sense of unpredictability in the child's situation. Some intensely attached fathers find intermittent fathering painful and withdraw from their children. On the other hand, a substantial number of fathers report that their relationship with their children improves after

divorce, and many fathers, previously relatively uninvolved, become competent and concerned parents.

The parents' response to divorce and the quality of the child's relationship with both parents immediately after divorce has a substantial effect on the child's coping and adjustment (Hetherington et al., 1976; Kelly, Note 1). In the first year after divorce, parents often are preoccupied with their own depression, anger, or emotional needs and are unable to respond sensitively to the wants of the child. During this period divorced parents tend to be inconsistent, less affectionate, and lacking in control over their children (Hetherington et al., 1978). However, they recover markedly in the second year after divorce.

Although in the early months following divorce fathers are having as much or even more contact with children as they did preceding the divorce, most divorced fathers rapidly become less available to their children. Fathers are more likely to maintain frequent contact with their sons than with their daughters (Hess & Camara, in press). Most children wish to maintain contact with the father, and in preschool children, mourning for the father and fantasies of reconciliation may continue for several years (Hetherington et al., 1978; Tessman, 1978; Wallerstein & Kelly, 1975). Unless the father is extremely poorly adjusted or immature, or the child is exposed to conflict between the parents, frequent availability of the father is associated with positive adjustment and social relations, especially in boys (Hess & Camara, 1979; Hetherington et al., 1978, Note 3; Wallerstein, Note 4). A continued mutually supportive relationship and involvement of the father with the child is the most effective support system for divorced women in their parenting role and for their children. The recommendation that has been made that the custodial parent have the right to eliminate visitation by the noncustodial parent, if he or she views it as adverse to the child's well-being, seems likely to discourage parents from working out their differences and runs counter to the available research findings.

DIVORCED MOTHERS AND THEIR CHILDREN

With time, the custodial parent in single-parent families becomes increasingly salient in the development of the child (Hetherington et al., Note 3). Fathers who maintain frequent contact and involvement with their children have more impact on the child's development than do fathers whose contacts are relatively infrequent or who are relatively detached. However, even highly involved noncustodial fathers are less influential than the custodial mother in many facets of the child's personality and social and cognitive development. The well-being of the divorced mother and the quality of mother-child relations thus become central to the adjustment of the child. However, this is not a one-way street, since the mother's sense of competence, self-esteem, and happiness is modified by the behavior of her children, particularly her sons. The mother who must cope with too many young children or with acting-out, noncompliant behavior in sons becomes increasingly distressed and inept in her parenting. Divorced adults have more health and emotional problems, even after the initial crisis period of divorce, than do married adults (Bloom, Asher, & White, 1978). This suggests that the child may be coping with a mother who is not only confronting many stresses but who may be physically and psychologically less able to deal with adversity.

In most divorcing families there is a period in the first year after divorce when mothers become depressed, self-involved, erratic, less supportive, and more ineffectually authoritarian in dealing with their children. Divorced mothers and their sons are particularly likely to get involved in an escalating cycle of mutual coercion. As was noted above, parenting improved dramatically in the second year after divorce; however, problems in parent-child relations continue to be found more often between divorced mothers and children, especially sons, than between mothers and children in nuclear families.

Different aspects of the divorced mother's relationship with her children are important with children of different ages. With preschool children, organization of the home and authoritative control, accompanied by nurturance and maturity demands, seem to be particularly important in the adjustment of the child. Young children have more difficulty than older children in exerting self-control and ordering their changing lives and thus require more external control and structure in times of stress and transition (Hetherington et al., Note 3). On the other hand, divorced mothers of older children and adolescents are more likely to rely on their children for emotional support and for assistance with practical problems of daily life. The children are asked to fulfill some of the functions of the departed father. There is great pressure for elementary-school-aged children and adolescents to function in a mature, autonomous manner at an early age. Weiss (Note 5) described the phenomenon of great self-sufficiency and growing up faster in one-parent families. If the mother is not making excessive or inappropriate demands for emotional sustenance, her greater openness about concerns and plans can lead to a companionate relationship between her and her children. However, being pushed toward early independence and the assumption of adult responsibilities leads to feelings of being overwhelmed by unsolvable problems, incompetence, and resentment about lack of support and unavailability of mothers, and to precocious sexual concerns in some school-aged children and adolescents (Kelly, Note 1; Wallerstein, Note 4).

Extrafamilial Support Systems

Willard Hartup (1980) discussed how little we know about extrafamilial social and affectional systems and the relationships among familial and extrafamilial systems. This is nowhere more apparent than in the area of divorce, where the focus of study largely has been confined to parent-child relations and where the emphasis has been on supports for the divorced parents rather than for the children. Even the role of siblings and the extended family as support systems for children going through family disruption has received only cursory examination. The research thus far indicates that extended family and community services play a more active role as support systems for low-income than for moderate-income families (Colletta, 1978; Spicer & Hampe, 1975). With preschool children, family relations are prepotent in the adjustment of the child. Disruptions in family functioning are associated with maladaptive behaviors both in the home and in other social situations (Hess & Camara, 1979; Wallerstein & Kelly, 1975; Hetherington et al., Note 3).

With older children, although the disruptive effects of divorce may flood over into other relations in the period immediately surrounding divorce, they are more rapidly able to circumscribe these effects. Older children are frequently able to confine their stress within the family arena and to use peers and schools as sources of information, satisfaction, and support (Hetherington et al., in press; Wallerstein, Note 4). The validation of self-worth, competence, and personal control are important functions served by peers, and positive school and neighborhood environments are to some extent able to attenuate the effects of stressful family relations (Hess & Camara, 1979; Hetherington et al., in press; Rutter, 1979b; Wallerstein, Note 4; Hetherington et al., Note 3).

SUMMARY

The best statistical prognostications suggest that an increasing number of children are going to experience their parents' divorce and life in a single-parent family. A conflict-ridden intact family is more deleterious to family members than is a stable home in which parents are divorced. An inaccessible, rejecting, or hostile parent in a nuclear family is more detrimental to the development of the child than is the absence of a parent. Divorce is often a positive solution to destructive family functioning; however, most children experience divorce as a difficult transition, and life in a single-parent family can be viewed as a high-risk situation for parents and children. This is not to say that single-parent families cannot or do not serve as effective settings for the development of competent, stable, happy children, but the additional stresses and the lack of support systems confronted by divorced families impose additional burdens on their members.

Most research has viewed the single-parent family as a pathogenic family and has failed to focus on how positive family functioning and support systems can facilitate the development of social, emotional, and intellectual competence in children in single-parent families. Neither the gloom-and-doom approach nor the political stance of refusing to recognize that many single-parent families headed by mothers have problems other than financial difficulties is likely to be productive. We need more research and applied programs oriented toward the identification and facilitation of patterns of family functioning, as well as support systems that help families to cope with changes and stress associated with divorce and that help to make single-parent families the basis of a satisfying and fulfilling life-style.

REFERENCE NOTES

1. Kelly, J. B. *Children and parents in the midst of divorce: Major factors contributing to differential response*. Paper presented at the National Institute of Mental Health Conference on Divorce, Washington, D.C., February 1978.
2. Hodges, F. H., Wechsler, R. C., & Ballantine, C. *Divorce and the preschool child: Cumulative stress*. Paper presented at the meeting of the American Psychological Association, Toronto, August, 1978.
3. Hetherington, E. M., Cox, M., & Cox, R. *Family interactions and the social, emotional and cognitive development of children following divorce*. Paper presented at the Johnson and Johnson Synposium on the Family: Setting Priorities, Washington, D.C., 1978.
4. Wallerstein, J. S. *Children and parents 18 months after parental separation: Factors related to differential outcome*. Paper presented at the National Institute of Mental Health Conference on Divorce, Washington, D.C., February 1978.
5. Weiss, R. *Single-parent households as settings for growing up*. Paper presented at the National Institute of Mental Health Conference on Divorce, Washington, D.C., February 1978.

REFERENCES

Bane, M. J. Marital disruption and the lives of children. *Journal of Social Issues*, 1976, *32*, 103–117.

Bloom, B. L., Asher, S. J., & White, S. W. Marital disruption as a stressor: A review and analysis. *Psychological Bulletin*, 1978, *85*, 867–894.

Brandwein, R. A., Brown, C. A., & Fox, E. M. Women and children last: The social situation of divorced mothers and their families. *Journal of Marriage and the Family*, 1974, *36*, 498–514.

Chess, S., Thomas, A., & Birch, H. O. Behavioral problems revisited. In S. Chess & A. Thomas (Eds.), *Annual progress in child psychiatry and child development*. New York: Brunner/Mazel, 1968.

Colletta, N. D. *Divorced mothers at two income levels: Stress, support and child-rearing practices*. Unpublished thesis, Cornell University, 1978.

Garmezy, N. The experimental study of children vulnerable to psychopathology. In A. Davids (Ed.), *Child personality and psychopathology*, Vol. 2. New York: Wiley, 1975.

Glick, P. G., & Norton, A. J. Marrying, divorcing and living together in the U.S. today. *Population Bulletin*, 1978, *32*, 5–38.

Graham, P., Rutter, M., & George, S. Temperamental characteristics as predictors of behavior disorders in children. *American Journal of Orthopsychiatry*, 1973, *43*, 328–399.

Hartup, W. Two social words: Family relations and peer relations. In M. Rutter (Ed.), *Scientific foundations of developmental psychiatry*. London: Heinemann Medical, 1980.

Hess, R. D., & Camara, K. A. Post-divorce family relations as mediating factors in the consequences of divorce for children. *Journal of Social Issues*, 1979, *35* (4), 76–96.

Hetherington, E. M. Effects of father absence on personality development in adolescent daughters. *Developmental Psychology*, 1972, *7*, 313–326.

Hetherington, E. M., Cox, M., & Cox, R. Divorced fathers. *Family Coordinator*, 1976, *25*, 417–428.

Hetherington, E. M., Cox, M., & Cox, R. The aftermath of divorce. In J. H. Stevens, Jr., & M. Matthews (Eds.), *Mother-child, father-child relations*. Washington, D.C.; National Association for the Education of Young Children, 1978.

Hetherington, E. M., Cox, M., & Cox, R. Play and social interaction in children following divorce. *Journal of Social Issues*, in press.

Kriesberg, L. *Mothers in poverty: A study of fatherless families*. Chicago: Aldine, 1970.

Marsden, D. *Mothers alone: Poverty and the fatherless family*. London: Allen Lane the Penguin Press, 1969.

Pearlin, L. I., & Johnson, J. S. Marital status, life strains, and depression. *American Sociological Review*, 1977, *42*, 704–715.

Pedersen, F. A. Rubenstein, J., & Yarrow, L. J. Infant development in father-absent families. *Journal of Genetic Psychology*, 1979, *135*, 51–56.

Porter, G., & O'Leary, D. K. Marital discord and child behavior problems. *Journal of Abnormal Child Psychology*, 1980, *8*(3), 287–295.

Ross, H. L., & Sawhill, I. V. *Time of transition: The growth of families headed by women*. Washington, D.C.: Urban Institute, 1975.

Rutter, M. Maternal deprivation 1972–1978: New findings, new concepts, new approaches. *Child Development*, 1979, *50*(2). (a)

Rutter, M. Protective factors in children's responses to stress and disadvantage. In M. W. Kent & J. E. Rolf (Eds.), *Primary prevention of psychopathology, Vol. 3. Promoting social competence and coping in children*. Hanover, N.H.: University Press of New England, 1979. (b)

Santrock, J. W. Father absence, perceived maternal behavior and moral development in boys. *Child Development*, 1975, *46*, 753–757.

Santrock, J. W., & Trace, R. L., Effect of children's family structure status on the development of stereotypes by children. *Journal of Educational Psychology*, 1978, *70*, 754–757.

Spicer, J., & Hampe, G. Kinship interaction after divorce. *Journal of Marriage and the Family*, 1975, *28*, 113–119.

Tessman, L. H. *Children of parting parents*. New York: Aronson, 1978.

Tuckman, J., & Regan, P. A. Intactness of the home and behavioral problems in children. *Journal of Child Psychology and Psychiatry*, 1966, *7*, 225–233.

Wallerstein, J. S., & Kelly, J. B. The effects of parental divorce: The adolescent experience. In A. Koupernik (Ed). *The child in his family: Children at a psychiatric risk*, Vol. 3. New York: Wiley, 1974.

Wallerstein, J. S. & Kelly, J. B. The effects of parental divorce: Experiences of the preschool child. *Journal of the American Academy of Child Psychiatry*, 1975, *14*, 600–616.

Weiss, R. *Marital separation*. New York: Basic Books, 1975.

Winston, M. P., & Forsher, T. *Nonsupport of legitimate children by affluent fathers as a cause of poverty and welfare dependence*. New York: Rand Corporation, 1971.

6. THE "ELASTIC MIND" MOVEMENT: RATIONALIZING CHILD NEGLECT?

Albert Rosenfeld

Would you believe that the way children are raised by their parents—and whether their homes are happy or not—has little or nothing to do with the way they turn out as adults? And, further, that their experiences in infancy have very little impact on their later lives—indeed, may simply vanish and be forgotten? I don't believe it either. At least, not yet. In fact, I find such ideas outlandish and disquieting. They directly contradict beliefs we have long cherished. Nevertheless, these are the ideas being espoused lately by some highly esteemed behavioral scientists who specialize in child development and child rearing.

I had discerned this, in my peripheral awareness, only as a slight, insignificant, and probably fleeting trend. But last November I got my first inkling that the trend had developed into what amounts to a virtual movement. The occasion was a seminar at Rockefeller University sponsored by the Council for the Advancement of Science Writing. One of the speakers was psychologist Bertram J. Cohler, of the University of Chicago, who has been studying the children of chronically depressed mothers. The effects of such upbringing, he reported, are clearly deleterious to a child's emotional life; moreover, the effects are still visible at the age of 10, which was as far as Cohler had followed his study group at that time. Yet Cohler is convinced that by adulthood all these troubles are dissipated and that no long-range

harm is done. Why this assurance despite his own results?

"Well," he explained, "all the longitudinal studies"—those studies that follow the same people through time, from childhood into their later years—"show that what happens in early childhood has no demonstrable impact on adult life. People who had an unhappy childhood do just as well later on and are just as happy as those who had a happy childhood." He further insisted that the way parents raise their kids and how troubled the parents themselves might be don't really matter very much because the kids will turn out the way they will turn out; people keep remaking their lives *all* their lives, and what happens to them later, including what they do for themselves, pretty well compensates for earlier disadvantages in upbringing. As for the current emphasis on " parenting" and on training young people for parenthood, Cohler scoffed at such programs as a waste of time, money, and energy. All this to an audience of science writers from around the country whose stories would soon be going out over the wires.

In the press room later, under sharp questioning, Cohler gently but firmly held his ground and emphasized that he and his colleagues at Chicago were far from alone in their views. He felt, rather, that he was expressing what would soon be the consensual stance among leading experts in the field. Among the names of those he said

This article is reprinted with permission from *Saturday Review*, April 1, 1978, 26–28.

supported his position was that of Harvard psychologist Jerome Kagan, whom I have long respected.

Before I had a chance to call Kagan for firsthand confirmation, I received in the mail an advance copy of the first issue (January 1978) of an interesting new magazine called *Human Nature*. In it, sure enough, was an article by Kagan called "The Baby's Elastic Mind," dealing with the very themes Cohler had sounded. I was actually more stunned to see such ideas in print under Kagan's by-line than to hear them expressed verbally by Cohler. Many of the beliefs that are still held by most experts of my own acquaintance, and that are still part of my own convictions, are here referred to by Kagan in the past tense, as though they already had a quaintly anachronistic flavor. A few examples:

Western scientists used to believe . . . that infantile autism, a form of childhood psychosis, could develop simply because a mother rejected her baby.

Many still believe that most of an infant's experiences have effects that reach many years into the future.

Accordingly, we have awarded certain early experiences as mysterious power. As a result, middle-class parents worry about providing sufficient stimulation to their month-old infant or wonder whether failure to unite the newborn with its mother immediately after birth might have harmful consequences.

Parents were supposed, through proper nurture, to prepare their children to be psychologically healthy adults.

Kagan's article concludes that new discoveries—which he details—about the human infant "imply that his first experiences may be permanently lost. . . . I suspect that it is not until a child is five or six years old . . . that we get a more reliable preview of the future. The infant's mind may be more like a sandy beach on a windy day than a reel of recording tape."

None of this is to be taken lightly, coming, as it does, from the likes of Jerome Kagan, who is indisputably one of the world's leading authorities on child development. While I was still trying to absorb the shock of Kagan's piece, the February 1978 issue of *Psychology Today* arrived. It contains an article called "The Myth of the Vulnerable Child." And the title states its message quite literally: The idea that children are vulnerable creatures is a myth— especially the idea that they are vulnerable to the vagaries of parental behavior. The author of this piece is research psychologist Arlene Skolnick of Berkeley's Institute of Human Development. "In the twentieth century," she writes, "this traditional American obsession with children has generated new kinds of child-rearing experts—psychologists and psychiatrists, clothed in the authority of modern science, who issue prescriptions for child rearing. Most child-care advice assumes that if the parents administer the proper prescriptions, the child will develop as planned. It places exaggerated faith not only in the perfectability of children and their parents but in the infallibility of the particular child-rearing technique as well."

In fact, very few of the experts who have recently been dispensing child-care advice make any such assumptions. Nor do they place such faith in the perfectability of either children or parents or in the infallibility of their techniques. Most of the advisers attempt, rather, to guide parents cautiously away from the more egregious errors that parents can and do make to keep the child from becoming any more of a mess than is absolutely necessary. The advice is usually offered more in this spirit (unless one is talking about a rare type like B. F. Skinner) than with the voice of rigid authority. Indeed, the more popular advisers, such as Dr. Spock, keep reassuring parents that if they follow their own feelings and instincts, they can't go too far wrong. Most child-rearing experts are reasonably modest in their pretensions. Even so, they have in general felt secure in the knowledge that the attitudes and the behavior of parents do constitute important factors in the child's later emotional life and that what happens to a child in those early, terribly vulnerable years from infancy to 5 or 6 can, and frequently does, have a shaping influence on that same person as an adolescent and as an adult. The best that Skolnick will concede in her article, however, is that "parental determinism," as she calls it, does contain "a kernel of truth—like all myths."

I have perhaps been guilty of oversimplifying the specific stands of this new movement (though not its overall stance). I have presented it this way in order to underline what troubles me about it. Before proceeding further in this vein, however, it bears emphasizing that the movement's general position contains a number of valuable ingredients when stated less extremely—as they are, for instance, by sociologist Orville G. Brim, Jr., head of the Foundation for Child Development. (I am not sure he would like to be included as part of any movement, though he is co-editing a book on some of this movement's themes with Kagan.) There is certainly no *necessary* connection between a disadvantaged childhood and a troubled adulthood. Many children do survive, and even thrive, in the face of every adversity, as so many biographies of the great readily attest. Parents—and especially mothers—have taken too much of the blame when children turn out "bad" (by whatever definition) and have had too great a burden of guilt laid upon them. Poor and disadvantaged parents have, as Skolnick points out, been faulted for consequences that more often result from the failings of the community at large.

Most important, perhaps, is Brim's point that damage of various sorts in childhood has all too often been looked upon as irreversible; and if something is labeled irreversible, then there is little incentive to try to turn it around. Yet, much of what is done to children *can* be undone—and has been shown to be undoable when the necessary effort is put forth. Cohler is right: people can and do often succeed in refashioning their own lives. In all these senses, I join Skolnick in deploring "parental determinism."

What is it that troubles me, then?

One source of disquiet is the conviction that if the movement's more extreme statements are taken seriously, they can all too easily let parents—and the community, in all its social and governmental manifestations—off the hook. If what happens in early childhood doesn't matter, if children aren't vulnerable after all, if kids are going to make it okay nevertheless, if poor parenting (whatever that can mean under the newly defined circumstances) is of no great consequence, then what's all the fuss about? Why orate about "child advocacy"? Why practice "child psychiatry"? Why give child-rearing advice at all?

Yet, look at what's really happening out there in our world. The statistics on child abuse are obscene. Family life is perceived to be increasingly fragmented. The landscape abounds with children in anguish. Many parents seem increasingly irked by the responsibilities of parenthood. Will the movement not give all of us license to care even less about children than we in our celebrated "child-centered society" now do? In a word, the movement appears to me to be a big step backward. And at whose expense? The children's.

To characterize such dedicated people as Kagan, Cohler, and Skolnick as being antichild would be most unfair; they spend their lives thinking about children and children's welfare. Just the same, the net effect of their pronouncements could turn out to be the inadvertent encouragement of antichild behavior. (Truly loving parents, of course, find it sufficiently rewarding to treat children well so they'll feel good now, regardless of later outcome.) If they were making their statements based upon a firm body of substantial evidence, I might feel that well, we just have to swallow hard and accept the consequences. But such studies are fairly tenuous at this point—much more so, it seems to me, than the case for the special vulnerability of early childhood and for the profound ill effects of certain kinds of defective parenting. Thus, these psychologists perform a disservice by the premature publicizing of what must be looked upon as tentative conclusions—a charge more usually directed at journalists.

The careful investigations of mother-infant bonding carried out by pediatricians Marshall H. Klaus and John H. Kennell, of the Case Western Reserve University School of Medicine, offer impressive and only recently accepted evidence that parent-child interaction even in the first hours of life can affect later emotional life. Apart from the intuitive conviction that one acquires from observing one's own and one's friends' children, the formidable accumulation of psychiatric and psychoanalytic case histories offers quantities of evidence (mostly retrospective, to be sure) of the connection between early childhood and adult troubles. Moreover, many longitudinal studies of the very kind cited by Cohler and Skolnick, studies made by respected investigators such as Rene Spitz, Ian Gregory, Margaret Fries, Elsie Broussard, Robert Skeel, Marie Crissey, Sylvia Brody and Sidney Axelrad, Stella Chess and Alexander Thomas, among others, point to the strong influence of what happens to children in their early, vulnerable years and its effect on their later emotional life. All this, and more, adds up to too strong a body of already-established evidence to brush aside so cavalierly. Those in the movement have every right to challenge any assumption they believe to be prevalent and challengeable. But one wishes they would frame their challenges less flamboyantly, considering the gravity of the possible consequences if they turn out to be wrong—as I so far believe them to be.

Analyst Gilbert W. Kliman, of the New York Psychoanalytic Society, is among those who deplore the new and in his view unwarranted direction the movement represents. He fears that the conclusions expressed will be latched onto all too eagerly by our contempories, parents and nonparents alike. "We have unequivocal long-term evidence," says Kliman, "that troubled children are often under the compulsion to repeat their early traumatic experiences as adults, to visit similar experiences upon their own children, and that babies who fail to get an adequate diet of 'stimulus nutrition' from a reliable caregiver are at great risk of developing later emotional problems." We have equally clear evidence that some very severe early-life problems can be reversed, even when due in part to pathological treatment by parents. But such reversal is achieved at great cost and only with great effort. Prevention would be so much better! And it too is achievable. That's why I hate to see any move afoot that will devalue or undercut the necessary preventive programs.

"We in our culture," Kliman goes on, "are finding it increasingly difficult to bear the pain of our children. We no longer have the excuse we used to have when people had large families and could say they were too busy to give each child a lot of individual attention. So we must rationalize our collective neglect of children by denying that the neglect does them any harm. Just as each of us has individually repressed all the painful memories of those earliest, most vulnerable years, we would like to be able to say of children in general: Early experience doesn't matter. It all just goes away and is forgotten."

Atypical Development

7. PERSONALITY DETERMINANTS IN THE BEHAVIOR OF THE RETARDED

Edward Zigler

David Balla

The behavior of retarded persons is not the product of low intelligence alone. In fact, a striking feature encountered among retarded individuals is the variety of behavior patterns displayed. We are not dealing with a homogeneous group, but rather with individuals who differ widely in regard to motives, educational experience, and experiential backgrounds. In research conducted to date, it has been strongly suggested that many of the reported differences between retarded and intellectually average children of the same mental age (MA) are a result of motivational and emotional differences which reflect variations in environmental histories and are not a function of intrinsic defects (Zigler, 1969). This is not to say that the cause of retardation is motivational: the cognitive functioning of retarded individuals unquestionably has a profound and pervasive influence on their behavior. The crucial questions are: just how great is this influence, and how does it vary across tasks with which retarded persons are confronted? What often is not realized is that the behavior of the retarded, as for all human beings, reflects formal cognitive processes, achievements, and motivational factors. In this article, we will review some research on motivational factors in retarded behavior.

SOCIAL DEPRIVATION

It has become increasingly clear that the performance of the institutionalized retarded is related to preinstitutional social deprivation (Clarke & Clarke, 1954; Kaplun, 1935; Zigler, 1961). The largest body of research has shown that social deprivation can result in a heightened motivation to interact with a supportive adult—an increased responsiveness to social reinforcement (Balla, Butterfield, & Zigler, 1974; Balla, Kossan, & Zigler, 1980; Zigler, 1961; Zigler & Balla, 1972; Zigler, Balla, & Butterfield, 1968). The heightened motivation to interact with an adult, stemming from a history of social deprivation, is consistent with the frequently observed behavior in the retarded of actively seeking attention and affection.

It should be noted that heightened motivation for social reinforcement has been used as an indicator of an important phenomenon discussed in the general child development literature, namely, dependency. Thus, with an almost imperceptibly slight shift in terminology, we might conclude that a general consequence of social deprivation is overdependency. We cannot place enough emphasis on the role of such overdependency in the behavior of the re-

This article was adapted from Zigler, E., & Balla, D., Personality factors in the performance of the retarded. *Journal of the American Academy of Child Psychiatry.* Winter 1977, *16*,(1), 19–37.

tarded. Given some minimal intellectual level, the shift from dependency to independence is perhaps the single most important factor which enables the retarded to become self-sustaining members of society (Zigler & Harter, 1969).

Some indication of the pervasiveness of the atypical dependency of the institutionalized retarded may be found in a study by Zigler and Balla (1972). In keeping with the general developmental progression from helplessness and dependence to autonomy and independence, both retarded and intellectually average children of higher MA were found to be less motivated for social reinforcement than those of lower MA. However, at every MA level the retarded children were more dependent than the nonretarded children. The disparity in dependency was just as great at the upper as the lower developmental level.

POSITIVE- AND NEGATIVE-REACTION TENDENCIES

A phenomenon which appears to be inconsistent with the retarded individual's increased desire for social reinforcement has often been observed, namely, the retarded child's reluctance and wariness in interacting with adults. The work of Zigler and his associates has indicated that social deprivation results both in a heightened motivation to interact with supportive adults (positive reaction tendency) and in a reluctance and wariness in doing so (negative reaction tendency).

This view was tested in a study in which groups of intellectually average and retarded children, matched on MA, were compared on an experimental task after initially experiencing either positive or negative reinforcement. The findings confirmed the prediction that both the nonretarded and retarded groups who played the experimental games under the negative reinforcement would be more wary of adults

than those children who had received positive reinforcement (Shallenberger & Zigler, 1961). Similar results were obtained by Weaver and his colleagues (Weaver, 1966; Weaver, Balla, & Zigler, 1971), who used a more direct experimental measure. These results were obtained for both institutionalized and noninstitutionalized retarded individuals. Thus, further evidence was provided that on certain tasks, differences in the performance of retarded and nonretarded individuals of the same MA can be attributed most parsimoniously to different environmental histories and resulting motivations.

Some evidence exists that institutionalized retarded individuals suffer from a generalized wariness of strangers, regardless of whether the strangers are adults or peers (Harter & Zigler, 1968). That socially depriving experiences can cause a generalized and persistent wariness of adults was indicated by the finding (Balla et al., 1980) that after approximately 8 years of institutional experience, individuals with a history of high preinstitutional social deprivation were still more wary than less deprived individuals.

FAILURE AND THE PERFORMANCE OF THE RETARDED

Another factor frequently mentioned as a determinant in the performance of the retarded is their high expectancy of failure. This expectancy has been viewed as a consequence of a history of frequent confrontations with tasks with which retarded persons are ill equipped to deal. The experimental work employing the success-failure dimension has proceeded in two directions. The first has been an attempt to document the pervasiveness of feelings of failure in the retarded. The work of Cromwell (1963), as well as that of MacMillan and his colleagues (MacMillan, 1969;

MacMillan & Keogh, 1971; MacMillan & Knopf, 1971), has lent support to the general proposition that retarded individuals have a higher expectancy of failure than those of average intellect.

The second line of research has focused upon the effects of success and failure expectancies on cognitive problem-solving behavior. Children with low expectancies of success, as gauged by aspiration level or need-achievement measures, have been found to have a lower expectancy of success in a problem-solving situation than children with high expectancies of success (Gruen, Ottinger, & Zigler, 1970; Kier & Zigler, 1977; Ollendick & Gruen, 1971). Retarded children have been found to exhibit a lower expectancy of success than children of average intelligence (Gruen & Zigler, 1968; Stevenson & Zigler, 1958). Gruen, Ottinger, and Ollendick (1974) attempted to determine whether the success-failure findings could be replicated in a more lifelike school setting. As predicted, retarded children in regular classes (presumably being exposed to repeated failure) were found to have higher expectancies of failure than retarded children in special classes (being exposed to relatively higher levels of success).

THE REINFORCER HIERARCHY

Due to experiential factors, the retarded individual's motivation for incentives may differ from that of intellectually average individuals of the same MA (i.e., the position of various reinforcers in the reinforcer hierarchies may differ in retarded and nonretarded children). Much of the experimental work on the reinforcer hierarchy has focused on tangible and intangible reinforcement (Havighurst, 1970). It has been argued that certain factors in the histories of retarded children cause them to be less responsive to intangible reinforcement than are nonretarded children of

equivalent MA (Zigler, 1962; Zigler & deLabry, 1962; Zigler & Unell, 1962). This work is of special importance, since intangible reinforcement (information that a response is correct) is the most immediate and frequently dispensed reinforcement in real-life tasks. When such a reinforcer is employed in experimental studies comparing retarded and nonretarded individuals, any group differences found might be attributable not to differences in intellectual capacity but rather to the different values that such reinforcement may have for the two types of individuals.

Clearest support for the view that the retarded child is much less motivated to be correct for the sake of correctness than is the middle-socioeconomic-status (SES) child (so typically employed in comparisons with the retarded) is contained in a study by Zigler and deLabry (1962). They tested MA-matched middle-SES, lower-SES, and retarded children on a concept-switching task (Kounin, 1941) under either a tangible or intangible (information that the response was correct) reinforcement condition. In the intangible condition, both the retarded and lower-SES groups were poorer in their concept-switching than the middle-SES children. However, no differences were found among the three groups who received tangible reinforcers. Furthermore, no differences in the ability to switch concepts were found among the three groups receiving what was assumed to be their optimal reinforcer (retarded, tangible; lower-SES, tangible; and middle-SES, intangible).

This study highlighted an assumption that has been noted as erroneous by many educators, namely, that the lower-SES child and the retarded child are responsive to the same types of reinforcers as the typical middle-SES child. However, although retarded children as a group may value being correct less than do middle-SES children as a group, this may not hold true for any particular child; the crucial factor is not membership in a particular social class or being retarded per se, but rather the particular social learning experience.

This point is aptly underlined in a study by Byck (1968), who examined the performance of groups of institutionalized Down syndrome and familial retarded subjects on a concept-switching task receiving either tangible or intangible reinforcement for their performance. Superior concept switching for the Down syndrome children was found in the intangible as compared to the tangible condition, whereas the reverse pattern was found for the familial group. This finding is consistent with the social-class and reinforcer-effectiveness literature noted above, if one remembers that the institutionalized familial retarded almost invariably come from a lower-SES background, whereas children with Down syndrome are more likely to come from middle-SES homes. It would appear that the social learning experiences acquired fairly early in the child's life and prior to institutionalization are particularly influential in determining the potency of various reinforcers.

In more recent work, attention has shifted to the more general phenomenon of the intrinsic reinforcement that inheres in being correct, regardless of whether or not an external agent dispenses a reinforcer for such correctness. This shift in orientation owes much to White's (1959) formulation concerning the pervasive influence of the effectance or mastery motive. A series of studies (Shultz & Zigler, 1970; Zigler, Levine, & Gould, 1966a; 1966b; 1967) has given some support to this view that using one's own cognitive resources to their fullest is intrinsically gratifying and thus motivating.

As with the case of intangible reinforcers, the strength of the effectance motive may be different for retarded and nonretarded children. Evidence on this point is provided by Harter and Zigler (1974), who constructed several measures of effectance

motivation. On these measures, intellectually average children demonstrated more effectance motivation than retarded children. Institutionalized retarded children were also found to be less curious than noninstitutionalized retarded children. In summary, retarded children seem to be both less responsive to intangible reinforcers and less motivated by intrinsic effectance motives than the child of average intellect.

OUTER-DIRECTEDNESS

Findings (Green & Zigler, 1962; Zigler, Hodgden, & Stevenson, 1958) that retarded children are more sensitive to cues provided by an adult than intellectually average children of the same MA have led us and our co-workers to the study of a general style of problem solving referred to as *outer-directedness* (Achenbach & Weisz, 1975; Achenbach & Zigler, 1968; Balla, Styfco, & Zigler, 1971; Sanders, Butterfield, & Zigler, 1968; Turnure & Zigler, 1964; Yando & Zigler, 1971; Zigler & Abelson, 1980). This style has been defined as the degree to which the individual uses external cues to solve problems rather than relying on his own cognitive resources.

Three factors have been advanced as important in determining the child's degree of outer-directedness—the general level of cognitive development, the relative incidence of success the individual has experienced when employing his cognitive resources in problem-solving situations, and the extent of the individual's attachment to adults (Balla et al., 1980; Zigler & Abelson, 1980). Either too little or too much imitation of adults is viewed as a negative psychological indicator. Some intermediate level of imitation is viewed as a positive developmental phenomenon reflecting the individual's healthy attachment to adults and responsivity to cues that adults emit which can be utilized in the child's problem-solving efforts.

In general, the developmental aspect of the outer-directedness formulation has received experimental support. With nonretarded children, outer-directedness has been found to decrease with increasing MA (MacMillan & Wright, 1974; Ruble & Nakumura, 1973; Yando & Zigler, 1971; Zigler & Yando, 1972). This developmental shift has also been found in institutionalized retarded persons (Turnure, 1970a, 1970b). In groups of noninstitutionalized mildly retarded people, decreasing outer-directedness with increasing MA has been found by Balla et al. (1971) and Gordon and MacLean (1977).

The success-failure aspect of the outer-directedness formulation has generated the prediction that retarded persons, because of their histories of failure, are more outer-directed in their problem-solving behavior than nonretarded children of the same MA. This prediction has been confirmed in several of the studies cited above. Both nonretarded and retarded children have been found to become more outer-directed following failure than success experiences.

To this point, outer-directedness or imitativeness has been discussed as if it were a unitary psychological dimension. Actually, in different studies, at least two somewhat conceptually different measures have been employed. These measures each bear somewhat differently on the success-failure aspect of the outer-directedness formulation. In some studies, a learning measure has been utilized where a cue extrinsic to the task could either help or hinder performance. There was clearly a right or wrong answer. It seems reasonable to expect that children living in an environment adjusted to their developmental level would be less imitative in this task than children living in an environment where they are confronted with their intellectual shortcomings and experience considerable failure. Indeed, Achenbach and Zigler (1968) found that noninstitutionalized retarded children were more reliant on external cues on this task than were institutionalized retarded children. A second measure of imitation that has been utilized has simply involved the extent of imitation of the experimenter's behavior. This task does not involve learning, and there are no right or wrong answers. This task may well tap the extent of conformity or compliance with adults. It seems reasonable to expect that in environments where a high degree of compliance has adaptive value, such as in total institutions, greater imitation would be found. In two studies (Lustman, Zigler, & Balla, 1979; Yando & Zigler, 1971), institutionalized retarded persons have been found to be more imitative on this task than noninstitutionalized retarded persons.

In regard to the attachment-to-adults aspect of the outer-directedness formulation, there is some evidence that individuals who have not formed healthy attachments to adult caretakers will have an atypically low level of outer-directedness (Balla et al., 1980). These investigators found that institutionalized retarded individuals whose caretakers had negative attitudes concerning them were less outer-directed than those whose caretakers had positive attitudes concerning them. Thus, individuals who are responded to in a negative manner may learn to ignore cues provided by adults and thus become less imitative.

SELF-CONCEPT

The self-concept construct has had a central role in general personality theory but, surprisingly, has received relatively little attention in the mental retardation literature (Balla & Zigler, 1979). Traditionally, a person's self-concept has been seen exclusively as a function of his life experience. An alternative view has been proposed by Zigler and his colleagues (e.g., Achenbach & Zigler, 1963; Katz & Zigler, 1967), who have advanced a developmental view of the self-image construct. They have argued that the growth and development of an individual must invariably be accompanied by an increasing disparity between assessment of the person's current self-concept and the way the person would ideally like to be. From the developmental point of view, the magnitude of self-image disparity is considered an index of the level of maturity attained.

Although there has been a relative emphasis on the developmental aspects of the self-concept in the above studies, we have also recognized that there is certainly an experiential component in the development of the self-image, and that any comprehensive understanding of the issue requires a synthesis of both developmental and experiential positions. In our studies involving the self-concept of retarded persons, both positions have received empirical support. In one study (Zigler, Balla, & Watson, 1972), we found that older nonretarded children had a more adverse self-concept than did younger nonretarded children, a finding consistent with the developmental approach to the self-concept. Consistent with the experiential position, however, was the finding that retarded individuals had lower ideal self-images than did the nonretarded individuals. This finding has since been replicated (Leahy, Balla, & Zigler, 1980). These findings concerning the ideal self-image among the retarded seemed to indicate that one consequence of being identified as retarded is a lowering of goals and aspirations, an interpretation certainly consistent with the expectancy-of-success literature cited above. In summary, both developmental and experiential interpretations of the development of the self-concept in retarded persons have received empirical support in our work.

REFERENCES

Achenbach, T. & Weisz, J. R. A longitudinal study of developmental synchrony between conceptual identity, seriation, and transitivity of color, number, and length. *Child Development*, 1975, *46*, 840–848.

Achenbach, T. & Zigler, E. Social competence and self-image disparity in psychiatric and nonpsychiatric patients. *Journal of Abnormal and Social Psychology*, 1963, *67*, 197–205.

Achenbach, T. & Zigler, E. Cue-learning and problem-learning strategies in normal and retarded children. *Child Development*, 1968, *3*, 827–848.

Balla, D., Butterfield, E. C., & Zigler, E. Effects of institutionalization on retarded children: A longitudinal cross-institutional investigation. *American Journal of Mental Deficiency*, 1974, *78*, 530–549.

Balla, D., Kossan, N., & Zigler, E. *Effects of preinstitutional history and institutionalization on the behavior of the retarded.* Unpublished manuscript, Yale University, 1980.

Balla, D., Styfco, S. J., & Zigler, E. Use of the opposition concept and outerdirectedness in intellectually-average, familial retarded, and organically retarded children. *American Journal of Mental Deficiency*, 1971, *75*, 663–680.

Balla, D. & Zigler, E. Personality development in retarded persons. In N. R. Ellis (Ed.), *Handbook of mental deficiency* (2d ed.). Hillsdale, N.J.: Erlbaum, 1979.

Byck, M. Cognitive differences among diagnostic groups of retardates. *American Journal of Mental Deficiency*, 1968, *73*, 97–101.

Clarke, A. D. B. & Clarke, A. M. Cognitive changes in the feebleminded. *British Journal of Psychology*, 1954, *45*, 173–179.

Cromwell, R. L. A social learning approach to mental retardation. In N. R. Ellis (Ed.), *Handbook of mental deficiency*. New York: McGraw-Hill, 1963, 41–91.

Gordon, D. A. & MacLean, W. E. Developmental analysis of outerdirectedness in noninstitutionalized EMR children. *American Journal of Mental Deficiency*, 1977, *81*, 508–511.

Green, C. & Zigler, E. Social deprivation and the performance of retarded and normal children on a satiation type task. *Child Development*, 1962, *33*, 499–508.

Gruen, G., Ottinger, D., & Ollendick, T. Probability learning in retarded children with differing histories of success and failure in school. *American Journal of Mental Deficiency*, 1974, *79*, 417–423.

Gruen, G., Ottinger, D., & Zigler, E. Level of aspiration and the probability learning of middle- and lower-class children. *Developmental Psychology*, 1970, *3*, 133–142.

Gruen, G. & Zigler, E. Expectancy of success and the probability learning of middle-class, lower-class, and retarded children. *Journal of Abnormal Psychology*, 1968, *73*, 343–352.

Harter, S. & Zigler, E. Effectiveness of adult and peer reinforcement on the performance of institutionalized and noninstitutionalized retardates. *Journal of Abnormal Psychology*, 1968, *73*, 144–149.

Harter, S. & Zigler, E. The assessment of effectance motivation in normal and retarded children. *Developmental Psychology*, 1974, *10*, 169–180.

Havighurst, R. J. Minority subcultures and the law of effect. *American Psychologist*, 1970, *25*, 313–322.

Kaplun, D. The high-grade moron. *Procedures of American Mental Deficiency*, 1935, *40*, 68–89.

Katz, P. & Zigler, E. Self-image disparity: A developmental approach. *Journal of Personality and Social Psychology*, 1967, *5*, 186–195.

Kier, R. J. & Zigler, E. Success expectancies and the probability learning of children of low and middle socioeconomic status. *Developmental Psychology*, 1977, *13*(5), 444–449.

Kounin, J. Experimental studies of rigidity: I. The measurement of rigidity in normal and feebleminded persons. *Character and Personality*, 1941, *9*, 251–272.

Leahy, R., Balla, D., & Zigler, E. *Role taking, self-image, and imitation in retarded and nonretarded individuals.* Unpublished manuscript, Yale University, 1980.

Lustman, N. M., Zigler, E., & Balla, D. *Imitation in institutionalized and non-institutionalized retarded children and in children of average intellect.* Unpublished manuscript, Yale University, 1979.

MacMillan, D. L. Motivational differences: Cultural-familial retardates vs. normal subjects on expectancy for failure. *American Journal of Mental Deficiency*, 1969, *74*, 254–258.

MacMillan, D. L. & Keogh, B. K. Normal and retarded children's expectancy for failure. *Developmental Psychology*, 1971, *4*, 343–348.

MacMillan, D. L. & Knopf, E. D. Effect of instructional set on perceptions of event outcomes by EMR and nonretarded children. *American Journal of Mental Deficiency*, 1971, *76*, 185–189.

MacMillan, D. L. & Wright, D. L. Outerdirectedness in children of three ages as a function of experimentally induced success and failure. *Journal of Educational Psychology*, 1974, *68*, 919–925.

Ollendick, T. & Gruen, G. Level of "n" achievement and probability in children. *Developmental Psychology*, 1971, *4*, 486.

Ruble, D. N. & Nakamura, C. Outerdirectedness as a problem-solving approach in relation to developmental level and selected task variables. *Child Development*, 1973, *44*, 519–528.

Sanders, B., Zigler, E., & Butterfield, E. C. Outerdirectedness in the discrimination learning of normal and mentally retarded children. *Journal of Abnormal Psychology*, 1968, *73*, 368–375.

Shallenberger, P. & Zigler, E. Rigidity, negative reaction tendencies, and cosatiation effects in normal and feebleminded children. *Journal of Abnormal and Social Psychology*, 1961, *63*, 20–26.

Shultz, T. & Zigler, E. Emotional concomitants of visual mastery in infants. *Journal of Experimental Child Psychology*, 1970, *10*, 390–402.

Stevenson, H. W. & Zigler, E. Probability learning in children. *Journal of Experimental Psychology*, 1958, *56*, 185–192.

Turnure, J. E. Reactions to physical and social distractors by moderately retarded institutionalized children. *Journal of Special Education*, 1970, *4*, 283–294. (a)

Turnure, J. E. Distractibility in the mentally retarded: Negative evidence for an orienting inadequacy. *Exceptional Children*, 1970, *37*, 181–186. (b)

Turnure, J. E. & Zigler, E. Outer-directedness in the problem-solving of normal and retarded children. *Journal of Abnormal and Social Psychology*, 1964, *69*, 427–436.

Weaver, J., Balla, D., & Zigler, E. Social approach and avoidance tendencies of institutionalized retarded and noninstitutionalized retarded and normal children. *Journal of Ex-*

perimental Research in Personality, 1971, *5*, 98–110.

Weaver, S. J. *The effects of motivation-hygiene orientation and interpersonal reaction tendencies in intellectually subnormal children.* Unpublished doctoral dissertation, George Peabody College for Teachers, 1966.

White, R. W. Motivation reconsidered: The concept of competence. *Psychological Review*, 1959, *66*, 297–333.

Yando, R. & Zigler, E. Outerdirectedness in the problem-solving of insitutionalized and non-institutionalized normal and retarded children. *Developmental Psychology*, 1971, *4*, 277–288.

Zigler, E. Social deprivation and rigidity in the performance of feebleminded children. *Journal of Abnormal and Social Psychology*, 1961, *62*, 413–421.

Zigler, E. Rigidity in the feebleminded. In E. Trapp & P. Himelstein (Eds.), *Readings on the exceptional child.* New York: Appleton-Century-Crofts, 1962, 141–162.

Zigler, E. Developmental versus difference theories of mental retardation and the problem of motivation. *American Journal of Mental Deficiency*, 1969, *73*, 536–556.

Zigler, E. & Abelson, W. *Is an intervention program necessary in order to improve economically disadvantaged children's IQ scores?* Manuscript submitted for publication, 1980.

Zigler, E. & Balla, D. Developmental course of responsiveness to social reinforcement in normal children and institutionalized retarded children. *Developmental Psychology*, 1972, *6*, 66–73.

Zigler, E., Balla, D., & Butterfield, E. C. A longitudinal investigation of the relationship between preinstitutional social deprivation and social motivation in institutionalized retardates. *Journal of Personality and Social Psychology*, 1968, *10*, 437–445.

Zigler, E., Balla, D., & Watson, N. Developmental and experimental determinants of self-image disparity in institutionalized and non-institutionalized retarded and normal children. *Journal of Personality and Social Psychology*, 1972, *23*, 81–87.

Zigler, E. & DeLabry, J. Concept-switching in middle-class, lower-class, and retarded children. *Journal of Abnormal and Social Psychology*, 1962, *65*, 267–273.

Zigler, E. & Harter, S. Socialization of the mentally retarded. In D. A. Goslin & D. C. Glass (Eds.), *Handbook of socialization theory and research.* New York: Rand McNally, 1969, 1065–1102.

Zigler, E., Hodgden, L., & Stevenson, H. The effect of support on the performance of normal and feebleminded children. *Journal of Personality*, 1958, *26*, 106–122.

Zigler, E., Levine, J., & Gould, L. Cognitive processes in the development of children's appreciation of humor. *Child Development*, 1966, *37*, 507–518. (a)

Zigler, E., Levine, J., & Gould, L. The humor response of normal, institutionalized retarded, and noninstitutionalized retarded children. *American Journal of Mental Deficiency*, 1966, *71*, 472–480. (b)

Zigler, E., Levine, J., & Gould, L. Cognitive challenge as a factor in children's humor appreciation. *Journal of Personality and Social Psychology*, 1967, *6*, 332–336.

Zigler, E. & Unell, E. Concept-switching in normal and feebleminded children as a function of reinforcement. *American Journal of Mental Deficiency*, 1962, *66*, 651–657.

Zigler, E. & Yando, R. Outerdirectedness and imitative behavior of institutionalized and noninstitutionalized younger and older children. *Child Development*, 1972, *43*, 413–425.

8. THE SYNDROME OF EARLY CHILDHOOD AUTISM: NATURAL HISTORY, ETIOLOGY, AND TREATMENT

Barbara K. Caparulo

Donald J. Cohen

In 1943 Leo Kanner identified a small group of children with a profound inability to establish meaningful emotional and social relationships, even with their parents, and who failed to develop language in the normal way (Kanner, 1973). He characterized this group as suffering from *early infantile autism*, a disorder which he considered to be an inborn vulnerability, similar to inborn errors of metabolism such as phenylketonuria (PKU). The choice of the term *autism*, suggested by the autistic withdrawal found in adult schizophrenia, was perhaps unfortunate. Over the past 40 years, research and clinical experience have demonstrated that autistic children have multiple cognitive and emotional handicaps that block acquisition of basic concepts of self, other, and mutuality and prevent recognition of the symbolic nature of language. When, later in life, autistic youngsters appear to withdraw from social contact, it is an expression of confusion and anxiety related to overly complex social demands rather than a retreat into the internal world of fantasy. Contemporary studies of autism continue to search for the biological basis of the disorder; analysis of the dysfunctions of autistic children has revealed disturbances in the preconditions for normal cognitive and emotional development and disruptions in the processes and skills emerging in the first year or two of life upon which later linguistic and social competencies depend.

Autism occurs in about 1 in every 2,500 children, making it far more common than PKU (1:15,000) and less common than Down's syndrome (1:700). It affects three or four times more boys than girls, and, while it is unusual for more than one child in a family to have autism, there are families with autism, language disorders, and other developmental disabilities in siblings and relatives which suggest some genetic contribution. Because of its severity and the continuing uncertainties surrounding its causes, diagnosis, and treatment, childhood autism has generated a great deal of scientific research and discussion and many treatment approaches.

THE EARLY YEARS

The behavioral and emotional disturbances of childhood autism are usually apparent from the first months of life. Failure to establish or maintain eye contact, to prepare for being picked up, and to smile

This article was adapted from Cohen, D., and Caparulo, B., Childhood autism. *Children Today*, July–August 1975, 3–6, 36.

socially are among the first symptoms of the disorder. The baby may be unusually good or cry inconsolably; he may become preoccupied with one object or toy, spend hours looking at his fingers, or repeatedly banging his head against his crib. The child's physical health during the first year of life is typically normal, although feeding difficulties, marked by strong preferences for only some foods, are common. Abnormal sleeping patterns, allowing the child and his family only 3 or 4 hours of sleep a night, are often reported. Activity level appears to be poorly modulated; extreme hyperactivity and overarousal to environmental stimulation mark the early years for many autistic children, although others show a hypoactive behavioral pattern and appear sluggish and almost apathetic to what goes on around them. The child often seems not to hear the speech addressed to him but panics at the sound of a washing machine or hair dryer. The most perplexing, and, for parents, devastating aspect of the young child's development, however, is the discrepancy between his gross motor and physical development and his growth in social and linguistic skills. The child's inability to relate to other human beings in the normal way becomes more noticeable as he grows older. Parents may be used as objects in order to satisfy basic needs, but the child shows no signs of closeness and enjoyment from mutual interaction with his parents. Physicians, finding the child's physical health and motor development to be normal, have typically dismissed parents' expressions of concern or have suggested a "wait and see" policy. By the age of 16 to 24 months, however, the child's history of failure to babble, play social games like peek-a-boo, and learn single words results in referral for developmental evaluation. Careful assessment of the preschool autistic child reveals a range of intellectual, linguistic, social, and behavioral abnormalities, each suggesting a single diagnosis such

as mental retardation, developmental language disorder, atypical personality development, and severe emotional disturbance (Cohen, 1976). While each label captures a particular facet of autism, none fully describes the range of deficits present in the disorder.

Differential Diagnosis
Diagnosis of childhood autism entails evaluation from several disciplines. Intellectual assessment requires procedures that must be adapted to the child's behavioral, linguistic, and attentional abilities. Many hours of observation are needed, and a careful developmental history must be obtained in order to chart the overall pattern of growth as well as the areas of relative strength and deficit displayed by the child. Typically, the child with primary autism does much better in areas involving visuospatial processing, rote memory, and gross-fine motor functioning than in those that call for sequencing, rule abstraction, and symbolic manipulation. Unlike the child with mental retardation, however, the autistic child's socioemotional development lags far behind his overall intellectual development.

Linguistically, the 4- or 5-year-old autistic child has a limited expressive vocabulary or has no expressive language at all. Children with severe delays in the development of language, and those with central language disorders such as dysphasia, present similarly retarded attainment of linguistic milestones (Cohen, Caparulo, & Shaywitz, 1976). The presence of echolalia, unusual intonational characteristics in whatever expressive language the child possesses, and intact articulation set the autistic child apart from one with a primary language impairment, however; furthermore, in disorders of the latter type, social communication through nonverbal channels emerges relatively smoothly (Caparulo & Cohen, 1977).

Behavioral observation reveals the presence of stereotyped motor patterns such as twirling, rocking, flicking of fingers in front of the eyes, or monotonous pacing. There is an intense need to preserve sameness in the physical environment or in daily routines; rearranging a bedroom or taking a different route to the supermarket results in a panic reaction that may involve extreme agitation, self-aggression, and screaming. During assessment, the child may perseverate in lining up toys or may insist that the evaluator follow the same routine during each hourly visit.

The medical evaluation, aimed at determining if the behavioral and intellectual difficulties are secondary to any known disease, should include careful examination of vision and hearing, neurological and pediatric physical examination, urine screening for metabolic and genetic diseases, and other laboratory studies. An electroencephalogram (EEG), x-rays of the skull and computed tomographic brain scanning, and blood screening tests are indicated to rule out diseases that may have symptoms similar to those in autism (e.g., untreated PKU, measles encephalitis, and congenital rubella). If such evidence is uncovered, the child's autism is said to be secondary to the organic disturbance; most autistic children, however, receive clean bills of health from their medical evaluations and are classified as having primary autism. As medical research discovers more biological causes of severe behavioral disturbances in childhood, some children now diagnosed as having primary autism may be moved to the category of secondary childhood autism.

Children with autism are difficult, uncooperative patients and frequently suffer from too limited pediatric, dental, and eye care. Their disorder puts them at risk for the development of other problems; many children, for example, suffer from pica, the ingesting of nonedible material such as dirt, newspaper, and paint (Cohen, Johnson, &

Caparulo, 1976). Pica often results in an elevation of blood lead levels, which, if untreated, can have major neurological effects. Others have undetected middle ear infections or severe dental problems. Good pediatric care under the supervision of a physician alert to the special health needs of autistic children is essential, especially for preventive purposes.

THE LATER YEARS

Research is just beginning to fill in the gaps in the natural history of childhood autism by studying the children, once physically attractive and motorically agile, as they move through middle childhood, adolescence, and into their adult years (Caparulo & Cohen, in press; Rutter & Schopler, 1978). Only 5 to 15% of older autistic persons develop useful communicative language and improved social and work skills that allow them to live in semi-independent or, rarely, independent, situations. Their behavior in social encounters, while not bizarre or disruptive, lacks spontaneity and reflects the hard work they, and their parents and teachers, have put into their education. In school, these persons show areas of high intellectual ability whose utility in terms of acquisition of practical skills, however, may be questionable. After extreme delays in learning basic linguistic structures, the higher-functioning autistic person becomes quite competent in using language but experiences major difficulties in understanding the social significance of interpersonal communication. As an adult, he appears anxious, fearful, and often depressed about his disabilities; when upset or excited, especially by social demands, he often engages in the stereotypic behaviors that first appeared years earlier. Friendships and emotional ties with adults remain superficial, despite his feelings of recognition that such relationships would help to ease his loneliness and sense of isolation.

For the less fortunate autistic child whose language does not progress, behavior during the school-age and adolescent years remains similar to that of the preschool years. Hyperactivity may decrease with maturation and training, but the child's ability to communicate, use symbols, follow commands, and relate to peers and adults is extremely limited. Some children become more aggressive toward others and destructive, symptoms that require thoughtful but firm attention through behavior modification. As the child becomes older, his intellectual and linguistic handicaps may become more obvious so that by the age of 17 or 18, they overshadow his social impairments. For the autistic child with greater intellectual impairments, intense efforts must be made to prevent stereotypic behaviors from dominating his waking hours by redirecting his attention toward basic skills and comprehension of simple instructions.

The upsurge of sexual drives during adolescence may lead to increased tension which the autistic man or woman does not know how to discharge. For some autistic individuals, parents and educators must consider teaching even basic sexual knowledge, such as how, when, and where to masturbate. The sexual curiosity and inappropriate behavior toward others lead to difficulties in school and residential programs. The autistic person cannot fully understand the feelings of others or navigate the subtle mutualities required for normal sexual relations; his normal sexual urges thus can find no socially acceptable avenue for expression. Curricula for sex education of autistic children recognize these special problems and suggest methods for teachers, parents, and the individual to deal with them (Lieberman & Melone, 1979).

CAUSES OF AUTISM

The cause of primary childhood autism is not known. Psychoanalytic and psychodynamic theories that were most prominent in the 1940s and 1950s have been rejected in favor of hypotheses emphasizing an organic basis of the disorder. In support of such biological theories are various kinds of evidence. Disturbances in sensory integration and in the sequential ordering of behavior appear to reflect abnormalities in central nervous system functioning. Autistic children's stereotypic behavior, disorganization, hyperactivity, troubles in feeling pleasure or pain, and other symptoms are consistent with some patterns of abnormalities that affect brain metabolism. Many autistic children have an abnormal or borderline abnormal brain wave pattern, and about 25% develop seizures. Autism is found throughout the world, in every social class, with a uniform clinical picture. And finally, in a high percentage of cases in which one identical twin has autism, the other also has this condition, suggesting a congenital, and perhaps genetic, basis for the disorder. All of this evidence supports the view that autism is like some of the now well-defined inborn errors of metabolism, but considerably more research is needed to investigate such a hypothesis (Young & Cohen, 1979).

Another promising field of investigation is the possible biochemical basis for severe developmental problems (Cohen, Caparulo, & Shaywitz, 1978). Recent research on manic-depressive disease and schizophrenia in adults, as well as on neurological diseases such as Parkinson's syndrome and chronic multiple tics of Gilles de la Tourette's syndrome, has greatly increased knowledge about the way in which messages are chemically transmitted by nerve cells in the brain. This process involves various chemicals—such as dopamine and norepinephrine—which are stored in nerve endings and then released when needed. There may be abnormalities in the way in which these chemicals are synthesized, released, or broken down after performing their function. Knowledge about these processes has been the bases for the treatment of Parkinson's disease with DOPA and for explaining the chemical action of medicines used in the treatment of depression, schizophrenia, and childhood attentional disorders.

TREATMENT

Just as the cause of autism is not known, its cure remains undiscovered. The mainstays of treatment are special education and vocational training, parental guidance, psychotherapy, drug therapy, and a structured, consistent living environment.

Educationally, the major advances in recent years have been in the use of behavior modification integrated with cognitive-developmental curricula, beginning in the preschool years and extending through to adulthood (see Rutter & Schopler, 1978, for review). Parents are taught to educate their own children, even at the age of 2 or 3 years, during the hours spent at home. Behavior modification is an effective method of both training the child's behavior and teaching him self-help, preacademic, and academic skills when used in the context of precision education, in which the child's capacities, the teacher-parent's objectives, and the teaching and measurement methods are precisely defined. Both educational techniques, however, are extremely complex and have been abused by even well-intentioned educators; their application requires sensitivity, experience, intuition, and intelligence, and their success depends on the establishment of close collaboration between parents and professionals who can maintain constancy from home to school. Their utility is increased when used in conjunction with a comprehensive language and cognitive development program aimed at providing the child with a range of concepts about objects, people, the world, and causality.

Prevocational and vocational training must be begun as the child approaches early adolescence. The development of a work, self-help, and social vocabulary, the acquisition of a range of vocational skills, and the learning of on-the-job behaviors (e.g., paying attention, keeping track of one's time spent at work, following instructions) are the three primary areas of training that must be addressed in a step-by-step, consistent way. For better-functioning persons with autism, the acquisition of vocational skills provides a channel for partial self-support, as well as for assuming an acceptable role in society, and makes a critical difference in the ultimate prognosis. For autistic persons who are more impaired, prevocational and vocational training offers the opportunity of participating in highly structured and well-supervised workshops where social and intellectual growth may continue well after formal education ends. The prognosis for severely impaired persons with autism remains guarded, although models now exist of adult living environments that offer reasonable alternatives to a life spent in an institution.

Parents require emotional support and practical, long-term guidance in relation to both their autistic child and their other children. As Josh Greenfeld (1973, 1978) describes in his chronicle of his own family's experiences, an autistic child may create extreme tension between a husband and wife, which, when coupled with exhaustion, anxiety, and guilt, can ultimately lead to separation and divorce. Counseling siblings of an autistic child is a critical part of the supporting professional's job, as is aiding in the development of a life plan for the child that allows the family to respond rationally to critical changes accompanying developmental transitions (e.g., preadolescence, entry into adulthood).

Psychotherapy plays a limited role for most children with autism, but for those who show the beginnings of being able to form social and affectionate attachments, and for some older, better-functioning youngsters, it offers the opportunity of expressing feelings of anxiety, happiness, and self-discovery. There are no firm data to support this belief, but several youngsters, studied through late adolescence and into adulthood, have appeared to benefit from the personal contact and feelings of relatedness thay have experienced in therapy with an empathetic and intuitive professional.

Although no psychoactive medication has proven to be especially useful for all symptoms or for long periods of time in autistic children (Campbell, 1978), judicious clinicians may suggest a trial of a medication with demonstrated value in the treatment of severe psychiatric disturbance, hoping to relieve a target symptom such as extreme self-aggression or to help a child make use of special education by relieving his hyperactivity or anxiety. Children should not be kept on medication for years, however, and close monitoring of the dose and side effects by a responsible physician, the child's parents, and his teachers is essential. Medication such as dextroamphetamine, which has traditionally been used in the treatment of hyperactivity, has not been found to be useful with autistic youngsters, since it increases the behavioral and mental disorganization the child experiences and appears to exacerbate other symptoms.

Finally, children with autism require continuity of care and stability in their lives. Residential special education programs often provide the best setting to meet these needs because of their ability to have 24-hour staffing by persons who can respond consistently to the child's behavior and emotional needs. The child's place within his family, however, must not be sacrificed; weekly or monthly visits home help the family remain engaged with the child. Alternatives to residential education include "extended day" programs within the local school system or in private schools such as Benhaven (Lettick, 1979; Simonson, 1979), where vocational, academic, and social training is offered on an 8-hour-day, 6-day-week, 50-week-year basis. Summer "vacations" should be avoided, since serious regression almost always occurs and the child's educational needs go unattended. Finally, artistic children should not be placed on general wards in institutions for the mentally retarded or seriously emotionally disturbed; they invariably do badly, lose areas of competence, and become more disorganized behaviorally.

Future Prospects

Until the causes of autism are understood, many children and their families face a long and exhausting course in trying to attain the diagnostic, educational, and treatment services that have been developed over the past 20 years. Perhaps the most exciting advances of the 1970s have been in the elucidation of the type of educational programs that most benefit persons with autism. In the future, interdisciplinary and parent-professional collaboration[1] must take the lead in assuring that such programs reach those who need them. Great work remains to be done in establishing adult living environments for persons with autism and in assisting families in planning for the long-term needs of their autistic

---

1. See various issues of the *Journal of Autism and Developmental Disorders.*

child. Groups such as the National Society for Autistic Children[2] now play a central role in advocacy on behalf of persons with autism and similar developmental disorders.

Research must continue in brain chemistry and physiology, in relation to both primary autism and those developmental disorders, such as central language disturbances, that may be related, and to the changes in brain functioning over the natural course of these disorders.

The development of social policies about the treatment of autistic persons, the improved provision of services, and the continuation of biological research require an intense interdisciplinary effort and collaboration with parents. With the expansion of knowledge in the neurosciences, linguistics, education, and other areas relevant to autism, sustained collaboration between professionals and parents promises to reveal new insights into the causes of, and treatments for, severe childhood disabilities.

REFERENCES

Campbell, M. Pharmacotherapy. In M. Rutter & E. Schopler (Eds.), *Autism: A Reappraisal of Concepts and Treatment.* New York: Plenum Press, 1978.

Caparulo, B. K. & Cohen, D. J. Cognitive structures, language, and emerging social competence in autistic and aphasic children. *Journal of the American Academy of Child Psychiatry*, 1977, *16*(4), 620–645.

Caparulo, B. K. & Cohen, D. J. Developmental language studies in the neuropsychiatric disorders of childhood. In K. E. Nelson (Ed.), *Children's Language.* Vols. 1 and 2. New York: Halsted Press, 1978 and 1979.

Cohen, D. J. The diagnostic process in child psychiatry. *Psychiatric Annals*, 1976, *6*(9), 404–416.

Cohen, D. J., Caparulo, B. K., & Shaywitz, B. A. Primary childhood aphasia and childhood autism: Clinical, biological, and conceptual observations. *Journal of the American Academy of Child Psychiatry*, 1976, *15*(4), 604–645.

Cohen, D. J., Caparulo, B. K., & Shaywitz, B. A. Neurochemical and developmental models of childhood autism. In G. Serban (Ed.), *Cognitive defects in the development of mental illness.* New York: Brunner/Mazel, 1978.

Cohen, D. J., Johnson, W. T., & Caparulo, B. K. Pica and elevated blood lead level in autistic and atypical children. *American Journal of Diseases of Children*, 1976, *130*(1), 47–48.

Greenfeld, J. *A child Called Noah.* New York: Warner Books, 1973.

Greenfeld, J. *A place for Noah.* New York: Holt, Rinehart, & Winston, 1978.

Kanner, L. *Initial studies and new insights.* Washington, D.C.: Winston & Sons, 1973.

Lettick, A. L. *Benhaven then and now.* New Haven, Conn.: Benhaven Press, 1979.

Lieberman, D. A. & Melone, M. B. *Sexuality and social awareness: A curriculum for moderately autistic and/or neurologically impaired individuals.* New Haven, Conn.: Benhaven Press, 1979.

Rutter, M. & Schopler, E. (Eds.). *Autism: A reappraisal of concepts and treatment.* New York: Plenum Press, 1978.

Simonson, L. R. *A curriculum model for individuals with severe learning and behavior disorders.* Baltimore, Md.: University Park Press, 1979.

Young, J. G. & Cohen, D. J. The molecular biology of development. In J. D. Noshpitz (Ed.), *Basic handbook of child psychiatry.* New York: Basic Books, 1979.

2. For more information, contact: The Director, Chapter and Member Service, National Society for Autistic Children, Suite 1017, 1234 Mars Avenue, N.W., Washington, D.C. 20005.

9. MAINSTREAMING:
THE PROOF IS IN THE IMPLEMENTATION

Edward Zigler

Susan Muenchow

Mainstreaming must be considered in context: Ten years ago, less than half of the estimated 8 million handicapped children in the United States were receiving special education services, and 1 million handicapped children were excluded from the public school system entirely (Kakalik, Note 1). The passage of the Education for All Handicapped Children Act of 1975 (P.L. 94–142, Note 2), which guarantees a "free appropriate public education" in the "least restrictive environment" to all handicapped children, therefore represents a major landmark in entitlement legislation. With the passage of the act, parents have gained a tool to hold the state accountable for providing some of the support services necessary to raise a seriously handicapped child at home. The handicapped have gained legitimate access to a major public system, whereas previously they had none. Perhaps the most revolutionary aspect of the legislation is its mandate for parent participation in developing an "individualized education program" for each handicapped child. This provision, if implemented, is a step toward involvement by parents in the education of their children to be envied by many parents of normal children.

Yet despite the law's clear intent to expand the options for handicapped children and their parents, it takes more than legislation to create a social revolution in the schools. Caught in the squeeze between the federal mandate to educate all handicapped children and state and local budget cutbacks, many school districts may interpret the "least restrictive" alternative as the least expensive alternative. The law's admonition that handicapped children be educated to the maximum extent feasible in regular classes could be abused by failing to provide sufficient special classes. If mainstreaming, like deinstitutionalization, is oversold, it may be reduced to its lowest common denominator—dumping vulnerable children in already overcrowded classes without any of the support services necessary to make such a policy work. Without adequate teacher preparation, the "individualized education program" could be dismissed as the "impossible education program" (Turnbull, Strickland, & Hammer, 1978). In short, as with any massive change in social policy, mainstreaming is unlikely to have effects on children that are unidirectional. It is the task of researchers to help determine those effects, both positive and negative. Now that the education of handicapped children with their nonhandicapped peers to the greatest extent possible has become the position of orthodoxy, mainstreaming could become, in Etzioni's

This article first appeared in *American Psychologist*, October 1979, *34*(10), 993–996. Copyright 1979 by the American Psychological Association. Reprinted by permission.

(1978) words, another "vastly oversold good idea." To guard against a backlash, feedback from research on mainstreaming is desperately needed. Research is needed to provide some basic knowledge about which children, with which handicaps, are likely to benefit from mainstreaming and about how to provide special training for teachers. Furthermore, research is needed to determine how the majority of school districts are interpreting and implementing the law. Mainstreaming must not be allowed to proceed along the same lines as deinstitutionalization, which has often amounted to the trading of inferior care for no care at all.

It is important to note that the treatment of the handicapped has frequently been buffeted between social trends with an apparent life span of about 10 years. Consider the recent history of retarded persons. During the last century, there was a period when the notion of mental orthopedics was in ascendance: the idea that given the right training experience, retarded children would be made "normal." State institutions were originally set up with the goal of "habilitation" in mind. But when retarded persons did not become normal, professionals quickly abandoned attempts to train them. State training schools became human warehouses, and the treatment of the retarded entered its darkest phase.

Some years later, the importance of special training was rediscovered. Workers in the field of mental retardation promoted special education as the solution to the problem of training the retarded. By the 1960s school psychologists were claiming that "regardless of outcome, special class placement is important from a humanitarian point of view . . . [for it] prevent[s] frustration and feelings of inferiority derived from undue competition" (Quay, 1963, p. 672). But in less than a decade, special education would become suspect on humanitarian grounds; special-class placement would be viewed as inherently stigmatizing. Under the banner of "normalization," deinstitutionalization and mainstreaming have become the policy slogans for treating mentally and physically impaired children.

We offer this perspective not to suggest that there has been no progress in this nation's treatment of mentally retarded children, but to underscore the precarious nature of that progress. Conceived during the civil rights movement and in reaction to the mislabeling of many minority children as retarded, mainstreaming appears to be based more on a political and philosophical zeitgeist than on any scientific evidence concerning the merits of particular educational placements for children with particular handicaps. The problem with social policy based largely on good intentions is that the pendulum can swing very quickly in the opposite direction.

To date, the data on the merits of educating retarded children with their nonretarded peers are simply inconclusive. Academically, it appears that mainstreamed retarded children fare no better or worse than children in special classes (Budoff & Gottlieb, 1976), with a few investigators finding some gains in reading but not in arithmetic (Walker, 1974). The results of studies exploring the effects of mainstreaming on self-image among retarded children are mixed. Some studies have shown improved self-image among the mainstreamed (Budoff & Gottlieb, 1976), some have shown few differences (Walker, 1974), and at least one study showed a higher expectancy of failure among retarded children in mainstreamed classes than among those in special classes (Gruen, Ottinger, & Ollendick, 1974). The expectation that mainstreamed retarded children would be less stigmatized by their peers than are children in self-contained special education classes has not been borne out (Gottlieb & Budoff, 1973; Goodman, Gottlieb, & Harrison, 1972; Iano, Ayers,

Heller, McGettigan, & Walker, 1974). However, as an excellent recent review pointed out, most of these studies have been conducted in elementary schools (Meyers, MacMillan, & Yoshida, 1979). "Seriously in need of replication," according to Meyers et al., is a study among secondary students (Sheare, 1974) which found that nonretarded peers who had been exposed to educable mentally retarded (EMR) students in their classes viewed these students more favorably than did nonretarded students who had not been exposed.

To sum up the data on mainstreaming, "there appears to be no unambiguous answer to the primitive question of whether segregated or integrated placement is superior" (Meyers et al., in press). Moreover, the research is complicated by the tremendous variation in the operational definition of mainstreaming. Some school districts, in order to qualify for federal funding, count the time a handicapped child spends in the cafeteria or in the halls as mainstreaming. In addition to this gamesmanship, some variation is unavoidable and inherent in the very principle of an individualized education program.

Despite the ambiguous nature of the current research on mainstreaming, a few points seem clear. First, the importance of appropriate training for teachers and other personnel who work with handicapped children cannot be overemphasized. As Sarason and Doris (Note 3) pointed out, although public policy now calls for placing handicapped children in the least restrictive environment, teacher-training centers continue to educate school personnel in the tradition of the most restrictive alternative. Second, without adequate support personnel to assist regular-class teachers with the education of handicapped (particularly EMR) students, mainstreaming is doomed to fail. Third, given the need for support teachers, any mainstreaming worthy of the name is likely to cost more, not less, than the old special classes. Taxpayers must not be deceived into thinking, as they were with deinstitutionalization, that mainstreaming is a bargain. As one Connecticut school superintendent put it, one of the chief problems with PL 94-142 is that the federal government is "better at mandating than at allocating." The federal government now mandates that states serve all handicapped children, but "the federal contribution to the costs of meeting that service and other requirements of PL 94-142 is only a fraction of the costs to be borne by the states and local education agencies if states decide to participate in the federal program" (ECS Policy Committee, Note 4).

Finally, mainstreaming and its evaluation are not taking place in a social science vacuum. How one perceives the effectiveness of mainstreaming in part depends on the criteria of measurement employed, criteria that are themselves influenced by values and assumptions. Some advocates maintain that mainstreaming, whatever its effects on academic achievement and social adjustment, at least forces society to acknowledge its own intolerance of handicaps.

Our own view is that normalization, the basic principle underlying both mainstreaming and deinstitutionalization, is not sacrosanct. For some children, normalization may mean a denial of the right to be different or to have special needs. A blind teacher scoffed at the mainstreaming advocates who congratulate themselves for having taught a blind child to color along with his or her classmates, using special guides: "Why? Does this teach concepts he must have? Colors? Forms? Or is it a kind of puppetry?" (quoted in Greenberg & Doolittle, 1977). Normalization can mean nonacceptance, an unwillingness to accept a child's blindness.

The principle of normalization can also lead educators astray if short-term benefits are pursued at the expense of the long-term ones. For example, the attempt to mainstream some deaf children in school may ironically reduce their chances to live and work in the mainstream as adults. "The paradox is that without the education I got in *deaf* schools I would be hopelessly lost in the hearing world now," explained a deaf teacher (quoted in Greenberg & Doolittle, 1977). The most significant research on mainstreaming is yet to come: how does mainstreaming affect a handicapped person's functioning in the adult world after graduation? Social competence should be the ultimate criterion for monitoring the effectiveness of mainstreaming.

The Education for All Handicapped Children Act of 1975 clearly attempts to increase the options for handicapped children and their families. The emphasis on the "individualized education plan," with provisions for parental involvement, is commendable. It is interesting that although the law uses the phrase "least restrictive alternative," the term *mainstreaming* never even appears. But the proof of this legislation will lie in its implementation. Mainstreaming can have many positive effects on handicapped children, but this policy will be an empty slogan, with many negative effects, if not accompanied by adequate teacher-training and support services. Furthermore, mainstreaming must not be presented as a panacea for handicaps. As Cruickshank (1977) aptly observed, the concept of least restrictive placement "will not, in and of itself, solve a single problem of a single child" (p. 193). Much more work is needed to determine not just which children, with which handicaps, can benefit from mainstreaming, but also what the environmental nutrients are that promote full development.

REFERENCE NOTES

1. Kakalik, J. S. *Improving services to handicapped children* (Report prepared for the U.S. Department of Health, Education, and Welfare, Office of the Assistant Secretary for Planning and Evaluation, R-1420-HEW). Santa Monica, Calif.: Rand Corporation, May 1974.
2. Public Law 94-142, Education for All Handicapped Children Act, November 29, 1975.
3. Sarason, S. & Doris, J. Mainstreaming: Dilemmas, opposition, opportunities. In M. C. Reynold (Ed.), *Futures of education for exceptional students: Emerging structures.* Minneapolis: University of Minnesota, National Support Systems Project, 1978.
4. Education Commission of the States Policy Committee. *Selected statements* (Pub. No. P.1). Denver, Colo.: Education Commission of the States, September 1977.

REFERENCES

Budoff, M. & Gottlieb, J. Special class students mainstreamed: A study of an aptitude (learning potential) X treatment interaction. *American Journal of Mental Deficiency*, 1976, *81*, 1–11.

Cruickshank, W. M. Least-restrictive placement: Administrative wishful thinking. *Journal of Learning Disabilities*, 1977, *10*, 193–194.

Etzioni, A. A vastly oversold good idea. *Columbia*, Spring 1978, pp. 14–17.

Goodman, H., Gottlieb, J., & Harrison, R. H. Social acceptance of EMRs integrated into a nongraded elementary school. *American Journal of Mental Deficiency*, 1972, *76*, 412–417.

Gottlieb, J. & Budoff, M. Social acceptability of retarded children in nongraded schools differing in architecture. *American Journal of Mental Deficiency*, 1973, *78*, 15–19.

Greenberg, J. & Doolittle, G. Can schools speak the language of the deaf? *New York Times Magazine*, December 11, 1977, pp. 50–102.

Gruen, G., Ottinger, D., & Ollendick, T. Probability learning in retarded children with differing histories of success and failure in school. *American Journal of Mental Deficiency*, 1974, *79*, 417–423.

Iano, R. P., Ayers, D., Heller, H. B., McGettigan, J. F., & Walker, V. S. Sociometric status of retarded children in an integrative program. *Exceptional Children*, 1974, *40*, 267–271.

Meyers, C. E., MacMillan, D. L., & Yoshida,

R. K. Regular class placement of EMR students, from efficacy to mainstreaming: A review of issues and research. In J. Gottlieb (Ed.), *Educating mentally retarded persons in the mainstream.* Baltimore, Md.: University Park Press, 1979.

Quay, L. C. Academic skills. In N.R. Ellis (Ed.), *Handbook of mental deficiency.* New York: McGraw-Hill, 1963.

Sheare, J. B. Social acceptance of EMR adolescents in integrated programs. *American Journal of Mental Deficiency,* 1974, *78,* 678–682.

Turnbull, A. P., Strickland, B., & Hammer, S. E. The individualized education program—Part *2:* Translating law into practice. *Journal of Learning Disabilities,* 1978, *11,* 18–23.

Walker, V. S. The efficacy of the resource room for educating retarded children. *Exceptional Children,* 1974, *40,* 288–289.

Child Rearing

10. ON BEING A PARENT

Edward Zigler

Rosa Cascione

Being a parent in our society is a difficult and often anxiety-producing job. The parent who is confronted with a tiny, helpless newborn is struck with the awesome responsibilities of helping the child evolve from a dependent, immature, and unsocialized infant into an independent, intellectually sophisticated, and socially competent human being. The conscientious mother and father are, without question, the most important agents in determining the specific course of their child's growth and development.

The job of parenting is a demanding one that requires considerable attention, knowledge, selflessness, and patience. One must work at it consciously and continually, and one must be prepared for the anxieties and doubts which arise when confronted with the question, "Am I a good parent?" The more one wants to be a good parent, the more anxious one becomes. Although a certain amount of anxiety is normal and understandable, many parents today tend to be *too* anxious, and this anxiety has detrimental effects upon the parents themselves, upon their children, and upon the parent-child relationship.

Some of this overanxiety can be attributed to the fact that many parents are not as well equipped for parenthood as parents have been in the past. Parents of today often do not have the support for parenting that was once generally available. The extended family is rare in con-

temporary society, and with its demise the new parent lost the wisdom and daily support of older family members. The increased mobility and new housing patterns of American families have all too often deprived the family of a variety of community activities that supported parenting and family life. Furthermore, as child development experts Myrtle McGraw and Urie Bronfenbrenner have been pointing out for many years, our society has become divided along age lines. Grandparents live far from their grandchildren, children form peer groups early, and older children have greatly reduced responsibilities in caring for the young. Indeed, the generally diminished interaction between adults and children in our society led participants at the 1970 White House Conference on Children to raise the basic issue of how children might be reintroduced into the world of adults.

As a result of these developments, most new parents tend to lack knowledge about how children grow and develop. Moreover, they rarely have immediately at hand loving and experienced adults to assist them through their apprenticeship. Faced with such a state of affairs, parents turn in ever greater numbers to the counsel of distant experts whose directives are often contradictory and confusing. The lack of knowledge and needed advice has resulted in a situation in which many parents misunderstand the real strengths and needs of

Presented March 31, 1980.

both their children and themselves. For example, many parents view their young child as more fragile than he or she really is. These parents have convinced themselves that one misstep in child rearing will result in horrible, lifelong consequences. For such parents, it would be reassuring to learn what experienced grandparents know intuitively: that even the very young child is a relatively tough, active human being with a personal capacity for growth that almost guarantees a normal course of development, provided the child is protected from physical harm and is given the love and care of ordinary, devoted parents.

As a result of their isolation and worries, too many parents experience the obligations of child rearing without the pleasures. In many homes, both parents and children walk about as if on eggshells. The parent-child relationship is characterized by apprehension, joylessness, and the pursuit of questionable goals. This state of affairs is in large part an outgrowth of the reliance by parents on the advice of people who claim special scientific expertise about child development.

Parental attitudes and child-rearing practices have always tended to follow the thinking of child development experts. Yet developmental psychology is like any other science. At any time, there are differences in opinion, changing viewpoints, and a mixture of sense and nonsense about the practical implications of any laboratory evidence. The parent who is neither familiar with the thousands of studies of child development nor trained in scientific inquiry can easily be steamrollered into believing a point of view which may turn out to be little more than a passing fad. This is usually exacerbated by journalists who rush to tell parents how to improve their children's well-being, generally basing their information on the latest sensational finding from this or that child development laboratory. What parents do not realize is that much of the so-called information

about children presented in the popular press is often no more than the writer's interpretation of a tentative hypothesis, a scientist's value judgment, or an unverified hunch. It is our belief that a large part of the current overanxiety of parents stems from just such fads and opinions based on tentative and incomplete views of the developing child.

Although psychologists and other scientists have far to go before arriving at a complete understanding of how a child develops, one of the most significant advances toward this goal is currently being made in the field of child development. From many laboratories in the United States and throughout the world, numerous research findings are converging upon a more comprehensive view of child development. What seems to be emerging is a recognition that the number of factors responsible for a child's growth is much greater than was formerly believed. In addition to the significance of the mother, the importance of the father and of the whole environment—from the influences of schools and television to the availability of medical care and part-time jobs—is being demonstrated. Moreover, studies are finding that the child may play an active role in its own development. Thus, according to the new research findings, a child's development is affected not merely by the mother, or both mother and father, but by a host of other factors over which parents may or may not have control. These new findings should change a number of ideas that experts and parents have held in the past about child-rearing practices.

One of the most long-standing limitations in our thinking about child development has been the notion that the mother is the exclusive agent in determining the child's behavior and psychological adjustment. This notion has been promoted and supported by various schools of thought in psychology. Freud and other psychoanalytic thinkers have exalted the influence of the mother by blaming her for children's neuroses. John Watson, the father of modern behaviorism, claimed that by applying the proper conditioning principles, mothers could train a child to become whatever the parents wished—doctor, lawyer, merchant, or artist. And John Bowlby, taking an evolutionary perspective, believed that "a warm, intimate, and continuous relationship" with the mother was an essential ingredient for producing mental health in children.

Although the mother's influence cannot be overestimated, psychologists are now discovering that the father also figures prominently in his child's development. Of course, the father has long been recognized as a biological and economic necessity to his children, but until recently his psychological influence was not very much appreciated. Currently, however, psychologists are discovering the significant impact that a father does have on his child. One of the most interesting findings is that young infants develop attachment bonds to their fathers as well as to their mothers. The infant's attachment to the father begins to develop at around the same time in the middle of the first year as its attachment to the mother, even though in the typical American family the father plays no major role in the care of his infant and interacts with the infant no more than an average of 10 hours a week. There is, however, a difference in the child's attachment to its mother and father. Michael Lamb (1976) found that generally children show no preference between mother and father, but in stressful situations they usually, though not always, prefer their mothers when both parents are available.

The father is not merely a potential substitute mother for times when the mother is looking after chores or is otherwise not available, but contributes qualitatively different experiences to the child. When Michael Lamb (1977) observed both mothers and fathers interacting with their 7- to 13-month-old infants, he found that the two parents played with their babies in different ways and held them for different reasons. Mothers more often played conventional games such as peek-a-boo and pat-a-cake, while fathers were more likely to play vigorous, physically stimulating, or unpredictable types of games. Mothers held their babies most often for caretaking purposes—to feed or diaper them, and for restricting their exploration. But fathers were more likely to hold their babies just to play with them or to satisfy the babies' desire to be held. By providing their children with different kinds of experiences than mothers do, fathers may actually broaden the scope of their children's social and intellectual competence.

Another difference between mothers' and fathers' behavior toward their children can be seen in the second year. Unlike mothers, fathers begin to treat the sexes differently. They pay special attention to sons but seem to withdraw from daughters (Lamb, 1979). As a result, children—particularly boys—develop a preference for the same-sex parent. This behavior on the part of the father may contribute to the development of the child's gender identity. Other research has shown that boys may become deficient in their sex-role adjustment when their fathers are absent during infancy (Biller, 1974).

As children grow older, fathers continue to contribute to sex-role development. For example, fathers who are highly nurturant enhance masculinity in sons and femininity in daughters (Lynn, 1976). Girls with absent fathers may not develop an adequate female role and as adolescents may have difficulties in their relationships with men (Hetherington, 1972). Fathers also contribute to their children's social and moral development, cognitive functioning, and achievement motivation.

The father's personality and behavior are as important as the mother's to the overall adjustment of the child. This fact was clearly established by a study which compared the behavior of parents whose children were well adjusted with those whose children had adjustment difficulties (Peterson, Becker, Hellmer, Shoemaker, & Quay, 1959). The investigators were surprised to discover that both mothers and fathers of children with adjustment problems were themselves less well adjusted, less friendly, and less democratic than parents of the well-adjusted children. The maladjusted children who were very aggressive tended to have weak and ineffectual fathers, whereas children who were shy and had feelings of inferiority tended to have fathers who were dictatorial and unconcerned about their children.

Fathers may also be helpful by compensating for the limitations of the mother. Sally Bloom-Feshbach, Jonathan Bloom-Feshbach, and Jane Gaughran (1980) studied how 3-year-old children of parents with different child-rearing styles adjusted to being separated from their parents at nursery school. These investigators found that when both parents were not very nurturant and were either very strict or very lax in controlling the child, the child had a difficult adjustment to nursery school. When either mother or father was nurturant and firm in child-rearing style, however, the child's adjustment was much easier.

In addition to having a direct impact on the child, the father also has an indirect influence on the child through his relationship with his wife. Marital strife can be very damaging to children. In fact, living in a house where parents are in discord may be more damaging to a child than living simply with one parent (Longfellow, 1979). Studies have shown, for example, that the quality of the marital relationship affects how a mother feeds the child. A mother is more effective in feeding a baby when the father is supportive of the mother and is less effective when there is tension and conflict in the marriage (Pederson, 1976). Parents who are critical of each other also express more negative feelings to their children (Pederson, Anderson, & Cain, 1980).

When a father is involved in child care, the mother's burden is reduced and the quality of her child care improves dramatically. A mother who is less burdened by tasks for her children is also more available as a wife. Research has shown that marital satisfaction is greater among husbands and wives who share many activities together. Typically, however, when a child is born marital satisfaction decreases because the mother becomes much more involved in child care and participates less in activities with her husband. But when a father shares in child care, it can become another activity for husband and wife to enjoy together and thus enhance rather than reduce happiness between them. This has indeed been found to be true in a study of first-time fathers by Jonathan Bloom-Feshbach (1979). In this study, fathers who became involved with their child reported that their marriages were improved by the birth of the child, whereas fathers who did not participate as much in their child's care felt that the birth of the child had detracted from the marriage.

We thus see how important the father is to the optimal development of his children. The father who is available to his children, who is warm, sensitive, and responsive to them, benefits them emotionally, intellectually, and socially. The research also demonstrates that the father helps his children not only directly but indirectly through his effect on the mother. A father who is supportive of the mother and participates in child care helps to improve her caretaking qualities since she will feel less overwhelmed by all the tasks that need to be accomplished for the child. And finally, a father who shares in child care with the mother enhances the quality of his marriage, which in turn affects the quality of child care that both parents provide the child.

The new findings showing the importance of the father are a needed corrective to the notion that the mother bears sole responsibility for the child's development. Another body of evidence which lightens mothers' burden, as well as fathers', is that which disputes the idea that the child begins life as a formless mass which parents shape to their own specifications. This idea gained popularity from John Watson and his disciples in American psychology. According to Watson, a child's mind is a *tabula rasa* or blank slate on which parents, by providing the right kind of experiences, write everything that the child is to become. In this climate of thought, it is no wonder that parents have taken seriously the messages coming from popular writings that they can give their children a superior mind, that children should be taught to read at the age of 2, or that IQs can be raised dramatically if only the child is engaged in this or that regimen. Supporters of this environmental mystique have relied heavily on Joseph McVicker Hunt's book, *Intelligence and Experience*. This book has become the credo, almost the bible of the environmental mystique. Dr. Hunt's book is a healthy, speculative, theoretical treatise, but the implications as they have been spelled out to the layperson are *not* so healthy. A number of years ago, *Reader's Digest* published an interview with Dr. Hunt. The article, in question-and-answer format, was heralded by a flier attached to the cover that read provocatively, "How to Raise Your Child's IQ by 20 Points."

The findings of an early compensatory program in New York City were reported in the New York press as having resulted in one point of IQ increase for every month the child had spent in the program. If IQs could indeed be increased this mechanically, one wonders why all parents would not immediately avail themselves of 30 or 40 months of such treatment for their children. In articles appearing in *Harper's* and the *New York Times Magazine* section, we were informed that the intelligence levels of poor children would be raised by subjecting them to an intellectually demanding "pressure cooker" form of education during the preschool years. An issue of *Life Magazine* carried a feature article reporting the work of a group of Harvard-MIT scientists on the effects of infant stimulation. Cited was the finding that putting mobiles and other moving objects over cribs of young infants caused them to do better on certain developmental tasks than infants who were not exposed to these objects. What was not pointed out was that there was no relationship between the developmental abilities measured and later intelligence. Shortly after this article appeared, a mobile (properly endorsed by one of these scientists) became available commercially. As a result, we now frequently encounter what may be called the "mobile syndrome." Some mothers are so anxiety-laden about not having placed mobiles over their infants' cribs that they wonder what they can do to rectify the tragic error now that their children are 17 and 18.

What must be honestly told to parents is that there is no short-term intervention, no gadget, no gimmick that clearly results in an elevated IQ at maturity. However, this fact has not deterred the suppliers of books and educational materials from inundating parents with their wares. Books on teaching children to read at the age of 2 are a case in point. Given all the developmental tasks that 2-year-olds must master to develop into competent human beings, one would wonder why parents would want to waste their children's time by having them perform what amounts to little more than intellectual tricks. We can only surmise that such activities usually have much more to do with the egos of parents than with the ego development of their children.

Parents of young children, who have been hearing so much about how malleable their children's minds are, are seen by industry as a ready market for educational toys. Where once mothers and fathers went to toy stores in the hopes of obtaining an object that their child would enjoy, they are now more interested in "toys that teach." Some of these toys are indeed constructed on the basis of sound pscyhological and pedagogical theorizing and research, but many of them are pure junk.

Throughout this period there have been, of course, persons with the good sense to insist that almost any toy could teach if parents took the trouble to use it to arouse the child's curiosity and interest, and if they made playtime an occasion for social interaction between parent and child. Some specialists even had the temerity to state, wisely in our opinion, that the cognitive development of very young children has less to do with a formal learning intervention than with the natural exchange between children and their physical and social environments. Young children can learn more by playing with pots and pans, especially if their parents play along with them, than with the rather expensive toys parents buy in the hope of raising their children's IQ.

Given our nation's love of gadgetry, one could look upon the parents' search for books and toys which promise instant genius with some amusement, except for the dire consequences it has had upon children and family life. Overemphasis on training the mind has led to a distorted view of parental tasks. The parent's job has come to be viewed as little more than programming a computer. In the process, we have lost sight of the child as a whole person with a unique personality, abilities, and needs. Today, parents must relearn that their goal should be to help their children achieve optimal development in all spheres—social and emotional as well as intellectual.

Parents must also be helped to recognize that their child's development is not entirely in their own hands to shape, but that the child is endowed by nature with indi-

viduality and unique potential. One *can* provide a child with experiences conducive to his or her full intellectual growth. But parents must be clearly aware that there are individual differences between children, even between children in the same family, and that the impact of a child's experiences is determined in large part by the child's own nature. After acknowledging this, we should not jump from such an obvious truth to talking about inferiority or superiority. Children differ in all their abilities, and these differences are part of the human condition.

Anyone who observes newborns in a nursery notices immediately how much the babies differ from one another. Some cry a great deal, others cry very little; some are always moving around, others appear calmer; some have regular rhythms of sleep and wakefulness, while others do not appear to have any regular patterns in these behaviors. These characteristics and some others make up what is known as the child's *temperament*. The child's temperament stabilizes by about 4 months of age and remains relatively constant throughout development. It is very important for parents to recognize, therefore, that they have very little control over the development of a number of traits of their children. These traits have been identified by Professors Alexander Thomas, Stella Chess, and Herbert Birch (1968) as the child's general *activity level*, the regularity of biological functions, mood, desire to approach or withdraw from new situations, attention span, persistence and distractability, sensitivity to sensory stimuli, and intensity of response to objects and events.

Thomas, Chess, and Birch traced the development of a group of individuals from infancy through adolescence. They identified three types of temperament in children, although many babies were not a pure type. The majority were identified as "easy" children. They had a pleasant mood, were regular in hunger, sleep, and excretion patterns, tended to approach new objects and persons, and generally had a low or moderate intensity of response. In the second category were "slow-to-warm-up" children. These children had a slightly negative mood, were somewhat variable in biological rhythms, were wary of new situations, and had a low intensity of response. The investigators found that about 1 in 10 babies could be placed in the third category, labeled "difficult" children. These children tended to cry often and quite loudly, seemed to be generally unhappy, were irregular in feeding and sleeping, and were slow to accept new foods or routines.

The fact that children were born with different temperaments has important implications for child development and child rearing. First, what should be reassuring to parents is that behavior patterns once thought to be the outcome of poor child-rearing practices may actually be constitutional characteristics of the child. Thomas, Chess, and Birch (1968, p. 191) explain it this way:

A child who stands at the periphery of the group in a nursery school may be anxious and insecure, but he may also be expressing his normal temperamental tendency to warm up slowly. An infant with irregular sleep cycles who cries loudly at night may possibly be responding to a hostile, rejecting mother, but he may also be expressing his temperamental irregularity. A six-year-old who exploes with anger at his teacher's commands may be aggressive and oppositional, but he may also be showing the frustration reactions of a very persistent child when he is asked to terminate an activity in which he is deeply absorbed. A mother's guilt and anxiety may be the result of a deep-seated neurosis, but they may also be the result of her problems and confusion in handling an infant with a temperamental pattern [of] a very difficult child.

Although parents may not be responsible for their children's difficult temperaments, their reactions to their children's temperaments may have important consequences in many areas of development. Just as a parent's behavior influences that of the child, a child's behavior influences that of the parent. Children are not simply passive objects, receptacles of all that parents wish to put into them. Rather, children actively influence the kinds of behavior the parents transmit to the child. The notion of reciprocal interactions between parent and child, which is currently being examined by Richard Q. Bell (1979) and others, should sensitize parents to the importance of recognizing how their children affect their behavior. It is possible that difficult children may arouse negative responses in parents which may, in turn, have detrimental effects on the children's psychological development. An example of how this may occur was described by Arnold Sameroff (1977) from his study of interactions of a group of children and their mothers. He found that children judged as difficult at 4 months of age had the lowest intelligence test scores at 30 months. When he observed the interactions of the mothers and their children at 12 months of age, Sameroff found that mothers of difficult children tended to stay away from them more and to look at, stimulate, and play with them less than did mothers of other children. In contrast, children whose mothers spent a great deal of time socializing with them had higher intelligence test scores at 30 months of age. Sameroff suggests that children's difficult behavior may "turn off" their mothers to interacting with them. If this happens, the mother's lack of attention may result in decreased intellectual competence in the child later on.

Since children's behavior can affect parents' behavior, parents must be especially careful not to allow their own behavior to become as negative as that of their children. Otherwise a vicious circle of bad child behavior and bad parent behavior may develop which can lead to maladjustment in children and a frustrating, tension-filled existence for parents. Thomas, Chess, and Birch (1968) predicted that difficult children would need psychiatric treatment later in life. They found, however, that only those difficult children whose parents had been unable to adapt to their children's temperaments and individual needs later required clinical help.

Thus an important principle for parents to remember is that child-rearing practices should be adjusted to each child's temperament. All children cannot be treated alike. By recognizing and understanding a child's individual temperament, however, parents may be better able to guide the growth of their children. For example, parents who have slow-to-warm-up children should not pressure them to accept and adjust to new situations quickly, for this may only strengthen their fears and tendency to withdraw. Parents can help these children to anticipate their fears and reassure them that they will be able to adapt to new objects and events. Otherwise, a slow-to-warm-up child may turn out like a boy named Bobby (Segal & Yahraes, 1978). Whenever Bobby rejected new food, his parents never gave it to him again; because he shied away from the kids at the playground, they kept him at home. At the age of 10, Bobby had no friends and ate only hamburgers, applesauce, and medium-boiled eggs! In contrast, the parents of a difficult boy named Carl (Chess & Thomas, 1977) learned to anticipate their son's frequently stormy responses to new experiences and to be patient with his tantrums without giving in to his demands. They encouraged and reassured Carl and modified their own expectations and behavior in accordance with their child's temperament. As a result, Carl never developed a serious behavior disorder.

Once parents and the rest of society begin to appreciate the uniqueness of each child, they will begin to see that children simply cannot be molded, as John Watson believed, into what others want them to become. This is not to say that children were born with a fixed personality which remains unchanged throughout life. The child is born with a rather fixed temperament, which means that he or she is predisposed toward reacting in certain ways. The child's personality, however, develops from all that the child experiences, as filtered and fashioned by his or her temperament. Personality, therefore, is a product of both the inborn temperamental style and external parental and environmental influences that reach the child.

As powerful as parents and the child's own behavioral predispositions are in influencing children's development, these are not the only contributing factors. Parents and children do not exist in a vacuum. They are located in an environmental setting containing, among other things, friends, and acquaintances, inanimate objects, and social institutions. The child will be affected by the neighborhood, the school, peers, the media, health care, the state of the economy—indeed, the whole of the physical and social environment to which the child is exposed.

Urie Bronfenbrenner (1979) has underscored the importance of the whole ecology or environment of the child in determining what the child becomes. He has also pointed out how parents' behavior is affected by the broader environment, too. In societies in which extended families are the norm, parenting does not appear to be as difficult or anxiety-provoking as in societies where nuclear families prevail. The presence of grandparents and other clan members may relieve many of parents' practical needs and provide emotional support to the parents. A tragic example of what can happen when such support is not available can be seen in many cases of child abuse. Although there are many factors that make parents neglect or strike out at children, one that emerges with great regularity is a parent's sense of alienation and aloneness. The abusing parent generally feels a great burden of responsibility which cannot be mitigated because there is no one the parent can turn to for help.

Another significant factor in the child's ecology has been shown to have an important impact on development by Kenneth Keniston and the Carnegie Council on Children in their book, *All Our Children.* This element is the economic system of the country. Children whose parents are chronically unemployed will undoubtedly be adversely affected. Children whose family incomes are below the poverty level will also suffer. Not only will these children be deprived of services and experiences that money can buy, but more importantly, as the Carnegie report points out, if a child sees too many doors closed to the adults he or she knows best, the child may learn "to expect failure of himself just as the world expects it of him." In addition, children are affected by the length of the work day in American industry and by industry's decision about whether its employees are to be moved from city to city every few years. They are influenced too by their parents' frequent inability to find or afford satisfactory day-care arrangements. And children are affected by the ever-changing regulations concerning the availability of food stamps as well as a thousand and one other decisions made by government at the federal, state, and local levels.

It is becoming clear that our society has a special responsibility to children. Since parents are not the only socializing agents for children, their efforts alone cannot ensure the best possible developmental outcome for their children. To promote optimal development, parents can no longer remain content to simply do their best for children at home. They must also begin to do their best for children in the public domain. They must speak out when the me-dia treat children as only consumers to be manipulated and exploited. They must also let their voices be heard when a governmental policy, either by omission or commission, threatens the well-being of children. They must do whatever they can to improve the national climate for child rearing. In short they must become nothing less than social activists and effective advocates on behalf of children.

An appreciation for the many elements contributing to child development suggests, therefore, that parents should expand their role. They should not only be private parents, trying to maximize their own personal effectiveness in helping their children grow, but they should also enter the public arena, speaking out and lobbying for a society more responsive and supportive of children's needs. This may be more work for parents, but it is work that must be done. The rewards that will emerge will be numerous. Parents will have the pleasure of knowing they are doing all they can for their children. Many of their anxieties will be reduced as the rest of society comes to share in the tasks of child rearing. And most importantly, children will benefit from being reared in an environment where all the conditions—from mothers and fathers to business hours and children's toys—are designed to foster their optimal development.

REFERENCES

Bell, R. Q. Parent, Child, and Reciprocal Influences. *American Psychologist,* 1979, *34,* 821–826.

Biller, H. B. *Parental deprivation: Family, school, sexuality and society,* Lexington, Mass.: Heath, 1974.

Bloom-Feshbach, J. *The beginnings of fatherhood.* Unpublished doctoral dissertation. Yale University, 1979.

Bloom-Feshbach, S.; Bloom-Feshbach, J.; & Guaghran, J. The Child's Tie to Both Parents: Separation Patterns and Nursery School

Adjustment. *American Journal of Orthopsychiatry*, 1980, *50*, 505–521.

Bronfenbrenner, U. *The ecology of human development: Experiments by nature and design.* Cambridge, Mass.: Harvard University Press, Massachusetts. 1979.

Hetherington, E. M. The Effects of Father Absence on Personality Development in Adolescent Daughters. *Developmental Psychology*, *7*, 1972, 313–326.

Hunt, J. McV. *Intelligence and experience.* New York: Ronald Press, 1961.

Keniston, K. and The Carnegie Council on Children. *All our children: The American family under pressure.* New York: Harcourt Brace Jovanovich, 1977.

Lamb, M. E. Effects of Stress and Cohort on Mother- and Father-Infant Interaction. *Developmental Psychology*, 1976, *12*, 435–443.

Lamb, M. E. Father-Infant and Mother-Infant Interaction in the First Year of Life. *Child Development*, 1977, *48*, 167–181.

Lamb, M. E. Paternal Influences and the Father's Role: A Personal Perspective. *American Psychologist*, 1979, *34*, 938–943.

Longfellow, C. Divorce in Context: Its Impact on Children. In G. Levinger and O. C. Moles (Eds.) *Divorce and separation: Context, causes, and consequences.* New York: Basic Books, pp. 287–306.

Lynn, D. B. Fathers and Sex-Role Development. *The Family Coordinator*, 1976, *25*, 403–410.

Pederson, F. A. *Mother, father, and infant as an interaction system.* Paper presented at the meeting of the American Psychological Association, Washington, D.C., September, 1976.

Pederson, F. A., Anderson, B. J., & Cain, R. L. An Approach to Understanding Linkages Between the Parent-Infant and Spouse Relationships. In F. A. Pederson (Ed.) *The father-infant relationship: Observational studies in a family context.* New York: Holt, Rinehart & Winston, 1980.

Peterson, D. R., Becker, W. C., Hellmer, L. A., Shoemaker, D. J., & Quay, H. C. Parental Attitudes and Child Adjustment. *Child Development*, 1959, *30*, 119–30.

Sameroff, A. Concepts of Humanity in Primary Prevention. In G. Albee and J. Rolf (Eds.) *Primary prevention of psychopathology*, Vol. 1. Burlington, Vt.: Waters, 1977.

Segal, J. & Yahraes, H. *A child's journey.* New York: McGraw-Hill, 1978.

Thomas, A. & Chess, S. *Temperament and development.* New York: Brunner/Mazel, 1977.

Thomas, A., Chess, S., & Birch, H. *Temperament and behavior disorders in children.* New York: New York University Press, 1968.

11. WHAT CAN "RESEARCH EXPERTS" TELL PARENTS ABOUT EFFECTIVE SOCIALIZATION?

Michael E. Lamb

One must always exercise caution in attempting to translate research findings into policy recommendations, but this is particularly true in the area of socialization. The present state of our knowledge makes me uncomfortable about efforts to transform this study or that into useful advice for parents. I am uneasy not because we know nothing of relevance, but because there is a distressing tendency for tentative findings to become hallowed principles, for essential qualifications to be forgotten, and for notions about one of the major inputs to the socialization process (the parents' contribution) to be portrayed as the *sole* essential input. Effective parenting and successful socialization depend on at least three considerations: (1) the goals and behavior of the parents, (2) the characteristics of the child, and (3) the practices and mores of the culture and subculture. Any prescription for parenting which fails to acknowledge the importance of the child's individuality, and the impact of other socializing agents (peers, schools, teachers, the media), is at best misleading; at worst it is dangerously counterproductive. Unfortunately, however, policy applications can seldom make extensive allowance for individual variations of this sort, and we know too little about these complex issues to permit universal recommendations.

To illustrate this dilemma, I will outline some of the principal components of effective parenting. By discussing only the conclusions for which there is substantial empirical support, I hope to show the problems involved in trying to turn even these fairly consistent findings into good sound advice. Thereafter, I will buttress my skeptical introduction with a brief discussion of the conceptual problems inherent in attempts to determine the characteristics of effective parents and to amend the process of socialization through the modification of parental styles. I will then hazard my views as to the place of research, and of the researcher, in the area of current public policy.

THE CAUTIOUS PRESCRIPTIONS

Although there is no easy formula which contains all the essential principles of parenting, it is possible to make some cautious generalizations based on what we know about the effects of parents on children. One key concept is clearly *sensitivity* or *emphatic understanding*. Much of the work on mother-infant interaction suggests that the mother's ability to interpret the baby's cues accurately and respond appropriately is a major predictor of the quality of the rela-

This article is a condensed version of one which appeared in Fantini, M. D., & Cardenas, R. (Eds.), *Parenting in a multicultural society*. New York: Longman, 1980.

tionship they develop (e.g., Ainsworth, Bell, & Stayton, 1974; Blehar, Lieberman, & Ainsworth, 1977; Schaffer & Emerson, 1964). Similarly, Baumrind's data suggest that the most effective parents "meet their children as persons, and maintain sufficient flexibility in the face of their child's individuality that they can learn from it the kind of parenting to which it best responds" (Lamb & Baumrind, 1978, p. 54). Though the specific parental behavior that is appropriate obviously changes in relation to the child's age, the importance of sensitivity/empathy appears constant. This implies that effective parenting involves guiding children and encouraging the flowering of their individual propensities, rather than stamping in alien behavior patterns, and recognizing when they would benefit from the challenge of performing independently.

Perhaps the most vexing dilemma for parents concerns discipline and punishment. On the one hand are those who believe in molding the child after the parents' image (the *authoritarian* viewpoint); on the other side are those who emphasize the self-actualizing propensity of children and the dangers inherent in squelching this inclination (the *permissive* viewpoint). Baumrind's (1975b) studies suggest that both extremes are undesirable. She found that socially competent children are more likely to have *authoritative* parents—those who direct or guide their child in a rational, issue-oriented manner and who are sensitive to the child's needs and capabilities. Unlike authoritarian or permissive parents, they realize that children are immature and that they need guidance (mediated both by reward and attention, and by punishment and limit setting) if they are ultimately to function optimally in society. They thus encourage independence while also valuing conformity to cultural mores.

Another proven influence is the *consistency* of parental demands. Nothing dis-

torts the acquisition of socially approved behavior more thoroughly than parents whose discipline is capricious, whose attention and response are unpredictable, and whose wishes are ill-defined. Effective parents should set reasonable and reasoned standards and should maintain these standards consistently thereafter. On the other hand—and this is why expert advice rapidly becomes confusing—they should not be inflexible and insensitive in formulating and enforcing their demands.

Successful socialization involves not only what parents do *to* their children but what they do *in front of* them. Most children—particularly those whose parents are nurturant and accessible—are motivated to emulate their parents (Bandura, 1977; Mussen, 1967). By imitating parental models, children learn many complex behavior patterns, particularly those related to sex roles and (perhaps) morality. Although earlier theories held that explicit reinforcement had little to do with these observational learning processes, it appears that the effectiveness of modeling is greatly enhanced by parental encouragement and approval of the identification. The ideal course is to reward the motivation while gently correcting the performance, bearing in mind the child's immature ability to render adult behavior patterns.

THE PRESCRIPTIVE CAUTIONS

Now let us address the cautions about any inferences that can be drawn from these research findings. The major problem concerns the correlational design necessary in studies of socialization: how can we determine the direction of effects? Eminent researchers like Diana Baumrind usually begin with some definition of the "perfect" child—the ideal outcome of the parenting process. They then seek to define parental characteristics that are correlated with the children's styles. For Baumrind, the ideal child is one who is assertive, autonomous, independent, socially competent, and not intrusive with adults; and her studies (1975b) have provided reliable and replicable evidence about the characteristics and attitudes of the parents of such socially competent preschoolers. In general, the most effective parents were those Baumrind called *authoritative* (see above). Permissive and authoritarian parents either provided insufficient guidance or thoroughly forbade independent effort, badly misjudging the developmentally appropriate needs of their children.

At first blush, then, it appears that we have here the answer: careful research indicating quite clearly which patterns of child rearing and parental behavior produce "appropriate" behavior patterns in young children. Yet Baumrind's follow-up (1975a) failed to substantiate these seemingly robust findings. Although only preliminary results from the longitudinal study have been reported, it appears that by the time the children reached 9 years of age, those with authoritative parents were no more socially competent than those whose parents had vastly different disciplinary styles.

Why the discrepancy? Despite the fact that the original studies were perhaps the best ever done, the troubling fact remains that they were dependent on correlational data. Baumrind had to assume that the social competence of the children at 5 years of age was a product of the behavior and attitudes of the parents. Yet it is quite conceivable that the apparent rationality and effectiveness of the authoritative parents were due, at least in part, to the fact that their children were significantly more socially competent, less intrusive—in short, more manageable. In other words, perhaps the parents' behavior is as much a response to the children's personality styles as a cause of them. This is not to say that cause and effect can never be elucidated in stud-

ies of socialization. Only longitudinal studies can yield the answers we seek, however, and the field's experience with such studies suggests that the answers are not easily attained.

Another critical problem with research on socialization as well as with parent-education projects is the implicit assumption that all children are equally malleable. More crudely, certain parental practices are portrayed as the necessary conditions for *forming* certain personality styles in children. This notion completely overlooks the innate differences in temperament and potential with which children are born. While parents are not without their influence, these inherent differences are not the sole determinants of a child's personality either. The outcome is dependent on an intimate and ill-understood *interaction* between the child's individual characteristics and the rearing environment. The findings of the New York Longitudinal Study (Thomas, Chess, & Birch, 1968) illustrate this most clearly, methodological inadequacies notwithstanding. Children who eventually needed psychiatric attention were not found to be characterized from early in life by their "difficult" temperaments, nor did their parents have particularly maladaptive styles; rather, there was a *mismatch* between the infants' temperaments and the parents' styles.

This type of interaction underscores why there can be no hard-written prescriptions for effective parenting. Parental behaviors that are effective in eliciting desired behavior will vary considerably depending on the nature of the individual child. To the notion that authoritative parenting may be most effective, then, we must emphasize a qualification: sensitivity to the needs, developmental level, and individual personality of the child is of crucial importance, as is the ability to monitor one's own behavior and demands so as to challenge but not overestimate the child's potential.

Another problematic issue is implicit in

most studies of socialization but is seldom considered directly. Is it the parents' *way* of posing demands in raising their children that is critical, or the *content* of the demands themselves? Most research in this area focuses on style rather than substance, examining the effects of punitiveness, permissiveness, nurturance, and so on. Yet there is little research directly relevant to the concrete problems with which parents must deal. One reason for our current ignorance may be that concepts like *punitiveness* are certain to be defined differently by various researchers, and this can almost assure discrepancies among research findings. Clear answers that are useful to parents may be possible only when we specify *what* demands are being made punitively or permissively, instead of papering over a multitude of parental styles and goals with labels and adjectives. It matters a great deal, I suspect, whether a parent punishes a 1-year-old or a 4-year-old for soiling; to call both punitive is to ignore the most important information. Classification of the content of demands is not easy, and this is probably why the issue has so often been avoided. Perhaps the value itself (for example, it is good/bad to fight back when someone hits you) is not as important as the age-appropriateness of the demand. This underscores the relation between the content of demands and parental sensitivity.

PITFALLS IN THE APPLICATION OF RESEARCH FINDINGS

We thus see that there are large gaps in our knowledge base and that most research findings simply cannot be tapered to "parents in general" or "children in general," for here no generalities exist. Next, I will mention examples where available research evidence and the best intentions of those who formulate policy together may foster policies that can be quite inappropriate.

Working Mothers

There is currently great concern about the children of working mothers and a related issue—the effects of day care on developmental processes. The topics have been debated vociferously by both proponents and opponents; meanwhile, the evidence shows that both extreme positions underestimate the complexity of the issues. The children (particularly daughters) of working mothers, we find, tend to avow less stereotyped sex roles than the children of full-time mothers (Hoffman, 1974; Vogel et al., 1970). In contemporary society, this is clearly a beneficial rather than a deleterious consequence. Second, children who are raised by dissatisfied women who would rather be working risk greater psychological damage than those whose mothers are able to combine career and family roles in the way they choose (Birnbaum, 1971; Hoffman, 1974; Yarrow, Scott, DeLeeuw, & Heinig, 1962). Thus the harm comes only when the mother feels guilty or resentful at the abandonment of either her family or her career (See Hoffman, 1974).

In other words, then, a policy that aims to keep mothers at home may harm some children even as it is beneficial to others. In such circumstances, it is probably unwise to institute policies that discriminate among family styles in order to encourage the maintenance of certain types. Any decision to do so must rest not on empirical but on philosophical and sociopolitical considerations.

Substitute Child Care

It is now fairly well established that the daily separations from parents and the associated substitute care are not *in themselves* inimical to the normal course of sociopersonality development (e.g., Doyle, 1975; Roopnarine & Lamb, 1977; Schwartz,

Strickland, & Krolick, 1974; Feldman, Note 1; Schwartz, Note 2). However, an important qualification is in order. Most research has been conducted in high-quality day-care programs, whereas fewer than 10% of the children receiving substitute care are enrolled in such places. The majority are cared for by relatives, babysitters, or in "family day care" (where a mother looks after other children in her own home). It is probably because children in centers are more accessible that researchers have focused on this comparatively small group, which is largely composed of the children of wealthier and better-educated parents. While it is comforting to know that these children are not at risk, it is troubling to note how little concern is expressed about the fate of the majority. The findings of one pioneering study are certainly unsettling. Saunders and Keister (Note 3) found that children in family day care suffered more frequent changes of caretakers, had less competent care in relatively unstimulating environments, and received less attention from adults than did children in group-care facilities. In the heat of the arguments about whether day care is good or bad, we seem to have forgotten that there is good and bad day care, and that the quality of the program may be more important to the child's fate than whether or not the mother works.

We thus know too little about the effects of various substitute-care arrangements to encourage or discourage knowledgeably any particular type. All we can say is that quality center day care is apparently not harmful to most children. Indeed, the experience with peers may be valuable. Quality day care, however, is extremely expensive. Unless we find that other types of substitute care are harmful and thus merit eradication (achieved by providing free day care), the major policy issue here is not whether there should be alternative modes of day care but whether they should be publicly funded. This question has nothing to do with research expertise; it has everything to do with sociopolitical philosophy. Researchers, of course, have political opinions, and many who study children may feel especially strongly about issues concerning children. Nevertheless, their opinions are manifestations not of some special knowledge but of their philosophical persuasion. Until we know more about this socially volatile issue, we must take special care to distinguish between recommendations based on empirical evidence and those based on personal feelings.

Do Researchers Lead or Follow?
This discussion highlights a vexing impediment to the fruitful application of research data in the formulation of social policy. However fascinating and extensive the studies on working mothers and substitute care, the findings will probably have little impact on the societal trends concerned. Investigators seldom engineer rearing environments in order to see what effects they have. They are left to study the environments created by others. This means that they do not guide the direction of the changes. Instead they declare, in retrospect, what the effects of the changes have been. This fact is likely to moderate the impact that researchers have.

This is not to suggest that researchers have no role to play in shaping public policy. Most researchers are in the field because they believe that the results of their investigations may have practical implications. Yet this is a relatively young science, and we need a great deal more basic research before policy recommendations can be wisely and confidently made. At this point, the interests of public policy and the credibility of researchers would best be served by humility and circumspection rather than by self-assured prescriptions.

REFERENCE NOTES

1. Feldman, S. S. *The impact of day care on one aspect of children's social-emotional behavior.* Paper presented to the American Association for the Advancement of Science, San Francisco, February, 1974.
2. Schwartz, J. L. Social and emotional effects of day care: A review of recent research. Paper presented to the Society for Research in Child Development Study Group on the Family, Ann Arbor, Mich., October, 1975.
3. Saunders, M. M. & Keister, M. E. *Family day care: Some observations.* Unpublished manuscript. University of North Carolina, Greensboro, 1972.

REFERENCES

Ainsworth, M. D., Bell, S. M., & Stayton, D. J. Infant-mother attachment and social development: Socialization as a product of reciprocal responsiveness to signals. In M. P. M. Richards (Ed.), *The integration of a child into a social world.* Cambridge: Cambridge University Press, 1974.

Bandura, A. *Social learning theory.* Englewood Cliffs, N.J.: Prentice-Hall, 1977.

Baumrind, D. M. The contribution of the family to the development of competence in children. *Schizophrenia Bulletin,* 1975, *14*, 12–37. (a)

Baumrind, D. M. *Early socialization and the discipline controversy.* Morristown, N.J.: General Learning Press, 1975. (b).

Birnbaum, J. A. Life patterns, personality style, and self-esteem in gifted family-oriented and career-committed women. Unpublished doctoral dissertation, University of Michigan, 1971.

Blehar, M. D., Lieberman, A. E., & Ainsworth, M. D. Early face-to-face interaction and its relation to later infant-mother attachment. *Child Development,* 1977, *48,* 183–193.

Doyle, A. B. Infant development in day care. *Developmental Psychology,* 1975, *11,* 655–656.

Hoffman, L. W. Effects of maternal employment on the child: A review of the research. *Developmental Psychology,* 1974, *10,* 204–228.

Lamb, M. E. & Baumrind, D. M. Socialization and personality development in the preschool years. In M. E. Lamb (Ed.), *Social and personality development.* New York: Holt, Rinehart & Winston, 1978.

Mussen, P. H. Early socialization: Learning and identification. In T. M. Newcomb (Ed.), *New directions in psychology III.* New York: Holt, Rinehart, & Winston, 1967.

Roopnaire, J. L. & Lamb, M. E. The effects of day care on attachment and exploratory behavior in a strange situation. *Merrill-Palmer Quarterly,* 1977, *24,* 85–95.

Schaffer, H. R. & Emerson, P. E. The development of social attachments in infancy. *Monographs of the Society for Research in Child Development,* 1964, 29, whole number 94.

Schwartz, J. C., Strickland, R. G., & Krolic, G. Infant day care: Behavioral effects at preschool age. *Developmental Psychology,* 1974, *10,* 502–506.

Thomas, A., Chess, S., & Birch, H. G. *Temperament and behavior disorders in children.* New York: New York University Press, 1968.

Vogel, S. R., Broverman, I. K., Broverman, D. M., Clarkson, F. E., & Rosenkrantz, P. S. Maternal employment and perception of sex roles among college students. *Developmental Psychology,* 1970, *3,* 384–391.

Yarrow, M. R., Scott, P., DeLeeuw, L., & Heinig, C. Child-rearing in families of working and non-working mothers. *Sociometry,* 1962, *25,* 122–140.

12. RELATION OF CHILD TRAINING
TO SUBSISTENCE ECONOMY

Herbert Barry III

Irvin L. Child

Margaret K. Bacon

Cross-cultural research on child training has generally grown out of an interest in how personality characteristics or trends typical of a people are brought into being. The customary child-training practices of a group are thought to be one important set of influences responsible for typical personal characteristics, and hence an important clue in tracing their causal background. But typical personal characteristics may also be viewed as an existing set of conditions that may exert an influence on later child-training practices. Indeed, any present feature of culture may influence future child-training practices, either directly or through an influence on the personality trends typical of members of the society. Thus child training may just as well, and with equal interest of another sort, be viewed as an effect in a series of cultural events rather than as a cause (being in fact, we presume, both at once). Moreover, even while considering child training as a cause of personal characteristics typical of a people, one is led to inquire: Why does a particular society select child-training practices that will tend to produce this particular kind of characteristic? Is it because these characteristics are functional for the adult life of the society, and train-

ing methods that will encourage them are thus also functional?

By a variety of routes, then, the student of child training is led to inquire into the relation of child training to the basic patterns of social life—to those aspects of culture, whatever they be, that set the scene for the rest of culture. Among the features likely to hold this sort of dominant or controlling position is the general nature of the subsistence economy, and it is to this aspect of culture that we will here relate child-training practices.

A HYPOTHESIS ABOUT ECONOMIC ROLE AND TYPE OF SUBSISTENCE

In considering the relation of economy to adult role, and hence to child training, we felt that perhaps a variable of great significance is the extent to which food is accumulated and must be cared for. At one extreme is dependence mainly on animal husbandry, where the meat that will be eaten in coming months and years, and the animals that will produce the future milk, are present on the hoof. In this type of society, future food supply seems to be best

This article was adapted and condensed from one which first appeared in *American Anthropologist*, 1959, *61*, 51–63. Additional results and discussion appear in the original publication.

assured by faithful adherence to routines designed to maintain the good health of the herd. Agriculture perhaps imposes only slightly less pressure toward the same pattern of behavior. Social rules prescribe the best-known way to bring the growing plants to successful harvest and to protect the stored produce for gradual consumption until the next harvest. Carelessness in the performance of routine duties leads to a threat of hunger, not for the day of carelessness itself but for many months to come. Individual initiative in attempts to improve techniques may be feared because no one can tell immediately whether the changes will lead to a greater harvest or to disastrous failure. Under these conditions, there might well be a premium on obedience to the older and wiser, and on responsibility in faithful performance of the routine laid down by custom for one's economic role.

At an opposite extreme is subsistence primarily through hunting or fishing, with no means for extended storing of the catch. Here individual initiative and development of high individual skill seem to be at a premium. Where each day's food comes from that day's catch, variations in the energy and skill exerted in getting food lead to immediate reward or punishment. Innovation, moreover, seems unlikely to be so generally feared. If a competent hunter tries out some change of technique and it fails, he may still have time to revert to the established procedures to get his catch. If the change is a good one, it may lead to immediate reward.

ECONOMY AND CHILD TRAINING

We have outlined above a hypothesis about economic behavior as an adaptation to the general type of subsistence economy. If the economic role tends to be generalized to the rest of behavior, predictions might be made about typical personal characteristics of adults in societies with different subsistence economies. In societies with low accumulation of food resources, adults should tend to be individualistic, assertive, and venturesome. By parallel reasoning, adults should tend to be conscientious, compliant, and conservative in societies with high accumulation of food resources.

If the economic role and personal characteristics tend to be appropriate for the type of subsistence economy, we may expect the training of children to foreshadow these adaptations. The kind of adult behavior useful to the society is likely to be taught to some extent to the children in order to assure the appearance of this behavior at the time it is needed. Hence we may predict that the emphasis in child training will be toward the development of kinds of behavior especially useful for the adult economy.

PROCEDURE

In the preliminary version of a classification by Murdock (1957), the subsistence economy of societies was divided into six categories, designated by the letters A, F, G, H, P, and R. We have considered societies as likely to be extremely high in accumulation of food resources, by our definition, if they were classified by Murdock as predominantly pastoral (P) or as agricultural with animal husbandry also important (A). Societies were considered likely to be extremely low in accumulation if Murdock designated them as predominantly hunting (H) or fishing (F).

Societies were considered intermediate in accumulation if Murdock designated them as predominantly agricultural, with either grain (G) or root (R) crops, with animal husbandry not important. The grain and root societies were for our purposes placed together, but were then subdivided according to another analysis with which Murdock provided us, of the degree of subsidiary importance of hunting and fishing in these predominantly agricultural societies. We averaged the rating of the importance of hunting and of fishing and then divided this average rating at the median. Societies above the median in importance of hunting and fishing were then classified as intermediately low in accumulation of food resources. Societies below the median in importance of hunting and fishing were classified as intermediately high in accumulation.

The authors of the present article obtained ratings on several aspects of child-training practices by their own analysis of ethnographic documents. The methods used are described and the ratings reproduced in Barry, Bacon, and Child (1967). Societies were rated separately for boys and for girls with respect to six aspects of training.

1. Obedience training.
2. Responsibility training, which usually was based on participation in the subsistence or household tasks.
3. Nurturance training, i.e., training the child to be nurturant or helpful toward younger siblings and other dependent people.
4. Achievement training, which was usually based on competition or imposition of standards of excellence in performance.
5. Self-reliance training, defined as training to take care of oneself, to be independent of the assistance of other people in supplying one's needs and wants.
6. General independence training. This was defined more generally than self-reliance training to include training not only to satisfy one's own needs but also toward all kinds of freedom from control, domination, and supervision. Ratings of general independence training were highly correlated with ratings of

self-reliance training, but were not identical to them.

For each of these six aspects of training, societies were rated on strength of socialization, which was defined as the combined positive pressure (rewards for the behavior) plus negative pressure (punishments for lack of the behavior). The ratings were for the stage of childhood, from age 4 or 5 years until shortly before puberty. Each rating was made by two separate judges, working independently, and the sum of their two judgments was used.

For each society, separately for boys and for girls, the ratings of the six aspects of strength of socialization were ranked, so that the score for each aspect depended not on its absolute rating but on its rank in comparison with the ratings of the other aspects for the same society. This device was used because in this article we are interested in the relative stress a society places on one rather than another aspect of socialization. Tied ratings were given the same rank. A society was included on this measure only if it had been rated on at least five of the six aspects. Each rating, at the time it was made, was classified as confident or doubtful. In order to have a sizable number of cases, we decided to use all instances where both analysts made a rating, regardless of whether it was confident or doubtful, despite the inevitable lowering of reliability.

The results to be reported are on 104 societies that are included in two separate samples: Murdock's sample of over 500 societies classified on economy and social organization, and 110 societies rated on socialization by Bacon and Barry. Most of these 104 societies are nonliterate, and they are distributed all over the world. Many cultures were omitted from some of the ratings because of insufficient information; such omissions are much more frequent for the socialization variables than for Murdock's variables.

RESULTS

Economy and Specific Variables of Socialization

As Table 1 shows, responsibility and obedience are positively correlated with accumulation of food resources; achievement, self-reliance, and independence are negatively correlated with accumulation. Nurturance shows inconsistent results, generally of small magnitude and in no instance statistically significant. The results are in the same direction both for the extreme and for the intermediate comparisons of economy, and as we might expect, the correlations are generally higher for the extreme comparison. The tests of statistical significance ($p < .05$ or $p < .01$) also give evidence that the results are more consistent for the extreme comparisons.

These results are all substantially alike for the training of the two sexes. The correlations between economy and child training are in the same direction for boys and girls for all the variables except nurturance. There seems to be no consistent difference between the sexes in the size of the correlations. An interesting sex difference was reported in the unabridged arti-

cle. The variables for which socialization pressures were strongest in societies with high accumulation of food resources (obedience and responsibility) were emphasized more strongly in the training of girls than boys, whereas the variables for which socialization pressures were strongest in societies with low accumulations of food resources (achievement, self-reliance, and independence) were emphasized more strongly in the training of boys than girls. A further description of sex differences for the same group of societies may be found in a prior paper by Barry, Bacon, and Child (1957).

There remains the question of whether the information used in making the child-training ratings was largely information about training in economic behavior, so that our results may not genuinely pertain to any more general variables of child training. The only way to answer this question with complete confidence would be to edit the material on socialization, removing all information about economic training, and then have other judges make the ratings again from the remaining information. It was not feasible for us to undertake this very expensive additional project. As a

Table 1 Relation of Child-Training Practices to Accumulation of Food Resources (Expressed as Coefficients of Association)

	Extremes in accumulation		*Intermediate in accumulation*	
	Boys	*Girls*	*Boys*	*Girls*
Responsibility	+.74**	+.62**	+.33	+.37
Obedience	+.50**	+.59**	+.66**	+.45
Nurturance	−.01	+.10	−.26	+.11
Achievement	−.60**	−.62**	−.32	−.12
Self-reliance	−.21	−.46*	−.19	−.53*
Independence	−.41*	−.11	−.21	−.42

*$p < .05$
**$p < .01$ } Two-tail tests, based on the Mann-Whitney U (Siegel, 1956:116–127).

substitute, however, we looked back at our notes on child training (made in the course of arriving at ratings) for the 20 societies showing the most extreme results in confirmation of the relationship reported in this paper. Our conclusion is that the information about the training of children in the predominant economy of the society played a much smaller role in determining the ratings than we might have supposed. For girls there was rarely any information about training in the predominant economy. For boys there was often (though not always) information about training in the predominant economy. This often played an important role in the judgments of responsibility, but it seemed almost always to be accompanied by important relevant information about noneconomic aspects of training. For other aspects of training (nurturance, obedience, self-reliance, and achievement), information about economic training rarely seemed to play an important role in determining ratings even for boys. Our review of these cases leaves us convinced that the associations we find between the economy and socialization apply not simply to direct training in economic functions but also to much more general aspects of child training.

Economy and a General Variable of Socialization

In their relation to the economy, the socialization variables (if we omit nurturance) fall into two distinct groups. This fact suggests that a single more general variable might be extracted for presentation of data on individual societies and for further exploration of results. We have called this variable *pressure toward compliance versus assertion*. It is based on the separate socialization variables and was derived in the following way: the sum of the rankings of responsibility and obedience training, for both boys and girls, was subtracted from the sum of the rankings of achievement and self-reliance, for both boys and girls. A plus

score meant that responsibility and obedience were ranked higher (i.e., were assigned lower numbers) than achievement and self-reliance, and for purposes of calculating a coefficient of association, any plus score was designated as predominant pressure toward compliance. A zero or minus score was designated as predominant pressure toward assertion. We dealt with cases of missing information as follows: in the several societies in which the achievement rating was not made, general independence was substituted for it in deriving this general measure of pressure toward compliance versus assertion. In the two societies where the obedience rating was not made, the responsibility rating was substituted for it. Eleven societies were omitted because some or all of the ratings had been made only for one sex.

Table 2 presents a list of societies, divided according to predominant economy and arranged in order of their score on relative predominance of compliance versus assertion in child-training pressures. The correlation portrayed in this table is very consistent. Societies with high accumulation of food resources almost always had predominant pressure toward compliance, whereas societies with low accumulation almost always had predominant pressure toward assertion. For the extreme comparison, 39 societies conformed to this result and only seven had high accumulation with assertion or low accumulation with compliance. The association coefficient for this relationship is .94. For the intermediate comparison, 26 societies conformed to this result and only seven were exceptions. The association coefficient is .93.

These results both show a high degree of statistical significance, which we have measured by the Mann-Whitney U Test (Siegel, 1956:116–127). The separate comparisons differ more in this respect than in their absolute value; for the extreme comparison p is less than .001, and for the intermediate comparison p is less than .02.

Table 2 Relation of Subsistence Economy to General Pressure Toward Compliance versus Assertion in Child Training

Extremes in accumulation		Intermediate in accumulation	
HIGH (animal husbandry)	LOW (hunting, fishing)	HIGH (agriculture only)	LOW (agriculture, hunting, and fishing)
Aymara (+13½)			
Tepoztlan (+13½)			
Lepcha (+11½)			
Swazi (+8½)			
Tswana (+8½)			
Nyakyusa (+8)			
Sotho (+8)		Hopi (+10½)	
Nuer (+7)		Azande (+8)	
Tallensi (+7)		Ifaluk (+6)	
Lovedu (+6½)		Wogeo (+6)	
Mbundu (+6½)		Samoans (+5)	
Venda (+6½)		Yoruba (+5)	
Kikuyu (+6)		Navaho (+4½)	
Zulu (+6)		Arapesh (+4)	
Pondo (+4½)		Wichita (+4)	Vanua Levu (+11½)
Chagga (+4)		Zuni (+4)	Lesu (+10)
Ganda (+3)		Papago (+3½)	Lau Fijians (+6)
Chamorro (+2½)	Teton (+4)	Ulithians (+3)	Yagua (+6)
Masai (+2½)	Yahgan (+1)	Ashanti (+1½)	Malaitan (+2)
Chukchee (+1)	Hupa (+½)	Nauruans (+1)	Tikopia (+½)
Tanala (0)	Chiricahua (0)	Alorese (−6)	Camayura (0)
Thonga (−2½)	Murngin (0)		Cuna (0)
Araucanian (−3)	Paiute (0)		Omaha (−1½)
Balinese (−3)	Arapaho (−2)		Kwoma (−3½)
	Kwakiutl (−2)		Mandan (−3½)
	Cheyenne (−2½)		Jivaro (−4)
	Kaska (−2½)		Trukese (−5)
	Klamath (−2½)		Winnebago (−5)
	Ojibwa (−2½)		Marquesans (−9)
	Ona (−3)		Ifugao (−9½)
	Aleut (−4)		Pukapukans (−12)
	Jicarilla (−6½)		Maori (−13)
	Western Apache (−10)		
	Siriono (−10½)		
	West Greenland Eskimo (−11)		
	Aranda (−12)		
	Comanche (−12)		
	Crow (−13½)		
	Manus (−15)		

Note: The societies are grouped in columns on the basis of economy and are listed within each column in descending order of degree of pressure toward compliance as compared with pressure toward assertion. The number in parentheses after each society indicates the degree of preponderance of compliance (plus scores) or of assertion (minus scores)

It is not surprising, of course, that economy shows a higher correlation with the combined measure of socialization pressures than with any of the separate child-training measures from which it is derived. The magnitude of the correlation is, however, surprising. We may conclude that a knowledge of the economy alone would enable one to predict with considerable accuracy whether a society's socialization pressures were primarily toward compliance or assertion.

DISCUSSION

Some readers may feel that our results are obvious to the extent of being therefore trivial. We believe that this is not the case, that we have instead obtained strong evidence for one hypothesis where some other quite different hypothesis might to some people seem more obvious in advance. For example, let us start the other way around and think of child training as the basic given. Pressure toward self-reliance and achievement should produce strongly independent people who hate to be dependent on others. This character tendency should render very rewarding all features of economic behavior that make it easier to avoid being dependent on others. Among such features, one of the most conspicuous might be the possession by each individual or family of an accumulated food supply (such as a herd or crop), which ensures that an unlucky hunt will not leave one dependent upon the neighbor's catch. Hence a child-training pressure toward assertion should motivate (perhaps unconsciously)

the quest for high-accumulation techniques of subsistence. But according to our findings, it evidently does not. If any such process operates, it appears to be completely obscured by the much more important process to which our results point.

Our findings then are consistent with the suggestion that child training tends to be a suitable adaptation to a subsistence economy. Pressure toward obedience and responsibility should tend to make children into the obedient and responsible adults who can best ensure the continuing welfare of a society with a high-accumulation economy, whose food supply must be protected and developed gradually throughout the year. Pressure toward self-reliance and achievement should shape children into the venturesome, independent adults who can take initiative in wresting food daily from nature and thus ensure survival in societies with a low-accumulation economy.

REFERENCES

Barry, H. III, Bacon, M. K., & Child, I. L. A cross-cultural survey of some sex differences in socialization. *Journal of Abnormal and Social Psychology 55*, 1957, 327–332.

Barry, H. III, Bacon, M. K., & Child, I. L. Definitions, ratings, and bibliographic sources for child-training practices of 110 cultures. In Clellan S. Ford (Ed.) *Cross-cultural approaches: Readings in comparative research.* New Haven, Conn.: HRAF Press, pp. 293–331.

Murdock, G. P. World ethnographic sample. *American Anthropologist 59*, 1957, 664–687.

Siegel, S. *Nonparametric statistics for the behavioral sciences.* New York, McGraw-Hill, 1956.

13. PATERNAL INFLUENCES AND THE FATHER'S ROLE: A PERSONAL PERSPECTIVE

Michael E. Lamb

It is by no means easy to review research and theory concerning the father's role in child development. For a start, the limited evidence available has come from studies of our own culture, which is not especially representative. Further, the West is currently in flux concerning gender and parental roles, and some long-established assumptions about children, their care, and their needs are changing. Since I heartily endorse most of these changes, the perspective in this article is unashamedly partisan: it represents my thoughts concerning the father's role—past, present, and future. I have not reviewed the literature systematically or provided references for most of the findings cited. Those who find this frustrating are invited to sample from a smorgasbord of reviews: Benson (1968), Biller (1971, 1974), Lamb (1976), Lamb and Frodi (1979), Lynn (1974), and Parke (1979) present perspectives so different that the need for future diligent research will be apparent to any reader.

FATHERS—PAST AND PRESENT

The Father-Infant Relationship

Not long ago, men in our culture neither sought nor assumed active responsibility for rearing their children. Infant care, in particular, was perceived as the province of women. Today, however, increasing numbers of men are participating more in child rearing, and a growing number of social scientists now recognize that for biological *and* social reasons, most children have *two* parents.

The era of paternal rediscovery may be seen as a reaction to the presumption (professional and popular) that mothers were the only socializing agents of significance to young children. Since mothers performed most caretaking activities, the argument went, they must be the most important influences on their children's development. This conclusion was bolstered by the prevailing belief in the special meaning of early experiences, since mothers seemed to be involved in an overwhelming proportion of the infant's activities. By considering only the greater quantity of mother-child contact, we neglected to acknowledge that it is the *quality* of experiences that makes them salient, and that fathers may make up in quality some of what they lack in quantity.

Because the notion of maternal preeminence was so pervasive, investigations of the importance of fathers to young infants began only within the last decade, but they have since become popular. To the surprise of many, all studies have shown that fathers can be quite as competent and responsive as mothers (Parke, 1979) and that infants develop attachments to both parents, although most babies seek comfort from their mothers when they are distressed (see Lamb, 1978). The two parent-infant relationships appear to emerge at roughly the same time in the middle of the first year of life. It is important to note that fathers in these studies had no major role in the care of their infants. In fact, the amount of father-infant interaction probably averaged less than 10 hours per week.

When parents assume traditional sex roles, they engage in different types of interaction with their infants. That is, mothers undertake the physical care, whereas fathers interact in play (Parke & O'Leary, 1976; Yogman, Dixon, Tronick, & Brazelton, Note 1). As a result, I suspect, mothers and fathers come to represent different types of experiences for their babies. The significance of this is that from early in their lives, children are exposed to salient models of traditionally masculine and feminine behavior. From the beginning of the second year, furthermore, the child's attention comes to focus on the behavior of the same-sex parent (Lamb, 1977). Fathers are most likely to initiate this sex-differentiating treatment, since it is they who begin to pay special attention to their sons and apparently withdraw from their daughters. The children—especially boys—respond to this in a predictable fashion: they develop preferences for the same-sex parent. This phenomenon may be one of the major factors in the acquisition of gender identity (Lamb, 1977), although the evidence here is far from conclusive.

Research on Fathers and Older Children
Inferences about paternal influences on older children are largely dependent on studies of father absence. Unfortunately, as a number of researchers (e.g., Biller,

1974; Herzog & Sudia, 1973; Lamb, 1976) have noted, these studies tend to confuse so many potential influences that they do little to elucidate the effect of fathers in intact families. For example, the lack of a parent figure and male model may directly alter the child's development. On the other hand, the departure of the father is usually a cause of emotional and economic distress for the mother, which is likely to affect her behavior. If the children later appear maladjusted, it may be only an indirect consequence of the father's absence. It would therefore be incorrect to conclude that the father has a key role in personality adjustment from the finding that children raised without fathers are more poorly adjusted than children raised in intact families.

Still, a handful of careful studies do indicate that we can place some credence in the findings of the father absence literature. Especially noteworthy is a study of Blanchard and Biller (1971) which showed that the effects of psychological father absence (which occurs when, for professional or attitudinal reasons, fathers seldom spend time with their children) and those of physical absence were qualitatively similar. Like most studies, these investigators focused on the effects of paternal deprivation on boys and found deviant or deficient sex-role development in at least some boys raised without fathers. Among girls, father absence appears to predict dissatisfaction with and maladjustment in the female role, as well as problems in interacting with males (Hetherington, 1972). These effects are often not evident until adolescence, however, whereas among boys the negative effects of father absence are apparent much earlier.

Confidence in the conclusions of the father absence literature would be bolstered if studies of intact families showed that identification with fathers indeed influenced sex-role development. Yet for the most part, researchers have failed to find significant father-son similarity. (The only relatively consistent finding is that paternal masculinity is correlated with daughters' femininity.) This tends to defeat the same-sex identification theory implicit in most research on father absence. As an explanation, Mussen's and Biller's studies suggest that the father's nurturance and not simply his masculinity must be taken into account when predicting a boy's desire to be like his father. In other words, fathers are salient models only when they are affectively appealing people whom their children would like to emulate, and this depends not on prescribed masculine traits but on the warmth of the father-son relationship.

This confusion underscores the single most important reason for our failure to progress further in understanding the nature of paternal (and for that matter, maternal) influences on child development. Quite simply, researchers have regarded relationships as if they were static entities, easily measured along one or a few orthogonal dimensions. Most investigations of paternal influence, for example, have focused on the father as a model of masculinity, career commitment, or achievement orientation. Yet it seems to me that we have placed too much emphasis on what the father does in front of the child (i.e., what sort of model he provides) and ignored what he does with or to the child (i.e., what sort of socializing agent and companion he is). We are dealing with complex and dynamic relationships between two personalities; if we are to understand the effect of either individual on the other, it is essential to know something about the ambiance of all their interactions.

Greater progress will also be made if researchers recognize that the father-child relationship exists within the context of a family system, where each member influences every other (see Hartup, 1979). Thus the effects of a father's leaving will differ depending on the nature of the preceding father-child, mother-father, and mother-child relationships. For example, hostility between the parents may be more detrimental to healthy personality development than is father absence (Lamb, 1976). Further, a father's leaving may have a different impact on the child who has a warm as opposed to a distant relationship with the mother. Rather than viewing this as evidence minimizing the significance of paternal influences, it can be viewed as an index of the complex nature of the socialization process.

Decontextualization of the father-child relationship has thus hampered analytic progress. Equally important, we have been so eager to identify the special contributions of the father that we have lost sight of the fact that he is, along with the mother, a major socializing agent in the child's life. He models and teaches not only sex roles, but other values and mores as well. His performance as a transmitter and enforcer of societal rules and expectations surely has a broader impact on development than does his role as the male parent. It is likely that the paternal and maternal influences supplement one another to such an extent that it is impossible to extract the father's unique influence. When both parents affect the same aspect of development, however, this does not mean that the paternal influence is insignificant by virtue of superfluity and redundancy. A socialization system that incorporates redundancy has a greater probability of success than does one that relies on a number of socializing agents, each solely responsible for providing certain information or experiences. Since the father-absent family cannot count on the usual redundancy, its performance as a socializing system can be considered at risk. Minor failures in the socialization process are more likely in such a family, but they are certainly not inevitable, particularly since the family itself is simply one (important) entity amid a complex array of institutions (e.g., school, the peer group) dedicated to the socialization of children.

FATHERS—PRESENT AND FUTURE

I have attempted to explain why we know so little about paternal influences on child development. Even as we investigate the traditional role of the father, however, the role itself is changing dramatically (although more major changes are occurring in female roles). Let us then consider the implications of moderate and radical changes in gender and parental roles.

Today's children are the first generation to be raised amid doubt about role prescriptions that have long gone unchallenged. Traditionally, socialization was a process of raising the young to fill niches in society when the present incumbents vacated them. Yet today we do not know what type of society our children will inherit or the roles for which they should be prepared. Even if parents were to presume simply that more egalitarian sex roles will prevail in the future (with men being more involved in child rearing and women more concerned about achievement and the career trajectory than they have been), the process of socialization would still be problematic for two reasons.

First, most parents, both traditional and nontraditional, wish their children to develop secure senses of *gender identity*—that is, confident views of themselves as a male or female. What parents who have nontraditional aspirations for their children are trying to avoid are stereotyped *gender roles*. Unfortunately, neither parents nor psychologists know which sex-differentiating aspects of socialization are necessary to ensure gender identity and which simply contribute to the adoption of restrictive sex roles. The likeliest response to this dilemma, I believe, is to adopt the most conservative strategy: sex-type just in case failing to do so will have adverse consequences. Unfortunately, there is no other simple solution.

Second, there are few models of nontraditional masculinity and femininity for the children of today to emulate. As a result, a special burden is borne by contemporary agents of socialization. Fathers, in particular, have an enormously important role to play in the socialization of "liberated" daughters and sons (see Lamb, Owen, & Chase-Lansdale, 1979). Many contemporary fathers disapprove of nontraditional aspirations (achievement motivation, career commitment) on the part of their daughters. If the fathers of the future instead communicate a belief that career dedication is not incompatible with femininity, fewer women will feel conflict about their social and occupational goals. For somewhat different reasons, paternal attitudes are also destined to facilitate or inhibit changes in the sex-stereotypic behavior and attitudes of sons. In contemporary society the masculine role is viewed as the most powerful; males surely stand to lose most from any redefinition of sex roles. Consequently, an acknowledgment by fathers of the need for such redefinition is likely to be more persuasive and more salient than similar beliefs on the part of women.

Another significant trend is that young fathers of today are seeking a more active role in the care, rearing, and socialization of their children. This gradual change represents a step toward a more egalitarian social structure. For children, it promises to bring increased exposure to one of the major socializing agents within the family, and this will surely increase the extent of paternal influence even if much of this appears redundant—duplicative of maternal influences. Men will also represent more nurturant models and a more humane brand of masculinity, and this may maximize the propensities of children to emulate their fathers. All of these factors speak for increasing paternal involvement in the processes of socialization.

These changes—the predictable changes —amount to minor modifications of the traditional sex roles. Far less likely (despite the amount of attention they receive) are instances of radical role redefinition, as in the cases of role sharing (both parents equally involved in child rearing and breadwinning) and role reversal (father as caretaker, mother as breadwinner). Here it is important not to equate conformity to traditional sex roles with secure gender identity or with mental health. The parents in "alternative families" are not necessarily confused or confusing models. Women may be secure in their femininity and still have occupational aspirations, and secure masculine identity does not preclude taking care of children. Thus, if children in nontraditional families identify with the same-sex parent and if that parent has a sound gender identity and evinces a coherent, if unusual, sex role, then no untoward consequences need occur.

I am considerably less sanguine about the prospects for the children of single parents. To be sure, deviant outcomes are not inevitable, but they are certainly more likely. Parenting can be a difficult job, but it is more so when either parent is absent. In the eyes of many, single fathers are in an especially invidious position, for they often must assume child-care responsibility without adequate training or supervision. Yet I believe that single fathers are a highly selected and self-motivated group who desire custody enough to fight for it amidst societal and judicial prejudices. They are thus quite likely to succeed in meeting the demands placed on them. However, as Eleanor Maccoby (Note 2) said, "Childrearing is something that many people cannot do adequately as single adults functioning in isolation. Single parents need time off from parenting, they need the company of other adults, they need to have other voices joined with theirs in transmitting values and maturity demands to their children" (p. 17). With this type of social and community support available, the socialization process need not

fail in all or even most single-parent families.

These predictions reflect my belief that the fathers of tomorrow will share in both the joys and the sorrows of parenthood much more than they have in the past. In my view, this represents a wholly admirable evolution within our society. And as the father's role changes, the formative significance of fathers in children's lives is likely to expand greatly. We can only hope for a parallel change in the methodological and conceptual sophistication evinced by social scientists attempting to understand the role of the father in child development.

REFERENCE NOTES

1. Yogman, M., Dixon, S., Tronick, E., & Brazelton, T. B. *Development of infant social interaction with fathers.* Paper presented at the meeting of the Eastern Psychological Association, New York, April 1976.
2. Maccoby, E. E. *Current changes in the family, and their impact upon the socialization of children.* Paper presented at the meeting of the American Sociological Association, Chicago, September 1977.

REFERENCES

Benson, L. *Fatherhood: A sociological perspective.* New York: Random House, 1968.

Biller, H. B. *Father, child, and sex role.* Lexington, Mass.: Heath, 1971.

Biller, H. B. *Paternal deprivation: Family, school, sexuality and society.* Lexington, Mass.: Heath, 1974.

Blanchard, R. W. & Biller, H. B. Father availability and academic performance among third-grade boys. *Developmental Psychology,* 1971, *4*, 301–305.

Hartup, W. W. The social worlds of childhood. *American Psychologist,* 1979, *34*, 944–950.

Herzog, E. & Sudia, C. Children in fatherless families. In B. M. Caldwell & H. N. Ricciuti (Eds.), *Review of child development research*, Vol. 3. Chicago: University of Chicago Press, 1973.

Hetherington, E. M. Effects of father absence on personality development in adolescent daughters. *Developmental Psychology*, 1972, *7*, 313–326.

Lamb, M. E. *The role of the father in child development*. New York: Wiley, 1976.

Lamb, M. E. The development of parental preferences in the first two years of life. *Sex Roles*, 1977, *3*, 495–497.

Lamb, M. E. The father's role in the infant's social world. In J. H. Stevens & M. Mathews (Eds.), *Mother/child, father/child relationships*. Washington, D.C.: National Association for the Education of Young Children, 1978.

Lamb, M. E. & Frodi, A. M. The role of the father in child development. In R. R. Abidin (Ed.), *Handbook of parent education*. Springfield, Ill.: Charles C. Thomas, 1979.

Lamb, M. E., Owen, M. T., & Chase-Lansdale, L. The father-daughter relationship: Past, present, and future. In C. B. Kopp & M. Kirkpatrick (Eds.), *Becoming female*. New York: Plenum Press, 1979.

Lynn, D. B. *The father: His role in child development*. Monterey, Calif.: Brooks/Cole, 1974.

Money, J. & Ehrhardt, A. *Man and woman, boy and girl*. Baltimore, Md.: Johns Hopkins University Press, 1972.

Parke, R. D. Perspectives on father-infant interaction. In J. D. Osofsky (Ed.), *Handbook of infant development*. New York: Wiley, 1979.

Parke, R. D. & O'Leary, S. E. Father-mother-infant interaction in the newborn period: Some findings, some observations and some unresolved issues. In K. Riegel & J. Meacham (Eds.), *The developing individual in a changing world*. Vol. 2.: *Social and environmental issues*. The Hague, The Netherlands: Mouton, 1976.

14. COME BACK, MISTER ROGERS, COME BACK

Jerome L. Singer

Dorothy G. Singer

No sane parent would present a child with a fire engine, snatch it away in 30 seconds, replace it with a set of blocks, snatch that away 30 seconds later, replace the blocks with clay, and then replace the clay with a toy car. Yet, in effect, a young child receives that kind of experience when he or she watches American television.

As psychologists who have been investigating television for the past decade, we have become concerned about the ways in which television's rapid-fire delivery may be affecting young children's capacities for imagination and reflective thought. Our research on imaginative play in early childhood suggests that private fantasy has significant benefits for a growing child. Children of 3 or 4 who engage in pretending or make-believe play not only appear to be happier but also are more fluent verbally and show more cooperation and sharing behavior. They can wait quietly or delay gratification, can concentrate better, and seem to be more empathic and less aggressive, thanks to their use of private fantasy.

Can television enhance or inhibit imagination in young children? We think the latter is true, and are increasingly disturbed about the emphasis in American television on extremely short-action sequences, frequent interruptions, and drastic changes in the visual field. Producers—even the producers of "Sesame Street"—argue that they need rapid change to hold children's attention. Yet it seems possible that they are actually creating a psychological orientation in children that leads to a shortened attention span, a lack of reflectiveness, and an expectation of rapid change in the broader environment. The pacing of television itself may be stimulating an appetite for novelty and lively action, as well as an expectation that problems can be resolved in a very short space of time.

The development of young children's imaginative skills requires that they periodically shift their attention away from a rich visual environment—television—and assimilate new information or engage in their own mental imagery. Television, with its constantly changing sequences, may well prevent the elaboration of such private images and preclude the inner rehearsal that is critical in transferring material from the short- to the long-term memory system.

In effect, the major result of watching television may simply be to train children to watch the screen in a fashion that permits surprisingly little subsequent retention. Learning numbers and the names of

Reprinted from *Psychology Today*, March 1979, *56*, 59–60. Copyright © 1979 Ziff-Davis Publishing Company.

letters by rote may be a useful outcome for children who watch "Sesame Street." But, according to psychologists Donald Meichenbaum and Lorraine Turk, children need to learn thinking strategies that will provide them with a variety of active learning attitudes for coping with new material. Fast-paced shows like "Sesame Street," "The Electric Company," and, of course, most commercial children's shows, leave little time for the response and reflection that are important ingredients of such strategies.

Children also need adult models who are thoughtful, who seem to listen, and who ask youngsters to think or to express themselves as part of a total learning process. One of our favorite programs for preschoolers does just this: "Mister Rogers' Neighborhood." Unfortunately, it has been limited to reruns for some years now. Mister Rogers' show is perhaps the best-thought-out program for young children from a psychological standpoint. It does not focus primarily on cognitive skills but attempts to reassure children about their own uniqueness and to convey to them a sense of security and personal worth. Significantly, Mister Rogers' manner is slow, and he repeats himself often. His sugary style irritates many parents. They feel his pace is too slow and that he is perhaps not sufficiently masculine in his manner. *But Mister Rogers is not talking to parents.* He is talking to 3- and 4-year-old children, who are still having lots of trouble making sense of the complexities of the outside world. Children seem to benefit enormously from his relaxed rhythm, the way he follows a subject over a period of days, his reassuring attitude, and his willingness to ask a question and then, in defiance of most television conventions, to say nothing for a few seconds—while children answer for themselves.

Independent research studies have shown that children exposed to about 2 weeks of watching "Mister Rogers' Neighborhood" become more willing to share with other children, more cooperative in their play behavior, and more imaginative. In addition, our own study, carried out with Roni Tower and Ann Biggs, found some interesting patterns in what young television watchers recall from Mister Rogers' program.

We compared the behavior of nursery-school children watching "Sesame Street" with that of children watching "Mister Rogers' Neighborhood." The children watching "Sesame Street" kept their eyes glued to the set, while children watching "Mister Rogers' Neighborhood" allowed their eyes to wander from the TV screen and occasionally walked away from the set. Nevertheless, when we measured recall of particular details from both programs, including story content, the children watching "Mister Rogers' Neighborhood" did as well as those watching "Sesame Street." There seemed to be distinct advantages in watching "Mister Rogers' Neighborhood" for children who were less intellectually gifted and less imaginative. Those children could follow Mister Rogers' material better than children of comparable intellectual capabilities who watched "Sesame Street." After 2 weeks of watching "Mister Rogers' Neighborhood" every day at school, they increased their level of imaginative play and showed more positive emotional reactions to the other children than did children who watched "Sesame Street" or a group of control films.

We are not plugging a specific show. Rather, we feel that the research evidence and an analysis of the cognitive properties of the television medium suggest that it would be far more useful for children if producers of children's shows learned the lesson of "Mister Rogers' Neighborhood" and began providing children with longer sequences, slower pacing, and more personal communication.

Children can actually learn a good deal from television and acquire some constructive social habits. But children, particularly preschoolers, need relatively simple material that lends itself to imitation in action or words. They need bits of time to "talk back" to the TV set. They need to be able to walk away from it, develop pictures in their minds, or try out for size something they have just watched by playing it out on the floor for a few minutes.

Currently, hearings are going on under the auspices of both the Federal Trade Commission and the Federal Communications Commission that deal primarily with commercials directed at children but that also are raising fundamental questions about the overall impact of television on children's information processing.

We think that, rather than attempt to ban commercials, it would be helpful if the networks and producers could use a larger percentage of the huge income derived from advertising to children to generate creative and imaginative programming. There should be continuous consultation with child-development specialists and careful research on children's reactions to programming and the clustering of commercials.

We think Mister Rogers had the right idea, and we'd like to see more of him. But there could be even better shows that would reflect a genuine awareness that 3- and 4- and 5-year-olds need the chance to sort out the complexity of images and to elaborate the information they must process. If television for preschoolers might become "boring," it's worth the chance. As a matter of fact, so powerful is the medium that if all of the networks agreed on a massive graduated slowdown of material being presented, preschool children would still watch and would adjust to the new rhythm.

One might well ask whether all Saturday morning television should be paced so slowly, but maybe 1 hour of such a morning's fare is all a child ought to be watching anyway. Above all, children need time with parents or other "live" caregivers who talk with them, listen to what they say, and encourage their imaginative development by telling stories, singing songs, or playing pretend games.

15. STOP PICKING ON BIG BIRD

Gerald S. Lesser

The Singers say there is a single best style of television for young children. I believe we serve children better by providing a variety of styles. I cannot find the logic in the Singers either/or argument that for young children, slower must be better than faster, longer better than shorter. In an effort to sustain the attention of preschoolers and to teach them effectively, "Sesame Street" mixes fast and slow segments, long and short ones, human as well as animated characters, and puppets. Surely there is room for programs with a variety of styles, as well as for "Mister Rogers' Neighborhood."

The Singers are not the first to express dismay concerning what they see as American television's increasing emphasis on "extremely short-action sequences, frequent interruption, and drastic changes in the visual field." But so far, I have found little research evidence to support the claim that any possible negative effects of such techniques outweigh the positive learning benefits.

Let's look first at the clinical evidence, based on children who were brought to a child-guidance center for a variety of behavior symptoms. Werner Halpern, director of the Children and Youth Division of the Rochester Mental Health Center, reported in 1973 that he had observed cases of a "revving up," or disorganized hyperactivity, in young children, which he attributed to viewing the "stimulus-rich, highly focused" programs of "Sesame Street." However, to check his original observation, Halpern continued his study during the following year and, by 1974, reported that for unclear reasons, "the number of 2-year-olds who manifested hyperactivity and echoic speech related to 'Sesame Street' dropped to the vanishing point in our clinic population."

Experimental research evidence also runs counter to the Singers' arguments. At the University of Massachusetts, Daniel Anderson, Stephen Levin, and Elizabeth Lorch compared the reactions of 72 4-year-olds to rapidly paced and slowly paced segments of "Sesame Street." The research team observed the children watching differently paced versions, tested them after viewing to measure their impulsive behavior and their persistence in completing a puzzle, and then observed them during a 10-minute free-play period. They concluded, "We could find no evidence whatsoever that rapid television pacing has a negative impact on preschool children's behavior. We were unable to find a reduction in 'sustained effort'; nor . . . an increase in aggression or in 'unfocused hyperactivity.'"

Anderson, Levin, and Lorch's research alerts us to another dubious distinction made by the Singers, who not only claim that slow and long are better than fast and short but also imply that fostering imagination is somehow more important than

Reprinted from *Psychology Today*, March 1979, 57, 60. Copyright © 1979 Ziff-Davis Publishing Company.

teaching young children the intellectual skills that will help them in school. Testing assertions made earlier by the Singers and other critics, Anderson and his colleagues declared that "if the 'Sesame Street' critics' assertions [about reduced attention span, aggression, and hyperactivity] have any basis, then the effects would seem to be small, subtle, and insignificant in comparison with the program's demonstrated educational benefits."

When the Singers and their colleagues conducted their own experimental comparison of children's responses to the "fast-paced" "Sesame Street" and the "low-key" "Mister Rogers' Neighborhood," they also failed to find evidence of the shortened attention span that they fear will result from rapidly paced programs: the tables in their 1977 paper reported the results of their work do not reveal significant differences in concentration.

However, when the Singers looked at the entire group of children they studied, and not just at the subgroup that was less intellectually gifted and less imaginative, they reported two other significant findings: while "Mister Rogers' Neighborhood" viewers increased significantly in "imaginativeness," "Sesame Street" viewers also increased, but not as much; "Sesame Street" viewers increased significantly in positive interaction with adults, while overall, "Mister Rogers' Neighborhood" viewers declined on that variable.

The Singers' research reveals another important distinction between "Mister Rogers' Neighborhood" and "Sesame Street" that they fail to mention in their present analysis. In comparing the two programs, the Singers guessed that the "simple, direct" format of "Mister Rogers' Neighborhood" would be better at teaching facts, while the "complex" format of "Sesame Street" would help a child learn to make inferences ("which requires the child to abstract meaning from situations"). Their research showed that the guess was correct: "Mister Rogers' Neighborhood" was better at teaching facts, such as the way a pitch pipe works; "Sesame Street" was better at teaching inferences.

Since I prefer not to regard different types of learning as competing alternatives, I will not claim that learning to make inferences is more important than learning factual information. Clearly, both are important to the young child. The Singers' data thus provide another convincing argument for diversity of television programs for children.

I share the Singers' sadness over the loss of "Mister Rogers' Neighborhood" in anything but reruns. The variety and quality of television programs for our children must be expanded, not diminished. But let us not assume that one style of television program is best for all young children. Don't we have enough ingenuity and commitment to children to provide programs in different forms, styles, and moods? Can't we give children and their parents the opportunity to watch "Mister Rogers' Neighborhood," "Sesame Street," and any other educational programs that we care enough to invent? Let's leave room to experiment, to discover the range and variety of programs that will most benefit our children.

16. CONTROLLING CHILD ABUSE IN AMERICA: AN EFFORT DOOMED TO FAILURE

Edward Zigler

THE PROBLEM

Child abuse is an area of concern that one has great difficulty approaching objectively and analytically. It is a phenomenenon that arouses moral outrage and other intense emotions associated with a number of poorly understood prejudices and anxieties.

To highlight the cultural relativism of most moral strictures, I have asked my students what particular behavior is inherently evil as assessed by any and all value stystems. A behavior regularly nominated as the ultimate of evil is the physical abuse of a child. It is interesting to me that these enlightened Yale undergraduates, who characteristically are willing to find so many reasons to excuse the perpetrator for socially unacceptable behavior, cannot bring themselves to view the child abuser as another victim of social forces beyond his or her control.

The great revulsion toward child abuse might help to explain why so many people react to it with the psychological mechanism of denial—either disbelieving that it takes place or believing that it takes place too rarely to constitute a major social problem. Even leading workers in the area of child abuse have called into question the view that child abuse is widespread. Yet, to me, the real question concerns the magnitude of the problem. The answer to this controversial question has been made murky by people's failure to specify whether they are making judgments on the basis of absolute or relative numbers.

Certainly, one can point to other negative events experienced by children, such as falls, which occur more frequently than child abuse. Thus, speaking relatively, one can argue that child abuse is not as large a problem as childhood accidents. But such a relative approach to designating social problems has serious dangers. Taken to its extreme, it would lead to total inaction in most of the problem areas in which child advocates are currently working to improve the status of America's children. I support the absolute approach to the problem of child abuse and argue that whether there are one thousand or one million abused children, child abuse constitutes a real social problem that merits our society's concern and intervention.

RESEARCH AND DEMONSTRATION PROGRAMS

There is general agreement that theoretical and empirical research in the area of child abuse remains primitive and rudimentary. The work done to date has been relatively recent, relatively limited in quantity, and poor in quality. It is the poor state of the-

This article is reprinted from Gil, David G. (Ed.), *Child abuse and violence*. New York, AMS Press, 1979.

ory and research in the child abuse area that led me, in part, to the pessimistic and apocalyptic title of this address. I believe there is a logical relation between the knowledge base in an area and the ability of workers in that area to mount effective interventions. Stated most baldly, I feel that the knowledge base in the child abuse area is much too limited to direct us to any socially acceptable and realistic interventions of far-reaching effectiveness.

I am greatly troubled by the restrictions placed on research funding by the Child Abuse Prevention and Treatment Act of 1974. I am afraid these restrictions reflect the negative attitude currently in vogue in Congress concerning behavioral science research. When will decision makers learn that our ability to help individuals cannot outdistance the relevant and valid information we have about them? The Act's emphasis on services partakes of the Washington dictum "Don't just stand there, do something." I would suggest that at certain junctures in history the wiser course of action might be "Don't do anything, just stand there."

If there is anything that must be done first and done quickly in the child abuse area, it would be the development of the knowledge base that is a prerequisite for cost-effective interventions. Since the research money provided in the Child Abuse Act is much too small for the task I have outlined, we must look elsewhere for the necessary research funds. I call on the National Center on Child Abuse and Neglect to use its pivotal position in HEW to lead a coordinated research effort in which the funds of several HEW agencies—such as NICHD, NIMH, and OE—are used to support research in the area of child abuse. The Office of Child Development has played such a successful coordinating role around the issue of early childhood education. It could and should do the same for the area of child abuse.

I must add that it would be absurd to delay action until the last bit of scientific evidence is in, and I implore you not to use the relatively poor quality of scholarship in the child abuse area as an excuse for inaction. Poor though our knowledge base might be, we already know more about effective intervention than we are implementing. At this level, the problem is less one of inadequate knowledge than of society's lack of resolve and commitment of resources to services known to be effective in at least reducing the incidence of child abuse.

Given the embryonic state of knowledge in the child abuse area, it is not surprising to discover that the area is more replete with myths than with well-validated facts. The danger here is that, when the emphasis is on social action, as it currently is, these myths become the guides to action; they are all that is available to inform social policy and intervention efforts. Since we have only recently turned our attention to the phenomenon of child abuse, one myth has grown that child abuse has but recently appeared on the human scene. In fact, however, the physical abuse of children has been commonplace for many centuries; it is less common today than it was during any earlier century. I consider the implications of this fact to be ominous in regard to our current efforts to reduce child abuse in America. This long history of child abuse has left a historical residue that makes the physical punishment of children an acceptable social form.

Of course, our immediate concern is whether child abuse is currently on the increase or the wane; and, for this, we have no reliable data. But there is a strong supposition that child abuse has increased over the past two to four decades. The National Center on Child Abuse and Neglect would be performing a real service if it would continuously collect reliable data on incidence. There has been much discussion in the social science area concerning social indicators. I propose that the incidence of child abuse in our society is one such important social indicator.

The single most telling indicator that the child abuse area is at an extremely primitive level of theory construction is that there is today no widely accepted definition of child abuse. How does one investigate a phenomenon that has no widely accepted definition? Resolving this definitional dilemma must become the first item of business among workers in the child abuse area.

One finds in the literature a vacillation between a narrow definition emphasizing serious physical abuse, a somewhat broader definition emphasizing maltreatment, and a broad definition, such as Alvy's, which focuses on the fulfillment of the child's developmental needs. Alvy's comprehensive definition has considerable appeal to me, since it not only flows unerringly from a sense of what children are and what they need, but also leads quickly to a plan of action for improving the lives of many children who are at risk because of a myriad of socially sanctioned practices that interfere with the fulfillment of their developmental needs. I am aware of how threatening Alvy's definition of child abuse would be to our society, since inherent in it is the view that, to the extent that we silently allow ills to befall our nation's children, we are all guilty of child abuse.

A major subproblem in the definitional dilemma is determining at exactly what point on the punishment continuum discipline ends and child abuse begins. We lack a differentiated and conceptually based classification system for child abuse. I believe we have gotten about all the mileage we can out of our simple two-category system of essentially discriminating between children who suffer abuse and those who do not.

Perhaps there would be some profit in searching for the correlates of circumscribed types of child abuse. A number of subcategories immediately come to mind: punishing a child to the point of physical damage, torturing a child, sexually abusing a child, starving a child. At a somewhat higher level, we might conceptualize a classificatory system that differentiates between acts of commission, which are currently used in the narrow definition of child abuse, and acts of omission, which are currently used in the definition of neglect.

Unfortunately, both the old and the recommended new classificatory systems seem to place total emphasis on actions of an adult as experienced by a child. While this has certain value for the tight formation of operational definitions, I believe this value has too high a conceptual price. What appears to be missing is concern with the adult's intentions or any recognition that child abuse is a phenotypic event having a variety of causes.

PARENTING AND PREVENTION

In this same vein, much of our work in the child abuse area is a matter of treating symptoms rather than causes, an issue related to primary versus secondary prevention. *Primary prevention* refers to the prevention of abuse before it occurs, while *secondary prevention* is after-the-fact intervention. It appears that our society is willing to engage in secondary prevention but is almost totally uninterested in primary prevention. It is this state of affairs that once again leads me to be pessimistic about our country's ability to solve the child abuse problem.

Primitive though the work in the child abuse area may be, some tentative information does emerge. For instance, there is considerable evidence that child abuse is more frequently found in a single (female) -parent home in which the mother works. Further, the mother in such homes experiences considerable stress, which is exacerbated by her sense of isolation from any effective social support system.

At a somewhat more tentative level, there is evidence that the lower-SES (socioeconomic status) and working classes are overrepresented among child abusers, even after corrections are made for the well-known SES bias in reporting. (Certainly, such a finding should not be used to further disparage the poor in our nation. The overriding majority of economically disadvantaged parents do not abuse their children, whatever definition of abuse is used.) The relation between SES and child abuse is intriguing. A promising line of research here would be to investigate further the willingness of different SES groups to engage in physical acting-out behaviors. Another approach would be to examine families of differing SES for variations in the amount of stress experienced. It may be that the amount of stress a family experiences, rather than its preferred child-rearing practices, mediates the relation between SES and incidence of child abuse.

We already have convincing evidence that an unemployed father in the home is associated with a higher incidence of child abuse. I need to await no further research to assert that if our nation really wants to reduce the incidence of child abuse, it should pursue a policy to provide employment for those who want it. Here again, you must see the reason for my pessimism concerning our nation's commitment to reducing child abuse. How can I be sanguine when I see a calculated government policy allowing a national unemployment rate of over 8%? But I wish to be fair. Decision makers who argue that high unemployment is the cost we must pay to reduce inflation are not evil people consciously bent on the abuse of America's children. They may feel that inflation is detrimental to family life, and that this concern must have priority over the concern of unemployment.

I urge decision makers to consider the health of families as a variable in their cost-benefit equations that lead our national

government to pursue one course of action over another. We have no explicit family policy in America, and we have yet to begin the critical task of determining the impact on families of policies implemented by our political leaders. My reading of the child abuse literature is that the single overriding factor in determining whether a child will experience abuse is the viability and strength of that child's family. How can our nation control child abuse if it currently does not even consider the strength of America's families, much less how a variety of social policies influence this strength?

Abusive parents often have unrealistic expectations about what behaviors their children are capable of, as well as a general lack of knowledge about child development. It appears that anything we do to teach the general population about child care and the normal course of child development would be helpful in reducing child abuse. I endorse the suggestion of many workers that our nation commit itself to teaching parents how to be parents, with courses on parenthood becoming part of the curricula of every high school in America. A model of such an effort is the Education for Parenthood program mounted jointly by the Office of Child Development and the Office of Education. This program should be greatly expanded to reach all students.

Not only would the national implementation of courses in parenting be effective in reducing child abuse, but the cost of such a program would be relatively small. Further, thanks to the work of George Hecht and others, I believe our society is prepared to support an effort to train all our young people to become better parents. Of course, I would expect some rumblings concerning government-subsidized education for parenthood programs and anticipate the charge that the government is intruding in the rearing of children. The credence given to such a charge will depend on how successful we are in constructing courses that emphasize hard information on child development rather than the inculcation of values.

I am not recommending courses in parenthood for the economically disadvantaged alone. Such training is needed by all our young people. Think for a moment about the fact that abusive parents tend to have unrealistic expectations of their children. The phenomenon can also be found among middle-class parents, so many of whom want to teach their children to read at age 2 or believe one can raise a child's IQ by 20 points or more. This lack of knowledge about children and unrealistic expectations of them is a form of child abuse. The child who cannot fulfill these expectations must encounter a lesser degree of acceptance by his parents.

Compared to the considerable work that has been done on the characteristics of the abusing parent, somewhat less but still substantial work has been done to describe the characteristics of the child who is prone to being abused. A relation has been found between abused children and mentally retarded children, but we do not know how to interpret this relation. Do parents physically assault children because the children are retarded, or do children become retarded as a result of abuse? If it is substantiated that a sizable number of retarded children are abused, this might be related to the parents having unrealistic expectations of these children.

Another finding is that premature children experience a greater incidence of abuse. Perhaps the very nature of premature birth produces considerable stress in a family's life, and this general stress may be what mediates the relation between prematurity and abuse. Also, premature infants probably exhibit a higher incidence of noxious behaviors such as crying, and it may be these unpleasant behaviors that precipitate the abuse.

But, again, we need await no lengthy

program of research to assert that we could reduce the incidence of child abuse in America if we were willing to mount a national effort to reduce the incidence of premature births. One would want to do this for many reasons in addition to the impact on child abuse. Yet I see no great national concern and no massive intervention effort to deal with prematurity. We already know how to markedly reduce the incidence of prematurity; what is lacking is the resolve and the commitment of needed resources.

We come now to what appears to be the most salient conceptual issue in the child abuse area: namely, whether child abuse is best conceptualized as a pathological phenomenon most appropriately understood in terms of the character traits or psychodynamics of individual parents, or whether it is most appropriately viewed as a sociocultural ecological phenomenon, with the causes seen as residing in the extremely stressful nature of the parent's ecological niche. In this latter view, special attention is given to the effects of poverty, alienation, and the lack of an effective social support system for the parenting function.

How this individual-versus-social conceptual issue is resolved has real implications for the social efforts we choose to mount to reduce the incidence of abuse. If we commit ourselves to the individual psychopathological approach and select psychiatric intervention as the treatment of choice, there are neither enough mental health workers nor money to treat all the adults guilty of even gross and severe child abuse.

Another intervention implication within the individual approach is that child abuse is a trait that the abuser needs help to deal with. I believe that workers have been too impressed with the phenomenon of some abusing parents coming forward to ask for help for themselves. It is a short step from this notion to the establishment of Parents Anonymous groups and hotlines. I feel that such interventions will prove ineffective because they are based on an inadequate conceptualization of the causes of child abuse. My colleagues, Urie Bronfenbrenner and Julius Richmond, have convinced me that such efforts, which do nothing to improve the ecological system's impacting on child abuse, will be ineffective.

It is already too late in the day to view child abuse totally from the individual perspective. We must concern ourselves with the social factors that contribute to the incidence of abuse, the abuser will be conceptualized as part of a family that is embedded in the social, economic, and political realities of its ecology.

But if child abuse is in large part caused by general ecological factors, I again have no choice but to be pessimistic about our society's determination to control abuse. Society has taken some tentative steps to correct environmental pollution. But it has done precious little to correct the social pollution of many Americans' ecologies—the polluted ecologies that drive many parents to child abuse.

The control of child abuse is much more likely to come from efforts to beef up our nation's general social service programs than from efforts specifically directed against abuse. So long as we attend only to the symptom of abuse and engage in token efforts flowing from this narrow concern, we avoid dealing with the underlying social determinants, which would of course be much more costly to correct.

The ecological approach directs us to certain aspects of or institutions in the family's ecology where intervention might have particularly high payoff in reducing the incidence of abuse. In view of the finding that abused children are often the products of unwanted pregnancies, family planning programs should be effective in reducing child abuse. Homemaker services, which could aid in the child rearing function of families who are experiencing difficulties, would also have a direct and immediate effect in reducing child abuse.

A logical consensus has developed that the incidence of abuse would decline if parents could more readily avail themselves of child care of various kinds. Our society appears to be extremely reluctant, however, to provide the child care that so many American families desperately need. It is only my dislike for hyperbole that prevents me from shouting "hypocrisy" at a society that claims to want to control child abuse and yet does so little to provide child care.

The single most important determinant of child abuse is the willingness of adults to inflict corporal punishment upon children in the name of discipline. Well over half of all instances of abuse appear to have developed out of a disciplinary action. All too often, an adult begins to discipline a child and ends up damaging the child much more than was intended. This situation is exacerbated by parents' lack of knowledge about the physical vulnerability of children.

Who is the real villain in this common scenario? Certainly not the child. Nor is it the parent, who often feels that, in disciplining the child, he or she is doing what society expects. The real villains are our child rearing practices, which permit corporal punishment, and a society that approves of such methods of child discipline. So long as corporal punishment is accepted as a method of disciplining children, children will be abused in our country. Once again, I am pessimistic about our nation's ability to control child abuse.

Again, I am tempted to point out the hypocrisy of a society that verbalizes its desire to stop child abuse but is nevertheless willing to countenance the well-documented abuse and neglect of children in settings funded by taxpayers' dollars—in institutions for the retarded, hospital settings for the emotionally disturbed, and our day-care system. This abuse of children is being purchased with your tax dollar and mine. I have looked closely at who is guilty of child abuse and have discovered it is I.

Where else may we find the legally and socially sanctioned abuse of children? I point to that social institution which, after the family, is the most important socializing agent in America: the school.

A family's ecology is best conceptualized as a rubric of interacting social institutions. The school is an important institution embedded in this rubric. Its practices not only reflect the values of America's families but also influence the development of familial attitudes and practices. If you wish to decrease the incidence of child abuse in America, make it illegal for school personnel to use corporal punishment against school children. I am troubled by the Supreme Court's recent decision upholding the right of school personnel to punish children physically. As a result of the example such punishment sets, children are much more likely to be abused in the home, where the more severe forms of child abuse currently take place.

This era of violence in the schools should not be attributed to an underuse of discipline in the home. Rather, it appears to reflect a growing acceptance of violence in our society. One finds violence, hostility, and aggression everywhere in our society. So long as these are tolerated and even glorified, we can expect child abuse both at home and in school.

The foregoing analysis leads me to conclude that we will make little progress over the next few years in reducing the incidence of child abuse. We simply do not have the knowledge and resources to deal very effectively with even the symptomatic treatment of abuse.

I even find myself conflicted about the value of the Child Abuse Prevention and Treatment Act of 1974. The Act promises more than it can possibly deliver. It provides too little in the way of resources and direction to make any significant impact on incidence figures for child abuse. We cannot legislate away major social problems with a single bill.

Social change is produced not by the stroke of a pen but by intensive and persistent efforts to change the human ecology in which the social target is embedded. Laws such as the federal Child Abuse Act do little more than give us a false sense of security. Such token efforts give the appearance that something meaningful has been done and thus interfere with the mounting of truly effective measures. A $20 million bill to fight child abuse in America amounts to little more than a Band-aid on a cancer. Given the current fiscal austerity in our nation, however, I am afraid that child abuse will have to take its place for the time being alongside lead-paint poisoning (which, by the way, is a socially tolerated form of child abuse) as another problem that our society has neither the commitment nor the resources to solve.

I am surprised at the depth of my pessimism concerning our ability to reduce child abuse. My pessimism should not be interpreted as some sort of plea for apathy or inaction. There is much that could and should be done in this area, including an invigorated research and data-collection program; increased efforts in the family planning area; the widespread implementation of education for parenthood programs; a massive effort to reduce the number of premature births in America; an increase in the availability of homemaker services; and an immediate increase in the availability of child care. Finally, and perhaps most important, if we are to be effective in stopping the abuse of children, we need to examine our society's value system and to reduce the acceptability of man's violence to man, of which child abuse is but one manifestation.

17. PROJECT HEAD START BECOMES
A LONG-DISTANCE RUNNER
Laura L. Dittmann

Editor's Note:
The following selection is a review of *Project Head Start: A Legacy of the War on Poverty*, edited by Edward Zigler and Jeanette Valentine. We have chosen to include the review here not for the evaluative comments it offers but because we believe it presents an excellent overview of the Head Start Program.

Project Head Start has been referred to as the country's biggest peacetime mobilization of human resources and effort (Brazziel, 1967). Implemented in June 1965, the program had been conceived only the previous November. A promising combination of ample funding and a conviction that environmental enrichment would eliminate the poverty cycle instilled enthusiasm in the early planners.

Instead of a pilot program to get 2,500 poverty-level children ready for school in the fall, the committee decided to provide a comprehensive preschool experience for 100,000 children that would include health services (medical, dental, nutritional, and mental health) and social services to their families. The program would involve the parents in both planning and participating in the program. The 100,000 children quickly became 500,000 as proposals flooded in from all parts of the country.

The first summer, there were 11,000 child development centers located from the Arctic Circle to Guam, from Indian reservations to migrant camps, from one coast to the other. More than 100,000 adults were involved. Sargent Shriver, then director of the parent agency, the Office of Economic Opportunity (OEO), recalls, "It was like wildcatting for oil in your own backyard and hitting a gusher" (p. 56).

The excitement, almost exaltation, created in launching this remarkable effort is captured fully in *Project Head Start: A Legacy of the War on Poverty*, edited by Edward Zigler and Jeanette Valentine. More than 40 individuals associated with Head Start in varying capacities contributed to this lengthy book. Its broad scope examines the years during which the project developed, its subsequent 15-year history, and the future of the program.

The enthusiastic narration of Head Start's beginning is particularly effective. Vivid anecdotes from Mrs. Lyndon B. Johnson and from Urie Bronfenbrenner are included. Shriver summarizes it all: "So, we figured, we'll get these kids into school ahead of time; we'll give them food; we'll give them medical exams; we'll give them the shots or the glasses they need; we'll give them some acculturation to academic work—we'll give them (this is where the

This article is reprinted by permission from *Young Children*, vol. 35, no. 6, September 1980, 2–9, copyright © 1980, National Association for the Education of Young Children, 1834 Connecticut Avenue, N.W., Washington, D.C. 20009.

name came in) a *head start.*" The original name Kiddy Corps, as a parallel to Job Corps, was abandoned. Shriver adds, "We did not want to start a program that took children away from their parents. . . . We felt that if these little children came to a school where in addition to a teacher there were parents from their own area, they wouldn't feel that they were suddenly being thrust into a totally alien environment. . . . Therefore, bringing the parents in was intended to be an immediately positive influence on the children, and also a start toward teaching the parents themselves" (pp. 52–53).

Julius Richmond, the first director of Head Start under OEO, recalls their offices that were virtually without furniture in an old hotel marked for demolition. Most of the meetings were held with everyone standing. He noted slyly, "It has often occurred to me since that much time could be saved if all meetings were held with people standing rather than sitting. I had no reason to believe that the decisions were any the worse for having been made in the upright posture" (p. 123).

At the first summer's conclusion, the planners moved immediately into organizing for a full-year program. High hopes kept work at a feverish pace for several years. But there followed, almost inevitably, a dismal stage. The early findings of IQ gains were reported to be eroded by second or third grade in the well-known Westinghouse Learning Corporation evaluation (1970). Unfortunately, this generally negative report was the most highly publicized of the numerous studies conducted thereafter (a veritable cottage industry, according to Zigler), which largely accounts for the fact that today many citizens are surprised to discover that Head Start still exists. Even though Westinghouse did find lasting gains for some groups of children, particularly for urban black children, the statement that cognitive gains

were often lost after the children had been in elementary school for a few years was interpreted as a case against Head Start rather than as an indictment of children's experiences in the years following Head Start.

The critics also lost sight of the multifaceted goals of the program—those of improving physical health and abilities; aiding the emotional and social development of the child by encouraging spontaneity, curiosity, and self-discipline; strengthening the sense of dignity and self-worth within the child and her or his family; and developing in the child and family a responsible attitude toward society as well as encouraging society to work with low-income citizens in solving their problems. All of these goals are difficult to measure, but they were seriously addressed.

Some programs were indeed slipshod and inadequate and served to fuel the indictment that this was another evidence of tokenism, offering a little something to deflect urban unrest rather than attacking the basic societal ills underlying family and community disorganization. At this juncture, however, all who embraced the Head Start idea—on the local, state, and national levels—settled down to work on the administrative and political conflicts, to strengthen the comprehensive nature of the program, and to create some semblance of uniformity from one site to another.

HEAD START AS A LABORATORY IN EARLY CHILDHOOD EDUCATION

Head Start has been a visible national experiment which has affected everyone in early childhood education and child development. Its struggles mirror such persistent issues as standards for operation, continuity in programming both before and after preschool, relationships with parents, relationships with the public schools, training and professionalization of personnel, inclusion of handicapped children, and choice of curriculum goals.

Head Start has addressed these stubborn themes over the years in a proliferation of experimental demonstrations. A description of some of these pilot programs illustrates the contents of the book and forms a bridge to the concerns of a more general readership.

Continuity in programming for children was approached first by establishing Follow Through in 1967. This large program continues under the sponsorship of the Office, now the Department, of Education. Follow Through extended into the elementary grades with a curriculum model selected by the local community. The objectives and content of the educational program were made explicit and maintained by the developer of the model.

Such specificity of the curriculum was in contrast to what had been going on in Head Start, which tended to offer a kind of traditional university-based nursery school point of view blended with local preferences and skills. Jeannette Stone points out that current nursery school education at that time was not considered traditional by anyone outside the field, but there was a kind of consensus that the child's social and emotional development were perhaps more important than intellectual achievement.

Implementation of a comparison of curriculum models was undertaken in Head Start in 1969. About 2,000 children each year were brought into a study of the results of 11 different plans covering curriculums taught through various methods. The approach varied from the highly specific academic strategies advocated by Bereiter, Engelmann, and Bushell to programs similar to Bank Street, Weikart, and the Responsive Education models, which focused more on problem solving and following up on child interests. Other programs relied on teaching the parents, as the Gordon model exemplified. In the book, Louise Miller gives an excellent explanation and description of the Head Start Planned Variation (HSPV) Study, and Lois-Ellin Datta includes the conclusions of this work with other comparison studies in her chapter on evaluation. The models and the outcomes are not readily summarized, but one can say that children tend to learn what adults care to teach them well, and that probably no one classroom can do everything equally effectively. Choices have to be made—choices that affect children in the long and short run.

Intellectual achievement is not the only outcome variable. *What* is taught does not necessarily relate to *how* it is taught. For example, Miller reports the finding that teachers in traditional classrooms were found to be low in most of the teaching techniques ordinarily used to convey information to children: straightforward verbal instruction, demonstration, modeling, and manipulation of materials. They had the lowest ratio of positive to negative reinforcement. Furthermore, teachers in the traditional programs were much more frequently engaged in attempts to control children's conduct, particularly in social behavior, rather than correcting errors in subject matter.

From this study and related research, early childhood educators have been able to consider more deeply the important questions of what to teach, when to teach it, what constitutes learning, what is universal for all children, and what is legitimate and desirable in adapting to cultural differences. Barbara Biber seems eminently correct in her statement that "it is fair to say that the Head Start program, national in scope and government supported, holds a unique position as a frontier movement in early childhood education" (p. 155).

IMPROVING STAFF PERFORMANCE

Along with the search for greater consistency from one classroom to another in educational standards, if not in curriculum itself, came the need to become more specific about the rest of Head Start's broad aims. By 1975, performance standards had been developed for nationwide use. Requirements for each of the components were spelled out, with sugggestions as to implementation strategies, including the requirement that at least 10% of the children enrolled be handicapped, as mandated by Congress in 1972. Every Head Start program conducts a self-assessment (SAVI) annually and must show how any deficiencies will be corrected.

As time goes by, program deficiencies are as likely to stem from financial shortages as from lack of knowledge or lack of good intentions. Recently, the administrator of a large urban program despairingly shared with me how the SAVI promise to obtain a playground gate, missing because of vandalism, was doomed. Three months after the assessment, the gate was replaced, but the next day, when a quarterly progress report was due, the gate was gone again. "From now on," announced the landlord, "there will be no gate at that playground."

Training of personnel has likewise been an important part of the drive to improve staff performance. Through various training programs, thousands of people, mostly low-income women, have moved into new jobs, and many have been given at least a start on college education. Head Start Supplementary Training, later dovetailed with the Child Development Associate Training program (CDA), has had a far-reaching effect on the way universities and colleges have conceptualized the skills needed to work with young children by leading the universities to adapt scheduling and classroom practices, as well as to formulate techniques, to reach a new type of student. In the book, Irving Lazar comments on similar changes in schools of social work. Frederick North acknowledges the influence of Head Start in training personnel for health and especially nutrition services, although North ruefully asserts that there has been little other institutional change in terms of school health or other public health activities. "Well-baby clinics and school health programs still have all the problems that Head Start demonstrated could be overcome, and school lunch programs fail to exploit the educational opportunities food service provides" (p. 249).

Funding and administrative difficulties have always plagued the career development aspects of training, however. Since the beginning of Head Start, the allocation of funds for training has not increased in direct proportion to the growth of the program. Recent developments in the administration of the Child Development Associate credentialing process have borne out the fears of many people from the beginning that placing professional certification into the hands of an independent, non-profit agency, almost totally dependent upon federal funding, renders the entire undertaking vulnerable.

MOVING UP INTO THE SCHOOLS

Two other demonstration programs have addressed preschool/elementary school relationships and have attempted to bring Head Start and subsequent experiences more into a continuum. In 1974, Project Developmental Continuity (PDC) was funded to allot about $100,000 annually to 13 sites in rural and urban communities, including an Indian reservation and a migrant locale. The multiple goals include construction of a sequenced and continuous educational program for children as they move through the primary grades, promotion of continuity in health and social services to the children, and special concern for bilingual (Arenas 1980) and handicapped children. All children in the demonstration classes and their families are included, not just Head Start graduates. The evaluation is still underway, as the first children involved are now completing third grade, but, in general, positive results are being documented.

As with any effort to infiltrate another social system, the viability of the program depends to a large extent on the espousal of PDC's aims, including active parent participation and decision making by the principal and other public school officials. This is not easy to do.

Most recently, Head Start has initiated a renewed emphasis on helping children acquire skills that will prepare them for greater achievement when they enter elementary school. Twenty-nine Head Start programs have been selected for the Basic Educational Skills Project (BES). The objectives of BES, less complex than those of PDC because they focus almost totally on cognitive, school-related aspects, may render the program more researchable. In its broadest terms, however, BES seems to be a restatement of Head Start 15 years ago.

ENROLLING THE FAMILY

Finally, there is a group of program alternatives which in one way or another include the family as the target unit. The earliest one of these is the Parent and Child Center (PCC), established in 1969 in 36 communities in an effort to reach the family of the child under 3 years of age—a head start on the Head Start approach. The PCC has always remained a low-profile demonstration, responsive to community needs, and most frequently has moved from center-based to outreach strategies in working with families. The Child and Family Mental Health Project was launched in 1975 in

14 communities to demonstrate innovative ways to provide psychological services to families, particularly in communities that lack local mental health facilities.

Much better known is the variation called Home Start, a demonstration program to provide Head Start's comprehensive services to children and parents in their own homes. Home Start was funded from 1972 to 1975 but has continued with a flexible mix of center-based and home-based programming using paraprofessionals from the families' own community as Home Visitors. More than 20,000 children are now receiving such services in approximately 400 full-year Head Start programs—about a third of all Head Start programs (Collins 1980). The evaluation of Home Start showed that mothers who were helped to promote the education and development of their own children at home did as well as if they had sent the child to a regular Head Start center (O'Keefe 1974). This finding is in agreement with numerous other studies which document the value of involving parents intensively in the education of their children (Bronfenbrenner 1974; Mann, Harrell, and Hurt 1978).

Most inclusive in scope is the Child and Family Resource Program (CFRP), which enrolls the family from the child's prenatal period through age 8. There are currently 11 of these demonstrations serving 1,200 families in a program that seeks to provide and integrate comprehensive services on an individualized basis. The service plan is developed cooperatively after an assessment of the family's needs is made. Valentine states, "In addition to providing a vast range of services, these programs have also furnished models for integrating and coordinating services to children and families in need. Unfortunately, the funding level . . . has not been commensurate with the mandate for services and the number of families in need of services. The budgets for CFRPs have averaged $125,000 per program" (p. 354).

THE LEGACY OF HEAD START

No one can doubt the success of this large-scale intervention program. Plenty of documentation for its value is available. (See also the report of other preschool intervention projects in Lazar and Darlington, 1974.) Of course, there are deficiencies and wide variations in quality from one location to another, but the broad education and health thrusts have had an enormously positive outcome for 7.5 million children and their families. In fact, the success of Head Start may be one of its problems because it is difficult to seize the attention of the press and the public when things are going well. Scandal or failure are much more quickly publicized.

However, the very number of small demonstration projects designed to respond to community needs or persisting national issues makes it hard to put one's finger on Head Start today. The administrative demands upon the small staff in the Head Start Branch of the Administration for Children, Youth and Families, furthermore, are so great that many of these programs do not receive the attention they need and deserve, either during the duration of the demonstration or at the conclusion. The complex aims and diversity of PCC, PDC, HSPV, Health Start, Child and Family Health, and CFRP make them difficult to "headline."

The pressure and desire to respond to the increasingly complicated needs of low-income families is causing Head Start officials to lean toward a model represented by the family-targeted CFRP. All aspects of family life, from conception to the child through the age of 8, are properly the concern of this effort. Such individualized program aims compound the problem of evaluation. In addition, however, there is the danger that such diffused goals will cause Head Start to become more closely identified with welfare strategies rather than remain educational in the broadest

sense. If this should occur, the program will become increasingly vulnerable—as would any program established to serve only one segment of the population in times of financial restriction and shifts in the national mood to antigovernment and anti-intrusion into the sanctity of family life.

It is sobering to realize that the announcement of such a program as Head Start would not be received today with the open enthusiasm recalled by Shriver: "We designed the program, announced it, and made it available to the American people according to specific criteria. But it was the American people who assured Head Start's success because of their fantastic nationwide response" (p. 55).

Today, Head Start and other child development programs are increasingly plagued by financial constraints. Only one in five of the eligible children can be enrolled. Instead of the ideal envisioned by Brazziel in 1967 of nearly 2 million children and some 70,000 teachers, Head Start has stabilized at around 400,000 children with about 70,000 paid staff, including aides and cooks. Despite the largess and devotion of many, the time is coming when only the dedicated can afford to strive under conditions that amount to exploitation of their willingness to work for low pay in the service of children and families.

Zigler and Valentine and their cohort of contributors have produced an excellent book that can help educators, health and social workers, citizen activists, and students focus on the tough social issues embedded in this program which is so firmly endorsed by its recipients but which, like solar energy, gets the wholehearted support of few of the powerful in political circles.

REFERENCES

Arenas, S. Innovations in bilingual/multicultural curriculum development. *Children Today*, May–June 1980, *9*(3), 17–21.

Brazziel, W. Two years of head start. *Phi Delta Kappan*, March 1967, *48*(7), 344–348.

Bronfenbrenner, U. *Is early intervention effective? A report on longitudinal evaluations of preschool programs*, Vol. 2. Washington, D.C.: Office of Child Development, Department of Health, Education and Welfare, 1974.

Collins, R. Home start and its implications for family policy. *Children Today*, May–June 1980, *9*(3), 12–16.

Lazar, I. & Darlington, R. *Lasting effects after preschool. A report by the central staff of the Consortium for Longitudinal Studies*. Washington, D.C.: U.S. Department of Health, Education and Welfare. DHEW Publication No. (OHDS) 80-30179. October 1979.

Mann, A. J., Harrell, A., & Hurt, Jr., M. A. *Review of Head Start research since 1969 and an annotated bibliography*. Washington, D.C.: U.S. Department of Health, Education and Welfare. DHEW Publication No. (OHDS) 78-31102. 1978.

O'Keefe, A. *What Head Start means to families*. Washington, D.C.: U.S. Department of Health, Education and Welfare. DHEW Publication No. (OHDS) 79-31129. September 1979.

Westinghouse Learning Corp. *The impact of Head Start: An evaluation of effects of Head Start on children's cognitive and affective development. Executive Summary*. Ohio Univ. Report to the Office of Economic Opportunity. Washington, D.C.: Clearinghouse for Federal Scientific and Technical Information, June 1969. (ED093497).

18. THE YALE CHILD WELFARE RESEARCH PROGRAM: IMPLICATIONS FOR SOCIAL POLICY

Leslie A. Rescorla

Edward Zigler

In the late sixties, there were a large number of intervention projects undertaken to help disadvantaged families and children (Bronfenbrenner, 1975; Day & Parker, 1977; Ryan, 1974). While these programs differed widely in research design, methodological sophistication, intervention philosophy, and program format, a common denominator was the hope and assumption that intervening early in the lives of disadvantaged children would help them make a more successful adjustment to school and hence to adult life. This article will focus on one such comprehensive intervention project, the Yale Child Welfare Research Program, carried out at the Yale Child Study Center from 1967 to 1972. We will first outline some major concerns in the field of early intervention in order to place the Yale project in historical perspective.

After a brief description of the project's goals and methods, the principal short-term and long-term effects of the intervention will be reviewed. The article will close with discussion of the social policy implications which can be drawn from interventions such as the Yale Child Welfare Research Program.

The fundamental issue in the early intervention literature has been the effectiveness of such massive programs. An important facet of this issue is the relative merits of center-based as opposed to home-based programs. Center-based programs ran the gamut from projects such as those of Heber (1977) in Milwaukee and the North Carolina Abecedarian program (1976), which provided full-time day care from infancy on, to programs such as that of Klaus and Gray (1968), which provided summer

The Yale Child Welfare Research Program received its financial support from the United States Children's Bureau, Office of Child Development, Department of Health, Education and Welfare (#PR900). A grant from the Ford Foundation, New York, supported the work on data organization and analysis.

The independent follow-up was supported by Grant PHS-90-C-912 from the Administration for Children, Youth, and Families and Research Grant HD-0 8008-13 from the National Institute of Child Health and Human Development.

The authors wish to thank the many dedicated people who worked in the Yale Child Welfare Research Program and the independent follow-up; the New Haven public schools for their cooperation; and the children and parents who shared their lives with us. Requests for reprints should be sent to Leslie A. Rescorla, Ph.D., Yale Child Study Center, 333 Cedar Street, New Haven, Connecticut 06510.

compensatory education programs. In his review of many programs, Bronfenbrenner (1975) concluded that IQ gains from center-based programs were not sustained beyond second or third grade and that programs with a strong parent involvement component have proved to be more effective than other projects. It should be noted that center-based projects varied widely in the degree to which they provided services to parents or involved them in the intervention.

A dimension which is important in classifying home-based programs is the degree of prescriptive programming involved in the intervention. While some projects involved a fairly didactic curriculum for parents (e.g., Levenstein, 1977; Schaefer, 1977), other programs were designed to offer more general child-rearing advice and to promote increased cultural enrichment. While some reviews have concluded that the more structured programs are most effective, Gray and Wandersman (1980) make the important point that assessment measures have generally been narrower than project goals, which perhaps slants the analysis in favor of the more didactic programs.

Thus, two important dimensions in early interventions are the degree to which the program provides services within the context of the child's family and the extent to which the project involves a prescriptive program of child care or education. Dichotomization of intervention programs as high versus low in extent of family context and high versus low with regard to prescriptive programming may be a useful way to consider their relative strengths and weaknesses as models of intervention.

A recurring theme in the literature has been dissatisfaction with existing criteria for program evaluation. Early evaluation studies such as the Westinghouse/Ohio University report (1969) and Bronfenbrenner's (1975) review focused on IQ gains in intervention children. Part of the skepti-

cism which has prevailed regarding the effectiveness of early interventions derives from the fact that initial IQ gains faded out as the children advanced through grade school. However, more recent evaluations, such as those reported by the Consortium for Longitudinal Studies (Darlington et al., 1980) and the Perry Preschool Program (Schweinhart & Weikart, 1980), have demonstrated that the most important and long-lasting effect of intervention programs is that fewer intervention children have been retained in grade and placed in special education throughout their school years than control children. Thus, the trend in intervention evaluations has been toward measures which reflect how the children actually adapt and cope in school. Zigler and Trickett (1978) have been among the main proponents of this broadening of evaluation criteria, arguing that gains in social competence rather than IQ score should be the ultimate criterion of program effectiveness.

In addition to a broadening of the evaluation criteria used to assess intervention children, there has also been a shift in recent years toward considering program effects on parents. A few projects have reported educational and occupational advancement in the intervention mothers (Gordon, Guinagh, & Jester 1977; Karnes, Zehrback, & Teska, 1974; Lally & Honig, 1977) or mothers' increased vocational aspirations on behalf of their children (Darlington et al., 1980). As the field of intervention research has matured, it has become increasingly acknowledged that interventions are successful to the degree that they make a significant impact on families' aspirations, expectations, lifestyle, and modes of interaction.

In addition to arguing for a strong parental component, Bronfenbrenner (1975) also contended that the best period for intervention was in the first 3 years of life. More recently, this theme has been elaborated by Gray and Wandersman (1980), who stress that the value of home-based intervention is its capacity to adapt to the needs and strengths of individual families and to create meaningful changes in parent-child interaction patterns. What is less well understood at this point are the dynamics of this intervention process, particularly the factors constraining the successful application of intervention services. This need for a stronger process orientation in intervention research has been recently emphasized by Ramey. (1981).

The Yale Child Welfare Research program was a small-sample comprehensive intervention project with a clinical orientation. It was a program with a strong family context, in which the aim was to provide supportive services rather than prescriptive programming. It has been evaluated using a broad range of socially significant criteria which assess both children and parents. Finally, the project findings touch on the issue of the factors limiting intervention effectiveness. For these reasons, consideration of the Yale project and the issues it raises can lead to some important implications for future social policy regarding early intervention.

THE YALE PROGRAM

The Yale Child Welfare Research Program has been fully described in *The Challenge of Day Care*, by Provence, Naylor, and Patterson (1977), as well as in two recent research reports (Rescorla, Provence & Naylor, 1981; Trickett, et al., 1981). Thus, only the main aspects will be outlined here. The goal of the Yale Program was to provide services to a group of disadvantaged families in order to help them improve their quality of life and foster the healthy development of their children. The intervention can best be described as an infant/toddler intervention program with a clinical-developmental approach. Clinical assessment provided the basis for individualizing ser-

vices to the child and family. The approach was developmental in its view of the child's physical, mental, social, and emotional growth. Concepts from psychoanalytic child psychology were central to the project, particularly propositions about the influence of the parent-child relationship on the relationships with others. The project shared with the Bank Street educational approach the assumption that the growth of cognitive functions is inextricably intertwined with the growth of emotional and interpersonal processes.

The intervention involved 18 children from 17 low-income families who participated in the program from birth to 30 months of age. All children were firstborn, with the exception of one younger sibling born during the project. The mothers were chosen on the basis of residence in the inner city and income below the federal poverty guideline. Twelve of the children were black, two were white, two were mixed (white mothers and black fathers), and two were siblings from a Puerto Rican family. There were 11 boys and 7 girls. There were eight intact and nine one-parent families. At the beginning of the project, six of the eight intact families were self-supporting and two were on public welfare. Of the single young women, one was entirely self-supporting, one was supported by her parents, and seven were supported by public welfare. The age range of mothers was 18–24, with a mean age of 20. Eleven of the mothers had completed high school; six had not.

The project was located in one of the inner-city slums of New Haven. The project staff consisted of experienced clinicians in social work, psychology, nursing, pediatrics, and psychoanalysis, as well as early childhood educators and research psychologists. There were four components to the intervention: (1) The home visitor, a professional clinician, met with each mother at least twice a month during the first year and monthly thereafter. The goal was to form a relationship with the parents, with help taking the form of assistance in dealing with social service agencies, psychological and emotional support, child care advice, or therapeutic counseling; the services were geared to the needs and wishes of the parents. (2) Pediatricians were responsible for care when children were sick and for well-child examinations, given monthly during the first year and every 3 months after that. (3) Developmental examinations using the Yale Developmental Schedules were administered at periodic intervals, helping parents to become more aware of their child's development, his problem-solving skills, and his sensitivities. (4) Full-time child care was available for families who wished to use it. The philosophy of the program was to arrange experiences which would enhance physical, intellectual, and emotional development. Five children spent 20 or more months in the day-care program; five had from 10 to 19 months in day care; two spent 5 months or less. Five of the six children whose parents did not wish day care attended a "toddler school" twice a week for 1½ hours with their mothers present, from 16 to 30 months of age.

About 1 year after the intervention project ended, a comparison sample of 18 children 30 months of age was selected from records in the same hospital clinic used to select the intervention mothers. Families were matched on income, marital status of mother, and race of parents; children were matched on sex and ordinal position. Each comparison mother was seen for a single in-depth interview by a psychiatric nurse who was part of the project staff, and each child in the comparison group was seen once for development evaluation.

In order to assess the long-term effects of the intervention, a follow-up was conducted by the Yale Child Study Center staff 5 years after the project ended, when the children were 7 to 8 years old. The 16 intervention families still resident in New England were contacted, and all but one family agreed to participate. Each mother was seen for an interview of about 1 hour's duration by her home visitor or by another familiar project staff member; each child was seen for one testing session using the Revised Wechsler Intelligence Scale for Children by a child psychologist who did not know the families. It was regrettably not feasible to follow up the comparison-group children at this same time, because they were 18 months younger.

To further assess the long-term effects of the Yale Child Welfare Research Program, an independent follow-up was conducted by Trickett and her colleagues (1981) in the same year as the Child Study Center follow-up. This follow-up involved 16 of the 18 intervention children (the two Puerto Rican siblings were seen in Puerto Rico) and two groups of control children. The two new control groups were recruited by sampling peers of the intervention children who attended public schools in both the original impoverished neighborhood of the intervention families ("Highpoint") as well as in the less impoverished neighborhood to which many families had moved by the time of follow-up ("Wilton"). Two contrast groups were chosen in order to control, to some extent, for the upward mobility achieved by the intervention families. The 33 children in Control Group I from Wilton were conceptualized as a "conservative-contrast" group, whereas the 31 children in Control Group II from Highpoint were conceived as a "liberal-contrast" group.

The dependent measures used in the independent follow-up were chosen to correspond with the general child developmental goals of the intervention and to reflect a belief that the most appropriate goal of early childhood interventions is to increase the overall social competence of the child and/or the parents (Zigler & Trickett, 1978). For the children, the Peabody Picture Vocabulary Test (PPVT) was used as a measure of verbal IQ, and the Peabody Individual Achievement Test (PIAT) was used to measure achievement in math, reading recognition and comprehension, spelling, and general information. Three motivational tasks were also given: the Box Maze (Provence, Naylor, & Patterson, 1977) to determine if children prefer to seek out variation when confronted with a repetitive task; the Sticker Game (Zigler, Abelson, & Seitz, 1973) to assess the child's tendency to use his or her internal resources rather than to rely on external cues from the examiner; and the Locus of Control scale (ETS, 1968) to measure the child's feelings of control over what happens to him or her. Shipman's (1972) rating scale was used to assess various aspects of the child's reaction to the testing situation (e.g., attentiveness, response speed, talkativeness). A School Performance Index was also computed for each child, indicating the child's grade level and report card marks in school. Finally, a subset of parents from the two control groups was interviewed with regard to family size, presence or absence of parents in the home, and parental education and employment history.

THE PROGRAM'S EFFECTS

The effects of the Yale Child Welfare Research program were examined at two points in time: at the conclusion of the intervention project and at follow-up 5 years later. For the evaluation at the project's close, the intervention children and their parents were compared to their comparison group counterparts on a variety of measures: the intellectual development and personality characteristics of the children, the demographic characteristics of the families, and the history and current functioning of the parents. There were several components to the follow-up evaluation. The intervention children were compared to two groups of control children. Additionally, changes in the intervention families were considered against the background of general demographic trends among disadvantaged families. Finally, there was an examination of the status and situation of the intervention parents relative to their condition before the project began.

In order to assess the immediate impact of the intervention on intellectual development, the intervention and comparison group children were compared on their performance on the Yale Developmental Schedules at 30 months of age, using analysis of variance on their test scores. The intervention children scored higher than comparison children on Total developmental quotient (105.3 vs. 98.1) and Adaptive developmental quotient (106.2 vs. 101.5), although these differences were not statistically significant. However, there was a highly significant difference between the two groups on their Language developmental quotient (99.4 vs. 85.5). As the scores indicate, the comparison group children were already delayed in their language development relative to their adaptive abilities. An item analysis showed that the intervention children's strength in language function was evident in both vocabulary acquisition and syntactic development. It is important to note that girls performed better than boys in both groups on all three sets of test scores, although the main effects for sex and the Group Sex interactions were not significant. Of particular interest is the extremely poor language performance of the comparison group boys, indicated by a mean score of 79.6. There were no detectable differences between the two groups of children on personality characteristics such as attention span, anxiety, coping skills, or presence of emotional problems, as assessed by the rating procedures used in the study.

When the intervention and comparison families were compared on demographic characteristics at the time the children were

30 months old, there were nonsignificant differences favoring the comparison families in the areas of father's employment, economic self-support, and presence of other adults in the home in addition to the mother. Thus, the significant intervention effect on language should be considered in light of the likely possibility that the matching procedure used resulted in a comparison group of slightly more advantaged inner-city families. It is interesting to note that despite the availability of free, high-quality day care in the intervention project, the same number of intervention and comparison mothers worked, namely eight mothers. This suggests that disadvantaged families, like any other group of individuals, show a diversity in life-style choice which must be considered in planning interventions.

A number of significant differences were found between intervention and comparison mothers in terms of their psychological adjustment and attitudes toward their children. Eight comparison group mothers were rated as having good psychological adjustment and coping skills, as opposed to only three intervention mothers. Once again, this makes the intervention effects on the children more striking. That is, the intervention children appeared to be at least as well adjusted as the comparison children and more advanced in their language, despite coming from families in which both fathers and mothers functioned less adequately and there were fewer other supportive adults available than appeared to be the case in the comparison families. A clue as to the basis of this intervention impact may be the significant finding that intervention mothers expected their children to be more mature than their age in behavior, habit training, or development and also that they were more likely to feel that their children had some problems in development. It is important to emphasize that while a main goal of the project was to help the intervention parents promote their children's development and achievement, another important goal was to help them be realistic in their expectations by increasing their awareness of child development. It may have been an inadvertent or paradoxical effect of the intervention that the parents tended to develop even higher expectations for their children than could realistically be achieved.

Correlational analysis was used to explore the relationships between characteristics of the intervention children and their parents and utilization of the project services. Among the variables most highly related to Total developmental quotient in the intervention children were ratings of the amount of cognitive stimulation and adequacy of play materials provided by their parents. Additionally, it appeared that Language developmental quotient was related in some measure to the enrichment provided by the day-care program as measured by the number of months the child had been enrolled in day care. Total developmental quotient was also significantly related to three areas of project utilization: parental involvement and interest in the child's developmental exam performance and in the day-care program and parental positive relation to the day-care staff. A pattern of significant correlations indicated that the families who were most involved and interested in the day-care program tended to be those in which fathers made an economic contribution, mothers were employed, mothers had been married, and the family was self-supporting. Similarly, families in which mothers had a more skilled level of employment and more education had stronger relations with the day-care staff, had better day-care attendance, used pediatric care more appropriately, and complied more with pediatric recommendations. Another important finding was that use of home visitor recommendations was significantly correlated with mother's psychological adjustment and coping, supporting the experience of clinicians that disturbed or poorly adjusted clients often have difficulty utilizing advice.

The 5-year follow-up of the intervention families indicated that the Yale Child Welfare Research Program had a sustained, long-term impact on the children's intellectual and academic development. The intervention children obtained an average WISC-R Full Scale IQ of 91.8, which is somewhat above the norm for inner-city disadvantaged children (Darlington et al., 1980). Assessment using the Peabody Picture Vocabulary Test at follow-up indicated that intervention girls scored significantly higher than girls in both of the control groups (111.8 vs. 88.1 in Control Group I and 81.2 in Control Group II); intervention boys scored higher than boys in the more disadvantaged control group (99.8 vs. 81.1 for Control Group II boys from Highpoint) and equivalently to boys from the less impoverished area of Wilton (96.1). On the Peabody Individual Achievement Test (PIAT) Total score, intervention children performed significantly better than control children from Highpoint, their neighborhood of origin, and equivalently to the more advantaged children living in Wilton. It is worth noting that girls performed better than boys on the PIAT in all three groups, with the girls in the intervention group and the Wilton group achieving near grade level.

Analysis of the three motivational task measures used in the independent follow-up did not reveal any significant differences between the groups. There was a nonsignificant tendency for the intervention children to be more internal in locus of control than the control children. Tester ratings indicated that the intervention children and the children in Control Group I from Wilton were significantly more relaxed and enthusiastic when tested than the children from Control Group II in Highpoint. While there were no significant sex or group differences in school grade level or report card marks, the intervention chil-

dren had significantly better school attendance than children in both of the control groups. Additionally, they had significantly lower within-group variance in attendance scores than the control children.

Stepwise multiple regression analysis was used to explore predictors of PPVT IQ and PIAT Total score for the intervention children. Results indicated that sex of the child was the best predictor of both dependent measures, accounting for 25% of the variance on the PPVT and 39% on the PIAT. For the PPVT, an index of the degree of poverty in the child's neighborhood at the time of intervention and the rating of mother's interest in the child's developmental exam performance during the intervention were also significant predictors.

The strongest findings documenting intervention impact pertain to the upward mobility achieved by the 17 intervention families. In the area of educational advancement, 10 out of 17 intervention mothers obtained some further education during the project. At the time of follow-up, eight mothers had continued to advance educationally. Changes in economic self-sufficiency were also dramatic: at the end of the project, the number of families on welfare had declined from nine to five, and at follow-up there were only three families still on welfare. Birth rate effects were also impressive, as shown by the fact that at the end of the project there were 14 families with only one child, and at follow-up there were still 10 such families.

Findings from the independent follow-up demonstrate that these qualitative changes in the intervention families were statistically significant as well as impressive. The intervention children had significantly fewer siblings than the children from Control Group II in Highpoint, with the Control Group I children in Wilton having intermediate-sized families. Intervention families were also found to have higher SES status than Highpoint control families. While the mothers in the three groups did not differ in educational status, more mothers were employed in the intervention group than in Control Group II.

Finally, a qualitative assessment was made of general improvement in quality of life for the intervention families. The criterion for improvement was positive change in one or more of the following areas: housing, medical care, socioeconomic status, educational or training status, social life, or engagement in community life. By the end of the project, 12 families had improved using these criteria. At the time of follow-up, 14 families showed clear evidence of tangible improvements in quality of life. Two others were not materially better off but seemed happier in their personal life and more positive in outlook. Only one mother had deteriorated in quality of life and general functioning.

DISCUSSION

The findings from the Yale Child Welfare Research Program constitute additional evidence documenting the effectiveness of early interventions for disadvantaged families. The research described here indicates that a broad-scope, clinically oriented intervention program can be effective in fostering child development for disadvantaged infants, an effect which can be seen as early as 30 months of age in the area of language development. Follow-up data indicated that intervention children scored higher on measures of IQ, school achievement, ease in the testing situation, and school attendance than children from their original neighborhood (Control Group II). The intervention children surpassed comparison children from the less impoverished neighborhood to which many project families had moved at follow-up (Control Group I) on school attendance and girls' IQ.

An important implication of the Yale project is that significant and long-standing effects were obtained by providing family support, medical care, and optional day care, rather than by replacing the parents of all the children for most of the daytime hours, as was the case in many center-based projects (Garber & Heber, 1977; Ramey et al., 1976). This implies not only that early intervention can be lastingly effective in improving the quality of life and educational prospects of disadvantaged children, but also that such intervention can be more flexible and oriented toward individual needs than many successful projects have been. Additionally, the project had a significant effect on early language and school achievement without having a curriculum targeted specifically on cognitive or speech development. Thus, the project results are consistent with Zigler's (1970; Zigler, Abelson, Trickett & Seitz, 1980) view that development of disadvantaged children can be best enhanced by directing intervention toward general social and personality development.

The results of the Yale Child Welfare Research Program are consistent with Bronfenbrenner's (1975) view that a project must significantly impact family patterns and attitudes to have a long-standing effect. In fact, the Yale project was highly similar to Bronfenbrenner's proposal for a mother-child interaction program during infancy, followed by a preschool enrichment program. Furthermore, the project underscores the importance of *early* intervention by showing that a difference between intervention and comparison children in language development could be detected as early as 30 months of age.

The children's gender proved to be a moderator variable on a number of dependent measures examined, a finding consistent with other evidence in the literature (Seitz, Apfel, & Rosenbaum, 1981; Zigler, Abelson, Trickett, & Seitz, 1980). Gender effects were seen most clearly in the regression analyses, where sex was found to be significantly related to both IQ and achievement scores, with the performance of girls being consistently higher than that of boys. Nonsignificant but clear differences in performance favoring girls were evident as early as 30 months of age. Thus, evidence seems to be accumulating that the deleterious consequences of growing up in impoverished circumstances may be greater (or less remediable) for boys than it is for girls (Garcie & Scheinfeld, 1968; Kessler 1966).

The long-term project impact on family patterns appears to be the most striking outcome of the research. The follow-up data revealed impressive changes in the families in terms of improvements in residence, educational advancement, economic self-sufficiency, and quality of life. The low birth rate in the intervention families at follow-up is a further suggestion of a change toward more autonomous control of important life decisions and striving for improved social circumstances. These demographic and socioeconomic effects of the Yale Child Welfare Research Program highlight the importance of using a multiplicity of outcome variables as an index of program effectiveness, such as advocated by Zigler and Trickett (1978).

The Yale Child Welfare Research program involved several intervention components. However, as with many intervention programs, the research design did not make it possible to tease apart the relative contribution of each component to the overall intervention impact. Clearly, the findings underscore the importance of working with parents as well as children. In fact, the data suggest that the intervention's primary effect was its impact on families—on their aspirations, life choices, and patterns of functioning. While the program served an educational role, it did not have a prescriptive curriculum to teach parents how to interact with their children, in the manner of some other projects (Levenstein, 1977; Schaefer & Aaronson, 1977). Rather, the program helped parents

achieve their own goals for themselves and their children. Thus, both its strong family orientation and its supportive rather than prescriptive approach make the Yale project especially attractive as an intervention model in the social and political climate of the 1980s.

The fact that significant project effects have been achieved in such a variety of intervention programs suggests that the crucial mediating factors of many interventions may be interpersonal and motivational. This may explain the relative lack of differential effects related to program specifics which has characterized the research literature. It would seem that a crucial effect of intervention is that the recipient comes to believe that the service providers value him as a person and consider his or her development and achievement as an important goal worth striving for. Perhaps of equal importance, the intervention helps parents to see that their own behaviors are important in influencing the course of their children's educational, social and emotional development.

The results of the Yale project are directly relevant to many of the issues raised by Gray and Wandersman, (1980), particularly a concern with the ecological factors promoting the development of competence in parents and children and influencing their capacity to utilize intervention. That is, an important aspect of the Yale Child Welfare Research Program was that effective utilization of the project services varied considerably. As reported, the data suggested that the families with better economic, educational, and social functioning tended to be more involved in the intervention program and to utilize services more effectively than less well-functioning families. However, examination of the individual intervention families reveals striking exceptions to this general pattern which illuminate the issue of why some were better able than others to utilize the program for helping themselves. Despite some similarities in members of this disadvantaged group, there were large variations in them, as in other groups, with respect to general adaptive abilities, personality characteristics, and capacity for relating, trusting others, and developing as parents. They also varied widely in their childhood experiences, including the strengths in their families of origin and the quality of their nurturance, conditions which influenced their capacities as adults. This psychological factor is central to the dynamic process linking service providers to program recipients. Thus, an important implication of this study is that once good services are made available by qualified personnel who respect their clients and understand human complexity, what will be utilized depends upon the participants, what they bring to the situation, and hence what each can use.

In conclusion, a major implication of this study for social policy is that intervention programs for disadvantaged families should provide a spectrum of quality services, offering options which are responsive to the needs of individual participants. The effectiveness of an intervention program is strongly influenced by the psychological and social strengths and weaknesses of its recipients and in turn by the degree to which the program can accommodate to the needs of the population it serves.

REFERENCES

Bronfenbrenner, U. Is early intervention effective? In M. Guttentag and E. Struening (Eds.), *Handbook of evaluation research*, Vol. 2. Beverly Hills: Sage Publications, 1975.

Darlington, R. B. et al. Preschool programs and later school competence of children from low-income families. *Science*, 1980, *208*, 202–204.

Day, M. C. & Parker, R. K. *The preschool in action: Exploring early childhood education programs* (2d ed.). Boston: Allyn and Bacon, 1977.

Educational Testing Service. *Disadvantaged children and their first school experience: Theoretical considerations and measurement strategies* (Report to Office of Economic Opportunity under Contract #4206 and Grant #C6-82-56). Princeton, N.J.: 1968.

Garber, H. & Heber, F. R. The Milwaukee Project: indications of the effectiveness of early intervention in preventing mental retardation. In P. Mittler (Ed.), *Research to practice in mental retardation*, Vol. 1: *Care and intervention*. Baltimore: University Park Press, 1977.

Garcie, J. E. & Scheinfeld, A. Sex differences in mental and behavioral traits. *Genetic Psychology Monographs* 1968, *77*, 169–299.

Gordon, I. J., Guinagh, B., & Jester, R. E. The Florida Parent Education Infant and Toddler Programs. In M. C. Day and R. K. Parker (Eds.), *The preschool in action: Exploring early childhood education programs*, (2d ed.). Boston: Allyn and Bacon, 1977.

Gray, S. W. & Wandersman, L. P. The methodology of home-based intervention studies: Problems and promising strategies. *Child Development*, 1980, *51*, 993–1009.

Harter, S. & Zigler, E. The assessment of effectance motivation in normal and retarded children. *Developmental Psychology*, 1974, *10*, 169–180.

Karnes, M. B., Zehrback, R. R., & Teska, J. A. The Karnes preschool program: Rationale, curricula offerings and follow-up data. In S. Ryan (Ed.), *A report on longitudinal evaluations of preschool programs*, Vol. 1. Washington, D.C.: DHEW Publication No. (OHD) 74-24, 1974.

Kessler, J. W. *Psychopathology of children.* Englewood Cliffs, N.J.: Prentice-Hall, 1966.

Klaus, R. & Gray, S. *The Early Training Project for disadvantaged children: A report after five years.* Monographs of the Society for Research in Child Development 33 (Whole No. 120), 1968.

Lally, J. R. & Honig, A. The Family Development Research Program. In M. C. Day and R. K. Parker (Eds.), *The preschool in action: Exploring early childhood education programs* (2d ed.), Boston: Allyn and Bacon, 1977.

Levenstein, P. The Mother-Child Home Program. In M. C. Day and R. K. Parker (Eds.), *The preschool in action: Exploring early childhood education programs* (2d ed.). Boston: Allyn and Bacon, 1977.

Provence, S., Naylor, A., & Patterson, J. *The challenge of day care.* New Haven: Yale University Press, 1977.

Ramey, C. T. Remarks as discussant at biennial

meeting at the Society for Research in Child Development. Boston, April 1981.

Ramey, C. T. et al. The Carolina Abecedarian Project: A longitudinal and multidisciplinary approach to the prevention of developmental retardation. In T. Tjossam (Ed.), *Intervention strategies for high-risk infants and young children.* Baltimore: University Park Press, 1976.

Rescorla, L. A., Provence, S., & Naylor, A. The Yale Child Welfare Research Program: Description and results. *American Journal of Orthopsychiatry,* 1981.

Ryan, S. ed. *A report on longitudinal evaluations of preschool programs,* Vol. 1. Washington, D.C.: DHEW Publication No. (OHD) 74-24, 1974.

Schaefer, E. & Aaronson, M. Infant Education Research Project: Implementation and implications of the home-tutoring program. In M. C. Day and R. K. Parker (Eds.), *The preschool in action: Exploring early childhood education programs* (2d ed.). Boston: Allyn and Bacon, 1977.

Schweinhart, L. J. & Weikart, D. P. *Young children grow up: The effects of the Perry Preschool Program on youths through age 15.* Ypsilanti, Mich.: High/Scope Press, 1980.

Seitz, V., Apfel, N., & Efron, C. Long-term effects of early intervention: The New Haven project. In B. Brown (Ed.), *Found: Long-term gains for early intervention.* Boulder: Westview Press, 1978.

Seitz, V., Apfel, N. H., & Rosenbaum, L. K. Projects Head Start and Follow Through: A longitudinal evaluation of adolescents. In M. J.

Begab, H. Garber, and H. C. Haywood (Eds.), *Prevention of retarded development in psychosocially disadvantaged children.* Baltimore: University Park Press, 1981.

Shipman, V. C. *Disadvantaged children and their first school experiences.* ETS-Head Start Longitudinal Study. Princeton, N.J.: Educational Testing Service, 1972.

Trickett, P. et al. A five-year follow-up of participants in the Yale Child Welfare Research Program. *American Journal of Orthopsychiatry,* 1981.

Westinghouse Learning Corporation & Ohio University. *The impact of Head Start experience on children's cognitive and affective development.* Springfield, Va.: U.S. Department of Commerce Clearinghouse, 1969.

Zigler, E. The environmental mystique: training the intellect versus development of the child. *Childhood Education,* 1970,46, 402–412.

Zigler, E., Abelson, W. D. & Seitz, V. Motivational factors in the performance of economically disadvantaged children on the Peabody Picture Vocabulary Test. *Child Development, 1973, 44,* 294–303.

Zigler, E., Abelson, W. D., Trickett, P. K. & Seitz, V. Is an intervention program really necessary to raise disadvantaged children's IQ scores? Unpublished manuscript, New Haven: Yale University, 1980.

Zigler, E. & Trickett, P. K. IQ, social competence, and evaluation of early childhood intervention programs. *American Psychologist, 1978, 33,* 789–798.

19. IQ, SOCIAL COMPETENCE, AND EVALUATION OF EARLY CHILDHOOD INTERVENTION PROGRAMS

Edward Zigler

Penelope K. Trickett

While there are serious shortfalls in our nation's delivery of services to children and their families, our tax dollars are currently being spent to fund some rather sizable and expensive programs. These programs include Title I of the Elementary and Secondary Education Act at a cost of approximately $1.5 billion annually; the Head Start program at a cost of over $400 million annually; day care, which, as limited as it is, still amounts to federal and state expenditures in excess of $2 billion a year.

Both taxpayers and decision makers are legitimately concerned with whether these programs succeed or fail—the slang word in governmental circles regarding this matter is "accountability." The desire for accountability typically takes a quantitative form and spells itself out in two types of evaluation. The first type is called process evaluation. An example of this is the monitoring effort in the Head Start program to guarantee that each Head Start center delivers the services mandated by the program. In this kind of evaluation, simple questions are asked, such as, "Do the children receive medical evaluation or not?" This type of evaluation presents little theoretical or methodological difficulty, which probably explains its popularity as well as the reluctance to do evaluations that go beyond the process type.

A much more demanding and difficult type of evaluation is outcome evaluation, which does not ask whether the services were delivered but attempts instead to assess the verifiable impact of the services. It is under the rubric of outcome evaluation that we encounter the government's beloved concept of "cost-benefit analysis." This elegant phrase, a creation originally of the Department of Defense, is usually translated as "How much bang do you buy per buck?" Since $10 million in the Department of Defense appears to be a rounding error, it is important to note that while a single buck may still be important to each of us, it has little meaning in federal governmental circles. The cost-benefit analysis concept has been adopted with a vengeance by government officials in the social services area, and the legitimate question they are asking is, "What is being accomplished as a result of the expenditure of hundreds of millions of dollars?"

Cost-benefit analysis presents at least two major problems. First, we never appear quite sure what variables to include and

Reprinted, by permission, from *American Psychologist*, September 1978. Copyright 1978 by the American Psychological Association, Inc.

317

what variables to exclude in our cost-benefit equation. For example, should the health and education improvements in a community that are the result of Head Start's being in that community be included? Or should the career development of the Head Start teachers be included in our cost-benefit equation? The second problem with cost-benefit analysis is that even after we decide which outcome measures are legitimately included in the equation, we often find ourselves at a loss in determining the exact dollar amount to attribute to particular outcomes. As has been pointed out before (Zigler, 1973), it is difficult to determine the dollar value assigned to warding off a case of measles or raising the measured IQ by 10 points.

One principle should emerge from this brief discussion: Our ability to perform outcome evaluation is enhanced to the degree that the goals of a program are clear and explicit and to the degree that these goals are held constant through the life of the program. The difficulty in evaluating the Head Start program stems largely from the fact that its goals were originally presented rather vaguely. The same is true of the Women, Infants, and Children (WIC) program in which more than $200 million per year is spent to improve the nutrition of pregnant mothers and very young children. As Solkoff (1977) pointed out, we cannot evaluate this program because no one has enunciated clearly what its circumscribed and measureable goals might be. Please do not mishear us. We are wholeheartedly in favor of pregnant mothers receiving the nutrition that is so crucial for the optimal physical development of the child in utero. Our context here is outcome evaluation. America's children and their families have so many unmet needs that we must champion the value of outcome evaluation so that decision makers can be informed as to whether they should perpetuate current programs or reallocate funds to other programs holding greater promise of achieving desired and explicit goals.

What then is the relationship of the social scientist to the constructor of social policy? Decision makers look to social science and outcome evaluation to provide some badly needed direction in how to spread a finite number of public dollars across what often appears to be an infinite number of possibilities. As Senator Proxmire (1977) has said, "Taxpayers' funds are not unlimited, and I would not be doing my job if I failed either to criticize spurious spending or to try to establish intelligent priorities for the spending of limited money" (p. 4).

THE IQ SOLUTION

In response to the pressure for accountability, without question, the most often utilized outcome measure over the 20-year history of childhood intervention programs has been the IQ score, or more typically, the magnitude of change in the child's IQ score. As a result of this misfortune, it became all too easy to avoid the rigors of goal-sensitive outcome evaluation and conclude that a children's program was a success if it resulted in higher IQs and was a failure if it did not. It is not possible in this article to provide a review of the theoretical and methodological problems raised when one decides to use the IQ score in this way. Suffice it to say that since the turn of the century, American social science has been terribly conflicted about the value of the standard intelligence test (Cronbach, 1971). Some have considered it psychology's greatest achievement; others have viewed it as a technological trap that has resulted in a calcification of our theoretical views and/or has misled us as to the essential nature of human development and the optimization of such development. (See McClelland, 1973, for a particularly telling critique of IQ testing.) Since this article deals with social policy construction, perhaps some special mention should be made of those critics of the IQ who have suggested or stated explicitly that the IQ score is easily employed as a tool of social injustice or political subjugation (e.g., Kamin, 1975; Pastore, 1949). To anticipate our argument somewhat, we do not feel the IQ score is as good as the IQ champions would seem to believe, nor do we feel it as bad as some of its critics have stated.

What then recommends the use of the IQ as a measure in the outcome evaluation of childhood intervention programs? There are several reasons why it became so popular. First, the standard IQ tests are well-developed instruments, the psychometric properties of which are so well documented as to allow the user to avoid difficult measurement problems. Second, the ease of administration adds to the attractiveness of such a measure. This attractiveness is enhanced further if one decides to employ the Peabody Picture Vocabulary Test, the Ammons Full Range Vocabulary Test, or the Otis-Lennon Mental Ability Test, justifying this decision on the basis of the relatively high correlations found between such 10-minute tests and the longer Stanford-Binet Intelligence Scale or the Wechsler Intelligence Scale for Children. Third, no other measure has been found to be related to so many other behaviors of theoretical and practical significance (Kohlberg & Zigler, 1967; Mischel, 1968). Since early childhood intervention programs are popularly regarded as efforts to prepare children for school, the fact that the IQ is the best available predictor of school performance is a particularly compelling rationale for its use as an assessment criterion. Beyond the school issue, if compensatory education programs are directed at correcting deficiencies across a broad array of cognitive abilities, the best single measure of the success of such programs is improvement on a measure re-flecting a broad spectrum of such abilities, namely, an IQ test.

The final reason for the attractiveness of the IQ as an outcome measure has less to do with the nature of this instrument than with the desire of those who mount intervention programs to demonstrate that these programs are beneficial (i.e., cost-effective). It is amazing how attractive as an outcome measure the IQ became, even to vehement critics of the IQ tests, once it became obvious that the most common outcome of just about any intervention effort was a 10-point increase in IQ (even a hastily mounted 8-week summer program). (See Eisenberg & Conners, Note 1.) Indeed, with such leading figures as Hunt (1971) reporting IQ improvements of 50 and 70 points as a result of early intervention, it became increasingly seductive for program people to bet on improvement in the IQ as the bedrock outcome measure. Along with a few other dissidents including the Clarkes (Clarke & Clarke 1967; Clarke & Clarke, 1976), Elkind (1971), Ginsburg (1972), Kamii and Derman (1971), and Kohlberg (1968), the first author has argued for the past 15 years that the level of intellectual functioning is much more constant and the level of cognitive development much less plastic than was suggested by such theoretical godfathers of early childhood intervention as Hunt (1961) in his book *Intelligence and Experience* or Bloom (1964) in *Stability and Change*. Indeed, we and our colleagues, taking seriously the capacity-performance distinction, have now presented considerable empirical evidence that IQ changes resulting from preschool intervention programs reflect motivational changes that influence the children's test performance rather than changes in the actual quality of cognitive functioning (Seitz, Abelson, Levine, & Zigler, 1975; Zigler, Abelson, & Seitz, 1973; Zigler & Butterfield, 1968; Zigler, Abelson, & Trickett, Note 2).

Given the impressive set of assets that

make the IQ test an attractive evaluation measure, why then do we feel that the IQ taken alone is an inadequate outcome measure? As has been stated many times, the quality and nature of formal cognitive processing typically assessed by the IQ test is but one factor in a myriad of factors that determine the quality and character of human functioning. Stated most simply, we believe that one can obtain a very high IQ score and still not behave admirably in the real world that exists beyond the confines of the psychologist's testing room. This fact is brought home to us in striking empirical fashion in the very modest relation that has been found between IQ scores obtained in childhood and everyday performance in life in the postschool period. McClelland (1973) estimates this correlation to be around .20.

The IQ score reaches its maximum efficiency as a predictor of everyday performance when it is employed to predict school performance. McClelland notes that it is not surprising to discover a correlation of approximately .70 here, inasmuch as good test performance and good school performance require superiority in playing the same type of pointless and/or irrelevant "little games." As will be discussed shortly, we disagree with McClelland on the issue of what exactly mediates the correlation found between IQ scores and school performance. In a science that appears much more concerned with significance levels than in how much of the variance in a behavior can be accounted for by a particular measure, we have chosen to allow ourselves to be dazzled by a correlation of .70. What does not receive sufficient attention is the fact that this correlation indicates that only *half* of the variance in school performance is accounted for by children's IQ scores. What then is influencing the other half of the variance? Clearly, it must include some collection of personal attributes or characteristics not very well assessed by our standard IQ test.

Given our usual contact with empiri-cally discovered correlations in the .30 to .50 range, we have become so impressed with a .70 correlation that we have glorified the IQ score and given it a primacy that it does not deserve. In the process we have even managed to bastardize the language of psychology and give names to phenomena that are paradoxical. Think for a minute, of those often-used labels *underachiever* and *overachiever*. (See, e.g., the book on this topic by Thorndike, 1963). In operational measurement terms, these labels mean no more than the disparity between the IQ score and school achievement, with the IQ score being utilized as the ultimate benchmark against which to assess school achievement. In everyday school practice, the specific operations utilized to define the constructs are conveniently forgotten, and unfortunate labels take their place. Thus, if a middle-class child does not do very well in school, both the school and the family appear more comfortable if we call the child an underachiever. If an economically disadvantaged child does poorly in school, we are tempted to call him or her stupid, using the school performance itself as the ultimate gauge of a child's intellectual level. This situation becomes even more ridiculous when we use the nonsensical label of overachiever. Our respect for the language is too great for us to be very tolerant of a label that essentially asserts that some individuals achieve more than they are capable of achieving. Does psychology really wish to argue that human capacity is reflected better in the IQ test than it is in the everyday school performance of a child? Only by adopting such a questionable assumption can we continue to employ the label of overachiever.

The IQ test appears to be most free of criticism when it is viewed as a measure of a collection of processes that, taken as a totality, constitutes an indicator of the individual's level of formal cognitive ability. But there are many who find this measure inadequate even as a measure of formal cognition. We must be aware that there are two distinctly different approaches to the development and assessment of human intelligence. One is the psychometric approach, with the standard intelligence test forming its foundation. The second is the developmental approach, championed most importantly by Piaget. The relation of these two approaches has been discussed by Elkind (1971). We now have some interesting efforts to synthesize the two approaches in the construction of instruments that incorporate both the sophisticated measurement techniques of the psychometric approach with the great sensitivity to sequential change in the nature of human information processing emphasized in the developmental approach (Laurendeau & Pinard, 1962; Tuddenham, 1971; Uzgiris & Hunt, 1975). At a practical level, perhaps we do not need to concern ourselves too much with the differences in the assessment of formal features of cognition generated by these two approaches. When both types of assessment are made, the correlation between the two is typically around .70. Both types of measurement are obviously tapping some of the same formal cognitive processes. However, consistent with our earlier argument, let us recognize that a correlation of .70 is far from representing an identity. We see little value in arguing now which of the two measures constitutes the most accurate assessment of the child's intelligence. The only point that we would like to make here as a criticism of the IQ test is that even as a measure of formal cognition, the IQ test raises questions, and the use of the scores poses still-unresolved problems.

WHAT DOES THE IQ TEST REALLY MEASURE?

The IQ test should not be viewed as a pure measure of formal cognition, but rather as a polyglot sample of behavior that is influenced by three empirically related but conceptually distinct collections of variables. First, it does measure a collection of formal cognitive processes such as abstracting ability, reasoning, speed of visual information processing, and all those other formal cognitive processes that appear and reappear with regularity in factor-analytic studies of human intelligence-test performance. Second, in keeping with the well-known process-content distinction, the standard intelligence test is also an *achievement* test highly influenced by the child's particular experiences, which determine whether particular knowledge is held by the child, without which he or she cannot pass the item in question. Since features of formal cognition and magnitude of achievement are themselves related, it might be worthwhile to draw a clear distinction between formal cognition and achievement. If we ask children what a "gown" is, and they reply that they do not know, we might assume that there is something inadequate about their memory storage and/or retrieval systems, which are aspects of their formal cognitive systems. On the other hand, if in the children's experience they never encountered the word *gown*, they will fail the item even though their storage and retrieval systems are perfectly adequate.

Finally, intelligence test performance is greatly influenced by a variety of motivational and/or personality variables that have little to do with either formal cognition or achievement variables. Again, perhaps a couple of simple but compelling examples might be helpful. The senior author once asked a child, "What is an orange?" The child replied that he did not know and then went on to do everything in his power to maximize the social interaction. This was a child residing in an institution, and what was conveyed was that, given the child's need system and motivation, he was much more interested in obtaining a warm human interaction than he was in playing some game of little interest to him concerning oranges.

We also often encounter a quite different phenomenon, especially among the economically disadvantaged children whose performance is assessed in our early childhood intervention programs. We are thinking here of the "I don't know" phenomenon, which reflects the lack of neither ability nor knowledge but rather the child's strong desire to terminate and/or minimize the interaction with the examiner. Why exactly do children insist on engaging in what our value system tells us to be such self-defeating behavior? Do they dislike the adult examiner or do they dislike the testing situation? Our best hunch is that they are fearful of both and therefore behave in an adaptive manner having as its goal the termination of an unpleasant experience. Clearly, given the demands of our society, children who have adopted the "I don't know" strategy are not very likely to utilize their cognitive systems optimally or, if they keep up their behavior, to obtain those rewards (e.g., high grades in school, high salaries, and attractive jobs after school) that society dispenses for behaving in the manner it prefers.

It is this tripartite conception of IQ test performance that explains why IQ test performance is a successful predictor of such a wide variety of behaviors. If one examines closely many of the criterion behaviors for which we would like the IQ to be a predictor, one discovers that they are themselves complex measures clearly influenced by the same set of factors that influence the IQ score. Does anyone seriously question that the child with superior formal cognitive abilities, rich experience in the middle-class world, and a high motivation to do well in school will display better school performance than the child who may have had more restricted or at least less middle-class-relevant experiences and who may also view the school experi-

ence as not only taking place in an alien and/or hostile environment but also involving a variety of activities that have little relevance? It is safe to conclude that the IQ test will always be a predictor of other variables, providing these other variables are influenced by the three factors that influence the IQ test. Thus, if conceptualized properly, the IQ can continue to be employed with profit in evaluations of early childhood intervention programs.

THE SOCIAL COMPETENCE ALTERNATIVE

We propose, as one of us has done several times before (Zigler, 1970, 1973), that social competence, rather than the IQ, should be employed as the major measure of the success of intervention programs such as Head Start. This proposal forces us to be explicit about the relation between IQ and social competence. The foregoing analysis should make it clear that we do not believe that the IQ and social competence are one and the same. However, we must also reject the inference that could be drawn from McClelland's (1973) paper—that the IQ and competence are very minimally related. The IQ and social competence are both influenced by some of the same variables, and thus, if approached properly, the IQ can act as a weak and relatively imperfect measure of social competence.

Some progress in the task of determining the relation of IQ and social competence has been provided by Schaefer (1975), who proposed a hierarchical relation between these two constructs. He developed a model in which *adaptation* is viewed as an even broader measure and is therefore treated as a third-order construct. While we are not in agreement with all aspects of Schaefer's model, this proposal of a hierarchical relation between intelligence and social competence does make sense and also provides a useful framework for the even more arduous task of rigorously defining social competence per se.

Efforts to arrive at such a definition are indeed difficult. This is so even though the use of the term in discussion with social scientists, public officials, or other lay-persons results in a general sense in both speakers and listeners that something meaningful is being transmitted. But what exactly is it? The construct seems to evaporate upon the application of the heat of even minimal debate. Social competence appears to be one of those constructs that is definable only in terms of other constructs whose own definitions are vague. Social competence theorists thus quickly find themselves adrift on a sea of words.

The senior author is not a newcomer to that sizable band of theorists who utilize social competence in their explanatory edifices. He has utilized the social competence construct in four distinctly different bodies of work during the last 15 years. These areas include (1) the previously mentioned work promoting the use of social competence as the only legitimate goal of programs in the compensatory education field (Zigler, 1970, 1973); (2) the relation between social competence and a variety of phenomena of theoretical and practical interest in the area of psychopathology (e.g., Phillips, Broverman, & Zigler, 1966; Zigler & Phillips, 1961); (3) the controversy in the mental retardation area over whether social competence should be included in our basic definition of mental retardation (Garfield & Wittson, 1960a, 1960b; Mercer, 1975; Zigler, 1967); and (4) the developmental etiology of effectance or mastery motivation derived from White's (1959) work (e.g., Harter, 1978; Harter & Zigler, 1974). Unfortunately, the use of the construct of social competence across these four bodies of work has not been consistent. It is with the knowledge that

has accrued from all these efforts, and with a recognition of their inconsistencies, that we say that we know of no rigorous or even mildly satisfying definition of the construct or term *social competence*. The intelligence variable, in contrast, presents no definitional dilemma to the extent that we are satisfied with the definition that intelligence is nothing more nor less than what standard intelligence tests measure.

We have witnessed no very wide adoption of the construct of social competence as the primary goal of early intervention programs for the very simple reason that there is little consensus as to exactly what measures should be employed to define social competence. It was with an eye to solving this problem that the Office of Child Development (OCD) funded a conference at the Educational Testing Service in which a sizable group of workers was brought together and given the task of constructing a definition of social competence that could be used by those agencies that desired to use social competence in their outcome evaluations. A report of this conference as well as a good analysis of the complexities involved in defining social competence was presented by Anderson and Messick (1974). While the group's analysis was sound, little progress was made in supplying OCD or the field with a definition of social competence or the methodology to assess it. The group delivered no less than 29 indicators of social competence, any one of which would require much greater refinement and solution of numerous difficulties. Even if all the measurement problems in this list were resolved, the sheer time needed to evaluate any child on the 29 items would make the task impossible. Finally, the list was so filled with our usual psychological jargon as to be for the most part incomprehensible to the taxpayer who foots the bill for our massive intervention programs and to policymakers who must continually make decisions concerning further funding allocations to these programs.

IS THERE A SOLUTION?

Hundreds of millions of dollars will continue to be spent on children's programs, and outcome evaluations will continue to be made. These evaluations will either be done badly or well. We are convinced that good social science and its offspring, good output evaluation, can play a useful and beneficial role in the construction of sound social policy. By the same token, bad social science and bad evaluation can undermine the construction of sound social policy and lead to serious detrimental effects on our citizenry. We refer you to the history of the Westinghouse evaluation (Westinghouse Learning Corporation/ Ohio University, Note 3) for a specific instance in which a poor evaluation came very close to causing our nation to jettison the most popular and highly regarded program ever mounted for children in America. However, the hour grows late, and unless the social sciences develop a practical and coherent measure of social competence, social competence will never replace the IQ as our primary measure of the success of intervention programs.

Decision makers now understand the need for a well-developed measure of social competence. The Administration of Children, Youth, and Family Services has contracted with Mediax Association, Inc., to develop a carefully defined and viable measure of social competence. The policy need for this measure is so pressing that we wish to offer some immediate definitions and suggestions.

We thus propose an arbitrary definition for social competence. We are not particularly concerned by our arbitrariness inasmuch as all definitions are arbitrary. In regard to definitions, the issue is not whether a definition is true or untrue but rather whether it is useful or not (Farber, 1975).

Since so many variables could be included in the definition, let us begin the task by asking the question of whether there are any conceptual schemas that would direct us to the particular variables that would finally be part of our definition. Building on the work of Kohlberg and Mayer (1972) and White (1959), Anderson and Messick (1974) provide us with a four-fold approach to the problem of defining social competence. We believe this four-fold approach can be reduced to a two-fold approach in which measures of social competence should reflect one of two major criteria. The first is that social competence must reflect the success of the human being in meeting societal expectancies. Second, these measures of social competence should reflect something about the self-actualization or personal development of the human being.

It is our early hunch that for the most part the social competence indexes meeting either of these criteria will prove to be positively related to each other. There is some early evidence in support of this hunch in Anastasiow's (Note 4) argument that children who display high exploration behavior (a personal development attribute) will do better in school achievement (a social expectancy variable) than children low in exploration behavior. However, as is usually the case, there is also evidence that such a straightforward and simple positive relation between these two facets of social competence does not exist. Certain personal development attributes may clash with meeting societal expectancies. Lytton (1972), for example, reviewed several studies indicating that teachers rate highly creative students as less likeable than those who are less creative. Possibly, being viewed as less likeable could affect a student's achievement. It also appears that an interactional relation between setting and personal development attributes can exist. For example, Kelly (1967) found that in high schools with low student turnover rates, students who were high explorers were more apt to be labeled as deviant by school personnel than were similarly high-exploring students at schools with high student turnover rates. Thus, the relation between these two aspects of social competence appears to be an open question.

What then are our candidates for inclusion in a social competence index? First, there should be measures of physical health and well-being, including appropriate weight for age, inoculation history, etc. (See North, 1979, for a review of physical health measures that have been used in the assessment of early childhood intervention programs.) We list physical health measures first since many thinkers in the social competence area have been so reluctant to view the physical health of the child as a major determinant of the child's social competence. Second, a social competence index should include a measure of formal cognitive ability. Here we would settle for either a standard IQ test or a Piagetian measure of level of cognitive functioning. Third, there should be an achievement measure. There are many good candidates for inclusion such as the Caldwell Preschool Inventory, the Peabody Individual Achievement Tests, and a variety of standard school-age achievement tests. Finally, the fourth component of social competence should be the measurement of motivational and emotional variables.

Obviously, there are numerous measures of motivational and emotional variables that could be included. We are aware of the measurement problems involved in assessing motivational and emotional attributes, but we do not view these problems as insurmountable. Relying on our own evaluation efforts, we suggest that emotional/motivational measures be selected from the following collection: (1) measures of effectance motivation, including indica-

tors of preference for challenging tasks, curiosity, variation seeking, and mastery motivation (Balla, Butterfield, & Zigler, 1974; Harter, 1978; Harter & Zigler, 1974); (2) outerdirectedness and degree of imitation in problem solving (Balla & Zigler, 1968; Turnure & Zigler, 1964; Zigler et al., Note 2); (3) positive responsiveness to social reinforcement (Robertson, 1978; Zigler, 1961; Zigler & Balla, 1972); (4) locus of control measured for both the children in the program and their parents (Coleman, Campbell, Hobson, McPortland, & Mood, 1966; Stipek, 1977); (5) expectancy of success (Gruen & Zigler, 1968; Ollendick, Balla, & Zigler, 1971); (6) wariness of adults (Weaver, Balla, & Zigler, 1971; Zigler et al., Note 2); (7) verbal attention-seeking behavior (Kohlberg & Zigler, 1967; Robertson, 1978); (8) aspects of self-image, including real image and ideal image (Katz & Zigler, 1967; Katz, Zigler, & Zalk, 1975; DeMott, Note 5); (9) measures of learned helplessness (Achenbach & Weisz, 1975; Weisz, 1975); (10) attitude toward school (Stipek, 1977); and (11) creativity (Yando, Seitz, & Zigler, Note 6).

Finally, we must insist that adequate social competence assessment can come about only if (1) we commit ourselves to assessing the long-term effects of our intervention programs, and (2) we commit ourselves not only to fine-grained analyses of developmental features, but also, to molar measures that are fully comprehensible and of great interest to both taxpayers and Washington decision makers. (For a particularly striking instance of such molar measures being employed in outcome evaluation, see Lazar, Hubbell, Murray, Rosche, & Royce, Note 7.) The molar behaviors we have in mind are related to our social expectancy criteria and include the following; (1) incidence of juvenile delinquency; (2) incidence of teenage pregnancy; (3) incidence of child abuse, either as a victim or a perpetrator; (4) being in school rather than out; (5) being in the appropriate grade for age; (6) being in a regular classroom rather than a special education classroom; and (7) being self-supporting rather than on welfare.

A FINAL WORD OF CAUTION

In light of the Anderson and Messick (1974) analysis, we see that an immediate problem with this early and tentative competence index is that it is hopelessly infused with values that are far from universal. We get a very clear indication of how the value issue undoes social competence theorists when we look at such premorbid social competence scales as those constructed by Phillips (1953) and Wittman (1941). In these scales, an individual gets a high score (i.e., is considered socially competent) if he engages in heterosexual behavior. Does this mean that a homosexual is a person of low social competence? We rather doubt it. Perhaps the value problem is not as great as we think and these scales can be rescued from their value-laden bias by drawing the distinction, in this instance, not between homosexual and heterosexual contact, but rather between the individual who has some other-person orientation versus the individual who is a loner. On the other hand, society is not value free, and useful measures of social competence will reflect some of the deeply ingrained values in which society invests its resources. Examples of such values include our commitment to education and our opposition to child abuse.

Despite the difficulties raised by the value issue, we believe it is possible to develop a useful scale of social competence quickly. Some of the measures we have suggested are already being employed in outcome evaluation of large-scale programs. For example, we are currently using many of these measures in a follow-up study of children who took part in an intensive infant intervention program.

We hope that social scientists will be skeptical and cautious about developing a useful social competence index, but not so skeptical and so cautious that they hand the field over to bureaucrats in Washington and in our statehouses. Social competence constructs will be employed in outcome evaluation and, given the critical importance of these evaluations to the future of early childhood intervention programs, they merit the attention of trained and sensitive social scientists.

REFERENCE NOTES

1. Eisenberg, L. & Conners, C. K. *The effect of Head Start on developmental process.* Paper presented at the 1966 Joseph P. Kennedy, Jr., Foundation Scientific Symposium on Mental Retardation, Boston, April 11, 1966.
2. Zigler, E., Abelson, W. D., & Trickett, P. K. *Is an intervention program necessary in order to improve economically-disadvantaged children's IQ scores?* Unpublished manuscript, Yale University, 1978.
3. Westinghouse Learning Corporation/Ohio University. *The impact of Head Start: An evaluation of the effects of Head Start on children's cognitive and affective development.* Springfield, Va.: Clearinghouse for Federal Scientific and Technical Information, U.S. Department of Commerce, June 12, 1969.
4. Anastasiow, N. J. Developmental parameters of knowledge transmission. In M. Scott & S. Grimmett (Eds.), *Current issues in child development.* Washington, D.C.: National Association for the Education of Young Children, 1977.
5. DeMott, D. P. *Children's self-concept disparity: Effects of age, race, social class and gender.* Unpublished master's thesis, Yale University, 1978.
6. Yando, R. M., Seitz, V., & Zigler, E. *Intellectual and motivational characteristics of children in differing social class and ethnic groups.* Unpublished manuscript, Yale University, 1978.
7. Lazar, I., Hubbell, V., Murray, H., Rosche, M. M., & Royce, J. *The persistence of preschool effects: A longterm follow-up of fourteen infant and preschool experiments* (Final report of the Consortium on Developmental Continuity, Education Commission of the States, Grant

18-76-07843). Washington, D.C.: U.S. Department of Health, Education, and Welfare, September 1977.

REFERENCES

Achenbach, T. & Weisz, J. R. A longitudinal study of relations between outer-directedness and IQ changes in preschoolers, *Child Development*, 1975, *46*, 650–657.

Anderson, S. & Messick, S. Social competency in young children. *Developmental Psychology*, 1974, *10*, 282–293.

Balla, D., Butterfield, E. C., & Zigler, E. Effects of institutionalization on retarded children. *American Journal of Mental Deficiency*, 1974, *78*, 530–549.

Balla, D. & Zigler, E. Cue-learning and problem learning strategies in normal and retarded children. *Child Development*, 1968, *3*, 827–848.

Bloom, B. *Stability and change in human characteristics*. New York: Wiley, 1964.

Clarke, A. D. B. & Clarke, A. M. Prospects for prevention and amelioration of mental retardation: A guest editorial. *American Journal of Mental Deficiency*, 1977, *81*, 523–533.

Clarke, A. M. & Clarke, A. D. B. (Eds.). *Early experience: Myth and evidence*. London: Open Books, 1976.

Coleman, J., Campbell, E., Hobson, C., McPortland, J., & Mood, A. *Equality of educational opportunity*. Washington, D.C.: U.S. Department of Health, Education and Welfare, 1966.

Cronbach, L. I. Five decades of public controversy over mental testing. *American Psychologist*, 1971, *30*, 1–14.

Elkind, D. Two approaches to intelligence: Piagetian and psychometric. In D. R. Green, M. P. Ford, & G. B. Flamer (Eds.), *Measurement and Piaget*. New York: McGraw-Hill, 1971.

Farber, I. E. Sane and insane: Constructions and misconstructions. *Journal of Abnormal Psychology*, 1975, *84*, 589–620.

Garfield, S. L. & Wittson, C. L. Comments on Dr. Cantor's remarks. *American Journal of Mental Deficiency*, 1960, *64*, 957–959. (a)

Garfield, S. L. & Wittson, C. L. Some reactions to the revised "Manual on Terminology and Classification in Mental Retardation," *American Journal of Mental Deficiency*, 1960, *64*, 951–953. (b)

Ginsburg, H. *The myth of the deprived child: Poor children's intellect and education*. Englewood Cliffs, N.J.: Prentice-Hall, 1972.

Gruen, G., & Zigler, E. Expectancy of success and the probability learning of middle-class, lower-class and retarded children. *Journal of Abnormal Psychology*, 1968, *73*, 343–352.

Harter, S. Effectance motivation reconsidered: Toward a developmental model. *Human Development*, 1978, *21*, 34–64.

Harter, S. & Zigler, E. The assessment of effectance motivation in normal and retarded children. *Developmental Psychology*, 1974, *10*, 169–180.

Hunt, J. McV. *Intelligence and experience*. New York: Ronald Press, 1961.

Hunt, J. McV. Parent and child centers: Their basis in the behavioral and educational sciences. *American Journal of Orthopsychiatry*, 1971, *41*, 13–38.

Kamii, C. & Derman, L. Comments on Englemann's paper. The Englemann approach to teaching logical thinking: Findings from the administration of some Piagetian tasks. In D. R. Green, M. P. Ford, & G. B. Flamer (Eds.), *Measurement and Piaget*. New York: McGraw-Hill, 1971.

Kamin, L. G. *The science and politics of IQ*. New York: Halsted Press, 1975.

Katz, P. & Zigler, E. Self-image disparity: A developmental approach. *Journal of Personality and Social Psychology*, 1967, *5*, 186–195.

Katz, P., Zigler, E., & Zalk, S. Children's self-image disparity: The effects of age, maladjustment, and action-thought orientation. *Developmental Psychology*, 1975, *11*, 546–550.

Kelly, J. G. Naturalistic observations and theory confirmation: An example. *Human Development*, 1967, *10*, 212–222.

Kohlberg, L. Early education: A cognitive-developmental view. *Child Development*, 1968, *39*, 1013–1062.

Kohlberg, L. & Mayer, R. Development as the aim of education. *Harvard Educational Review*, 1972, *42*, 449–496.

Kohlberg, L. & Zigler, E. The impact of cognitive maturity on the development of sex-role attitudes in the years four to eight. *Genetic Psychology Monographs*, 1967, *75*, 89–165.

Laurendeau, M. & Pinard, A. *Causal thinking in the child*. New York: International Universities Press, 1962.

Lytton, H. *Creativity and education*. New York: Schocken Books, 1972.

McClelland, D. C. Testing for competence rather than for "intelligence." *American Psychologist*, 1973, *28*, 1–14.

Mercer, J. Psychological assessment and the rights of children. In N. Hobbs (Ed.), *Issues in the classification of children*, Vol. 1. San Francisco: Jossey-Bass, 1975.

Mischel, W. *Personality and assessment*. New York: Wiley, 1968.

North, F. Health services in Project Head Start. In E. Zigler & J. Valentine (Eds.), *Project Head Start: A legacy of the war on poverty*. New York: Free Press, 1979.

Ollendick, T., Balla, D., & Zigler, E. Expectancy of success and the probability learning of retarded children. *Journal of Abnormal Psychology*, 1971, *77*, 275–281.

Pastore, N. *The nature-nurture controversy*. New York: King's Crown Press, 1949.

Phillips, L. Case history data and prognosis in schizophrenia. *Journal of Nervous and Mental Disease*, 1953, *117*, 515–525.

Phillips, L., Broverman, I. K., & Zigler, E. Social competence and psychiatric diagnosis. *Journal of Abnormal Psychology*, 1966, *71*, 209–214.

Proxmire, W. Funding research. *Newsweek*, June 13, 1977, pp. 4; 7.

Robertson, A. B. *Group day care and children's social-motivational development*. Unpublished doctoral dissertation, Yale University, 1978.

Schaefer, E. S. Factors that impede the process of socialization. In M. J. Begab & S. A. Richardson (Eds.), *The mentally retarded and society: A social science perspective*. Baltimore, Md.: University Parks Press, 1975.

Seitz, V., Abelson, W. D., Levine, E., & Zigler, E. Effects of place of testing on the Peabody Picture Vocabulary Test scores of disadvantaged Head Start and non-Head Start children. *Child Development*, 1975, *46*, 481–486.

Solkoff, J. Strictly from hunger. *New Republic*, June 11, 1977, pp. 13–15.

Stipek, D. J. *Changes during first grade in children's social-motivational development*. Unpublished doctoral dissertation, Yale University, 1977.

Thorndike, R. L. *The concepts of over- and underachievement*. New York: Columbia University Teachers College, 1963.

Tuddenham, R. D. Theoretical regularities and individual idiosyncracies. In D. R. Green,

M. P. Ford, & G. B. Flamer (Eds.), *Measurement and Piaget*. New York: McGraw-Hill, 1971.

Turnure, J. E. & Zigler, E. Outer-directedness in the problem-solving of normal and retarded children. *Journal of Abnormal Social Psychology*, 1964, *69*, 427–436.

Uzgiris, I. D. & Hunt, J. McV. *Assessment in infancy*. Urbana: University of Illinois Press, 1975.

Weaver, S. J., Balla, D., & Zigler, E. Social approach and avoidance tendencies of institutionalized and non-institutionalized retarded and normal children. *Journal of Experimental Research in Personality*, 1971, *5*, 98–110.

Weisz, J. R. *A developmental analysis of relations among hypothesis behavior, helplessness and IQ*. Unpublished doctoral dissertation, Yale University, 1975.

White, R. C. Motivation reconsidered: The concept of competence. *Psychological Review*, 1959, *66*, 297–333.

Wittman, M. P. A scale for measuring prognosis in schizophrenic patients. *Elgin State Hospital Papers*, 1941, *4*, 20–33.

Zigler, E. Social deprivation and rigidity in the performance of feebleminded children. *Journal of Abnormal Psychology*, 1961, *62*, 412–421.

Zigler, E. Mental retardation. *Science*, 1967, *157*, 578–579.

Zigler, E. The environmental mystique: Training the intellect versus development of the child. *Childhood Education*, 1970, *46*, 402–412.

Zigler, E. Project Head Start: Success or failure? *Learning*, 1973, *1*, 43–47.

Zigler, E., Abelson, W., & Seitz, V. Motivational factors in the performance of economically disadvantaged children on the Peabody Picture Vocabulary Test. *Child Development*, 1973, *44*, 294–303.

Zigler, E. & Balla, D. Developmental course of responsiveness to social reinforcement in normal children and institutionalized retarded children. *Developmental Psychology*, 1972, *6*, 66–73.

Zigler, E. & Butterfield, E. C. Motivational aspects of changes in IQ test performance of culturally deprived nursery school children. *Child Development*, 1968, *39*, 1–14.

Zigler, E. & Phillips, L. Social competence and outcome in psychiatric disorder. *Journal of Abnormal and Social Psychology*, 1961, *63*, 264–271.

20. A VISION OF CHILD CARE IN THE 1980s

Edward Zigler

Matia Finn

Webster's dictionary defines *care* as "close attention or careful heed; a liking or regard, to take charge of; look after; attend to; provide for; to feel concern about or interest in; to protect against trouble, want, etc." What is the status of *child care* in America? As a nation, do we look after, attend to, provide for our children? Do we feel concern and interest in what is happening to children? We do not. The state of children in this country is poor. What is more, all too many of us are not aware of the problems facing children in America.

In the area of health care, for example, our nation fails its children even before they are born. The United States is the richest and most technologically advanced country in the world. Yet, among 42 nations keeping comparable statistics, it ranks 12th in the incidence of infant mortality (*U.N. Demographic Yearbook*, 1977) and 13th in the incidence of deaths of mothers in childbirth (*U.N. Demographic Yearbook*, 1975). Research has shown that where proper nutrition and prenatal care are provided, the incidence of prematurity and related deaths and handicaps drops dramatically. However, over 30% of American women do not receive such care during the first trimester of pregnancy (Advisory Committee on Child Development, 1976), thus condemning many infants still in the uterus to death at birth or to a variety of handicaps which no amount of intervention can fully remediate.

Teenage pregnancy in this country has reached epidemic proportions. The phenomenon of children having children is associated with complications during pregnancy and delivery that are the result of biological and/or societal factors (Mednick, Baker, & Sutton-Smith, 1979). The risks associatd with teenage pregnancy do not end with the birth of the child. Over 93% of girls choose to keep their babies (Zelnick & Kantner, 1978). These infants often face a life of neglect and poverty because their mothers lack the emotional and financial capabilities to raise a child.

America's health care record does not improve much for older children. An estimated two-thirds of America's children receive inadequate medical care. About 25% of the children do not receive medical examinations over the course of the year (Advisory Committee on Child Development, 1976). In 1978, 82.7% of all children under five and 29.4% of all children under 17 have never visited a dentist over their entire childhood (*National Health Interview*

This article was adapted from Zigler, E., and M. Finn, "A Vision of Child Care in the 1980's," in L. A. Bond and J. M. Joffee (Eds.), *Facilitating Infant and Early Child Development*. Hanover, N.H.: University Press of New England, 1981, and is reprinted by permission. Copyright (1981) by the Vermont Conference on the Primary Prevention of Psychopathology.

Survey, 1978). And, despite our ability to eliminate infectious diseases through immunizations, 20–25% of all children between the ages of 1 and 4 have not been immunized against crippling, sometimes fatal childhood diseases such as diphtheria, pertusis, tetanus, measles and polio (*U.S. Immunization Survey*, 1980).

Our nation's neglect of its children is further evidenced by deaths and injuries inflicted on children. Childhood accidents constitute the single major cause of death for children between the ages of 9 and 15 years. Among Western nations, America ranks second in the rate of childhood deaths due to accidents and is ranked first in childhood deaths caused by firearms and poisonings (Furrow, Greundel, & Zigler, 1979).

Child abuse constitutes another national disgrace. The number of these cases is estimated conservatively at 1 million a year. Two thousand children die from abuse annually (Martinez, 1977). While there have been attempts, both at the federal and state levels, to combat child abuse, the U.S. Supreme Court in 1977 ruled the constitutionality of corporal punishment in our schools (Ingraham *vs.* Wright, 1977). By this decision, the Court gave not only legal sanction to the use of physical punishment in the classroom but also implicit social sanction to the use of force as a method of disciplining children at home. The Court made this decision despite our knowledge that over one-half of the incidents of child abuse develop out of disciplinary actions by parents.

As a nation, we allow numerous assaults on children's mental health. Despite the emotional scars that result from moving children from home to home, some 350,000 children remain adrift in America's foster care system. These children, who are supposedly placed in foster care *temporarily*, spend an average of nearly 5 years in different homes (Keniston, 1977). Public policies actually provide incentives for our present foster care system. For example, the federal government spends $250 million a year to keep children in foster care, yet very little money, if any, is available for support services such as homemaker, crisis intervention, or day care that would keep the family together and prevent the need for placement.

Day care is another source of problems. Day-care facilities are in critically short supply, and the quality of some day-care centers leaves much to be desired (Keyserling, 1972). However, federal and state governments fail to acknowledge the need for increased day-care services (Martinez, 1977) despite the fact that 2 million children between the ages of 7 and 12 years come home each day to an empty house (*Congressional Record*, 1979). Reports of children encountering burglars or being victimized are not uncommon. In a recent study in Detroit, an investigator discovered that one-sixth of the fires in that city involved an unattended child (Smock, 1977).

Efforts to guarantee quality child care in centers across the country and to enforce uniform standards have been going on for over a decade (Cohen & Zigler, 1977; Zigler & Heller, 1980). After a lengthy moratorium on the implementation of day-care regulations and in the face of considerable opposition, Health and Human Services Secretary Patricia Roberts Harris had the courage to approve the Federal Interagency Day Care Requirements (FIDCR) (*Federal Register*, March 19, 1980). These requirements, representing the absolute minumum standards, impose nothing on children except nutritious meals, protection from fires, and the right to be cared for by competent adults. Yet several weeks before the requirements were to take effect, their implementation was deferred for yet another year, this time due to so-called budgetary restraints (Zigler, 1980; Zigler & Goodman, 1980).

Finally, our children's social and emotional development presents cause for concern. Children spend less and less time with their parents or other adults. In contrast to children in the 1950s, who encountered several adults over the course of a day and who were involved in community activities, many children during the 1970s reported spending most of their time when not in school alone or with other children, mainly watching television, eating snacks, or fooling around (Boocock, 1977). Researchers found that children today have a greater dependency on their peers than they did a decade ago (Condry & Siman, 1974). They note also that attachment to age mates is more influenced by a lack of attention and concern at home than by any positive attraction of the peer group (Condry & Siman, 1976). The rising rate of juvenile crime (Advisory Committee on Child Development, 1976) and the increase in the incidence of childhood depression (Kashani & Simonds, 1979) and suicide (*Mortality Advance Report*, 1980) are but several possible consequences of the changing way children are growing up today.

THE FUTURE OF CHILD CARE

During the past decade, in particular during the 1979 International Year of the Child, we were forced to educate each other on these and other problems facing children. It is obvious that the time for action has come. But how are we to reverse the trend in this nation of neglect of children and disinterest in their welfare? We believe that the solution lies not in federal directives and massive social changes, but rather, in small changes within the social institutions that are most critical in determining the quality of life of children in this country. These institutions, in order of their importance in influencing the lives of children, are: the family, the school, and child care outside the home. We order our

recommendations for the future of child care around these institutions.

The Family
The family will remain the first and foremost institution in determining what is going to happen to children. It is imperative, however, that we acknowledge the multiple forms that now constitute a family. Whereas our national policies and rhetoric are directed to the traditional nuclear family in which the husband is the breadwinner, the mother the housewife, and two or more children are living at home, not all Americans live in this kind of family arrangement (U.S. Bureau of the Census, 1979). Other arrangements include both parents who are wage earners, with one or more children living at home; married couples with no children, or none living at home; single-parent families; unrelated persons living together; and one person living alone.

There have been deep and far-reaching changes in American society in recent years that contribute to the changes in family structure. These are significant in that they influence not only the way children are being raised and educated but also our attitude toward young people.

First, ours has become an aging society with relatively few children and mounting numbers of the elderly. While the number of adults over 60 years is increasing, the number of children under 15 is rapidly decreasing (U.S. Bureau of the Census, 1979). It is important for us to consider what will be the role of children and youth in an aging society. Will taxpayers be more responsive to children, or will the needs of the young be seen to conflict with adult goals? It may be of interest to the readers to note, as an example, that the President includes among his staff a Counselor on Aging. No similar staff member exists who routinely advises the President on children's issues.

Second, there have been great changes

in the economic realm. Rampant inflation, sluggish growth, increased energy costs, and balance-of-payments problems have contributed to pressures on family life and to people's loss of confidence in the economy and the future (Yankelovich et al., 1975). Accompanying these changes has been the increase in the number of working mothers. They now constitute a substantial portion of the labor force. Not only are mothers of young children working, 30% of working women hold more than one job (Brozan, 1980).

Many more children than ever before are living in single-parent families. Single parents grew by nearly 2 million between 1970 and 1978 (Norton, 1979). The majority of single-parent families are headed by low-income women and are likely to include children below age 5 (Comptroller General, 1979). Divorce is one reason cited for the increase in single-parent families. After divorce, the most rapidly growing category of single parenthood involves unmarried women (*Advisory Committee on Child Development*, 1976). Whatever the reasons, the consequences of this way of life do not escape children. In a recent study, it was found that elementary school children who are learning disabled or who exhibit behavior problems in schools are likely to be children from single parent families (Heschinger, 1980).

Preceding these social changes is the demise of the extended family. With the transition from an agrarian to an industrial society and in the process of multiple moves, the extended family was lost as a resource in time of trouble and as a natural teaching and socializing agent. Families no longer have immediate access to the experience and wisdom of their elders or the support systems for child care they once could count on. Not only are families separated from their kin, they also face increased isolation and alienation within their own communities, and they rarely interact with their neighbors (Yankelovich et al., 1975).

FAMILY SUPPORT SYSTEMS

For the family to remain viable during these times of transition in the face of changing demographic and socioeconomic conditions, we must commit ourselves to supporting and strengthening family life. As we have shown in the beginning of this section, an important element missing in families today is support. With this in mind, our recommendations for the future of child care are consistent with the notion of family support systems. There are several concrete and inexpensive ways to achieve this. We must realize, however, that these are but suggestions, only some of which may work well. It is important that as a nation we commit ourselves to an experimental approach to social reform (Campbell, 1969). In such an approach, we try out new programs and learn from the experience whether or not they are effective.

REFERRAL CENTERS

One of our recommendations in support of family life involves the planning and implementation of referral/information centers in each community. Parents often are not aware of day care, nutrition, legal aid, and health services that may be offered in their community. Referral/information centers would provide the links between families and the community. A network of such services would also provide us with important data—how many people need day care for their children; what are some of the concerns parents have—so that we can document changes in child and family life over time.

HOME VISITOR PROGRAMS

Another suggestion is to institute home visitor programs for all families regardless of their socioeconomic status. Families today function in isolation. They experience a sense of aloneness, alienation, and helplessness. We know that this isolation and sense of helplessness are contributing factors in many cases of child abuse, for example (Maden & Wrench, 1977; Kempe & Helfer, 1972). With the home visitor programs, families who wish to could have someone visit them occasionally to discuss how they are doing, what they may need, etc., and provide them with emotional support and any information they may need. For the home visitor programs we could utilize an important resource—this nation's senior citizens. Such programs could prove to be useful not only to families but also to many older retired people who are themselves isolated and lonely. There are several examples of successful home visitor programs. One is Henry Kempe's program in Denver (Kempe & Helfer, 1972); the other is the Home Start program, which was started at the instigation of the senior author during his tenure as Director of the Office of Child Development (Zigler & Valentine, 1979; Scott, 1974).

FOSTER CARE

Next to support of the family, we recommend that changes be instituted in our present foster care system. Our recommendations are that as many children as possible be kept at home and preventive services to families at risk, as well as adoption subsidies, be made in order to insure a permanent home for children. Preventive services and adoption subsidies are cost effective. Out-of-home care for a child between the ages of 2 and 18 years is $100,000. The alternative we recommend is cheaper. The Children's Bureau, for example, has developed several models for preventive services that have been instituted in several communities (e.g., Burt, 1976). These models show conclusively that minimal financial support to families in

times of need as well as other services, coupled with counseling and follow-up support, can reduce substantially the number of children placed in foster care.

Subsidizing adoption is also important if we are to achieve permanent homes for children, especially older children, black children, or retarded or otherwise handicapped children. There are many fine families who would adopt such children if only they could afford to. Instead of spending money on foster care or institutionalization of these children, why not subsidize their adoption? Senator Cranston, among others, recently proposed this idea in legislation to provide increased adoption assistance (Cranston, 1979).

The School

The second most important socializing institution is the American school. Consistent with the notion of family support systems, we envision the school of the future to serve children before they are born. Research studies are indicative of the importance of early intervention and our ability to prevent some handicapping conditions. If parents enroll in the school during pregnancy, they may receive support and education relevant to prenatal care that would prevent unnecessary disabilities in children. After birth, parents and children would continue to receive educational services that would further enhance adult-infant interaction and promote optimal development of the child. Should there be anything wrong with a child—speech impediment or hearing difficulty, for example—these would be identified during the preschool years and help provided before the problem compounded itself to the detriment of both the child and the family. We have available to us screening and other identification devices, as well as programs for handicapped infants and young children. Yet children with disabilities often go undiagnosed until they reach school age simply because their families do not come in contact with an institution such as the school until then.

The types of school services we are referring to are already in existence. The Brookline Early Education Project in Massachusetts is one example (Pearson & Nicol, 1977). Also, many states are cognizant of the school's failure to help preschool and younger children and are developing new programs to combat the problem. The Minnesota legislature, through the Minnesota Council on Quality Education, has been funding pilot early childhood and family education (ECFE) programs in Minnesota elementary schools. By law, the programs have geographic boundaries to their service area. *All* families and expectant parents of children zero through kindergarten within a program's service area are eligible to participate. Services offered by the programs include parent/family education, concurrent child development activities, family resource libraries, early health screening and referral, parenting education for adolescents and expectant parents, and coordination of community services for families (see Note 1).

Through these types of services, there occurs a natural situation wherein parents and schools act in partnership. As it stands now, parents do not have to send children to school until the child reaches the age of 5 or 6. By that time, school is viewed as an alien and often hostile environment. Teachers and parents are often at odds or, at best, parents are unaware of what schools are trying to achieve. An important outcome of Head Start and other early childhood education programs of the 1960s has been the realization that the parent is the child's primary teacher. Any help schools try to give children must be in conjunction with the parent if it is to be at all effective (Bronfenbrenner, 1975; Valentine & Stark, 1979).

EDUCATION FOR PARENTHOOD

Besides reaching out to would-be parents and parents of young children, schools should also offer education for parenthood classes to students of all ages. With the demise of the extended family and the increase in two-paycheck families, children no longer benefit from learning about child rearing and development. To compensate, we should include in school curricula courses relevant to the role and responsibility of parents. Such courses should also offer options of internship in child care. For example, high school students could be sent out to work at Head Start programs and day-care centers. There are Education for Parenthood model programs instituted in 2,000 school districts that include internship experiences in child care. These were developed by the U.S. Office of Child Development in 1972.

CORPORAL PUNISHMENT

As we mentioned earlier in the article, corporal punishment in schools is not only a barbaric form of discipline, it also serves to further child abuse in the home. We recommend that the practice be abolished. There is absolutely nothing in favor of corporal punishment. Studies are conclusive in the indication that corporal punishment is the least effective way of shaping human behavior (National Education Association Task Force on Corporal Punishment, 1972). Furthermore, it escalates aggression in children and promotes violent tendencies, factors which may contribute to the already rampant crime among our nation's youth. Many states require teachers to report parents suspected of child abuse. Yet, very few states have statutes that make schools accountable to the parents by banning corporal punishment and requiring school personnel to use other forms of discipline.

Child Care Outside the Home

The institution which overlaps the school (for the purposes of this discussion, we refer to it as a separate institution) is child care outside the home. As we have seen, more and more women are entering the work world, and child rearing, once the responsibility of the family, is increasingly delegated to include babysitters and other nonrelatives in publicly supported or private child-care facilities, day-care centers, and family day-care homes.

While the need for more day-care facilities remains acute, there are other problems associated with child care outside the home. We offer suggestions to the solution of some of these problems in two separate, albeit overlapping, sections, one dealing with publicly supported programs for low-income families and the other dealing with the child-care needs of all families, regardless of income or structure. The latter section will be discussed under the heading "Work and Family Life."

PUBLICLY SUPPORTED CHILD CARE AND EARLY INTERVENTION PROGRAMS

Federal spending on child care amounts to more than $2 billion a year. This includes expenditures for Head Start and other related early childhood programs (e.g., Home Start) and subsidizing day-care facilities for low-income families through Title XX of the Social Security Act. Intervention programs during the preschool year may prevent unnecessary retardation and/or other complications to development later in the life of children. While some of the programs, Head Start in particular, have been shown to work well (Palmer & Andersen, 1979; Zigler & Seitz, 1982) and are cost effective, only a percentage of those families eligible for services actually participate. One of the problems associated with publicly supported programs is, then, the need for more services to accommodate the number of low-income families requiring such services. It may not be realistic to expect that all those eligible receive some sort of preschool experience or day-care placement, but priority should be given to those who are most in need, including children of bilingual background, children of single parents, and handicapped children. These children are at a high-risk for developmental delays and associated learning and other disabilities, so services should be offered to them regardless of income.

Child and family resource programs The notion of family support systems that may be featured in the future is exemplified in the Child and Family Resource Program (CFRP), which has been experimentally implemented in 11 locales across the nation. This model approach to early intervention has been praised by the Comptroller General in a report (1979) as comprehensive and cost effective. Briefly described, CFRPs are designed to offer a variety of services tailored to the unique developmental needs of children. The services are provided from the prenatal period through the child's eighth year and include health, nutrition, and education components. What is unique about CFRPs is not only that they offer comprehensive support services for the entire family as well as the child, but that they utilize existing community services and act as a referral system and linkage between families and public agencies. According to the Comptroller General's report (1979), the benefits of CFRPs include better preventive health care and nutrition for young children; rapid assistance to families during crises; correction of problems such as inadequate housing; and general improvement in overall quality of life.

Child-care professionals Another important change, already in the offing, is the professionalization of child-care workers. This applies not only to federally subsidized centers but to all child-care centers. The most important aspect in determining how a child is going to develop rests in the nature of that child's interaction with adults (Abt Associates, 1979). Providing optimal care to a group of 15 or 20 children is not as simple as caring for one, maybe two children in a home setting. Those who work with children in group situations should be trained in the principles of child development and should be cognizant of their influence on the children's growth and socialization. It is imperative, if we are to have quality child care, that we spend additional funds on training child-care workers.

In the same vein, parents must be assured that their children are taken care of by competent adults. To this end, the senior author in 1972 was supported by several national organizations concerned with child development and welfare who sought the establishment of a consortium whose sole focus was to upgrade the quality of care children receive. Known as the Child Development Associate Consortium (CDAC), this nonprofit organization, with the help of the nation's leading psychologists and early childhood educators, developed an assessment and credentialing system for child-care workers (Ward, 1976). Those child-care workers who receive the Child Development Associate credential are regarded, in the eyes of the profession, as competent to take care of preschool children in group situations. Since 1972, close to 7,000 child care workers received the CDA credential. While significant, the number is low given our needs today. We not only need a greater number of CDAs, but the CDA concept should be expanded to meet the needs of our changing society. We need, for example, to develop a similar assessment and credentialing system for infant day-care workers, school-age day-care workers, and family day-care "mothers."

Regulating day care centers Another realm of responsibility that falls within the ru-

bric of the federal government is the regulation of day-care centers and the establishment of national day-care standards that would be adhered to by all child-care facilities. Despite an increase in federal involvement in day care in the last decade and the $2 billion plus price tag that it entails, the principle of federal responsibility for day care has not yet been established. The history of moratoriums and revisions of Federal Interagency Day Care Requirements (FIDCR) is explained in other publications (Beck, 1979; Cohen & Zigler, 1977; Zigler & Heller, 1980). Suffice it to add here that child-care advocates have been fighting for very basic standards that would do no more than ensure compliance with health and safety codes and a reasonable staff:child ratio. These have not been forthcoming for over 10 years.

A victory was scored recently with HHS Secretary Patricia Harris' announcement that implementation of the revised standards would take effect October 1980 (*Federal Register*, March 19, 1980). Several weeks after the Secretary's announcement, the House and Senate Appropriations committees delayed FIDCR implementation, this time due to budgetary reasons. There is considerable dispute as to how much, if anything, will actually be saved by this delay. In the meantime, children and families suffer the consequences. Ironically, 2 weeks after the committee's vote, four children and one adult died in an explosion in an Atlanta (Ga.) day-care center (*New York Times*, October 14, 1980, p. 16). At the time of the explosion there were 83 children and 9 adults at the center, which means that each caretaker had to take care of at least nine young children and bring them to safety—a rather awesome task. As the tragedy in Atlanta indicates, the stakes are great, and they will increase as the use of day care becomes more widespread. It is imperative that the American press and the American public impress upon this nation's leaders that day care is not an issue to be treated lightly. When so many American children are in day care, it should be tailored to their needs and safety (Zigler & Goodman, 1980).

WORK AND FAMILY LIFE

With the two-paycheck family the norm rather than the exception, and the increase in single parenthood, the impact of the workplace on family life becomes an issue of concern. The relationship between the two institutions has been the subject of several recent studies which emphasize an important point: work and family life are not separate worlds, as has been assumed, but are, rather, interdependent and overlapping, with functions and behavioral rules within each system influencing processes within the other (Kanter, 1977; Brim & Abeles, 1975).

To the extent that there are children present, life for the dual-career family is stressful. Day-care arrangements must be made for the infant and preschool child; before- and after-school facilities have to be found for the older child; school vacations and days when the child is sick bring with them the need for yet other solutions. Since worker satisfaction and productivity have been found to be a function of family stability and other processes within the family system (Kanter, 1977), it behooves industry to offer relevant services and benefits that would facilitate family life.

The role of industry in facilitating family life has been slow to develop. However, some of our suggestions with regard to work and family life have been tried by several of the major corporations. These include changes in the work structure to accommodate flexible working arrangements, part-time work opportunities, and job sharing. Companies are required by law to offer maternity leaves (Bureau of Business Practice, 1979). At best, these constitute 3 months, although school teachers, for example, are able to take up to a year's leave of absence without pay in order to

stay with their newborn infants. Some school systems offer maternity and paternity leave so as not to exclude the father from child rearing. However, as a nation we lag far behind other countries. According to Kamerman and Kahn (1976), European nations' pronatal policies include 6 to 12 months' maternity or paternity leave with pay in order to facilitate childbearing, and provisions for child care are made when both parents work.

Several major corporations instituted a variety of day-care programs in support of their employees. Stride Rite Corporation, in Boston, has a company-based day-care center as one of its employee benefits package. Employees pay at the rate of 10% of their salary for the day care to a maximum of $25 a week (McIntyre, 1978). Levi Strauss & Co., in San Francisco, after 7 years of research and experimentation, concluded that day-care services should be close to where people live rather than where they work (McIntyre, 1978). As a result of these findings, Levi Strauss' policy is to "advocate the concept" of home day care. However, the company, while it is supporting research on the issue, does not have a reimbursement program for employees who use family day-care homes.

Since company-based day-care centers may not be entirely satisfactory and subsidizing such centers is expensive, several businesses, such as a hospital, a telephone company, etc., could together support programs central to where their employees work. This would prove convenient to the employees as well as inexpensive since several businesses would contribute to the cost of one center. Part of the costs for child care may be paid by employees, with the rest subsidized either by companies or unions. Children from low-income families who attend the facility may be subsidized by the state or federal government.

Industry could also support other activities that would promote interdependence among families within neighborhoods. For example, a PTA block mother type arrangement (Mead, 1970) may be facilitated wherein parents take turns looking after children, as was done during World War II when the nation depended on the labor of women. Such an arrangement will work only in conjunction with flexitime or other types of restructuring of the traditional work week. This service will be important not only in alleviating the stresses families currently face but in promoting neighborhood stability.

Another option may be supporting a referral center or a network of senior citizens who could serve, for pay, as housekeepers or child-care workers. This could be done in a center-based location or through referring families in need to those older citizens who wish to work in such capacities. This service may prove especially useful in alleviating the school-age day-care problem, since it involves fewer hours per day of care or the times when children are sick or vacationing. With grandparents usually not in the same locality, the use of senior citizens may also add another important dimension to the lives of children.

Support from philanthropy Much of the literature calling for business support of family life is related to industry's involvement through restructuring of working arrangements and including other relevant services as part of employee benefits. Industries could also channel support dollars through their corporate funding program (Zigler & Anderson, 1979). By law, corporations can generally donate as much as 5% of their net profits for charitable causes. However, they choose to contribute less than 1% (Cmiel & Levy, 1980), despite the fact that these contributions are tax deductible. Furthermore, money that is donated by industry is channeled to sources which have little to do with family life. According to a recent analysis of corporate philanthropy (Cmiel & Levy, 1980), 49.1% of corporations changed their policies to reflect the impact of inflation and the retrenchment of government programs. Of those listing some changes, the most commonly cited changes were increased aid to higher education, followed by increases in the size of grants and more aid to cultural organizations. This means not so much a change as a reaffirmation of traditional priorities of corporate philanthropy (Finn, 1978). In terms of urban programs and community groups (these include children's programs) that might lose government programs, Cmiel and Levy (1980) note that "expressed corporate interest has not yet been translated into action." This is unfortunate considering the investment, in terms of employee satisfaction and productivity, corporations would be making if they provided financial aid in support of family life.

CONCLUSION

We have outlined in this article several ideas that may be tried out in response to problems facing children and families. It would be unrealistic to expect at these times of financial restraints revolutionary changes that involve eliminating societal stresses through the provision of jobs and adequate housing for everyone, or the restructuring of our entire economy, as has been suggested by some writers (e.g., Keniston, 1977). We must acknowledge, however, that new patterns of family life are just now beginning to emerge that affect all people, but especially our children. The social transition we are experiencing is difficult: a simple response is not the solution; instead, a broad spectrum of options is needed, options that may be tried out without vast organizational expenditures.

Our nation cannot be transformed into a child-oriented society overnight. Progress and change are gradual processes, and the first steps are undoubtedly the most difficult. We must work together toward becoming a nation which is concerned with, and responsible for, the optimal development of our most valuable resource, our children.

REFERENCE NOTE

1. For more information on the early childhood and family education programs in Minnesota, refer to *A policy study of issues related to early childhood and family education. A report to the Minnesota Legislature*, January 15, 1979. Available from the Minnesota Council on Quality Education, 722 Capitol Square Building, St. Paul, Minn. 55101.

REFERENCES

Abt Associates, Inc. *Final report of the national day care study: Children at the center.* Executive Summary. Cambridge, Mass., March 1979. (Contract No. HEW 105-74-1100.)

Advisory Committee on Child Development. *Toward a national policy for children and families.* Washington, D.C.: National Academy of Sciences, 1976.

Beck, R. Child Care: Story of neglect. *American Federationist*, 1979, *86*, 9–13.

Boocock, S. S. A cross-cultural analysis of the child care system. In Lillian G. Katz (Ed.), *Current topics in early childhood*, vol. 1. N.J.: Ablex, Norwood, N.J., 1977.

Brim, O. G., Jr. & Abeles, R. P. Work and personality in the middle years. *Social Science Research Council Items*, 1975, *29*, 29–33.

Bronfenbrenner, U. Is early intervention effective? In H. J. Leichter (Ed.), *The family as educator.* New York: Teacher's College Press, Columbia University, 1975.

Brozan, N. Women now hold 30 percent of second jobs. *New York Times*, June 24, 1980, B6.

Bureau of Business Practice. *Fair Employment Practice Guidelines*, 1979, 170(9).

Burt, M. R. The Comprehensive Emergency Services System: Expanding services to children and families. *Children Today*, 1976, *5*(2), 2–5.

Campbell, D. T. Reforms as experiments. *American Psychologist*, 1969, *24*, 409–429.

Cmiel, K. & Levy, S. *Corporate giving in Chicago: 1980.* Chicago: Donors Forum Library, 1980.

Cohen, D. J. & Zigler, E. Federal Day Care Standards: Rationale and recommendations. *American Journal of Orthopsychiatry*, 1977, *47*, 456–465.

Comptroller General of the United States. *Report to the Congress; Early childhood and family development programs improve the quality of life for low-income families.* Washington, D.C.: U.S. Government Accounting Office, February 6, 1979. (Document No. (HRD) 79-40.)

Condry, J. C. & Siman, M. A. Characteristics of peer and adult-oriented children. *Journal of Marriage and the Family*, 1974, *36*, 543–544.

Condry, J. C. & Siman, M. A. *An experimental study of adult versus peer orientation.* Unpublished manuscript, Cornell University, 1976.

Congressional Record, January 15, 1979, S76-77.

Cranston, A. (Testimony.) U.S. Congress. Senate Committee on Finance, Subcommittee on Public Assistance. *Proposals related to social and child welfare services, adoption assistance and foster care*, Ninety-Sixth Congress, September 24, 1979.

Edelman, M. W. Newsletter distributed by Children's Defense Fund. June, 1980.

Finn, M. Focus on foundation giving: Education. *The Philanthropy Monthly*, *XI*(8), 1978, 20.

Furrow, D., Gruendel, J. & Zigler, E. *Protecting America's children from accidental injury and death. An overview of the problem and an agenda for action.* Unpublished manuscript, Yale University, 1979.

Heschinger, F. M. "One parent household a handicap for pupils?" *New York Times*, September 30, 1980, pp. C1–C5.

Kamerman, S. B. & Kahn, A. J. *European family policy currents: The question of families with very young children.* Unpublished manuscript, Columbia University, School of Social Work, 1976.

Kanter, R. M. *Work and family in the United States: A critical review and agenda for research and policy.* New York: Russell Sage Foundation, 1977.

Kashani, J. & Simonds, J. F. The incidence of depression in children. *American Journal of Psychiatry*, 1979, *136*, 1203–1205.

Kempe, C. H. & Helfer, R. E. (Eds.). *Helping the battered child and his family.* Philadelphia: Lippincott, 1972. (a)

Kempe, C. H. & Helfer, R. E. Innovative therapeutic approaches. In C. H. Kempe and R. E. Helfer (Eds.), *Helping the battered child and his family.* Philadelphia: Lippincott, 1972. (b)

Keniston, K. *All our children.* New York: Harcourt, 1977.

Keyserling, M. D. *Windows on day care.* New York: National Council of Jewish Women, 1972.

Maden, M. F. & Wrench, D. F. Significant findings in child abuse research. *Victimology,* 1977, *2*, 196–224.

Martinez, A. (Testimony.) U.S. Congress. House Committee on Education and Labor, Subcommittee on Select Education. *Proposed extension of the Child Abuse Prevention and Treatment Act,* Ninety-Fifth Congress, March 11, 1977.

McIntyre, K. J. Day care: An employer benefit, too. *Business Insurance,* December 11, 1978, pp. 11–36.

Mead, M. Working mothers and their children. *Childhood Education,* 1970, *47,* 66–71.

Mednick, B. R., Baker, R. L. & Sutton-Smith, B. Teenage pregnancy and perinatal mortality. *Journal of Youth and Adolescence,* September 1979, *8*(3), 343–357.

Mortality Advance Report, 1978, National Center for Health Statistics, PHS/DHHS (September 17, 1980).

National Education Association Task Force on Corporal Punishment. *Report of the Task Force on Corporal Punishment.* Washington, D.C.: National Education Association, 1972.

National health interview survey. National Center for Health Statistics, PHS/DHHS, 1978. Unpublished data.

Norton, A. Portrait of the one-parent family. *The National Elementary Principal,* 1979, *59,* 32–35.

Palmer, F. H. & Andersen, L. W. Long-term gains from early intervention: Findings from longitudinal studies. In E. Zigler and J. Valentine (Eds.), *Project Head Start: A legacy of the War on Poverty.* New York: Free Press, 1979.

Pearson, D. E. & Nicol, E. H. *The fourth year of the Brookline Early Education Project: A report of progress and plans.* Unpublished report, 1977, Brookline Early Education Project, 987 Kent Street, Brookline, Mass. 02146.

Scott, R. Research and early childhood: The Home Start Project. *Child Welfare,* 1974, *53,* 112–119.

Smock, S. M. *The Children: The Shapes of Child Care in Detroit.* Detroit: Wayne State University Press, 1977.

United nations demographic yearbook, 1975.

United nations demographic yearbook, 1977.

U.S. Bureau of the Census. *Current population reports.* Series p-23, No. 84. Washington, D.C.: U.S. Department of Commerce, 1979.

U.S. Department of Health, Education and Welfare. *Monthly vital statistics report.* Provisional Statistics, June 30, 1976, *24,* 13.

U.S. Immunization Survey. Center for Disease Control, U.S. PHS/DHHS, 1980.

Valentine, J. & Stark, E. The social context of parent involvement in Head Start. In E. Zigler and J. Valentine (Eds.), *Project Head Start: A legacy of the War on Poverty.* New York: Free Press, 1979.

Ward, E. H. CDA: Credentialing for day care. *Voice for Children,* 1976, *9*(5), 15.

White House Conference on Children. *Report to the president.* Washington, D.C.: U.S. Government Printing Office, 1970.

Yankelovich, Skelly, White, Inc. *The General Mills American family report 1974–1975.* Minneapolis: General Mills, 1975.

Zelnick, M. & Kantner, J. First pregnancies to women aged 15 to 19: 1971 and 1976. *Family Planning Perspectives,* 1978, *10*(1), 11–20.

Zigler, E. Must budget ax fall on children. *New York Times,* July 30, 1980, 24.

Zigler, E. & Anderson, K. Foundation support in the child and family life field. *The Philanthropy Monthly,* 1979, *12,* 12–14.

Zigler, E. & Goodman, J. On day care standards—again. *The Networker: Newsletter of the Bush Programs in Child Development and Social Policy.* New Haven, 1980, *2*(1).

Zigler, E. & Heller, K. A. Day care standards approach critical juncture. *Day Care and Early Education,* 1980, *7*(3), 7–8, 47.

Zigler, E. & Seitz, V. Social policy implications of research on intelligence. In R. J. Sternberg (Ed.), *Handbook of human intelligence.* New York: Cambridge University Press, 1982.

Zigler, E. & Valentine, J. (Eds.). *Project Head Start: A Legacy of the War on Poverty.* New York: Free Press, 1979.

Index

Abortion. *See also* Pregnancy, Sterilization
  conception, 213
  laws governing, 216
Achievement
  cultural effects, 122
  and IQ tests, 321
  individual differences in, 67
  parental influences on, 67–68, 69
  social class differences and, 108
  teacher influences on, 69, 87, 89
  and social competence, 325
Acculturation, 70, 78. *See also* Culture
  effect on social learning by, 28–31, 117–26
Adolescence, 225, 230
  father's absence during, 97
  peers and, 86
  sex-stereotyped behavior, 58, 60–61
  and teenage pregnancies, 214, 215, 216–17, 329
Adoption, 132, 333
Age, 136. *See also* Mental age
  and attachment, 93–94
  and cognitive development of morality, 62, 64–65
  cross-cultural cognition studies and, 123
  developmental changes in esthetic sensitivity, 202–5
  and development of sex roles, 58–61
  early childhood intervention and, 307
  as factor in imitation, 40, 41

as factor in maturation, 32
  and moral behavior, 65
  relationship to gender identity, 55–57
  and response to divorce, 225, 227, 230
Aggression, 47–48, 82, 108, 148, 226
  conditioned cues to, 72–73
  definition, 70
  learning patterns of, 71–72
  and television viewing, 83–85
Alcohol, and fetal alcohol syndrome, 217
Altruism, acquiring, 84
Animal behavior
  cognition studies, 186
  peers, 86–87
  studies, 35
Anthropology, and social learning theory, 28–29, 188
Attachment, 11, 35, 92, 150, 186, 191, 237
  age and, 93
  "anxious," 189
  development of, 51–53, 92–93
  and outerdirectedness, 236
  trust and, 53–54
Attribution theory, 88, 109
Attributional styles, 69
Autism
  adolescent and adult, 248–49
  causes, 249–50
  diagnosis, 247–48
  early childhood, 246–52

Autism (*continued*)
   early infantile, 128, 235
   symptoms, 246–47
   treatment, 250–51

Behavior, 4–5, 21. *See also specific behaviors*
   adaptive, and mental retardation, 130–31
   and autism, 246–49
   in cultural context, 118
   and development of morality, 64–66
   in divorce, 227
   genetics, 32–34, 35, 38, 186–87
   goal oriented, 72
   imitation and, 11
   language and, 4
   learned patterns of, 27–28, 38, 39
   and mental retardation, 132–33
   origins of social, 13–15, 17, 66
   patterns of mentally retarded, 238
   self-described, 45, 66
   similarities in separated identical twins, 209,
      211
Behavior modification, 26, 129, 250
Behaviorist Manifesto, 25
Biological influences. *See also* Genetics; Heredity
   in puberty, 60–61
   research trends in, 186–87
   on sex-linked characteristics, 46–47
Biological needs, and personality development,
   17–18
Birth process, 219–20
Bonding. *See* Attachment
Brain, wave patterns in autism, 248, 249–50

California Growth Studies, 32
Caretaker(s), 94, 95, 271–72
   and infant relationships, 51
   and intervention program, 114
   multiple, 53
Child abuse, 292–98, 330, 333. *See also* Corporal
   Punishment
   definition, 144, 150–51, 294
   discipline and, 294, 297
   education and, 146
   incidence, 144, 145, 149
   intervention, 151–53, 190, 293
   medical model of, 147–48
   national social policy, 145–46, 295, 296–97
   parents' risk factors, 151–52, 189
   prevention, 189, 294
   psychiatric model, 148
   research, 189–90, 292–93
   schools and, 90, 145–46
   sexual abuse in, 149
   social-situational model, 150–51, 296–97
   sociological model, 148–49
   support systems and, 265–66
Child neglect, 236–37, 329

Child raising
   and cognitive ability, 123–24
   and cultural differences and, 120–26
   early intervention programs, 307–308
   economic influences on, 120–21, 274–80
   effects of expert advice on, 102, 153, 235, 236
   effects of social class differences on, 101–2,
      103
   and family patterns, 121, 187
   and gender distinction, 121–22, 260, 277–78
   and group day care, 94, 191
   and prediction of adult success with
      techniques of, 234
   and personality development, 122–23, 276–80
   and techniques of parent-child play, 260
   theories of, 26
   recent research relating to, 188
   and values, 124–25
Children
   achievement motivation of, 68–69
   aggression in, 70–72
   behavior of, and child abuse, 150–52, 264
   characteristics of, and child abuse, 189–90
   and child care programs, 190–91, 329–38
   cognition, 41–42, 186
   competence, 42
   curiosity, 25
   developing gender identity, 55–59, 260
   development of morality in, 79, 147–48
   developing sex roles, 55, 57, 58–59, 79
   early intervention programs for, 317–26
   effects of divorce on, 223, 224–31
   and family interaction, 185
   gifted, 135
   imitation and learning, 40–41, 47, 59, 79
   and intellectual development, 263–66, 312,
      314
   mentally retarded, 133–38, 253–56
   and parental behavior, 44–45, 78, 227–28
   peer reinforcement, 59, 85–86
   school influences on, 87–88, 141–42, 143–44,
      353–54
   self-activating socialization of, 19, 33, 57,
      154–55, 187–88
   television as influence on, 83–85, 287–91
   and television viewing, 83–85
Cognition
   and acculturation, 29, 123–24
   and attachment, 52
   and autism, 246, 250
   definition, 4, 186
   in developing esthetic appreciation, 201, 204
   development of, 16, 27, 41–43, 263, 308
   as factor in giftedness, 138–39, 140–41
   guilt and, 106
   humor and, 42
   in mental retardation, 133, 238
   and morality, 62–63
   and motivation, 43

prevention of in social learning, 32
"scripts" in, 32, 41
stages of, 29–30, 31, 35, 37, 62–63
Contraception, 214
    social class issues and, 215–16
Competence, 41–42. *See also* Social com-
    petence
Competence theory, 40
Conditioning, 25–26
Conformity, 11–12, 63, 108
Consanguinity study, 33
Conservation (as cognitive ability), 56–57
Corporal punishment, 145–46, 152, 298, 334
Creativity
    definition, 140
    as function of giftedness, 138, 139–42
    play and, 143
Culture(s), 200, 202
    cross-cultural comparison studies of child
        rearing, 122–26, 186, 274–80
    definition, 29
    differences and IQ, 130–31
    economy and adult roles, 274–80
    maintenance systems of, 119
    structure of child raising, 120
    values and, 124–25, 326
Culture changes, and socialization, 102–3
Cultural-familial retardation. *See* Mental retar-
    dation
Crying, 11, 51, 52, 150

Day care, 81, 311, 330. *See also* Children, and
    child care programs
    alternatives, 191
    compared to substitute-care, 471–72
    developmental concerns and, 29–31, 471–72
    government regulation of, 336–37
    kibbutz, studies of, 191
    national social policy and, 92
    need for, 190
    as socializing agent, 91, 191
Defense mechanisms, 107–8
Dependency, and mental retardation, 238–39
Determinism, 24, 50–51
Developmental structures, 24
    biological determinants of, 186
    cognitive, 29–30, 37, 39, 43
    and determinism, 24
    and legal definition of child abuse, 151
    research modes, 185–86
    and self-concept, 243
    and social class, 105–6, 110
    and social learning theory, 27, 44
    and theories of parenting, 259
    "universal" phases, 29
Developmental psychopathology, 125
Discipline. *See also* Child abuse; School(s)
    and children's moral behavior, 65, 66
    and social class differences, 102, 106

Divorce, 8, 81, 96–98, 223–31
    crisis model of, 224
    family changes after, 226–27
    stages of reaction to, 229, 230
Drive reduction theory, 26–27, 39, 43
Drugs. *See also* Substance abuse
    taken during pregnancy and birth, 218, 219

Economic influences, 120–21, 220, 274–80, 332
    in child abuse, 295
    in child ecology, 266
Economic problems, in divorce, 226–27
Education. *See also* Educational performance;
    Prenatal care; School(s)
    early childhood, 301, 302–3
    parenting, 190, 214–16, 299, 333–34
Education for Parenthood Program, 190
Educational performance
    of autistic children, 248, 249–50
    correlation with adult success, 141–42
    and early intervention, 5–6, 307, 319
    Head Start and, 112, 192–93
    mainstreaming and, 89, 137, 192, 194, 253–56
    special education and, 254
Effectance motivation. *See* Competence; Moti-
    vation
Environment. *See also* Acculturation; Culture(s)
    behavior-genetics research and, 187
    influences on socialization, 13, 14–15, 18–19,
        29, 113–14
    and intelligence, 132–33, 192, 262
    pollutants and prenatal development, 217–19
    self-selection of, 15–16
    study of separated identical twins and, 207
Esthetic sensitivity, study of development of,
    201–5
Ethology, 186
    and social learning theory, 35–36, 38
    and theory of aggression, 70
Ethnicity, and social class, 110
Ethnography, 125

Failure
    expectation of, 134, 136
    and motivation to learn, 87–88
    and problem solving, 68–69
Family, 92, 150, 260–61, 283, 285. *See also*
    Parent-child relationship
    child care and, 335
    cultural influences on, 121, 188–89, 265
    demographic characteristics of, 89
    destruction of traditional social setting and,
        28, 331–32
    extended, 258–59, 332
    and father's absence, 228–29
    in Head Start, Home Start programs, 299, 303
    with industry, 337–38
    interaction of members, 185, 187–88, 227
    intervention programs, 307–15

Family (*continued*)
  mental retardation in, 136–37
  multi-, after remarriage, 223
  single-parent, 150, 187, 223, 224, 228, 230,
    231, 332
  support systems, 231, 308, 332–33
Fathers, 52–53, 55–56, 260–61, 281–85
  absence, 80–81, 96, 97, 98, 282, 283
  and achievement of children, 68
  and divorce, 223, 229–30
  and gender appropriate behavior, 60, 80
  and infant relationship, 281–82
  and moral development, 65
  and role in family, 187, 228–29
  and sex role development, 81, 260
Foster care, 330, 333

Gender distinction. *See also* Sex differences
  and patterns of socialization, 121–22, 276–79,
    282
Gender identity, 55–56, 59, 284
Gender role, 55. *See also* Sex roles
Genetics
  behavioral differences of social class and,
    104–105
  in childhood mental disorders, 128
  and disorders effecting intelligence, 131–33
  and factors in autism, 246–49
  and influence on behavior, 32–34, 35, 38, 53,
    186–87
Gifted children, 138–44
  and creativity, 140–42
  and education, 142–44
  and psychological disturbances, 139
  and social isolation of, 144
Guilt, 107

Handicapped children, mentally retarded, 192,
  253–54, 255–56
Head Start, 5, 111–13, 115–16, 299–304
  comparison programs, 301, 302–3
  family participation, 303
  goals, 300
  Westinghouse Learning Corporation evalua-
    tion of, 192–93, 300
Health care, 112, 113, 325, 299, 329
  of autistic children, 248
Hermaphroditism, 55
Heredity. *See also* Genetics
  and influences on socialization, 13–14, 15,
    16–17
  and study of separated identical twins, 143
Home Start, 303, 332–33
Humor, 42

IQ tests, 108–9. *See also* Intelligence
  behavior-genetic investigation of, 186
  as behavior predictor, 322
  and correlation with adult success, 141–42

cultural differences and, 130
  and giftedness, 138, 140
  as measure of early childhood intervention,
    307, 310, 317–22
  mental retardation and, 129–31, 136
Identification, 17–18, 26–27, 35, 62, 67, 71
Infant development
  attachment, 260
  and autism, 128, 235
  correlated with adult success, 235–36, 237
  and day care, 92–94
  development of temperament in, 34, 270
  fathers' role in, 281–82
  feeding and personality, 50–51
  indulgence during, and cultural stability, 122
  imitation in, 39–40
  intelligence, 262
  mortality, 219
  prenatal care and, 217
  self-realization in, 54
  sex and gender role identities, 57
  social and political influences on, 213, 220–21
  socialization and, 15, 24, 26, 50, 54, 78
  surrogate parents and, 27
  survival behaviors, 35
  trust in caretakers and, 78
Imitation, 26–27, 40, 76, 241
  and acquisition of behaviors, 40–41, 71–72,
    83–85
  and performance, 27, 40
  and sex-role modeling, 30–31, 39
Imprinting, 35
Intelligence. *See also* IQ tests; Mental retardation
  correlated with creativity, 138, 139–40
  giftedness, 138
  Head Start and, 112–13
  and parenting activities, 262–63
  and social competence, 322–24
  and social class, 108
Interacting
  of autistic children, 247
  of mentally retarded children with adults, 238
  parent-child, 59–60, 282
Intervention, 306–15. *See also specific programs*
  (e.g. Head Start)
  components of Yale program, 308–9, 314
  demographic factors in, 310–11, 314
  early childhood programs of, 317–26
  educational, 89–91
  effects on family patterns, 311
  effects on parental behavior, 307–8
  evaluating effectiveness, 192–94, 306–7,
    310–15
  legal, in child abuse cases, 150–52
  in social class differences of child develop-
    ment, 111–16
Instinct, role of in socialization, 35
Institutionalization, 251
  child abuse and, 145, 297

and mental retardation, 135–36, 238–39, 241, 242
Isolation, 87, 148–49, 332, 333
   of autistic children, 248
   of gifted children, 143–44
   parental, 114, 258

Kohlberg's Stages of Moral Reasoning, 63–64

Laboratory of Comparative Human Cognition, 123
Language, 493
   animal research and, 186
   development in autistic children, 246–47, 250
   early intervention, 310, 311
Learning theory, 15–16, 17, 18, 21. *See also* Social learning theory
   and adaptive behavior, 18
   and moral development, 64, 65
   and pre-school children, 287–88, 288–89, 290–91
Locus of control, 109

Mann-Whitney *U* Test, 278
Maturation, 21, 32, 38
   Gessel's theory, 14
Mental age, 42, 133, 239, 241, 242
Mental retardation, 42, 129–38
   and child abuse, 190
   cultural-familial, 132–33, 240–41
   determination of, 129–32
   education, 137
   and effectance motivation, 240–41
   failure expectation, 239
   family context, 136–37
   and institutionalization, 135–36, 254, 238–39, 241, 242
   mainstreaming and, 253–56
   and outerdirectedness, 241
   personality characteristics in, 133–35
   self-concept, 242–43
   and social deprivation, 238–39
   special education and, 254–55
Mr. Roger's Neighborhood, 85, 287–91
Model(s): 67, 269
   and aggression, 71, 72
   influences on roles, 27
   and moral behavior, 66
   sex-appropriate, 27–31, 42, 59–60
Morality, 191
   developmental stages in, 30, 65, 106
   Kohlberg's theory of stages, 63–64
   learning patterns of, 30–31, 62, 65–66
Mothers, 82
   and attachment of pre-school children, 294, 331
   as custodial parent, 230
   effect of father's role on, 228–29
   mortality of, during delivery, 220

"sensitivity" of, 51–52, 268
   and sex-role development, 81
   working, 60, 91, 92, 191, 271
Motivation, 27, 30, 43, 142–43, 321
   for achievement, 67, 87–88, 133–34, 240–41
   early intervention and, 193, 312, 314
   as measure of social competence, 325
   and sex-role modeling, 88
Motor Skills, and autism, 248

National social policy. *See also* Intervention
   and autism, 252
   and child abuse, 293, 295, 297, 298
   and day care, 92, 272
   and handicapped children, 255
   and Head Start, 111–16
   and mentally retarded, 137–38, 254
   and school segregation, 191–92
   and social problems correlated with social sciences, 154, 194
Newborn, 10–11. *See also* Infant development
Neurosis, 128
   symptom-determined syndromes, 129
New York Longitudinal Study, 34, 270
Nutrition, and fetal development, 218
Nurturance, 82
   and model effectiveness, 47, 60, 83

Oedipal complex, 62
Outer-directedness, 15, 40, 42, 89, 241–42, 325

Parent-child relationship. *See also* Caretaker(s) Children; Fathers, Mothers
   adaptive behavior in, 264–65
   as agency of mental health, 331
   and autistic children, 250
   bidirectional, 187–88, 227, 265, 269–70
   canalization model of, 188
   in child abuse, 149–50, 151–52, 189, 190
   data gathering, 45–46, 102
   in development of child's intelligence, 189, 190, 263
   divorce and, 96–98
   effect of marital relationship on, 82
   effect of other socializing agents on, 82
   in families after divorce, 227–28, 229, 230
   and parenthood preparation, 190, 213
   as socializing agent, 18–19, 26, 27, 29, 78–82, 187–88
   transactional model of, 188
   unidirectional, 16, 45
Parental behavior
   and achievement of children, 67–69
   and aggression in children, 71–72
   authoritarian, 270
   child abuse and, 144–45, 147–52, 189–90
   and conflict between parents, 227–28
   corporal punishment and, 145–46, 152

Parental behavior (*continued*)
  demands on children, 11, 80, 190, 268–69, 270–71, 311
  development of children's gender identity, 55–56, 59–60
  and development of children's sex roles, 57–58
  education of parents and, 150
  and emotional development of children, 234–37, 265
  and intervention programs, 114–15, 307, 314–15
  involvement in children's education, 90–91, 111–14
  and mental retardation, 136–37
  and moral development of children, 65–66
  and personality development of children, 24, 44–45, 53, 155, 269–70
  and psychological adjustment of parents, 311
  and social class attitudes, 103
Parental values, 90
  class differences in, 106–7
  and day care, 94–95
Parents Anonymous, 296
Patterning, 39
Peer(s), 69, 191, 231, 254, 272, 331
  behavior reinforcement and, 85–86
  and sex-appropriate behavior, 59, 86
Perception, 200
  definition, 3
Personality, 15, 49, 79, 82, 118, 154, 265
  and characteristics of esthetic appreciation, 201, 205
  and characteristics of mental retardation, 133–35, 238–43
  "core," 5
  creativity and, 141
  developmental continuity of, 16–17
  deviation from "normal" development of, 8
  effect of culture on development of, 117, 122–23, 126, 191
  effects of early intervention on, 310
  effects of institutionalization on, 140–41
  Freudian theory of development, 21–23, 24, 26, 50
  genetic inheritance and, 32–34, 105
  good vs. evil theories of, 16–17
  individual differences in, 18, 263–65, 270
  Piaget's view of development, 30
  self-actualization and, 24
  social class and development of, 100
  Watson's view of development, 25
Phobia(s), 25–26
Play
  developmental value of, 143
  differences in parent-infant, 81
  imaginative, 287
Politics, factors that relate to development, 213, 215, 216–21, 231
Poverty, 89, 91, 111

Pregnancy, 217–21. *See also* Birth process; Contraception
  among adolescents, 214
  incidence, 213
Prematurity, and child abuse, 189
Prenatal care, 217–29
Pre-school intervention, 192–94
Problem solving, 68, 134, 240, 287
Psychic determinism, 21
Psychoanalysis, 32, 43, 51
  behavior modification and, 17, 20–25, 38
  and determinism, 24
  Freudian theory, 17, 21–23, 38, 62
  model of aggression, 70, 72
Psychosis, 128. *See also specific disorders*
  symbiotic, 128
Puberty. *See* Adolescence
Punishment, 106, 152. *See also* Corporal punishment
  in learning behaviors, 27, 39

Quality of life, 308, 313

Reinforcement, 26, 27, 43, 67, 134
  complementary response and, 35
  in learning behaviors, 39, 40, 58–59, 104
  tangible/intangible, 240–41
Rewards, 26, 83, 106, 244
Role(s), 19. *See also* Sex roles
  learning, 27, 79, 107

Schizophrenia
  adult, 246
  childhood, 128
School(s). *See also* Educational performance
  behavior and, 334
  child abuse/corporal punishment in, 145–46, 298
  and developing self-concept, 143–44
  as socializing agency, 78, 87–91, 191–92
Self, 17, 61
Self-concept, 242–43, 325
  child abuse and, 190
  development, 191
  and giftedness, 143
  image disparity, 42
  in infancy, 14, 81, 88–89
  and motivation, 87–88
  and retardation, 135, 243
  and social class, 105–6
Sesame Street, 84–85, 287–91
Sex differences
  and early intervention programs, 312, 313–14
  in responding to divorce, 225–26
Sex education, 213, 214
Sex roles, 8, 23, 42, 43
  identity, 186
  learning, 30–31, 42, 55, 56–57, 60–61, 79, 125, 191

and parental differentiation in treatment of infants, 57–58, 260
peer influences on, 86–87
related to aggression, 67–68
and relationship to father, 80–81, 97, 282–83, 260–61
Sex taboos, cultural, and socialization, 120–21
Siblings, 136–37, 250
Single parents. See Family
Situational analysis, 14–15
Smiling, 51
Smoking, and fetal development, 217–28
Social class
    data gathering techniques, 102–3, 109–10
    effect of differences on socialization, 99, 104–9, 110–11
    effect on by intervention programs, 312
    effectance motivation and, 240–41
    factors in child abuse, 149, 150, 295
    history of studies of, 100–102
    and infant development, 214, 219
    intelligence tests and, 108–9
    intervention programs, 111
    and unwanted pregnancies, 215–16
Social competence, 86–87, 113, 193, 270
    in childhood, 322–26
    definition, 323
    and mental retardation, 130, 131, 136, 192
Social deprivation, 136, 238–39
Social learning theory
    cognitive mediators in, 31
    developmental psychology and, 27, 29
    drive-reduction, 26–27
    identification and, 65
    imitation, 26–27, 31, 104
    patterning, 39
    reinforcement, 40
    survival factors in, 35–36
Socialization. See also Social competence; Social learning theory
    abnormal intelligence conditions and, 134
    acculturation and, 28–29, 120–23, 276–80
    activity/passivity in, 15–16
    behaviorism and, 25–26
    biological determinants, 186
    causality studies, 48
    cognitive development and, 29–31, 39, 41
    conformity, 11–12
    continuing nature of, 102–4
    cross-cultural research on, 123–26
    cultural changes and, 118–19
    definition, 4, 118
    economic influences on, 104–5
    fathers's role in, 288–29
    history of study of, 44–46
    infant instinct-response and, 35

inherited traits and, 33–34
interactionist theory, 14–15
intervention of, 111–16
maturational development theory, 32
methods, 47–49
moral behavior, 107–10
nature-nurture issues, 13–16
parental influences on, 78–83, 84, 268–72, 283. See also Parental behavior; Parent-child relationship
research applications of, 271–72
research trends, 186
roles in, 104
school's role in, 191–92
social class differences and, 99–103, 106–8
stimulus-response theory of, 26
time acquired, 18–19
transactional approach to study of, 38
unidirectional, 16
Social policy. See National social policy
Societalism, 118
Sociobiology, 17
Special education, 251, 253–54
Sterilization, 216
Stress
    as factor in child abuse, 149, 150
    as factor in divorce, 224, 225, 226
Substance abuse, 190
Survival
    needs, 35
    significance in development, 35

Teachers
    and children's aggressive behavior, 71
    and children's self-image, 88
    and children's sex-role development, 88
    as socializing agents, 87–89, 90
Television
    and aggressive behavior, 72, 83–84
    as behavior model, 83–84
    effect on pre-school learning, 287–91
Temperament, 34, 263–65
Thematic Apperception Test, 67
Theology, and theories of personality development, 16–17
Toilet training, 11, 22–23
Toys, 262–63
Transactional analysis, 32
Trauma, 16
Trust, development of in infancy, 53
Twins, studies of identical, 33, 206–12

Values. See culture(s); Parental values

Yale Child Welfare Research Program, 306–15